Fertile Crc

Cross / Cultures

Readings in the Post/Colonial Literatures in English

53

Series Editors:

Gordon Collier (Giessen)

Hena Maes-Jelinek (Liège)

Geoffrey Davis (Aachen)

Amsterdam – New York, NY 2002

Fertile Crossings

Metamorphoses of Genre in Anglophone West African Literature

Pietro Deandrea

Publication co-funded by the *Centro Piemontese di Studi Africani* (Palazzo Chiablese, Piazza San Giovanni 2, 10121 Turin, Italy)

The paper on which this book is printed meets the requirements of "ISO 9706:1994, Information and documentation - Paper for documents - Requirements for permanence".

ISBN: 90-420-1478-4 (bound)

Contents

Acknowledgements

This work[1] is the outcome of three years of intense research in Italy and abroad – three years that offered me the opportunity to delve into literatures, cultures and worlds my country is still largely ignorant of, in an age when immigrants of African and non-African origin are showing my fellow countrymen the way to our future multicultural society.

True, I could repeatedly quench my thirst for knowledge. Nevertheless, I realize with joy and shame that no book, essay, play or conference is comparable to the people I have met during my research and who helped my progress with their erudition, warmth and sympathy; that no fount of knowledge is comparable to the milk of human kindness. The joy is owing to my certainty that they represent an eternal treasure to be cherished in the days to come; the shame accompanies these few hurried lines I dedicate to them while I am perfectly aware of how much more they deserve.

This work was made possible by generous grants from the Centre for the Study of the Literatures and Cultures of the Emerging Areas, University of Turin, Italy. The author wishes to thank its director, Professor Sergio Zoppi, and all his staff for their human and technical support.

My thanks go also to: Professor Claudio Gorlier, who has constantly stimulated my passion for anglophone literatures; the Head of the PhD Programme, Professor Alfredo Rizzardi, University of Bologna; my two fellow PhD students, Roberta Gefter Wondrich and Rita Monticelli; all the academics from the University of Turin who have helped me enjoy these years inside the architectural eyesore known as the "Palazzo Nuovo": Paolo Bertinetti, Carmen Concilio, John Douthwaite, Antonella Emina, Valeria Guidotti, Ruth Anne Henderson, Alessandra Marzola, Isabella Mininni, Alessandro Monti, Renato Oliva, Pierpaolo Piciucco, and Isabella Maria Zoppi; my comrades in the 1990 Panther Movement, with whom I squatted that same building; those living in Italy who have facilitated my work in the most diverse ways: Kevin Armstrong, Shaul Bassi, Francesco

[1] Portions of which quote from, re-formulate and / or are inspired by the author's already published essays and interviews as included in the Bibliography.

Casotti, Pia Chiappella, Giorgio Davì, Zaria Greenhill, Elsa Linguanti, Aine Neville, Maria Grazia Orsi, Costanza Prada of the Piedmontese Centre for African Studies; Ben Okri, who kindly accepted to grant me two long interviews before and after his Booker Prize fame; Ben Tomoloju's Kakaaki and Bode Sowande's Odu Themes for the unforgettable fun we all had at the 1992 Chieri Theatre Festival; the writers and scholars who briefly visited Turin: Francis Bebey, Chaman Nahal, Kole Omotoso and the late Jacqueline Bardolph.

I am deeply indebted to several people for making my sojourns in Ghana and Nigeria (1993, 1997) happy and trouble-free: the late Kofi Agovi, who patiently guided my first discovery of West Africa; the Agovi family for making me feel at home; John Collins, for our endless bubra-fuelled discussions; James Gibbs, Patience Addo and Kofi Sarkodee's family, for their hospitality in Madina New Road; Kojo Laing, whose words opened my eyes; Ama Ata Aidoo and her motherly care; Kwadjo and Naana Jane Opoku–Agyemang for welcoming me in Cape Coast; Femi Osofisan and Sanni, who facilitated my stay in Ibadan; Bode Sowande's Odu Themes, for the welcome they gave me five years after our first encounter; Niyi Osundare, for his breathtaking humanity; Charles Olokpa, for our breakfasts in Agbowo; the great Jahman Anikulakpo and Ben Tomoloju, who led me around Lagos; Jide Ogungbade, who reappeared in the night; Emmanuele Ranesi, my fellow traveller extraordinaire; and also Temilola Abioye, Kobena Eyi Acquah, William Addo, Dapo Adelugba, Toyin Adewale, Kofi Agyekum, Bernice Ahlijah, Jare Ajayi, Femi Ajibode, Agatha Akonor–Mills, Nana Yaa Ampomfi and her family, Charles Angmor, Kofi Anyidoho, Sandy Arkhurst, Jane Naafia Asante, Yaw Asare, Muyiwa P. Awodiya, Marlon M. Bailey, Mohammed ben Abdallah, Kofi Boateng, Stefano Boni, Kwesi Brew, R.A. Cantey, Margaret Cudjoe, Gianna Da Re, Mary Esther Kropp Dakubu, J.O. DeGraft–Hanson, Aloysius Denkabe, Doris Abla Dzbodi Hormenoo, Yao Egblewogbe, Emmanuel Gawuga, Dzifa Glikpoe, Dzifa Gomashie, Kwame Gyekye, Linda Igbe, Carlos Jacques, Kwasi Korateng, Kojo Kyei, Dele Layiwola, Bernth Lindfors, Daniele Luccini, Bill Marshall, Efo Mawugbe, Carlton W. and Barbara J. Molette, Joe Ngozi Mokwunyei, Peter Kweku Nti and his family, Eric Ofei, Esther Ofei, Odia Ofeimun, Akoss Ofori Mensah, Wale Ogunyemi, Ama Ohene, Atukwei Okai, the staff of the Ona Ara Guest House (Agbowo), Nduka Otiono, Minna Otoo, Martin Owusu, Atta Owusu Xornam, Naa Qualey Dove, Jide Shodiyan, Tunji Sotiminrin, Efua Sutherland, Esi Sutherland–Addy, Florence Torson, Kwesi Yankah, Asiedu Yirenkyi, Mary Yirenkyi and, finally, the members of staff at the Institute of African Studies, School of Performing Arts and Department of English (University of Ghana at Legon), Department of Theatre Arts, Department of English and Institute of African Studies (University of Ibadan) for patiently putting up with my daily pestering.

London (1994–1995) was another place where I felt inspired to carry out my research with the much treasured support of my loving and formidable flatmate Bettina Pfanmöller, my brothers in arms Raffaele Colucci and Alan Maddock (glad all over...), my beloved Elaine Ee and Sarah Left, my mates Chris Brealey, Steve Buckley and Claire, Margaret Burmester and Thankam, Tim and Lindsay, Alessandro Capodanno, Cesare Davolio, Paul Gready, Paola Marchionni, Cathy McCann, Cathy McCarthy, Emily McElroy, Lara Sabella, Carlotta Saconney and Sebastian and Julia, Laura Savio. I also wish to thank Osofo Kwadjo Amaning, Elizabeth Gunner, Eldred Durosimi Jones and Ronald Warwick for their academic support.

Finally, the Centre of West African Studies (CWAS), University of Birmingham, an oasis of happiness and enthusiasm in the middle of dreary Birmingham, where I spent three wonderful months (1996). It is hard to convey the human bounty I found there, starting with Stewart Brown, my mentor in African and Caribbean literature, five-a-side football (long live the Golden Codgers!), squash and modesty; Karin Barber, Paulo F. de Moraes Farias, Tom McCaskie, Lynne Brydon and Hannah, always ready to give me some precious advice and encouragement; all those who contributed to the daily enlivening of the CWAS Study Room: the great Jasper "Orso" Morgan Chalcraft, Mawuli Adjei (whom I never managed to beat at table tennis), David Kerr, Adrian Ouvry, Stuart Smith, Edward Tewiah, Alison and Benjamin Torrens, Nancy Van Leyden and Yinka, Souad Zanati. I also wish to thank all the scholars and writers I exchanged views with during my stay at CWAS and later: 'Biyi Bandele–Thomas, Buchi Emecheta, John La Rose, Femi Oyebode, Alain Ricard, Lawrence Scott. A big hug to Stephanie Newell for her boundless patience, advice and affection.

And, first and last and always, I wish to express my love and gratitude to my parents, Francesco Deandrea and Clotilde Mosca, and to my sister Irma, for their constant affection and patience in the face of my trips abroad. What they have given me is indeed impossible to return.

This study is dedicated to the loving memory of my grandmother Adele Costanzo, who died in 1992, and of Ornella Togniaccini, who left us so soon. The final dedication is for my baby nephew Martino; may he grow happily and learn to love and respect his neighbour.

A tutti voi, un abbraccio.

The painting by Erhabor Ogieva Emokpae on the cover is reproduced from Okwui Enwezor, *The Short Century: Independence and Liberation Movements in Africa 1945–1994* (Munich: Prestel-Verlag, 2001), pages 84–85, with kind permission of Prestel.

PIETRO DEANDREA

Introduction: Metamorphoses of Genre

> A good prose writer is also a good poet; a good poet must be able to write good prose; and neither prose nor poetry can reach its heights without some elements of drama. (Osundare, Ibadan, 1 August 1997)[1]

THE PRESENT STUDY traces the growth and development of a phenomenon that has been touching a portion of anglophone West African literature: the interpenetration of prose, poetry and drama, the three main literary genres usually considered and analysed as discrete domains by large sectors of Western culture. The study as a whole is centred on the conviction that the relationships among these three main forms are marked by a high degree of incorporativeness.

The inspirational source behind the process in question appears to be of a syncretistic nature, stemming from the encounter between imported Western models and the traditional conception of literature, where the fluid characteristics of orality create a continuum of genres or, to use Ato Quayson's term, "a conceptual arena of flux."[2] In other words, a 'holistic vision.' Karin Barber's study of Yoruba oral genres is a case in point: in her paper on *Alo* (folktales), *ese Ifa* (Ifa divination verses) and *oriki* (praise poetry or appellations), she states that they "draw on the same thematic and linguistic material; [...] they draw to a considerable extent on each other, for Yoruba oral genres tend to be highly incorporative and porous."[3] This study, therefore, can also be seen as focusing on the tendency on the part of modern African writers to identify with the literary traditions of their people. I have

---

[1] Where quoted material is followed by parentheses including surname, location and date, this refers to one of the interviews listed at the close of the Bibliography below.

[2] Ato Quayson, *Strategic Transformations in Nigerian Writing: Orality and History in the Work of Rev. Samuel Johnson, Amos Tutuola, Wole Soyinka and Ben Okri* (Oxford: James Currey; Bloomington & Indianapolis: Indiana UP, 1997): 13.

[3] Karin Barber, "Multiple Discourses in Yoruba Oral Literature," *Bulletin of the John Rylands University Library of Manchester* 73.3 (Autumn 1991): 13.

attempted here to trace parallelisms between traditional and contemporary literature with regard not so much to specific borrowings of content, but mostly as part of a general strategic attitude towards literary genres and techniques.

The path I have followed has also been foreshadowed by Karin Barber's emphasis, in her studies of the popular arts in Africa, on a phenomenon similar to the one I shall be examining. Among the forms of art taken into consideration, Barber shows the existence of porosity in the realm of Onitsha market literature:

> the genres into which the pamphlet writers poured their imaginative effort – drama, novel, poem, and, of course, letter – also derive not from indigenous culture, where these concepts have no exact counterparts, but from the literary tradition of the metropolitan countries. But the use they make of these forms is (literally) unconventional. The requirements of consistency and unity of form are often totally disregarded.

Barber takes as exemplary R. Okonkwo's *The Game of Love*, which freely mixes the most diverse of styles. It displays a dramatic format in which stage directions turn into passages typical of the psychological novel, occasionally switching to the epistolary format and to a final authorial poem regarding the theme of the work.[4]

Still in the realm of popular literature, Stephanie Newell notes how the didactic thrust of market literature leads its authors to stop their narrative in order to "actively interpret and offer counsel," mixing the fictional with the 'how-to' text.[5] In another of her works, she focuses on a book which attacks the practice of the bride price as immoral: similarly to the case discussed above by Karin Barber, its author alternates dramatic dialogue with long, narrative and interpretative stage directions. *Money Marriages* by Eze Ebisike thus freely admixes theatrical and prose formats. In turn, the pedagogic dimension mixes with the fictional one in both stage directions and dialogue, where the characters read long passages aloud from other texts to drive their point home.[6]

Bearing in mind such examples from other fields, I started investigating an analogous occurrence: the cross-contaminations among prose, poetry and theatre formats in anglophone West African literature.

The first part of this book analyses the techniques through which the novel and the short story have been 'poeticized' or rendered highly lyrical. Chapter 1 estab-

---

[4] Karin Barber, "Popular Arts in Africa," *African Studies Review* 30.3 (September 1987): 36.

[5] Stephanie Newell, "From the Brink of Oblivion: The Anxious Masculinism of Nigerian Market Literatures," *Research in African Literatures* 27.3 (Fall 1996): 57.

[6] Eze Ebisike, *Money Marriages: Mammon Marriages (Stop Mammon Marriages)* (Lagos: Beteze, 1992): 14–17.

lishes the forerunners of metamorphosis, such as Amos Tutuola's folktales, Ayi Kwei Armah's ancestral cantor's style, Ama Ata Aidoo's mix of prose and verses and her re-creation of popular orality, ending with Kofi Awoonor's lyrical novels reproducing the mood of Ewe dirges. Chapter 2 concentrates on the literary mode that has sprung from those four departure models – West African magical realism. To my knowledge, a comprehensive definition of this has been attempted only by Brenda Cooper, with whom I interact critically, elaborating on relevant categorizations and characteristics before reflecting on the novels written by its three exponents: Syl Cheney–Coker, Ben Okri and Kojo Laing, each developing his own variation on magical-realist narrative. Chapter 3 takes into consideration the daring works by Okri and Laing which can hardly be labelled magical realism as such and which constitute a new mode going beyond it.

The second part focuses on the drive of Ghanaian poetry towards the theatrical, the shift from written verse to the live stage. In this case, the precursor, thanks to his live recitals which ignited the 'movement' from the early 1970s, is Atukwei Okai, examined early in Chapter 4. His successors Kofi Anyidoho and Kobena Eyi Acquah further developed this practice, devising shows for theatrical companies representing their own verse; what they established in the 1980s is anticipated in the poems of Kojo Kyei staged in the early 1970s. Chapter 5 discusses the development of poetry on stage in the 1990s before analysing the highly oral style of three Ghanaian poets: Kojo Laing, Abena Busia and Kwabena Osei–Boahene.

The third part considers anglophone drama – 'élite', 'art' and 'literary' drama are other qualifiers normally applied – and the various influences that have been at work on it: ie traditional theatre, popular theatre and theatre for development, examined in all their cross-fertilizations. Chapter 6 treats the pioneering work of Efua Sutherland and her fellow Ghanaian playwrights from the very beginning of independence in 1957, while Chapter 7 concentrates on the author whom I hold to be the true heir of the trend they launched, Mohammed ben Abdallah. In both chapters, comparisons are traced with authors from other West African countries, with special attention to the highly innovative theatre of the Nigerian Femi Osofisan.

This tripartite structure, dedicated to each of the three genres, may seem to be a paradox: in a way, it structurally reaffirms the divisions that the main concept behind the whole book tries to negate. However, I have tried to maintain a high degree of fluidity with the help of the examined authors, whose suppleness sometimes allows them to appear in more than one chapter.

Furthermore, it will eventually become obvious how the concept of porosity is not limited to the interpenetrations of the three main genres. First of all, several authors also write books for children as a way to diversify their social engagement through literature. Secondly, most of them are producers of an impressively fertile critical literature – I actually received the most illuminating insights on the subject of my research from such essays, where artists often manage to blend creativity and in-depth analysis. A case in point is undoubtedly Femi Osofisan's essay "Warriors of a Failed Utopia?" (1996), which to my view represents one of the best overviews of the developments in anglophone West African literature since the 1970s; the essay begins with a touching remembrance of some recently deceased writers:

> I am constrained to speak to you with anguish as my primary drumstick. Especially, I speak with the wound of loss. [...] For all these ghosts, who will always remain among us because of the books they left behind, I beg your indulgence to sing this dirge from one of my plays.[7]

The widespread double role of creative writer-cum-critic in contemporary West Africa can be accounted for in different ways. First, the present state of the West African literary realm is able to guarantee financial survival only to the happy and fortunate few; academic posts may thus answer to a basic need, as they do to a good number of the authors examined here. Secondly, the Achebian precept of the novelist as teacher still exerts a pervasive, penetrating influence; if in 1965 Achebe envisaged his role as "to help my society regain belief in itself and put away the complexes of the years of denigration and self-abasement,"[8] one only need think of the neocolonial self-abasement that has been accumulating in the past thirty years to grasp the urgency of this statement.

Such an affirmation of the function of literature certainly calls forth a clarification of the critical standpoint of this book. From what has been said so far about the porosity of literary genres, readers might tend to expect a rigorously formalistic focus on stylistic techniques. On the contrary, I wish to avoid any poststructuralist highlighting of the text's primacy, of the way it constantly deconstructs its own intended meaning – in tune with Niyi Osundare's rejection of poststructuralist theories as inadequate to the contemporary African condition:

> many aspects of poststructuralist theorising have made the humanization of discourse impossible, as a result of their fetishization of the text and its theory. The over-abstract, reified process of contemporary theorising have hitherto not shown any efficient

[7] Femi Osofisan, "Warriors of a Failed Utopia? West African Writers since the '70s," *Leeds African Studies Bulletin* 61 (1996): 11.

[8] Chinua Achebe, *Morning Yet on Creation Day* (London: Heinemann, 1975): 44.

> medium of recognizing, analysing and representing the urgent concrete specificities of the developing world.[9]

The same accusation is levelled by the late critic Richard Bjornson:

> the social, economic, political and environmental crises facing the world in general and Africa in particular are so serious that new patterns of thinking must be elaborated if we hope to preserve the possibility of a decent future for the human race. The tendency of contemporary literary theory to dismiss the relevance of this problem to its area of specialized knowledge strikes me as morally irresponsible and ultimately schizophrenic in its consequences. [...] it seems to me that scholars of African literature cannot afford to ignore the moral dimension of their theoretical activity.[10]

The critical trend decried by Osundare and Bjornson is also known as 'postcolonial theory'. Its three principal exponents (the 'Holy Trinity') are Edward Said, Gayatri Spivak and Homi Bhabha, whose theoretical leanings are predicated on the tenets of French 'high' theory – represented in turn by a further trinity: Derrida, Lacan and Foucault. In his *Postcolonial Theory*, Bart Moore–Gilbert subtly analyses similarities and variations among the three; he particularly emphasizes the divide separating them from the great iceberg of postcolonial criticism, which rejects the poststructuralist retreat from social import.[11]

I have chosen to offer one concrete instance of such misplaced critical paradigms. In Chapter 1, I opted to exclude Ato Sekyi–Otu's essay on Armah's *Two Thousand Seasons*, even though it was published in one of the most prestigious journals of African literature. Armah's novel represents an impressive imaginative effort to construct the history of the Ghanaian people through the voice of an oral bard, whose lyrical thrust shaped by a novelistic frame produces one of the finest examples of the porosity mentioned above, and whose purpose is to reinforce a set of collective values and visions in his communitarian narratees. This ancestral voice rejects "the tricks of making up sure knowledge of things possible to think of, things possible to wonder about but impossible to know in any such ultimate way. We are

---

[9] Niyi Osundare, *African Literature and the Crisis of Poststructuralist Theorising* (Ibadan: Options Book and Information Services, 1993): 10. An identical view is expressed by Osofisan, "Warriors of a Failed Utopia?," 15, and by Stephen Slemon & Helen Tiffin, *After Europe: Critical Theory and Postcolonial Writing*, ed. Slemon & Tiffin (Mundelstrup & Sydney: Dangaroo, 1989): Introduction.

[10] Richard Bjornson, "Theory and Moral Commitment in the Study of African Literature," in *Literary Theory and African Literature*, ed. Joseph Gugler, Hans–Jürgen Lüsebrink & Jürgen Martini (Beiträge zur Afrikaforschung 3; Münster & Hamburg: LIT, 1994): 34–35.

[11] Bart Moore–Gilbert, *Postcolonial Theory: Contexts, Practices and Politics* (London: Verso, 1997): 1.

not stunted in spirit."[12] This quotation can be interpreted as a refusal of dogmatic truths before the unknown, paralleled by a rejection of the origins frozen in writing imposed by Arabic and Western cultures on traditional oral philosophies. In any case, one should not spend too much time on the issue, just as Isidore Okpewho does not: he rightly states that Armah's original *way* is "unlocated in time because the narrator knows only that it has been a living heritage of the race from an indeterminate past, a past that it is pointless to probe."[13] Rather, one is supposed to shift to the core of the novel, that is to say the narrator's pathos and moral urgency in the transmission of his lore, in the face of a secular oppression by foreign people: the things "possible to wonder about" are treated very seriously. Sekyi–Otu, though, quotes Kristeva and Derrida to hold that the narrator's

> epistemic and political gesture is internally subverted by a scornful disavowal of "sure knowledge" of the "ultimate origin" [...] What does the first chapter's opening satire on the formal and semantic conventions of "epic logic" signify if not a prefigurative deconstruction of the narrative's fictive proposition and allegorical certitudes?[14]

It is hard to find such a deconstructive tone in Armah's novel. The critic's tools are to be blamed here, because they are unsuitable to the object of their criticism; they patently belong to that postmodernist tendency to debunk "*all* efforts to speak of origins, collectivities, determinate historical projects," in the words of the Marxist critic Aijaz Ahmad.[15] Sekyi–Otu's analysis of *Two Thousand Seasons* actualizes a dangerous tendency pointed out by Slemon and Tiffin: "a poststructuralist refutation of the referent can underscore a theoretical dismissal of some of the basic survival strategies of subordinated and colonised peoples."[16]

On the one hand, therefore, there is the "permanently deferred meaning" dominant in the theories of the "High Canonical West"; on the other, "the theories of the peripheral social formations [...] deeply embedded in discourses and construction of

---

[12] Ayi Kwei Armah, *Two Thousand Seasons* (1973; Oxford: Heinemann, 1979): 3.

[13] Isidore Okpewho, "Myth and Modern Fiction: Armah's *Two Thousand Seasons*," *African Literature Today* 13 (1983): 16.

[14] Ato Sekyi–Otu, "'Toward Anoa... Not Back to Anoa': The Grammar of Revolutionary Homecoming in *Two Thousand Seasons*," *Research in African Literatures* 18.2 (Summer 1987): 192, 194.

[15] Aijaz Ahmad, *In Theory: Classes, Nations, Literatures* (London: Verso, 1992): 38. Moore–Gilbert (*Postcolonial Theory*, 75) aptly suggests that Spivak, on the other hand, has been engaging with actual manifestations of counter-discourse.

[16] Slemon & Tiffin, ed. *After Europe*, i.

collective destinies, of national cultures and identity."[17] From what has been said above, it should be clear that this study openly espouses the latter viewpoint. All the writers examined in the following chapters – and the metamorphoses of genre they operate in their works – deal with social issues of their times that can be associated with specific geographical and historical situations. Despite floating freely among received literary genres, they are a far cry from belonging to that figure of the migrant writer and / or intellectual who inhabits the interstitial spaces in-between the various cultures; such writers have long been championed by influential critics of 'postcolonialism' like Homi Bhabha, who asserts that "the truest eye may now belong to the migrant's double vision."[18] The critic Arun P. Mukherjee's fear of a homogenizing postmodern / postcolonial theory "which erodes or elides this difference in our [the ex-colonies'] historical or material circumstances" is closer to the spirit of these pages.[19]

The questions at issue are summed up perfectly by Niyi Osundare:

> We are talking about a continent with very little control over its economy and politics, whose intra-continental interactions are still dominated by the same old colonial languages – a continent so heavily indebted to the finance houses of the advanced industrialized world, that many of its governments are virtually under foreign receiverships.

Consequently, the label 'postcolonial' will not be employed for the authors' works, in complete agreement with Osundare – "How can we talk so glibly, so confidently about the 'postcoloniality' of a place so *neo*-colonial?"[20]

The generic metamorphoses and the various styles consequently adopted by each author are not considered here as pure formalistic devices, but as more (or less) effective ways of articulating the pressing issues mentioned above. This dissertation intends to attain and maintain a balance between stylistic features, the content these features bring to the fore and the context in which they are expressed. My ideal model may be described by what the Marxist critic Chidi Amuta writes: "a rigorous sociology of literature perceives the context of literature, its content and form as dialectically interconnected areas for comprehending the social essence of literature."[21]

---

[17] Biodun Jeyifo, "Literary Theory and Theories of Decolonization," in *Literary Theory and African Literature*, ed. Joseph Gugler, Hans–Jürgen Lüsebrink & Jürgen Martini (Beiträge zur Afrikaforschung 3; Münster & Hamburg: LIT, 1994): 18, 29.

[18] Homi K. Bhabha, *The Location of Culture* (London: Routledge, 1994): 5.

[19] Arun P. Mukherjee, "Whose Postcolonialism and Whose Postmodernism?," *World Literature Written in English* 30.2 (1990): 2.

[20] Osundare, *African Literature and the Crisis of Poststructuralist Theorising*, 8.

[21] Chidi Amuta, *The Theory of African Literature: Implications for Practical Criticism* (London: Zed, 1989): 9.

Despite stating that "the notion among bourgeois critics that sociological criticism [...] eschews formal considerations is false,"[22] Amuta's excessively deterministic readings of particular texts does not meet the expectations raised by his promising theoretical paradigms. I have attempted to avoid this fatal mistake by placing formal considerations at the pivotal point of my discussion, thereby leaving unspoilt the aesthetic pleasure inherent in literary creation, consumption and criticism. As the francophone writer Henri Lopes states, "it is more important for literary works to be 'engaging' than to be 'engaged'."[23] Marxist criticism of African literature has sometimes fallen prey to a 'take-up-arms' attitude which eventually reduces the unique potentialities of literature to arid sloganeering. One of its most emblematic instances (again, concerning Ayi Kwei Armah) is Ode S. Ogede's view of *The Healers*: according to Ogede, the novel's weak point is its "absence of an interventionist political ethic [...] to achieve the revolution."[24]

As far as context is concerned, I am indebted to the non-literary secondary sources employed here. My concern for context also accounts for the fact that this work displays an evident Ghanaian focus; Ghana was the West African state where I resided and researched the longest, and this necessarily influenced the geographical scope of my study.[25] Nevertheless, an effort has been made not to neglect any possible parallel with authors from the rest of anglophone West Africa, and, when suitable, with literary products from other parts of the world. More than mere comparisons, each chapter shows how – to different degrees – Latin American or European literary movements have functioned as catalysts of the West African generic porosity, giving rise to a rediscovery of one's artistic roots. Beside literary genres, then, the holistic vision of this book manifests itself in a geographic scope going beyond the West African region. I will return to this topic in due course, in each chapter as well as in my conclusion.

For my part, I offer here a small contribution to these various dilutions of confines by interspersing the interviews I had with some of the authors, as exemplified by the epigraph above. Too often interviews and essays have been kept neatly separated by critics and publishers of African literature; their blend may help under-

---

22 Amuta, *Theory of African Literature*, 9.

23 Bjornson, "Theory and Moral Commitment in the Study of African Literature," 31.

24 Ode S. Ogede, "The Rhetoric of Revolution in Armah's *The Healers:* Form as Experience," *African Studies Review* 36.1 (April 1993): 46.

25 Since it considers several writers producing in the 1980s and the 1990s, this work could also be seen as a modest complement to Charles Angmor's *Contemporary Literature in Ghana 1911–1978: A Critical Evaluation* (Accra: Woeli, 1996).

stand more thoroughly the factors working behind creative productions. Such a reliance on the interviews can sound too indulgent with authorial intentions, but I have made an effort to probe constantly into my own perplexities.

PROSE: THE POETICIZED NOVEL

1 Orality and the Novels of the First Generations

IN AN ANALYSIS OF INTERPENETRATIONS among anglophone West African prose, poetry and theatre, recourse to fiction as a starting point may sound bizarre. If, as posited in the introduction of this work, the syncretistic influence of the oral literary heritage is one of the main factors contributing to such a phenomenon, at first glance the novel should play a comparatively marginal role.

In fact, drama and poetry easily involve communal participation – that is, the basis of oral arts – unlike the isolated creation and consumption of the novel.[1] In his essay on Nikolai Leskov, Walter Benjamin identifies the decline of storytelling with the rise of the novel, made possible by the invention of printing: "What differentiates the novel from all other forms of prose literature – the fairy tale, the legend, even the novella – is that it neither comes from oral tradition nor goes into it."[2] Benjamin prophesies the end of the art of storytelling, while Femi Osofisan similarly states that "the modern age is [...] the storyteller's nightmare."[3]

In the same essays, though, all three critics throw their initial pessimism overboard by discussing those novelists who retained oral features in their prose. Benjamin delves into the Russian writer Leskov's enchanting prose, which points at the inadequacies of the modern civilization to come; Osofisan, in his highly literary style, attempts a daring comparison between African and European masters, grouped under the term "Tutuolans"; Sackey concentrates on African authors, most of whom are included here in Chapter 1 as precursors of the later magical-realist

[1] Edward Sackey, "Oral Tradition and the African Novel," *Modern Fiction Studies* 37.3 (Autumn 1991): 389.

[2] Walter Benjamin, "The Storyteller: Reflections on the Works of Nikolai Leskov," in *Illuminations*, ed. Hannah Arendt, tr. Harry Zohn (1955; London: Collins / Fontana, 1992): 87.

[3] Femi Osofisan, "Wonderland and the Orality of Prose: A Comparative Study of Rabelais, Joyce and Tutuola," in *The Genre of Prose Fiction: Two Complementary Views* (Ile-Ife: Ife Monographs on Literature and Criticism, 4th series, 3, 1986): 2.

generation: in his view, these writers "represent a sophisticated continuation of African storytelling and other oral traditions in dialectic tension with the novel form."[4]

In the field of African literary criticism, the tendency to look for such continuities is as widespread as it is old. Eileen Julien traces its origin to Léopold Senghor, and interprets it as an understandable reaction against the previous eurocentric appropriation. She shows very little sympathy for those critics who reinforce the dichotomy *novel=West vs. orality=Africa*: "Does the absence or presence of a literary form in one's past determine the extent to which it might exist in one's future?"[5]

Julien further exposes some critical clichés very sharply. The most dangerous among them seems to be another absurd opposition, that is to say, *realist novel= West* versus *'oral' novel=Africa*, even though realism has dominated – and it still dominates, in a way – anglophone West African prose.[6] On one hand, as she says, the Western novel is not to be considered as one monolithic essence grounded in realism and linearity, given its diversity and historical development.[7] Such stereotypes could be overcome by comparative approaches like the one by Osofisan mentioned above, analysing both African and Western writers who are "half-surrenders" to "the conspiracy of prose."[8]

On the other hand, the risk implied in that manichaean antinomy could lead to an unjustifiable idealization of the oral elements constituting some African novels: "*Orality* has become a metonymy for *African*," she warns, rejecting as well any "prescriptions for authenticity."[9] This chapter does not intend to point at supposedly superior novelistic standards, either, but merely try to examine the trends and poetics of some West African novelists. In the case of Ghana, the tendency to poeticize narrative works seems to have dominated in the 1970s, since the three Ghanaian authors examined in Chapter 1 – Ayi Kwei Armah, Ama Ata Aidoo and Kofi Awoonor – are the only Ghanaians included in Bernth Lindfors's "Famous Authors' Reputation Test": ie, among the twenty most popular anglophone African writers.[10]

4 Edward Sackey, "Oral Tradition and the African Novel," 390

5 Eileen Julien, *African Novels and the Question of Orality* (Bloomington: Indiana UP, 1992): 9. "For the same kind of reason I shouldn't know how to drive a car because I am no descendant of Henry Ford," Achebe quips on the topic (Achebe, *Morning Yet on Creation Day*, 54).

6 See Richard K. Priebe, *Myth, Realism and the West African Writer* (Trenton NJ: Africa World Press, 1988): 2.

7 See Julien, *African Novels and the Question of Orality*, 29–33.

8 Osofisan, "Wonderland and the Orality of Prose," 2.

9 Julien, *African Novels and the Question of Orality*, 10, 24.

10 Bernth Lindfors, *Comparative Approaches to African Literatures* (Cross / Cultures 14; Amsterdam & Atlanta GA: Rodopi, 1994): 131–40.

Amos Tutuola: the folktale revisited

The Palm-Wine Drinkard (1952), by the Nigerian writer Amos Tutuola (1920–97), is generally considered as the inception of anglophone West African fiction, and it has been thoroughly sifted by numerous critics. The drinkard's adventures in search of his dead palm-wine tapster struck the critical world because of their originality, primarily grounded in Yoruba language and oral traditions.

Tutuola's imperfect command of the English language[11] is revitalized to such an extent by the oral features of his mother language Yoruba[12] that the final result bears strong marks of musicality. The following otherworldly encounter – one among many – may serve as an example:

> there we saw a man who was walking towards his back or backwards, his both eyes were on his knees, his both arms were at his both thighs, these both arms were longer than his feet and both could reach the topmost of any tree; and he held a long whip too.[13]

Refrains, capital letters and repetitions in parentheses to reproduce an imaginary audience's response[14] are only some of the devices lending the novel that peculiar atmosphere called by Osofisan "orality's soundscape" and "percussive literature."[15]

As far as oral genres are concerned, Tutuola's borrowings are multifarious; Ato Quayson singles out the following:

> riddles, proverbs and etiological tales [...] his narratives become concatenations of several elements from Yoruba storytelling traditions and thus cannot be easily limited to one mode or genre.[16]

The 'porosity' of Yoruba oral genres brought to the fore by Karin Barber and mentioned here in the introduction, then, thrives in Tutuola's novels. In such a net of different traditional elements, the function of each is developed beyond its usual role, since its formulaic ending is made more open by the wider context.[17]

---

[11] For Tutuola's biographical data and modest level of literacy, see Bernth Lindfors, "Amos Tutuola: Debts and Assets" (1970), in Lindfors, ed. *Critical Perspectives on Amos Tutuola* (1975; London: Heinemann, 1980): 224–55.

[12] For the linguistic influence of Yoruba pervading Tutuola's English, see E.N. Obiechina, "Amos Tutuola and the Oral Tradition," 1968, in Lindfors, ed. *Critical Perspectives on Amos Tutuola*, 112–14; A. Afolayan, "Language and Sources of Amos Tutuola" (1971), in Lindfors, ed. *Critical Perspectives on Amos Tutuola*, 148–62.

[13] Amos Tutuola, *The Palm-Wine Drinkard* (1952; London: Faber & Faber, 1961): 56.

[14] See Laura Lasagna, "The Logos of the African Trickster," *Africa America Asia Australia* 16 (1994): 33–34.

[15] Osofisan, "Wonderland and the Orality of Prose," 8.

[16] Quayson, *Strategic Transformations in Nigerian Writing*, 59.

[17] See Quayson, *Strategic Transformations in Nigerian Writing*, 58.

Furthermore, Western fiction and criticism are not to be excluded from the range of Tutuola's sources: as Osofisan writes about the Tutuolans, "their fantasy world is a mosaic of other people's bits and pieces. Just like the griot's world."[18] First, the grotesque creatures swarming in and out of his writings clearly show how he was influenced by D.O. Fagunwa's Yoruba novels, with his hunters/heroes having to overcome similarly supernatural obstacles. Fagunwa, in his turn, was inspired by his own Christian beliefs, and the structure of his works are often compared with Bunyan's *Pilgrim's Progress*.[19] The influence of Christianity in western Nigeria may account for the pervasive grisly beings in both writers' works. In his essay on Yoruba folktales, Val Olayemi states that "though encounters with supernatural agencies are numerous in Yoruba folktales, the supernatural element is not of major significance."[20] The origin of the ghastly dimension is traced by Quayson:

> [in] an uncommon type of cautionary tales told to children [...which] involve the most frightening aspects of life outside the village community [...] It is possible to argue, then, that both Fagunwa and Tutuola settled on these types of tales precisely because it was these residues from childhood which challenged their new found Christianity. In a way, settling on them was a way of coming to terms with the awe and terror that their new religion asserted was inherent in the relationship between man and the spirit-realm.[21]

Secondly, Tutuola's lavish employment of metamorphosis could be construed in terms of Bakhtin's concept of the carnivalesque. It is significant that Osofisan describes as "carnival" a passage from *The Palm-Wine Drinkard* and associates Tutuola with Rabelais, a writer that Bakhtin analyses at length.[22] The idea of the carnivalesque will also show its usefulness later on in this chapter, with regard to magical realism.

---

[18] Osofisan, "Wonderland and the Orality of Prose," 10.

[19] "Fagunwa was a dominant figure on much of Yoruba literature from the mid-1940s when his books were introduced into the curricula in the then Western Nigeria"; Quayson, *Strategic Transformations in Nigerian Writing*, 45. With regard to an analysis of the similarities and differences between Tutuola and Fagunwa, Lindfors argues that "Tutuola does not moralize and he is never sentimental. Fagunwa is much more a Christian writer" (*Comparative Approaches to African Literatures*, 5), while Quayson notes that Tutuola's protagonists are "decidedly anti-heroic," if compared to Fagunwa's hunters (*Strategic Transformations in Nigerian Writing*, 51).

[20] Val Olayemi, "The Supernatural in the Yoruba Folktale," in *Yoruba Oral Tradition: Poetry, Music, Dance and Drama*, ed. Wande Abimbola (Ife African Languages and Literatures Series 1; Department of African Languages and Literatures, University of Ife, 1975): 969.

[21] Quayson, *Strategic Transformations in Nigerian Writing*, 46, 61.

[22] Osofisan, "Wonderland and the Orality of Prose," 20.

In general, Tutuola's "fresh distillations of the original material"[23] – from traditional and Western sources – appear to be his major achievement. His weak points, on the other hand, have been widely discussed by critics. In emphasizing the active presence of African languages in some europhone West African novels, Chantal Zabus excludes Tutuola from the process of 'relexification', which is meant to be

> a conscious, deliberate method of indigenization. Tutuola is for the most part inadvertently calquing, yet safeguarding the rhetoric, word play and bizarre imagery cherished by the Yoruba.[24]

In other words, Tutuola did not master the English language, therefore he could not fully subvert it. Since I am interested not so much in a strictly linguistic examination as in a study of style, structures, techniques and themes, Zabus's judgement is less relevant to my purpose.[25] The thematic liabilities stressed by several critics, unsatisfied with the novel's lack of connections with contemporary issues, sound more convincing.[26] Even Osofisan, Tutuola's staunch supporter, agrees with that view: "Is the modern griot free of the burden which his traditional counterpart carried, of commitment to his society?"[27] Quayson expresses a similar opinion on *My Life in the Bush of Ghosts* (1954),[28] Tutuola's second novel, where "social concerns can only be glimpsed as underdeveloped possibilities."[29]

This may account for the fact that Tutuola was hardly ever imitated, considering the social-realist trend that dominated the first generations of West African novelists. His paradox, then, consists in being the founder as well as a temporary dead-end for anglophone African literature. Years ago, Gerald Moore believed that

> there are not likely to be two Tutuolas in Africa today, and to write in his manner without comparable visionary power and imaginative intensity would not only be foolish but, for a more educated writer, affected as well.[30]

---

23 Osofisan, "Wonderland and the Orality of Prose," 10.

24 Chantal Zabus, *The African Palimpsest: Indigenization of Language in the West African Europhone Novel* (Cross / Cultures 4; Amsterdam & Atlanta GA: Rodopi, 1991): 113.

25 This is also the reason why Gabriel Okara's *The Voice* (1964), where the experimentalism mainly consists of an English language rendered according to Ijaw structures, is not examined in this chapter.

26 "Tutuola fails us in his inability to make use of his private myths to describe real life situations [... he is] frozen at the level of the tale"; Charles E. Nnolim, "The Nigerian Tradition in the Novel," *The Commonwealth Novel in English* 2.2 (1983): 24.

27 Osofisan, "Wonderland and the Orality of Prose," 35.

28 See also Chapter 7 (p. 244) below, for the dramatization of this novel by Bode Sowande.

29 Quayson, *Strategic Transformations in Nigerian Writing*, 73.

30 Gerald Moore, "Amos Tutuola: A Nigerian Visionary" (1957), in *Critical Perspectives on Amos Tutuola*, ed. Bernth Lindfors (London: Heinemann, 1980): 42.

Chapter 2 attempts to show how Ben Okri, in his three *abiku* novels, displays the same hallucinatory energy with a great control of the English language, and without overlooking the unquestionable role of the novel as a commitment, as the field where the "formidable problems and social inequities that Africa now faces become quite visible."[31] In the light of Okri's debt to Tutuola, one can easily agree with Lindfors's assessment of Tutuola's work:

> His originality set an excellent precedent for later writers who might otherwise have followed too parasitically the literary fashion of Europe. [...] Although few of his innovations were conscious or calculated and many were borrowed from Fagunwa and Yoruba oral tradition, he deserves to be called the father of experimentation in Nigerian fiction in English.[32]

Ayi Kwei Armah's griotization of the novel

The 1970s brought several writers – most of them Ghanaian – whose experiments steered away from the dominant social realist novel.

The first three works by Ayi Kwei Armah (b.1939) dive deep into the alienation of independent Ghana and Africa, the crisis of the neocolonial subject unsuccessfully looking for an intellectual rebirth abroad, the disillusionment caused by the failure of revolutionary ideologies and the need to recover traditional values. Their style and technique, though, do not show any particular breakthrough in relation to experimental later works. His subsequent development is represented by two courageous attempts at fusing those values with a new concept of 'oral' novel, "a revolution," Robert Fraser writes, "not only in Armah's art in particular, but for the African novel in general."[33]

Two Thousand Seasons (1973) is a history of the people who inhabit contemporary Ghana, according to the myth that tracks down their origin to the tenth-century African empire bearing the same name and which was located in the western Sudan.[34] The narrator mourns the loss of the traditional *way*, constituted by a balance between giving and receiving. The dominance of the former opens the

31 Julien, *African Novels and the Question of Orality*, 157.

32 Lindfors, "Amos Tutuola: Debts and Assets," 255.

33 Robert Fraser, *The Novels of Ayi Kwei Armah: A Study in Polemical Fiction* (London: Heinemann, 1980): 11. According to Lindfors's "Famous Authors' Reputation Test," Armah's popularity has constantly increased since this decisive turn in his writing; Lindfors, *Comparative Approaches to African Literatures*, 131–40.

34 See also Fraser, *Novels of Ayi Kwei Armah*, 71.

way to the invasion of the *predators* (the Arabs). Thus the originally cohesive black people are scattered for centuries, causing mass migrations southward, with their spiritual welfare already threatened by the mental enslavement that creates producers and parasites, the latter including kings as well. The narrator belongs to a group of twenty youngsters who, inspired by the seer Isanusi, have to be initiated as *fundi*. Thanks to a trick supported by King Koranche, they are imprisoned in the *destroyers*' (whites') slave ship, but they manage to escape and recruit more people in a guerrilla war fought against the European invaders, eventually conquering Poano Castle and killing the king himself.

The narrator's point of view is certainly the most original feature of the book: it is an all-pervasive first-person plural which stylistically reflects the communal thrust of his own collective philosophy. The narrator's *way*, in fact, is an organic and harmonious society which does not allow any kind of disconnection: "Pieces cut off from the whole are nothing but dead fragments. From the unending stream of our remembrance the harbingers of death break off meaningless fractions."[35] In his book on Akan philosophy, Kwame Gyekye states that "The good is identical with the welfare of society, which is expected to include the welfare of the individual."[36] Such a social theory has ancestral origins, according to *Two Thousand Seasons*, and ten years later Armah will demonstrate in an essay how European Marxism can teach Africa nothing new.[37]

His employment of the pronoun 'we' in the book is unrelenting to the point of disorientating some critical habits: when searching for the narrator's true identity, Sackey writes that "the narrators [are] the group of twenty"[38] – those inspired by the seer Isanusi. Actually, the narrator admits to being only one of them, but never says which one; to be precise, two of the followers are lost during the course of events, so that Sackey's claim should be modified to only eighteen.

Such a search seems to be quite unnecessary, since Armah's 'we' represents an attempt to build a traditional artist's historical narration, an oral bard carrying within himself "the vocation of those who used to be the soulguide of our people, the rememberers of the way" (88). In his book on Armah, Derek Wright asserts that "*Two Thousand Seasons* is the kind of 'novel' that a griot would have written if he had

---

[35] Ayi Kwei Armah, *Two Thousand Seasons* (1973; Oxford: Heinemann, 1979): 1. Further page references are in the main text.

[36] Kwame Gyekye, *An Essay on African Philosophical Thought: The Akan Conceptual Scheme* (Cambridge: Cambridge UP, 1987): 132.

[37] Ayi Kwei Armah, "Masks and Marx," *Présence Africaine* 131 (1984): 35–65.

[38] Sackey, "Oral Tradition and the African Novel," 397.

access to literary form."[39] Thus the 'we' is undoubtedly to be interpreted as something including the whole people, rather than the twenty proposed by Sackey. Such a highly responsible role carries the novel far beyond the realm of literature: *Two Thousand Seasons* is a compound of a people's history, myth, philosophy, pedagogy and politics, albeit a subjective one.[40]

If, as Kofi Awoonor writes, "the function of the [traditional] artist is close to that of a priest,"[41] the narrator's language accordingly shows enchanting, mesmerising qualities:

> Receiving, giving, giving, receiving, all that lives is twin. Who would cast the spell of death, let him separate the two. Whatever cannot give, whatever is ignorant even of receiving, knowing only taking, that thing is past its own mere death. It is a carrier of death. Woe the giver on the road to such a taker, for then the victim has found victorious death. (xii)

This lyrical chronicle moves the novelistic genre closer to poetry, as if the traditional artists's perspective transcended such categories. This is a phenomenon that Armah shares with the authors analysed in the following paragraphs and with West African magical realists in particular.

The storytelling features of the language are a supporting skeleton for the whole book.[42] The narrator addresses his imaginary audience ("who is it calling for examples?," 6), reassures it ("we shall not halt our main remembrance long," 56), and quite often intrudes with meta-narrative comments, calling for a pause, more swiftness, an end to a digression, and so on.[43] The following quotation illustrates this:

> We should not stay too long with them [the kings]. Let us make haste to move beyond them and their stinking memory. The smallest arrowpoint they occupy in our thought is too much space. (64)

---

[39] Unlike the term 'griotization' included in the title of this chapter, Wright coins 'griotature' and 'griotarary narrator'; Derek Wright, *Ayi Kwei Armah's Africa: The Sources of His Fiction* (New Perspectives on African Literature 1; London: Hans Zell, 1989): 226, 228, 244.

[40] Edward Sackey rightly defines it as "encyclopedic"; Sackey, "Oral Tradition and the African Novel," 402.

[41] Kofi Awoonor, *The Breast of the Earth: A Survey of the History, Culture and Literature of Africa South of the Sahara* (Garden City NY: Doubleday / Anchor, 1975): 62.

[42] Armah "recaptures the oral dimension in the textual performance, and formalizes orality without infringing orality's codes"; Claudio Gorlier, "The Haunted House of National Literature: Individual Malaise and Communal Plight in the Making of a Literary Discourse in A.K. Armah's Novels and G. Okara's *The Voice*," in *Literature and National Consciousness*, ed. Ernest N. Emenyonu (Calabar Studies in African Literature 4; Ibadan: Heinemann Educational, 1989): 19.

[43] See also 128, 163, 179, 192.

The language is also replete with refrains and repetitions. Consider, for instance, how often "our way, the way" is repeated in all its variants. In his study of African oral literature, Isidore Okpewho writes that such a stylistic quality has an aesthetically incantatory as well as utilitarian value; there is thus perfect agreement between the lyrical and the didactic purpose of Armah's novel.[44]

On the whole, then, the book should be considered an oral utterance to be heard: 'utterers' is often employed as a synonym for 'seers', while the last but one paragraph reads: "Soon we shall end this remembrance, the sound of it" (206).

The temporal structure of the book also goes against realistic prescriptions: "a non-Western sense of time."[45] It embraces an infinite span, from myths of origin through the narrator's age in order to look far into the future, never mentioning a single date:

> The linking of those gone, ourselves here, those coming; our continuation, our flowing not along any meretricious channel but along our living way, the way: it is that remembrance that calls us. (14)

Armah's originality, then, resides in his avoidance of expected genre categorizations as well: as a *novel* revolutionary, *Two Thousand Seasons* does not fit perfectly in the pigeon-hole of *epic*, either, which is considered by Bakhtin (in such essays as "Epic and Novel") as something closed, self-sufficient, without room for future openness. Actually, Armah's novel is well rooted in its vision of the future: Kofi Anyidoho notes that "the words Vision and Seer recur with as much frequency as Remembrance or Rememberers."[46]

Anyidoho elsewhere accurately identifies the temporal route followed by Armah's work: given that his first three novels are a sort of cul-de-sac for the neo-colonial subject, the only way out is to retreat into the deepest recesses of history.[47]

---

[44] Isidore Okpewho, *African Oral Literature: Backgrounds, Character and Continuity* (Bloomington & Indianapolis: Indiana UP, 1992): 78. It is not by chance that Okpewho has written one of the most stimulating essays on the novel, focusing on the author's Janus-faced attitude of respect and irreverence towards orality. The latter facet embraces the absence in Armah of eulogistic commentary on kings / heroes and of authorial proprietorship; Isidore Okpewho consequently defines *Two Thousand Seasons* as "tradition revised"; Okpewho, "Myth and Modern Fiction: Armah's *Two Thousand Seasons*," *African Literature Today* 13 (1983): 1–23.

[45] Peter Nazareth, "Time in the Third World: A Fictional Exploration," in *Awakened Conscience: Studies in Commonwealth Literature*, ed. C.D. Narasimhaiah (New Delhi: Sterling, 1978): 203.

[46] Kofi Anyidoho, "Historical Realism and the Visionary Ideal: Ayi Kwei Armah's *Two Thousand Seasons*," *Ufahamu* 11.2 (Fall 1981): 113.

[47] Kofi Anyidoho, "Ayi Kwei Armah and Our Journey of the Mind," in *Literature and National Consciousness*, ed. Ernest N. Emenyonu (Calabar Studies in African Literature 4; Ibadan: Heine-

Such a movement backwards is to be seen in a wider perspective, as a tool to guide one's ideology forward: besides teeming with warnings about the future in general, *Two Thousand Seasons* employs history and fiction to delve into neocolonial alienation as well, an age the narrator does not explicitly touch on; several pages, for instance, are dedicated to the mental enslavement produced by *predators* and *destroyers*. In addition, the power-craze seizing Kamuzu after the conquest of Poano Castle cannot but remind readers (apart from the Malawian dictator Kamuzu Banda) of the excesses of Nkrumah's regime. His lust for praise appellations – including "Osagyefo" ('Saviour-at-War'), attached by Nkrumah to his own presidential title – and his obsession about the castle are significant:

> Kamuzu thought we should aim to keep the stone place permanently. He even called it, after the manner of the white destroyers, his castle. In his opinion, the stone place was the new seat of power over our people in the new arrangements brought by the whites, and whoever held it would be the person in ultimate control. (171)

The castle image is a recurrent one in Armah's writings. He never concealed his shock after Kwame Nkrumah – the first president of independent Ghana – settled down in Christianborg Castle, one of the many fortresses used as prisons during the slave trade: "his first major act," complained Armah, "was to occupy the colonial castle which symbolises slavery."[48]

The spatial range of *Two Thousand Seasons* is huge as well, trying to involve, as it does, all black people, on the grounds of their common origin. After escaping from the ship, slaves from other lands join the guerrilla war. Their names, like those of the twenty youngsters, cover a pan-African toponymy that includes artists, scholars and fictional characters.[49] The novel's ending confirms this pan-African drive:

---

mann Educational, 1989): 116–17. Armah declared in one of his rare interviews his intention of "digging into history [... As] a means of finding a clearer perspective on how to solve the problem"; Dimgba Igwe, "Armah: The Reluctant Novelist," *African Concord* (7 May 1987): 19. His interest in Ancient Egyptian literature is an obvious demonstration of this; see Armah, "Masks and Marx," 38; Armah, "The Caliban Complex: 2," *West Africa* (25 March 1985): 571. Evident here is the influence of the Senegalese scholar Cheikh Anta Diop. This 'back-to-Egypt' thrust will surface again in Chapter 7 when I treat Mohammed ben Abdallah.

[48] Igwe, "Armah: The Reluctant Novelist," 17. See also Armah, *The Beautyful Ones Are Not Yet Born* (Oxford: Heinemann, 1968): 92.

[49] The name Isanusi is presumably taken from Chaka's seer, as Okpewho notes in "Myth and Modern Fiction," 13. Armah also dedicated a praiseful essay to Thomas Mofolo's epic on Chaka; Armah, "The Definitive *Chaka*," *Transition* 50 (October 1975).

> What a hearing of all the confluence of all the waters of life flowing to overwhelm the ashen desert's blight! What an utterance of the coming together of all the people of our way, the coming together of all the people of the way. (206)

The undeniable innovations for the African novel introduced by *Two Thousand Seasons* led to a few bizarre critical reactions to some of its facets, apart from the aforementioned narrator's identity. Some complain about its lack of psychological insight and development,[50] one of the most common expectations in the novelistic genre, because, as some critics have argued, the novel's character has to be a mutable one.[51] On the other hand, this feature, often invoked by critics, "has no inherent literary value."[52] It should be added that it has very little value in a novel like this one, given its eternal setting, pedagogic purpose and particularly its collective stance. After all, Ian Watt's notorious definition of the eighteenth-century middle-class novel as featuring "the development of its characters in the course of time" is largely based on the primacy of *individual* experience in the works of Defoe, Richardson and Fielding.[53]

Lindfors also finds fault with the novel's virulent stance towards *predators* and *destroyers*, detecting an excessively manichaean attitude on the part of the author.[54] But the point is certainly arguable: how can one awake one's people from centuries of mental and physical shackles without maintaining a fierce stance against any kind of enslavement? C.L. Innes implicitly supports Lindfors's criticism when she notes that the crumbling of communal values is caused by foreign influences only,[55] which is quite incorrect: the novel does not lack self-criticism regarding some topics, such as the loss of reciprocity before foreign invasions, the internal division between parasites and producers, the role that some natives played in the slave trade.[56]

Armah's next novel, *The Healers* (1978), covers a shorter historical period: namely, the *sagrenti-sa*, the Anglo-Asante war of 1873–74. Since it is a mixture of

---

[50] See Bernth Lindfors, "Armah's Histories," *African Literature Today* 11 (1980): 90.

[51] See Ian Watt, *The Rise of the Novel: Studies in Defoe, Richardson and Fielding* (1957; Harmondsworth: Penguin, 1963): 23.

[52] Julien, *African Novels and the Question of Orality*, 37.

[53] Watt, *The Rise of the Novel*, 13–15, 23.

[54] Lindfors, "Armah's Histories," 90.

[55] C.L. Innes, "Conspicuous Consumption: Corruption and the Body Politic in the Writing of Ayi Kwei Armah and Ama Ata Aidoo," in *Essays on African Writing 2: Contemporary Literature*, ed. Abdulrazak Gurnah (Oxford: Heinemann, 1995): 13.

[56] See Armah, *Two Thousand Seasons*, 16–17, 58–59, 115–16, 146. Cf Innes's viewpoint in "Femi Abodunrin, "Black Literature and Literary Theory," *Wasafiri* 14 (Autumn 1991): 9.

real and fictional characters and events, the author subtitled it *An Historical Novel*. In the Fante village of Esuano, the young and valiant Densu is unjustly accused of having killed Prince Appia, slain by Ababio – Densu's guardian – who is attempting to seize power with the whites' support. He thus flees to join the healer Damfo in the Eastern Forest. Damfo is trying to cure both Appia's mother, Araba Jesiwa – who nearly died when her son was attacked – and Asamoa Kwanta, commander of the Asante army. The latter is a figure worshipped by his troops, but has fallen into severe depression after his favourite nephew was killed during a barbaric ritual established by the Asante royalty. Damfo makes him see deeper into the evil of such customs: the novel, according to the historian T.C. McCaskie, is "a meditation on [...] the rhetorics of power that lie at the heart of Africa's past, present and future."[57] Finally cured, Asamoa Kwanta devises a plan to crush the British army and the other ethnic groups fighting for them, but he is betrayed by the Asante King and Queen Mother, frightened by the commander's growing power. The Asante capital of Kumase is taken; once again internecine divisions have led to defeat. Later, in Esuano, Densu is about to be condemned for the killing of the prince, but with a final *coup-de-théâtre* Appia's mother reappears in court to exculpate him.

The first-person plural is replacd here by sparser and less intrusive omniscient third-person narration, leaving more room for dialogue. The narrating voice, though, is still very much akin to an oral bard's style: "But now this tongue of the story-teller, descendants of masters in the art of eloquence, this tongue flies too fast for the listener."[58] There is only one further instance of self-reference in the whole novel (51–52). But the work is full of oral devices, including refrains, digressions, rhetorical questions, praise names and exclamations.[59] It is certainly a griot's voice the readers are 'listening' to between the stretches of character-dialogue.

Even though the time-span of the novel is restricted if compared to *Two Thousand Seasons*, an eternal temporal perspective comes up again in the healer Damfo's work and way of life. The remote past is a state of pan-African unity, therefore the Fante and the Asante are only two parts of the Akan who, in their turn, are "just a little piece of something whole – a people that knew only this one name we so seldom hear these days: Ebibirman. That was the community of all black

---

[57] Tom McCaskie, "Armah's *The Healers* and Asante History," in *Images of Africa* (Stirling: University of Stirling / Centre of Commonwealth Studies, 1990): 44.

[58] Ayi Kwei Armah, *The Healers: An Historical Novel* (1978; Oxford: Heinemann, 1979): 2. Further page references are in the main text.

[59] Armah, *Healers*, 5, 77–78, 242–52, 255, 260, 261, 275, 282, 284.

people" (84). The present includes the healing of individuals, a work made of discussions with the sick subject on his/her dreams, recollections, sensations: Damfo emerges as a blend of medicine man, psychologist and homeopath.

In the future there is hope –though feeble – of final reunion: "That highest work, the bringing together again of the black people, will take centuries" (83). Such a distant objective has to be linked with Damfo's refusal to follow the commander, the latter still being a slave of that biased power which caused so many intertribal wars: "We healers do not fear power. We avoid power deliberately, as long as that power is manipulative power" (270). His uncompromising stance saves his life, since he is not present when the other healers are massacred but, in the end, establishes an atmosphere of political impotence and sterility. Densu's refusal when he is offered Esuano's kingship after the trial, for instance, looks as though he is missing a chance to occupy the limited spaces offered by history, like a taxidermy of one's principles – not supple enough to answer present and future needs.[60]

On the other hand, such opportunities – and the hope to reunite the black people – are suggested in the final scene of the novel, where a colonialist paradox is pointed out by another healer, Ama Nkroma. At the departure of the white general, a procession of West Indian soldiers start dancing through Cape Coast, involving some locals and soldiers from other tribes: "Does it not amuse you, that in their wish to drive us apart the whites are actually bringing us work for the future? Look!" (309).

By and large, Armah's vision mirrors a highly anthropomorphic notion of society. *Two Thousand Seasons* sees European religious beliefs as children's fables:

> there is indeed a great force in the world, a force spiritual and able to shape the physical universe, but [it] is not something cut off, not something separate from ourselves. It is an energy in us. (96)

According to Gyekye, Akan humanism, unlike the Western variety, is supernaturalistic, but good and evil are decreed "not by a supernatural being as such, but by human beings within the framework of their experiences in living in society," this being due to the non-revealed nature of Akan religion.[61]

Armah appears to espouse these principles; his reaction to colonialism amounts to a counter-myth not based on an ethnic pantheon, but "a consistent pattern of perceiving reality or relating with it."[62] The logical force Armah displays in his novels

---

[60] No point here in calling for a revolution, anyway, as the critic Ode S. Ogede does (see Introduction above, p. xx).

[61] Gyekye, *Essay on African Philosophical Thought*, 132, 135, 143.

[62] Chidi Amuta, "Ayi Kwei Armah and the Mythopoesis of Mental Decolonization," *Ufahamu* 3 (Spring 1981): 45. On these grounds, Okpewho states Armah's 'tradition revised' as superior to

is often crushingly convincing. Such an attitude is evident in his admitted penchant for Cheikh Anta Diop's rationalist theories, as opposed to Léopold Sédar Senghor's stress on emotions and "pseudophilosophy of negritude."[63]

Therefore, even though Armah certainly paved the way for what the magical realists did in the 1980s and 1990s – in terms of the indigenization of the novel – he seems to keep at a distance from that later current on a thematic level.

Ama Ata Aidoo's storytelling squint

Among those writers from the 1970s who experimented with diverse ways of recovering oral strategies in their written prose, Ama Ata Aidoo (b. 1942) is unquestionably the most versatile. Her short-story collection *No Sweetness Here*[64] brought to the fore the wide variety of techniques she makes use of.

In the story "In the Cutting of a Drink," the first-person narrator recounts his trip to Accra in search of his sister Mansa, who, he will eventually discover, has become a prostitute. This is a topic pervading Aidoo's works, where "the colonial and neocolonial mentality [...] is intelligently tied up with the status of women in society."[65] The narrator's tale is often interrupted by direct addresses to his primary audience or narratees, viz. his extended family: "These are useless tears you have started to weep, my mother. Have I said anything to show that she was dead?"[66] The primary audience's reactions, then, are integrated into the speech of the narrator: it is from the interaction between the two that readers grasp the shock caused by the contact

---

Soyinka's 'tradition refined', the latter being too limited in its vision by the Yoruba gods and the tales he refers to; Okpewho, "Myth and Modern Fiction," 2–3, 19–20.

63 Ayi Kwei Armah, "Battle for the Mind of Africa," *South* (August 1987): 62.

64 During our interview, she said that there is an Akan saying that goes: "Wiase nye de (the world is not sweet)." The same adjective is implicitly associated with life in the title of Kojo Laing's first novel (see Chapter 2). In his book on Armah, Fraser writes that the expression "No sweetness here" was borrowed from Armah's *The Beautyful Ones Are Not Yet Born*, but during our interview Aidoo claimed that the contrary is true; Fraser, *Novels of Ayi Kwei Armah*, 26; Armah, *Beautyful Ones*, 67.

65 Chimalun Nwanko, "The Feminist Impulse and Social Realism in Ama Ata Aidoo's *No Sweetness Here* and *Our Sister Killjoy*," in *Ngambika: Studies of Women in African Literatures*, ed. Ann Adams Graves & Carol Boyce Davies (Trenton NJ: Africa World Press, 1986): 153. Aidoo extended her social commitment through direct involvement in politics, too, working as Ghanaian Secretary for Education for eighteen months in the early 1980s.

66 Ama Ata Aidoo, *No Sweetness Here* (Harlow, Essex: Longman, 1970): 32. Further page references are in the main text.

with the ugliness and modernity of Ghanaian city life.[67] Milfred A. Hill–Lubin describes Aidoo's skills as follows:

> In terms of narrator-audience participation, this modern day griot moves us from the individual, passive, solitary act of reading a story [...] on a printed page into a larger, more communal experience.[68]

In the stories of the collection, the author shows that she is able to re-create this communal atmosphere in other ways, apart from the first-person storytelling session: the development of a plurality of voices is a case in point. "For Whom Things Did Not Change" is composed mainly of exchanges between the old servant Zirigu, his wife Setu, and his new 'massa'. The old couple has not benefited at all from independence, and the core of the story resides in the dialogue between Zirigu and the young sympathetic master he has to serve, where two opposite walks of life momentarily find a point of contact. Dialogue is the body of the narration, apart from some passages in the first person disclosing the master's thoughts.

The same could be said about "The Message," another story about a clash of cultures. The old villager Esi Amfoa is told that her grandchild's stomach has been 'opened up' during her delivery: being unaware of caesarean birth, she believes her grandchild is dead, and travels to Cape Coast hospital. Aside from a few thoughts in the first person, direct speech is dominant again, but this time a cacophony of voices – sometimes anonymous – takes hold of the narration in the village, on the bus and at the hospital:

> – O, Nana do not weep ....
> – Is the old woman weeping?
> – If the only child of your only child died, won't you weep?
> – Why do you ask me? Do I know her grandchild is dead?
> – Where have you been, not in this lorry? Where were your ears when we were discussing it?
> – I do not go putting my mouth in other people's affairs ....
> – So what?

---

[67] See Esi Sutherland–Addy, "Narrative Technique and the Role of Commentators in Ama Ata Aidoo's Works," *Research Review* (Institute of African Studies, University of Ghana at Legon) New Series 5.2 (1989): 62. When linking this short story with the Akan traditional concept of *amanee* ('message'), Naana Jane Opoku–Agyemang states that the latter customarily "allows the audience to comment on the delivery"; Opoku–Agyemang, "Narrative Turns in Ama Ata Aidoo's *No Sweetness Here*," in *Emerging Perspectives on Ama Ata Aidoo*, ed. Ada Uzoamaka Azodo & Gay Alden Wilentz (Trenton NJ: Africa World Press, 1999): 129.

[68] Milfred A. Hill–Lubin, "The Storyteller and the Audience in the Works of Ama Ata Aidoo," *Neohelicon* 16.2 (1985): 227.

– So go and die.
– *Hei, hei,* it is prohibited to quarrel in my lorry. (43)

In stories like these, including "Something to Talk About on the Way to the Funeral," which is made up solely of dialogue, Aidoo's prose acquires a dramatic quality that confirms how the influence of traditional narrative forms[69] seems to approach a fusion of different genres, as the author confirmed during our interview:

> My impressions of oral literature – at least of what we have received through the oral tradition – are multi-dimensional, multi-generic, multi-this, multi-that. It seems to me a much more holistic way of dealing with life and art. I would want to think that my tendency I got as a writer to mix my forms is a throwback directly to African oratorial practices. For me it's a much more acceptable way of dealing with life, because life is not ever just a song or a dance or drama. (Aidoo, Legon, 10 June 1997) [70]

Another way of conveying that multi-dimensionality on paper is the switch from third- to the first-person narration. The Ghanaian critic Kofi Agovi applies this concept to some of his short stories, explaining in the introduction to his collection *A Wind from the North* (1989) that the storyteller usually identifies himself through this technique with various characters.[71] In Aidoo's "A Gift from Somewhere," a wandering mallam is asked to save a dying child: certain of the ineffectiveness of his rites, he runs away. The point of view is initially based on third-person description, dialogue and the mallam's unmediated train of thought; then it switches to the child's mother's tale in the first person, recounting how the baby survived and how she was surprised at how the mallam vanished.

The publication of her 'novel' *Our Sister Killjoy or Reflections from a Black-Eyed Squint* (1977) constituted – like Armah's *Two Thousand Seasons* – something unheard-of in African written prose, "a new thing in structure [...] a fresh approach to fiction-writing in Africa."[72] The European misadventures of the Ghanaian Sissie

---

[69] For oral features in this short story, see Chioma Opara, "Narrative Techniques and the Politics of Gender: Ama Ata Aidoo's *Our Sister Killjoy* and *No Sweetness Here*," in *Writing African Women: Gender, Popular Culture and Literature in West Africa*, ed. Stephanie Newell (London & New Jersey: Zed, 1997): 139.

[70] Her dramatic skills also show a considerable variety of speech variants; see Kofi Agovi, "A Dual Sensibility," 262; Angmor, *Contemporary Literature in Ghana*, 65.

[71] Kofi Agovi, *A Wind from the North and other stories* (Tema: Ghana Publishing Corporation, 1989): 12. According to Isidore Okpewho, it is common for the artist in oral literature "to weave his personality into that of his characters" and to "mesh his voice with his material"; Isidore Okpewho, *The Epic in Africa: Towards a Poetic of the Oral Performance* (New York: Columbia UP, 1975): 238.

[72] Oladele Taiwo, *Female Novelists of Modern Africa* (London: Macmillan, 1984): 21.

are described in a mixture of poetry and prose: the lyrical dimension, though, is not given a unified frame as in Armah's or Awoonor's novels; verse and fiction alternate: "*Killjoy* is actually a multi-media book" (Aidoo, Legon, 10 June 1997). Sometimes a few lines occupy the whole page; occasionally a single word is enough.[73]

In the first part, "Into a Bad Dream," Sissie gets ready for her journey abroad and then lands in Frankfurt, becoming the object of everybody's curiosity:

> But what she also came to know was that someone somewhere would always see in any kind of difference, an excuse to be mean.
>
> A way to get land, land, more land.
> Valleys where green corn would sway in the wind.
> A grazing ground for highland cattle.
> A stream to guggle the bonnie bairns to sleep.
> Gold and silver mines,
> Oil. (13)

In this as in the two following parts, the various dilemmas facing the neocolonial subject – especially the feminine subject[74] – are dissected in turn by third-person prose and first-person poetry. In regard to the latter, the author explained: "Life is not always a straight narrative. We stand aside and we pause and we look at things. So, for me, it is a sum of the pauses that we need in any kind of narrative" (Aidoo, Legon, 10 June 1997). Just like her short stories, *Our Sister Killjoy* gives voice to a series of points of view, not to mention abundant dialogue. The second part, "Plums," is about Sissie's stay in Bavaria:

> As for the African miss, ahh...h...h....look at her costume. How charming. And they gaped at her, pointing at her smile. Her nose. Her lips. Their own eyes shining. Not expecting her to feel embarrassed.
>
> That's why, my brother,
> You and I
> Shall see
> Impressed with
> Aeronautics and all such
> Acrobatics when they
> Bring us a
> Breathing Martian or a

---

[73] Ama Ata Aidoo, *Our Sister Killjoy or Reflections from a Black-Eyed Squint* (Harlow, Essex: Longman, 1977): 3–5, 14–16. Further page references are in the main text.

[74] Some feminist critics have highlighted links between the novel's protean structure and gender issues; see Arlene A. Elder, "Ama Ata Aidoo: The Development of a Woman's Voice," in *Emerging Perspectives on Ama Ata Aidoo*, ed. Azodo & Wilentz, 140.

> Ten-eyed
> Hairy drummer from the
> Moon. (43)

The atmosphere of Germany, Sissie's friend Marija's German accent, the zombie-like academic culture and Africa's dependence on the West are the themes of the second part, including the physical attraction between Sissie and Marija. Homosexual love still appears to be a sort of taboo in contemporary African literature; Sissie eventually recoils from Marija's approach, but the attraction she initially feels is instrumental in broaching the subject.

The third part, "From Our Sister Killjoy," which is set in London, focuses more intensely on the alienating experience of Ghanaians abroad:

> So when they eventually went back home as 'been-tos', the ghosts of the humans that they used to be, spoke of the wonders of being overseas, pretending their tongues craved for tasteless food which they would have vomited to eat where they were prepared best.
>
> Fish and Chips.
>
> They lied.
> They lied.
> They lied.
> The Been-tos lied.
>
> And another generation got itself ready to rush out. (90)

The fourth and final part, "A Love Letter," is an epistle in prose written on the plane taking Sissie back to Ghana. It is addressed to the man she loves, who has decided to stay abroad:

> My Beloved, looking at and listening to the perfected versions of our loss of perspective here would wipe the bravest grin from anyone's face. We have become past masters at fishing out death, no matter what package it comes in. (120)

The last three pages shift from the epistolary first person to the third person again. Being back home feels like "fresh honey on the tongue" –

> a mixture of complete sweetness and smoky roughage. Below was home with its unavoidable warmth and even after these thousands of years, its uncertainties. (133)

The alienation of the neocolonial self, then, is the main theme of the novel. This peculiar mixture of prose and poetry helps deal with it in a more manifold and enriching way. Kwaku Larbi Korang writes that Aidoo, "adapting and transforming the novel form, aims at breaking through the false forms that confine the modern

African consciousness."[75] He links her experiments with the traditional poetics of the oral performance, in this regard quoting Kofi Owusu, who sees

> the future of African literature in a judicious return to an African tradition that has always underscored the fundamental 'unity' of the vast continuum of verbal discourses.[76]

Aidoo's second novel, *Changes* (1991),[77] focuses again on the gender question in contemporary Ghana through the story of Esi Sekyi, a university career woman who decides to abandon her husband and later marry Ali, the man she loves, even though he already has one wife. As in her previous works, Aidoo refuses "to subordinate sexual to neo-colonial politics."[78] In the case of *Changes*, readers have a chance to taste the specific priorities that an African feminist novel may point at; in her search for happiness and professional gratification, Esi does not rule out the value of polygamy in enabling women to organize their life more independently:

> I suspect this is one of the reasons why even European feminists don't like *Changes*. Or some of them. Because I don't come out condemning polygamy. How are you going to condemn it, when the society you come from has found it a workable principle for centuries, and still hasn't abandoned it? What kind of an arrogance is that? Now, more generally, I have a problem with marriage and that problem is present in monogamies and polygamies. (Aidoo, Legon, 10 June 1997) [79]

As for the novel's form, it is evidently less disruptive than *Our Sister Killjoy*: "I almost wrote *Changes* to demonstrate to everybody, including myself, that I could write a 'normal' novel" (Aidoo, Legon, 10 June 1997). The attempt has proved successful, because the novel is praiseworthy for its depth of character psychology, the true-to-life dialogue and the range of issues it touches on.

Even then, the narrative of *Changes* is far from following the precepts of orthodox, linear prose.[80] Aidoo still enjoys switching to poetry when a character pauses to think, or of centering prose passages when the need to highlight a character's reflections (or her own) arises. See, for instance,

---

75 Kwaku Larbi Korang, "Ama Ata Aidoo's Voyage Out: Mapping the Coordinates of Modernity and African Selfhood in *Our Sister Killjoy*," *Kunapipi* 14.3 (1992): 54.

76 Kofi Owusu, "Canons under Siege: Blackness, Femaleness and Ama Ata Aidoo's *Our Sister Killjoy*," *Callaloo* 13.2 (Spring 1990): 356.

77 Winner of the 1992 Commonwealth Writers Prize – Africa Division.

78 Derek Wright, "Returning Voyagers: The Ghanaian Novel in the Nineties," *Journal of Modern African Studies* 34.1 (1996): 190.

79 Ironically, a few years before the book appeared it was complained that polygamy did not appear "within the scope of Aidoo's discourse"; Chimalun Nwanko, "Feminist Impulse," 158.

80 On this topic, see also Elder, "Development of a Woman's Voice," 166–67.

> Ali had sensed that Esi was struggling to feel easy about him watching her. [...] He had slept with a great number of women in his time, but he knew very few women from his part of the world who even tried to be at ease with their own bodies. The combination of forces against that had been too overwhelming –
>
> traditional shyness and contempt for the biology of women;
>
> Islamic suppressive ideas about women;
>
> English Victorian prudery and French hypocrisy imported by the colonisers ....
>
> All these had variously and together wreaked havoc on the mind of the modern African woman: especially about herself.[81]

At some points Esi's reflections are conveyed through a dialogue with herself (151–52) or anonymous voices take up the narrative and comment on it:

> the burden of bringing him [Ali] into this world had been too much for his mother. Poor Fatmatu.
>
> "Was she not fifteen when Ali was born?"
>
> "That was all she was."
>
> "Then how could she have lived?"
>
> "She could not live. She did not live."
>
> "I saw it all. She looked at the baby Ali very well. You would have though she just wanted to be sure that everything was fine with him."
>
> "Then what happened?"
>
> "Ah my sister, may Allah preserve us. She sat quietly and bled to death." (21–22)

Aidoo's gift for writing compelling dialogue makes her switch to exchanges written as scripts in Part II of the novel: one between two characters, and another between two wits, Ama and Aba, commenting on gender relationships (98–99, 109–10). In the latter case, she employs a device common to several works of contemporary Ghanaian drama – commentary on the story by characters external to it.

In her second story collection, *The Girl Who Can*, Aidoo makes sparing use of her typical multi-generic devices. It is interesting that two of the stories, "Payments" and "Newly-Opened Doors,"[82] follow the structure of her earlier "In the Cutting of a Drink" by integrating the narratees' reactions with the narrator's words.

<>

[81] Ama Ata Aidoo, *Changes* (1991; Accra: Sub-Saharan, 1994): 73. Further page references are in the main text.

[82] Ama Ata Aidoo, *The Girl Who Can and other stories* (Accra: Sub-Saharan, 1997): 93–105, 120–28.

Kofi Awoonor's novelistic dirges

Considering the already mentioned lyricization of prose, *This Earth, My Brother* (1971), by the Ghanaian writer Kofi Awoonor (b.1935), represents a stylistic apex among these authors breaking new ground for future generations: "although it is generally considered a novel," writes Kofi Anyidoho, "none of the conventional terms of classification fits it perfectly."[83] The novel is divided into an untitled prologue plus an additional fifteen chapters, probably due to the fact, as Gerald Moore argues, that sixteen is a basic number in the Ewe (Awoonor's ethnic group) system of divination called Afa.[84] What follows, though, will focus on how the chapters of the novel are internally organized, rather than on their global symbolic structure.

The untitled prologue is a flow of interior monologue marked by a high degree of musicality, where some facts can be glimpsed: the narrating "I," apparently re-living a supernatural childhood experience, faces the sea in the company of a mermaid:

> We followed the tracks laid by infant fisher feet of the tegayi where a shiny shoal of fish in the mud and the long line of retrievers followed bringing home the harvest of fish of the following feet.[85]

When a crowd of worshippers emerges from the sea – the mythic ancestors of the Anlo–Ewe are believed to have done the same – the mermaid follows them:

> they all moved to the single jangle of the leader's rattler. She was the last to go.
> And I was alone. But not for long. (6)

Stylistically speaking, the subsequent chapters are subdivided into third-person narration of the protagonist Amamu's life, going back and forth temporally, and a first-person section which is much more poetic and less linear. Chapter 1, for instance, is about Amamu's birth in the village of Deme, whereas the corresponding 1a includes a first-hand experience of a foetal passage, re-created by devices such as repetition, onomatopoeia and spare punctuation:

> The flash point of creation, birth before birth long tunnels tunnels roads of womb darkness stilled the mind's eye cannot behold, prescience prenativity of total darkness, the foreknowledge of the grave the exhilaration and impatience of the emergence. (13)

---

[83] Kofi Anyidoho, "Kofi Awoonor," in *Dictionary of Literary Biography* 117: *Twentieth Century Caribbean and Black African Writers, First Series*, ed. Bernth Lindfors & Reinhard Sander (Detroit MI: Bruccoli Clark Layman / Gale, 1991): 85.

[84] Gerald Moore, *Twelve African Writers* (Hutchinson University Library for Africa; London: Hutchinson, 1980): 40.

[85] Kofi Awoonor, *This Earth, My Brother* (London: Heinemann, 1971): 4. Further page references are in the main text.

Kofi Anyidoho describes the (a) segments as "poetic interludes that draw upon a variety of images and powerful symbols of myth and ritual to provide a running commentary and a larger vision concerning the [...] main narrative."[86] Once again, 'alienation' is a key word, if one wants to reach the thematic core of the novel. After his university studies in Britain, Amamu becomes a successful lawyer in contemporary Ghana, but ends up feeling disgusted by the moral, spiritual and physical decay of his country. As in some of Armah's novels, the nadir of this widespread ruin is reached in the historically significant Leader's Castle:

> Some said he had bought a submarine which was all set ready to go through a tunnel that led into the sea in order to escape when the revolution came. It was, they said, an improvement on the same tunnel through which the slaves were shipped in ancient days. (27)

This pervasive feeling touches on the repressive role of the law, Amamu's unsuccessful love stories and journalistic job, and the madness besetting war veterans. The dominant atmosphere is one of paralysis and death: "It was so very right that we should be the fashioners of our own scaffold, and our fingers should weave the final noose" (150). It is as if Amamu were continually longing for reunion with his lost mermaid: "Dear one, hold on, for I come," reads the close of Chapter 4a (60).[87]

This general mood is linked to the Ewe tradition of funeral dirge poetry.[88] Awoonor, who is chiefly a poet, translated and experimented with traditional oral forms in his verses, and *This Earth, My Brother* clearly reveals such a background. One of Awoonor's poems – published in the same year as *This Earth, My Brother* – is given the same title as his novel.[89] It is telling that the magical realists taken into consideration in Chapter 2 of the present study – Cheney–Coker, Okri and

---

[86] Anyidoho, "Kofi Awoonor," 85. Awoonor similarly infuses one of his short plays with his poetic talent, showing that he is at ease with the mixing of literary genres: in his "Lament," in *Short African Plays*, ed. Cosmo Pieterse (London: Heinemann, 1972), three voices speak by quoting some of his poems.

[87] The Ghanaian poet Atukwei Okai considers this a defeatist attitude, renaming it "Amamu-osis"; Okai, "Vision, Image and Symbol in Ghanaian Literature," in *African Writing Today: A Special Issue of Pacific Moana Quarterly* 6.3–4 (July–October 1981): 57–58.

[88] Richard K. Priebe, "Kofi Awoonor's *This Earth, My Brother* as an African Dirge," in *Ghanaian Literatures*, ed. Priebe (Contributions in Afro-American and African Studies 120; Westport CT: Greenwood, 1988).

[89] Kofi Awoonor, *Night of My Blood* (Garden City NY: Doubleday, 1971): 78–81. Kofi Yankson traces the similarities between the two works with a special focus on the historical figure of Kwame Nkrumah; Yankson, "*This Earth, My Brother*: A Study in Despair," *University of Cape Coast English Department Workpapers: Critical Essays and Reviews* 4 (July 1972): 68.

Laing – evince a similarly close connection with their own modes of poetic composition, which is often indicated as the creative source of their fictional prose.

The novel's inspirational literary forms, though, are not bound to traditional genres only, since the book is interspersed with paraphrases of or quotations from Western literature, including the Bible, Shakespeare, Kierkegaard, T.S. Eliot and, most of all, Dante Alighieri. The opening of Dante's *Inferno*, in fact, is employed as an introductory epigraph:

> In the middle of the journey of our life I came to myself within a dark wood where the straight way was lost. Ah, how hard a thing it is to tell of that wood, savage and harsh and dense, the thought of which renews my fear! So bitter is it that death is hardly more.

A situation of paralysis, despondency, rejection: this passage embodies all the main themes of the novel in embryo, including the looming prospect of death.[90] Furthermore, this translation from Dante is significant to the novel's structure, since it is a rendition in prose of a work originally written in verse.

Amamu's tenuous mental balance tips over in Chapter 12, when he has to search for Yaro, his watchman. His visit to Nima, the degraded ghetto of the capital of Accra, where Yaro lives, leads him to lose his already precarious control on reality – accordingly, the subsequent chapters lack their 'a' counterparts, and their narration is developed wholly through a lyrical style. Yaro's uncle is beaten up by the police, and eventually dies. Amamu starts walking along the coast until he finally reaches his home village, to put an end to his life there. He is back to where he feels he belongs, where his mermaid rises from the sea to take him away:

> The sea was real [...] like a scene in that waking dream of fever. It seemed suddenly that the centuries and the years of pain of which he was the inheritor, and the woes for which he was singled out to be the carrier and the sacrifice, were being rolled away, were being faded in that emergence. Here at last, he realized with a certain boyish joy, was the hour of his salvation. (180)[91]

In his essay on Awoonor, Kofi Anyidoho links this mermaid with the West African myth of Mami Wata, who takes human beings into the depths of the sea but sends them back into society after endowing them with healing wisdom:

> It is within the context of this myth that Amamu's career falls into a coherent, meaningful pattern [...] Amamu's death at the scene of his childhood dreams is a return to his

[90] Charles Angmor notes how Dante's "our" reflects the national concern of Awoonor's novel; Angmor, *Contemporary Literature in Ghana*, 70.

[91] Awoonor's homonymous poem significantly contains images of sacrifice and ritual scapegoats; Awoonor, *Night of My Blood*, 79.

> eternal woman of the sea, the mythical principle of creativity and healing that must come to fertilize a despoiled earth.[92]

The way out of neocolonial alienation, then, is not to be found within a naturalistic frame, an ideological stance Awoonor shares with the magical realists examined in Chapter 2. His second novel, *Comes the Voyager at Last* (1992), is contemporaneous with those novelists' works, despite its gestation as far back as 1975. Three different narrators alternate in carrying the plot forward. The first is an unnamed 'I', captured as a slave and led in chains with his fellow prisoners through desert, forest and river, and eventually taken away on a slave ship. It is certainly the most lyrical and least factual part of the three:

> And this desert, once ploughed by our feet, fashioned the eternal frenzy and the howling waves of our history.
>
> The trees would swoon now with a solemnity that was the signal of distress in their heaven high above our sorrow.[93]

The second narrator is Marcus Garvey MacAndrews (aka Sheik Lumumba Mandela), who recounts with a touch of African–American slang his difficult childhood and adolescence in Virginia, his move to New York in 1956, his undeserved experience in jail, and his conversion to Elijah Mohammed's Harlem Mosque: "a rather unconvincing, inauthentic rendition of the 1950s black American experience – a derivative pot-pourri of Richard Wright, Malcolm X and James Baldwin."[94]

The third narrator is an autobiographical Ghanaian who has just been fired in the aftermath of a military coup. In a nightclub he meets Sheik, who stabs a man during a fight. The third narrator escapes with Sheik to his home village. Once there, Sheik undergoes a trance-like experience in the course of a ceremony. In the last three pages of the book, the African–American describes his spiritual rebirth: "So the invulnerable arena of my soul was part of the landscape, of the magical leaping feat of the Fish, the purest witness to my primordial pain" (136).

Obi Maduakor, after inexplicably defining *This Earth, My Brother* as "critical realism," places *Comes the Voyager at Last* under the entry "Magical Realism": "Awoonor reconnects Lumumba to his slave past by means of dream and flashback

---

92 Anyidoho, "Kofi Awoonor," 86.

93 Kofi Awoonor, *Comes the Voyager at Last: A Tale of Return to Africa* (Trenton NJ: Africa World Press, 1992): 2, 44. Further page references are in the main text. The author elsewhere writes that the desert is a recurrent image in his poetry, too, being a remembrance of past migrations; Awoonor, *Breast of the Earth*, 205.

94 Wright, "Returning Voyagers," 171.

and he uses magic and fantasy to telescope this dance of cosmic harmony."[95] The definition of magical realism is a complex task that will occupy the next section of this chapter. Suffice it to say here that the magic of Awoonor's novel is too oneiric, mediated and subjective to be placed in such a category. Sheik, for instance, has a recurrent dream about a funeral procession changing into a chain gang, an obvious hint at the unnamed narrator's captive experience that occurred centuries earlier. The parallelism is strengthened by some similar events that they both witness,[96] but there is nothing more to suggest a conspicuous presence of the supernatural alongside the real. Sheik's final ecstatic visions, sometimes reminding one of Tutuola and Okri's creatures, is too subjective as well:

> The people were of all the colours of the earth [...] Among them were some with heads reaching to the skies, some whose feet were turned inside out, some were dwarfs whose nearness to the earth hardly afforded them somersaulting room. (137)

What can be said about the novel in question is that it attempts to evoke the collective unconscious of a whole race through its lyrical dimension, "a poetic consciousness as a mythic collective memory."[97] As with *This Earth, My Brother*, the dirge mood furthers that goal: "the fluidity of the Ewe dirge form lends itself to the cyclic, episodic, and mosaic structure of the novel."[98]

Notwithstanding the author's opinion that this is a better work than *This Earth, My Brother*,[99] the book is less successful for a number of reasons. First, the lyrical inspiration that made his first novel one of the best pieces of writing from anglophone Africa has abated. Both Sheik and the Ghanaian narrator flaunt their poetic skills, but to little effect.[100] The novel is "thin in texture [...] without the aid of the earlier work's enriching poetic lyricism and visionary mythology."[101]

Secondly, Sheik comes to the nightclub with a caricatured hyper-ideologized Ghanaian intellectual whose artistic and biographical data are an evident allusion to Ayi Kwei Armah. The latter, in turn, pilloried Awoonor through one of his

---

95 Obi Maduakor, "Novel (West Africa): Magical Realism," in *Encyclopedia of Postcolonial Literatures in English*, ed. Eugene Benson and L.W. Conolly (London & New York: Routledge, 1994): 1163.

96 Awoonor, *Comes the Voyager at Last*, 41, 51, 63–65, 130; compare also the woman at pp. 25–29 with the young girl at p. 48.

97 Kelly King Reidt, review of *Comes the Voyager at Last*, *Wasafiri* 20 (Autumn 1994): 79.

98 Esi Dogbe, review of *Comes the Voyager at Last*, *Uhuru* 5 (1994): 57.

99 See Jane Wilkinson, *Talking with African Writers* (London: James Currey; Portsmouth NH: Heinemann, 1990): 28.

100 See 34,89,102.

101 Wright, "Returning Voyagers," 180.

characters in his second novel *Fragments* (1970). Some critics have detected elements of the Ewe poetry of abuse (*halo*) in the satirical passages from both Awoonor's novels,[102] but he pushes his retaliation too far when calling his fictitious Armah "a pompous ass" (75). Thirdly, Sheik's feeling of communion with the Ewe village sounds like an over-exploited element, especially when the narrator's uncle, an Afa priest, points to Sheik's astonishing resemblance to a distant cousin of his (113). If Derek Wright recalls the same thing happening in Alex Haley's *Roots*,[103] one might also mention Maya Angelou's autobiographical book set in Ghana, *All God's Children Need Travelling Shoes* (1986): in a moving scene just before the ending, she is recognized by some market women as a descendant of the enslaved people from Keta, an Ewe coastal town.[104]

---

102 Mawuli Adjei, "Tradition and Continuity in Contemporary African Poetry in English: The Case of Kofi Awoonor and Anlo–Ewe Oral Tradition" (M.Phil. thesis, Department of English, University of Ghana at Legon, 1994): 106; Dogbe, review of *Comes the Voyager*, 57.

103 Wright, "Returning Voyagers," 181.

104 Maya Angelou, *All God's Children Need Travelling Shoes* (1986; London: Virago, 1991): 202–206.

2 The Rise of West African Magical Realism

THE FOLLOWING SECTIONS concentrate on the authors who inaugurated magical realism in anglophone West African prose, beginning in the mid-1980s: the Sierra Leonean Syl Cheney–Coker, the Nigerian Ben Okri and the Ghanaian Kojo Laing. Before grappling with their texts, it is necessary to make clear what is meant here by magical realism, among the intricate – at times somewhat confusing – maze of definitions fashioned by critics. The term was first applied in 1925 by the German critic Franz Roh to post-expressionist painters: "turning again to reality, they were contemplating the world as if it had just sprung up again from the void in a magic re-creation."[1] Such an attitude towards reality might be associated with the fictional works of the Argentinian writer Jorge Luis Borges, who "stresses the same extreme objectivity and ultraprecision employed by the [original] magical realists to invest reality with a touch of magic."[2]

Jean Weisgerber exhaustively traces the spread of Roh's definition into four different geographical areas: Germany, Italy, the Lowlands and Latin America, this last being of greatest importance to the topic of this chapter. Applied to some European authors in the literary circles of Buenos Aires in 1928, the formula reappeared in 1948 and 1955 thanks to, respectively, Arturo Uslar–Petri and Angel Flores: the first referring to the mystery inherent in reality, the second making up an all-embracing definition comprising the fantastic as well.[3]

The theoretical-cum-fictional statement of considerable import to West African literature, though, was elaborated in the Cuban Alejo Carpentier's novel *The King-*

---

[1] Enrique Anderson Imbert, "'Magical Realism' in Spanish-American Fiction," *International Fiction Review* 2.1 (January 1975): 1.

[2] Seymour Menton, "Jorge Luis Borges, Magic Realist," *Hispanic Review* 50 (1982): 414.

[3] Jean Weisgerber, "Le réalisme magique: la locution et le concept," *Rivista di Letterature Moderne e Comparate* ns 35 (January–March 1982): 38–39.

dom of This World (1948). In his prologue, he employs a modified definition, the *real maravilloso*: 'marvellous realism' or, as translated by Harriet de Onís, "the marvellous in the real." Carpentier claims that its origins are to be found in mythic ontologies, based on the most rigorous documentation regarding ethnic cosmogonies and differing radically from the literary ruses of European surrealism. His conception of marvellous realism involves whole world-views, rather than demanding an isolated effort by readers to attain a Coleridgean "suspension of disbelief."[4]

In *The Kingdom*, the world-view introducing the marvellous element originates on "the Other Shore" and is brought to the New World by African slaves; thanks to them, a whole culture was transplanted into the Caribbean. The hero Macandal, for instance, displays to the other plantation slaves

> his narrative arts, when, with terrible gestures, he played the part of the different personages, held the men spellbound, especially when he recalled his trip, years earlier, as a prisoner before he was sold to the slave traders of Sierra Leone.[5]

Others, such as Miguel Ángel Asturias and Carlos Fuentes, employ autochthonous American-Indian myths. Not all Latin American writers experimenting with this mode root their magical / marvellous in specific cosmogonies, though. The Colombian Gabriel García Márquez is the writer who spread its fame throughout the world, especially thanks to his acclaimed *One Hundred Years of Solitude* (1967), where readers can find

> many supernatural motifs such as flying carpets and levitation that have no more connection with an indigenous world-view than the transformation of Gregor Samsa into an insect in Kafka's *Metamorphosis*.[6]

Quite obviously, it would be a mistake to associate every single writer with either the ethnic myth or the generally magical orientation: Carpentier made use of the latter, too,[7] whereas in García Márquez's *Of Love and Other Demons* (1994) the marvellous elements clearly reveal West African origins, thanks to the servant

---

[4] David Lodge, "Magic Realism," in *The Art of Fiction*, ed. Lodge (Harmondsworth: Penguin, 1992): 115.

[5] Alejo Carpentier, *The Kingdom of This World*, tr. Harriet de Onís (1949; London: André Deutsch, 1990): 32, 14.

[6] Amaryll Chanady, "The Origins and Development of Magic Realism in Latin American Fiction," in *Magic Realism and Literature: Essays and Stories*, ed. Peter Hinchcliff & Ed. Jewinski (Proceedings of the Conference on Magic Realist Writing in Canada; Waterloo: University of Waterloo / Wilfrid Laurier University, May 1985): 50.

[7] See Chanady, "Origins and Development of Magic Realism," 56.

Dominga De Adviento, who brings up the protagonist Sierva Maria in the Yoruba language and dedicates her to the Yoruba sea-god Olokun.[8]

In *The Kingdom of This World* the marvellous has profound relevance to everyday reality and social matters. The runaway slave Mackandal is believed to have superhuman powers enabling him to transform himself into any animal; although he is executed, his fellow slaves believe in his metamorphic escape from the burning stakes, and his legend is passed on to the next generations. At the end, after the fictionalization of Henri Christophe's historical kingdom of freed slaves, the protagonist Ti-Noël follows Mackandal's example by turning into a goose and finding himself in an orderly, well-structured, truly democratic society. Nevertheless, he is kept at a distance because of his cowardice, his refusal of reality:

> Mackandal had disguised himself as an animal for years to serve men, not to abjure the world of men. [...] In the Kingdom of Heaven there is no grandeur to be won [...] beautiful in the midst of his misery, capable of loving in the face of affliction and trials, man finds his greatness, his fullest measure, only in the Kingdom of This World.[9]

The same stress on the marvellous as a means of interpreting human reality is evident in another seminal theorization of the concept by the Haitian writer Jacques–Stephen Alexis: "Art is fundamentally linked with life. We are dreamers, yes, but also infinitely realist. [...] To us, art is essentially linked with real life."[10] Like Carpentier, Alexis strives to acknowledge the connections of his "marvellous realism"[11] with African culture, and to distinguish it from the

> Intellectualist constructions of some kind of decadent West, its coldly surrealist research [...] Haitian art, like the art of the people of African descent, is always based on man, on fights and on hopes, not on the gratuitousness of the ivory tower.[12]

---

[8] Gabriel García Márquez, *Of Love and Other Demons*, tr. Edith Grossman (Harmondsworth: Penguin, 1994): 43.

[9] Carpentier, *The Kingdom of This World*, 111–12.

[10] "L'art est foncièrement lié à la vie. Nous sommes rêveurs, oui, mais réalistes infinitement [...] L'art pour nous est essentiellement lié à la vie pratique"; Jacques–Stéphen Alexis, "Du réalisme merveilleux des Haïtiens," *Présence Africaine* 9–10 (juin–novembre 1956): 259–60 (my tr.).

[11] "réalisme merveilleux" (my tr.).

[12] "constructions intellectualistes d'un certain Occident décadent, ses recherches surrealistes à froid [...] l'art haïtien, come celui des peuples d'origine nègre, amène toujours à l'homme, à la lutte et à l'espoir et non pas à la gratuité et à la tour d'ivoire"; Alexis, "Du réalisme merveilleux," 264 (my tr.). Regarding the comparison between Surrealism and magical realism, Wendy B. Faris states that the former is virtually unmotivated and resists interpretation, whereas the latter variants, "while projecting a similar initial aura of surprising craziness, tend to reveal their motivations – psychological, social, emotional, political – after some scrutiny": Faris, "Scheherazade's Children:

Two decades later, these common points shared by Carpentier and Alexis surfaced again for the first time in West Africa: in *The Form of the African Novel* (1979), the Nigerian novelist, playwright and critic Kole Omotoso employs the same definition of "Marvelous Realism." He invokes the rejection of any form of escapism, inasmuch as his Marvelous Realism must be assessed "side by side with the material condition of the characters. If the novelist uses this approach, the possibility of a radical use of marvelous realism exists."[13] The concept in question is interpreted in its ontological and historical implications, as the "juxtaposition of the belief system of one archaic economic and social system side by side with the belief system of another economic and social system, this time capitalism."[14]

Such a syncreticity of different world-views, characteristic of the contemporary West African condition in all walks of life, is the definition employed in the following parts of Chapter 2, since it certainly includes the context and content of the novels by Syl Cheney–Coker, Ben Okri and Kojo Laing. It is a juxtaposition that has to be seen as a variedly balanced cohabitation of the two equally valid realities: in her study of Latin American "Magical Realism," Amaryll Chanady likewise describes the rapport between the two as a "resolved antinomy" where the two poles constitute "no hierarchy," being two conflicting but autonomously coherent perspectives.[15]

So much for this attempt to delve into the genealogy and development of the concept of magical realism up to its contemporary manifestations in anglophone West African literature. As said above, the vagueness and confusion surrounding the concept have always represented a hard task for the critic. Brenda Cooper's *Magical Realism in West African Fiction* (1998) – which studies the same three authors of the present chapter – certainly constitutes an interesting case, being the first book to offer a comprehensive approach to both West African magical realism and its principal exponents. The book provides some insights into the nature of magical realism which correspond to what these pages infer, such as the syncretic union of capitalistic development and precolonial society and the sociopolitical foundations of the

---

Magical Realism and Postmodern Fiction," in *Magical Realism: Theory, History, Community*, ed. Lois Parkinson Zamora & Wendy B. Faris (Durham NC: Duke UP, 1995): 171. The same could be said about the novels examined in this chapter.

[13] Kole Omotoso, *The Form of the African Novel* (Akure & Ibadan: Fagbamigbe, 1979): 57.

[14] Omotoso, *Form of the African Novel*, 26. See also Fredric Jameson's similar definition in "On Magic Realism in Film," *Critical Inquiry* 12 (1986): 311.

[15] Amaryll Chanady, *Magical Realism and the Fantastic: Resolved Versus Unresolved Antinomy* (New York & London: Garland, 1985): 21, 104.

authors' projects.[16] Furthermore, other analyses by Cooper which I find congenial are re-employed as models later in my study.

At the same time, Cooper's book might disappoint those who expect it to outline the origins of magical realism and the way it branched out towards today's West Africa, be its source native or Latin American. Cooper's first three chapters offer a series of theoretical suggestions which fall short of providing a clarifying frame, as if they had succumbed to the critical looseness surrounding magical realism. Surprisingly enough, Omotoso's seminal text is never cited, nor are Carpentier's and Alexis's historic essays. Cooper's critical references are mainly oriented towards issues of hybridity raised by postcolonial theory, ranging from Bhabha's interstitial spaces (albeit "fully conceptualized within an understanding of oppression") to the idea of nomadic identity (through Sidonie Smith and Spivak's standpoints).[17] Such tenets are used as a matrix to explain the multi-faceted nature of magical realism. Her choice of critical cornerstones provides an example of the dangers inherent in postcolonial 'high' theory (already mentioned in the Introduction to the present study), inasmuch as it does not help her focus on the sociocultural specificities of her topic. When arguing that "ironical distancing is a crucial feature of the magical realist narrative point of view,"[18] for instance, she seems to apply an extremely facile template of poststructuralist/postcolonial theory. The rest of Chapter 2 will demonstrate how irony is a crucial feature of Laing's narrative but has little to do with the solemnity of tone in Okri and Cheney–Coker.

Before starting in on analysis of their novels, three further points need specifying. First of all, when it comes to practical examples Omotoso's groundbreaking book applies its own definition too broadly.[19] Elechi Amadi's novels with precolonial settings belong to an age which does not involve one of the two world-views at the basis of Omotoso's Marvelous Realism, but represent a society where magic is considered as identical – and not juxtaposed – with the real. The more suitable definition 'Ancestral Realism' is therefore proposed for such novels, which are not included in this chapter.

Omotoso also mentions Amos Tutuola among the exponents of the magical realist mode, but he should be seen as a precursor.[20] As shown later in Chapter 2,

---

[16] Brenda Cooper, *Magical Realism in West African Fiction: Seeing with a Third Eye* (London & New York: Routledge, 1998): 15, 52.

[17] Cooper, *Magical Realism in West African Fiction*, 3, 8–10.

[18] Cooper, *Magical Realism in West African Fiction*, 49.

[19] Omotoso, *Form of the African Novel*, 57.

[20] See Cooper, *Magical Realism in West African Fiction*, 44, 49.

Ben Okri is the writer most influenced by Tutuola. The reason why the latter cannot be considered a magical realist proper resides in the neatly drawn boundary he traces between human and supernatural worlds; the same boundary continuously blurs in Okri's *abiku* novels, where the two dimensions interact throughout the narrative.[21] Tutuola's pioneering role was prophesied by the Nigerian critic Chinweizu in 1978:

> In view of the Latin American achievement, it should be easier to see that Tutuola may well represent a main archway to the development of a modern African fiction powerful enough to explore the conditions and absurdities of neo-colonial Africa.[22]

Other novels chosen by Omotoso to exemplify his theory are hardly recognizable as belonging to his marvellous realism: Femi Osofisan's *Kolera Kolej* is a caricatured satire of neocolonial African politics, while his own *The Combat* is an allegory of the Nigerian Civil War. On the other hand, Omotoso could not possibly write in 1979 about Cheney–Coker, Okri and Laing, whose magical-realist works fit perfectly into his theorization but only appeared after the mid-1980s.

Secondly, one should be aware of the critical confusion in the labelling of the mode: 'Magic(al) Realism' and 'Marvellous Realism' have sometimes been allocated to contradictorily different spheres of influence. Should one call 'marvellous' whatever is rooted in ethnic mythologies – following Carpentier's use of the term – and 'magical' that which is generally mysterious, as Uslar Petri does? Or, rather, should one agree with the opposite theory put forward by Irlemar Chiampi, which distinguishes between the 'magic' practices of indigenous myth and the theoretical 'marvellous' of Tzvetan Todorov?[23] Further, John La Rose makes the interesting claim that the most faithful translation of Carpentier's *real maravilloso* should be

---

[21] As with Tutuola, reality and supernatural world belong to completely different locales in two early Ghanaian short stories departing from naturalism: Adolph Agbadja's "Down Below the Volta River," in *Voices of Ghana: Literary Contributions to the Ghana Broadcasting System, 1955–57*, quoted in Kofi Agovi, "A Dual Sensibility: The Short Story in Ghana, 1944–1980," in *Literature and Black Aesthetics*, ed. Ernest N. Emenyonu, 257–58; and Selma Al-Hassan's "Tanofia," in *The Cowrie Girl and Other Stories*, various authors (Tema: Ghana Publishing Corporation, 1971). Both stories narrate the adventures of humans briefly entering benevolent and peaceful underwater worlds.

[22] Unspecified quotation in Maduakor, "Novel (West Africa)," 1162.

[23] See Chanady, "Origins and Development of Magic Realism," 53, 56–57. See also the distinction between epistemological and ontological magical realism in Faris, "Scheherazade's Children," 165.

"the marvels of reality," instead of "marvellous realism."[24] In the light of this, the most common term 'magical realism' is used here in order to identify its different strains and forms of expression in West African anglophone novels through an actual study of each work, rather than by fiddling with labels of relative importance. After all, the foundations of a novel's magical quality in an ethnic world-view can reveal varying degrees of intensity, as Ben Okri's novels will prove, or may not be declared in the novel's content but manifest themselves mainly in the author's linguistic strategies, as in the case of Kojo Laing.

Thirdly, from what is written above it is evident that there is a Latin American influence on West African magical realism, one that enlarges the porosity or 'holistic vision' of this book from a generic to a geographic dimension, whereby the same effect is produced by the interaction between the different societal structures underpinning magical realist representations. The following pages will show whether and how direct literary connections between the two continents exist. The culture of the Americas, in turn, was historically affected by philosophies imported through the slave trade. The whole phenomenon, therefore, constitutes a curious sort of 'transatlantic feedback cycle' (also detectable in Chapter 6, on the origins of Ghanaian Concert Parties).[25] Such cultural links are seen here as prevailing over linguistic ones, whereas several critics tend to draw parallels between West African magical realism and instances of the same phenomenon from other anglophone areas with completely different historical and social backgrounds. Once again, as with regard to Brenda Cooper's book, distinctions need to be made, rather than searching for generic similarities. Stephen Slemon's acclaimed essay "Magic Realism as Postcolonial Discourse" (1988), for instance, bears a title that sounds too generalizing, intimating a massive critical hotpot that goes under the label 'postcolonial'. Slemon's definition of magical-realist texts is highly significant:

> In the language [...] a battle between two oppositional systems takes place, each working toward the creation of a different kind of fictional world from the other. Since the ground rules of these two worlds are incompatible, neither one can fully come into being, and each remains suspended, locked in a continuous dialectic with the 'other', a situation which creates disjunction within each of the separate discursive systems, rending them with gaps, absences, and silences.[26]

---

[24] John La Rose, "About *New Beacon Review*: A Statement," *New Beacon Review* 1 (July 1985): 2.

[25] The definition is drawn from Karin Barber, John Collins & Alain Ricard, *West African Popular Theatre* (Bloomington & Indianapolis: Indiana UP; Oxford: James Currey, 1997): 21.

[26] Stephen Slemon, "Magic Realism As Postcolonial Discourse," *Canadian Literature* 16 (Spring 1988): 10–11.

Not unlike Chanady, Slemon negates the existence of any hierarchy between the two systems, but the substance of the opposing views goes to the heart of the matter. Omotoso's definition as appropriated here concerns historically experienced belief-systems, whereas Slemon calls them "worlds," but also "narrative modes," "discursive systems" which create an opposition that "forestalls the possibility of interpretive closure":[27] the poststructuralist reification of the text – discussed in my introduction – is once again at work. Slemon extends his own attitude from the Canadian literary context to the whole 'postcolonial' world, regardless of the specific historical, social, and cultural milieux. West Africa's syncretic cultures are based on a profoundly experienced recognition of the validity of all its components, rather than, as Slemon writes about Jack Hodgins, on a myth-deconstructing "destabilization of the fixity of origins."[28]

At the same time; some non-West African critical theories will also come into play, whenever they prove helpful to the interpretative work in question.A case in point is Mikhail Bakhtin's theory of the carnivalesque, already employed by David K. Danow to construc Latin American magical realism and Second World War novels.[29] When the spirit of carnival permeates literature, Danow writes, it

> regards the supernatural as natural [...] makes the extraordinary or 'magical' as viable a possibility as the ordinary or 'real', so that no true distinction is perceived or acknowledged between the two.[30]

The magical element in the three West African novelists' writings may make up for a drawback lamented by the critic Kofi Agovi in 1974 about the "excessive realism which dominates the modern short story," and may move them closer to the spirit of traditional storytellers, since

> it was expected of him that his creative imagination should be a delicate balance between reality and fantasy. The more he was able to maintain this balance the more he was acclaimed a successful artist.[31]

---

[27] Slemon, "Magic Realism As Postcolonial Discourse," 12.

[28] Slemon, "Magic Realism As Postcolonial Discourse," 17.

[29] See also Cooper, *Magical Realism in West African Fiction*, 24–27.

[30] David K. Danow, *The Spirit of Carnival: Magical Realism and the Grotesque* (Lexington: UP of Kentucky, 1995): 3.

[31] Kofi Agovi, "Traditional Storytelling and the Modern Short Story," in *Out of the Writers' Workshop* (Accra: Arts Council of Ghana, 1974): 24, 19. See also Agovi, "Preliminary Observations on the Modern Short Story and the African Folktale Tradition," *Research Review* (Institute of African Studies, University of Ghana at Legon) 9.1 (1973): 126.

The same magical element shared by the three authors leads them to compose in an extremely lyrical style, akin to the lavish use of metaphors, similes and sound-play characteristic of African oral literature.[32] Generic porosity as a sustaining idea thus re-surfaces. Cheney–Coker, Okri and Laing are considered here as the true heirs of the writers examined in Chapter 1; as Chanady writes about Latin Americans, "magic realists do more than try to express their reality. In an attempt to draw the reader's attention to the richness of their continent, they often poeticize it."[33]

Syl Cheney–Coker's Creole perspective

In his first novel, *The Last Harmattan of Alusine Dunbar* (1990), the Sierra Leonean poet Syl Cheney–Coker narrates the history of the fictional community of Malagueta on the West African coast, sweeping widely across continents and generations for four hundred pages. The tone he imposes through his omniscient narrator is solemn, epic and lyrical, as in the following passage:

> On that fateful day, he walked from the first flickering fires of the inferno that was to engulf the island rising behind him. If they tormented him, Alphonso Garrison did not give any signs of being alarmed. Personal disasters took a long time coming to him. He was an eel who knew how to slide through the mud of change, a cat licking his body clean of the slime of upheaval until his good luck ran out.[34]

Both scope and tone are reminiscent of García Márquez's *One Hundred Years of Solitude* (1967), a similarity often remarked by critics.[35] In both novels, the inception depicts an army officer recalling his past in a moment of utter defeat. Compare the opening of Cheney–Coker's novel:

> Two nights after his failed coup, General Tamba Masimiara sat on a cold slab in his island prison cell and thought about the series of events that had led to his moving against the corrupt government in Malagueta. (vii)

---

[32] See Okpewho, *African Oral Literature*, 70–104.

[33] Chanady, "Origins and Development of Magic Realism," 52.

[34] Syl Cheney–Coker, *The Last Harmattan of Alusine Dunbar* (Oxford: Heinemann, 1990): 267. Further page references are in the main text.

[35] See Cooper, *Magical Realism in West African Fiction*, 115. Paolo Bertinetti notes that in both novels the main characters are among the founders of their fictional towns (Malagueta and Macondo), while the longevity of women in both families ensures narrative continuity; Bertinetti, "Reality and Magic in Syl Cheney–Coker's *The Last Harmattan of Alusine Dunbar*," in *Co-terminous Worlds: Magical Realism and Contemporary Post-Colonial Literature in English*, ed. Elsa Linguanti, Francesco Casotti & Carmen Concilio (Cross / Cultures 39; Amsterdam & Atlanta GA: Rodopi, 1999): 200.

with García Márquez's: "Many years later, as he faced the firing squad, Colonel Aureliano Buendía was to remember that distant afternoon when his father took him to discover ice."[36]

The Colombian writer's stylistic influence was partially conceded by Cheney–Coker himself. In the interview he gave Brenda Cooper, he acknowledges the importance of Carpentier's theory and the African origins of the latter's magical realism, thereby implying the transatlantic feedback cycle mentioned earlier:

> Inevitably the question arises, you know, is your novel magical realist? Were you inflamed by [García] Márquez? The answer is yes and no. If we are discussing form, yes, but if we are discussing an idea then the answer is, no. Before [García] Márquez there was the Cuban novelist, Carpentier, and Carpentier in turn was influenced by perceptions of an African world.[37]

When he claims his thematic difference from García Márquez, he highlights the hope present in his novel against the hopelessness of *One Hundred*: this point will be taken into consideration later on. Another basic – and more relevant – dissimilarity between the two novels is constituted by the ethnic origin of the magical element. Even though neither of them exploits a single mono-ethnic world view, García Márquez's marvellous is based on a melting-pot of fantastic events which often have no precise geographical origin, whereas Coker is more at pains to indicate the origin of most of the fantastic tesserae composing his mosaic of world cultures meeting in Malagueta.

Book One is set in America at the end of the eighteenth century, where Jeanette, a mulatto brought up by a black preacher who "had a deep knowledge of herbal lores" (5), marries Sebastian Cromantine, a slave who fought for the Colonial Army during the Independence War. The omniscient authorial voice informs the reader that the coming of Jeanette to West Africa has been prophesied by an unspecified "looking-glass of the Nubian, a hundred years before" (5). And that Sebastian, too, has strange dreams connected to "what a magical looking-glass had predicted a long time ago in a place far removed from where he was living" (9).

On the ship taking them to West Africa, the connection is unveiled thanks to Fatmatta the Bird-Woman, who, before dying on board, narrates her life-story to

[36] Gabriel García Márquez, *One Hundred Years of Solitude*, tr. Gregory Rabassa (1967; Harmondsworth: Penguin, 1972): 1.

[37] Cooper, "Syl Cheney–Coker: *The Last Harmattan of Alusine Dunbar*, and an Interview," *African Literature Association Bulletin* 20.3 (Summer 1994): 10. The roots of García Márquez's magic are in African folklore, too; see David Mimicks, "Derek Walcott and Alejo Carpentier: Nature, History and the Caribbean Writer," in *Magical Realism*, ed. Zamora & Faris, 375, 400.

Jeanette: she was the daughter of a mysterious magician, Sulaiman the Nubian, also known as Alusine Dunbar, who arrived one day in her mother's land of Kasila with a looking-glass where "everything was mirrored" (25). And with which he predicted the coming of black people from across the sea. Fatmatta inherited strange powers from her father: "she could open doors merely by looking at them, and change the colour of water by touching it" (33). As for Sulaiman, he mysteriously disappeared for good when kidnapped by a herd of baboons, reappearing to his disciple Ahmed the Elephant "through the door of the mirror" (41) and later going "back to his world amidst a cloud of smoke, engulfed by the mirror which began to shake in Ahmed's hands" (42). Ahmed was distraught by his unrequited love for Fatmatta: when Sebastian Cromantine arrives to Kasila, he is witness to the joyous dance of an elephant and a scorpion (the animal Fatmatta was associated with):

> They started to dance as if they had known each other in another world. When they were exhausted, the elephant kneeled down and let the scorpion climb on its back and, gently this time, the great beast went back to the woods, trumpeting the memory of former times when he had seen the proverbial eyes of the woman, who no longer tormented him as he bore her triumphantly into the silver light of morning. (70–71)

Cheney–Coker does not trace the connections explicitly, and the reader has to unite various hints from different chapters to grasp the overall situation. But it seems clear that Ahmed and Fatmatta have been reincarnated in the animals they are associated with, and that their troubled relationship has found some peace; just as it is obvious that Alusine's prophecies concerned the coming of the Cromantines and their fellow settlers from America.

In Book One the main characteristics of Cheney–Coker's magical realism – and, generally speaking, of several other writers employing the mode – are already present: a strong communion of human society with nature and an unbroken relationship with the dead, a feature common to all African cultures. Sulaiman the magician is not the only one who returns: when Jeanette gives birth to her son Emmanuel, Fatmatta reappears to keep her company and help her through the painful ordeal (109). Wendy B. Faris states that in magical realism "Fluid boundaries between the worlds of the living and the dead are traced only to be crossed."[38] The first novel she mentions in this regard is *One Hundred Years of Solitude*, where the crossing of boundaries is continuous: in the house of the Buendías, the living are "awakened by the traffic of the dead."[39]

---

[38] Wendy B. Faris, "Scheherazade's Children," 172.

[39] García Márquez, *One Hundred Years of Solitude*, 416. In applying Bakhtin's carnivalesque (where "boundaries do not exist") to Juan Rulfo's *Pedro Páramo*, Danow likewise shows that

Moreover, Book One displays part of that cultural mosaic mentioned above, due to the intcursion of African–American lore plus Alusine Dunbar and Fatmatta's "powers that had their origins in the ancient arts of manipulating mirrors perfected by the Nubians in the wide expanse of the Sudanese desert" (62). Before the end of Book One another former slave brings to Malagueta the wisdom of a native American ethnic group: Sister Louisa, after years of rape and violence, is rescued by

> some antediluvian Indians who initiated her into the ancient mysticism of Torlino, the priest of Hozonihatál, into the origins of death, and the poetry of the lamentation of the fox. They taught her how to mourn for the dead without being sad, how to be stoical and passionate without fear and cowardice as no one could escape death. (117–18)

African culture from the Caribbean is present, too. Thomas Bookerman, one of the leaders of Malagueta, was determined to return to Africa from Canada because of his people's exploitation, but also thanks to what he had heard about the historical events fictionalized in Carpentier's *The Kingdom of This World*:

> the revolt in Santo Domingo, of Macandal the Left-Handed whose name and that of Toussaint L'Ouverture were associated with the most fearsome tales of demonic powers and cleverness that their race had created in the hearts of the French. (102)[40]

An autobiographical interpretation of Cheney–Coker's magical-realist sources cannot but stress the relevance of his country and group of provenance, the Creole community of Sierra Leone: Cooper rightly states that "his Creole past has provided Cheney–Coker with a breadth, a humour, an insight into other cultures and perspectives that deepen and enrich his fiction."[41] The Creoles developed "from the intermarriage of settler Africans from a number of different ethnic groups" and knew very little about their ancestors. Sulaiman's role in the novel is therefore akin to efforts made by the Creoles to fill this gap by tracing their own cultural genealogy "back to what they believed to be the general black African past [...] Roman Africa, ancient Egypt, and the greatness of the Biblical Middle East."[42] It is not by chance that an unnamed mulatto in *The Last Harmattan* mentions Abyssinian Christianity and Hannibal's achievements (149–150). Evidently, therefore, the cultural patch-

---

"commonly conceived boundaries are destroyed – beginning with those between the living and the dead"; Danow, *Spirit of Carnival*, 25, 26.

[40] For another powerful novelistic rendition of that historical period, see Madison Smartt Bell, *All Souls' Rising* (New York: Pantheon, 1995).

[41] Cooper, "Syl Cheney–Coker," 9.

[42] Leo Spitzer, *The Creoles of Sierra Leone* (Madison: U of Wisconsin P, 1974): 120, 122, quoted in Cooper, "Syl Cheney–Coker," 6.

work supporting the novel's plot has a broad historical base,[43] rather than being an intellectual construction. The author holds that "the novelist must use his or her perception of the world, whether real or unreal, but in the process ground the magic in a form of reality."[44]

In the following Books of the novel, the integration of the living and the dead continues: Sebastian Cromantine wants to build a House for the Dead, meets with a funeral where he sees "the dead man trying to sit up" (142), and decides to honour the departed with a collective feast during which Thomas Bookerman performs libations and food offerings:

> The whole community – or what was then the community nearest to the Cromantines – was there. Sebastian passed around glasses filled with rum, to reconcile people who had gone apart, because the Cromantines were a peaceful couple and the dead were peaceful and demanded honour at their gatherings. (144)

When the British garrison led by Captain Hammerstone is established at Malagueta, the departed souls of the community take part in the anticolonial struggle alongside the living. During the first riots, Hammerstone shoots at Bookerman, but Fatmatta saves him, in a passage that displays the author's epic lyricism:

> instead of Bookerman, he saw the most beautiful woman he had ever seen, looking straight at him with the deadly eyes of a scorpion. He heard the bullet ricochet against the shell of an animal that had swam in the deepest rivers, over the longest resources of time, before surfacing to the shore to torment men like him and others who had the temerity to interfere with the dance of the spirits on their journey to a different home. (169)[45]

Cheney–Coker's style certainly draws on his collections of poems, which confer to the whole book an "intensity of verbal expression."[46] He recollects its writing thus:

> To be quite honest, I didn't feel I was up to the task. I started rather hesitantly and showed the first draft to my wife, who was a very perceptive teacher and critic, and she looked through it and said: this is very dense, you're a poet, you have to clean this up quite a bit.[47]

---

[43] Eldred Jones praised the book's "epic dimension whilst recreating history. Though much historical details are brought in, Dr Jones said, the novels does not strictly conform to historical details"; Arthur E.E. Smith, "Dreams from the Mind," *West Africa* 3842 (22–28 April 1991): 632.

[44] Cooper, "Syl Cheney–Coker," 11.

[45] See also 185.

[46] Chimalun Nwanko, review of *The Last Harmattan of Alusine Dunbar*, *African Studies Review* 35.1 (1992): 135.

[47] Cooper, "Syl Cheney–Coker," 10.

Some critics, though, did not appreciate the consequent slowing of the narrative.[48] Actually, readers must be prepared to take their time and let the action settle whenever Cheney–Coker launches himself in his long but often haunting digressions about the background, thoughts and feelings of each character. In any case, he never loses control of the narrative thread; *The Last Harmattan*'s plot has a solid backbone, without the episodic structure of Okri's novels; nor does its language ever attain the experimental extremes to be found in Laing's.[49]

Cheney–Coker depicts the Malaguetan community in its growth. The local language, for instance, develops by acquiring new words from a varied series of idioms. In Book Two, in the chapter entitled "Garbage," two new characters, Isatu and Gustavius, cannot have children and decide to visit Isatu's home village in the interior: readers are thus immersed in the rural culture of a local ethnic group. Isatu's father has recently died, but his presence is felt by his family; only Gustavius, the former slave from America, is unaware of the traces that his father-in-law leaves about. Nonetheless, the decaying village is revived by Gustavius' vitality, in a curious resemblance to Efua Sutherland's play *Foriwa*, where the stranger Labaran accomplishes an identical feat.[50] As for Isatu's barrenness, two astonishing dwarves who claim to be "the last members of a race of dwarf children who had been trapped in a grove by an evil spirit" (205) offer to perform a purification ceremony that Isatu's mother strongly recommends to Gustavius:

> Let me tell you, this is as it was before your time, because we are all segments of the dirt of the world, and an inescapable part of living is recognising our relationship to spirits, to nature and these creatures of the underworld. (206)

During the rite,

> the woman felt the encrustation of the dirt and garbage that years of marriage to a man without the roots of the forest had imposed on her, while the man felt the garbage of the world across the sea of blood running off his body. (206)

Their son is called Garbage, "so that he will not forget his roots" (206).

In Book Three, Thomas Bookerman starts writing his *History of the Founding of Malagueta*, also in the light of some recently unearthed materials of a past civiliza-

---

[48] See the review in the *Publisher Weekly* (21 December 1990): 49.

[49] See the rest of Chapter 2. When comparing these authors, Femi Osofisan rightly writes that "the magical realism of [Cheney–Coker's] novel is controlled and channelled towards a discernible narrative purpose, and hence less normatively incoherent"; Osofisan, "Warriors of a Failed Utopia?," 26.

[50] See Chapter 6 (pp. 210–11) below.

tion: graves of giant skeletons, bronze pagan statues and documents on the religious customs of the former inhabitants of the area, including the prophesies of Alusine Dunbar.[51] Such prophesies contain in embryo the much-criticized fatalistic concept of history conveyed by the novel:

> [the mystic] had seen the destruction of the area that was now part of Malagueta because the town was in the direction of a cyclical wind that blew once every fifty years, unleashed by the imponderable hand of a remarkable king. (212)

Some critics have shown little appreciation for this philosophy as it pervades the novel; Chimalun Nwanko points out a "subterranean fatalism and even nihilism."[52] The second coming of the colonialists in Book Three – forcing Bookerman into exile – must be seen in this light, and the same seems true for other invasions such as the Arab traders', "just as Sulaiman the Nubian, otherwise known as Alusine Dunbar, had seen them in the magical mirror many years earlier" (258).

Isatu's and Gustavius' son Garbage is another of the characters who develop a profound relationship with Sulaiman and magical forces. At the age of ten, he one day ends up at the abandoned shop of Theophilus the apothecary while following a column of black ants. There he meets Sulaiman, who declares his return to be favourable to the oppressed Malaguetans: "I have seen the leopards going for the goats and I had to come before they ate of all them" (288). From this moment on Garbage will visit him regularly, while Sulaiman in turn visits Sebastian Cromantine and prophesies "a new reign without honour but with the embellishment of falsehood" (304). Through the rays of light emanating from his testicles, Sulaiman shows Garbage the new phase in the anti-colonialist struggle, where Emmanuel Cromantine kills Hammerstone and is subsequently shot dead. Fatmatta, in the shape of an angel-woman, catches Emmanuel's falling body and gently leaves him at the feet of his mother Jeanette, who recognizes her old friend descending from the clouds.

The cyclical reappearance of Sulaiman as a source of wisdom recalls the similar function performed by the gypsy Melquíades in *One Hundred Years of Solitude*;[53] moreover, Melquíades's writings in Sanskrit on parchment reveal the whole history of the Buendías, a written prophecy akin to Sulaiman's oral predictions about the destiny of Malagueta.

From Book Four – corresponding to the early twentieth century – the novel assumes an increasingly political dimension; nonetheless, this is not meant to have a decisive influence on the novel's philosophical core. Garbage becomes a very

---

[51] The two dwarfs in Isatu's village mention him, too (205).

[52] Nwanko, "Review of *The Last Harmattan*," 135.

[53] See Cooper, *Magical Realism in West African Fiction*, 148.

talented writer who constantly denounces the abuses of the colonial regime, and is therefore hailed as the people's leader. One day he receives by mail a parcel of books, a collection of texts on various African cultures, and realizes Sulaiman is the sender: "he recognized the telluric preoccupations of the man who had introduced him to the magic properties of gold and the incantatory powers of strange eyes." As for politics, he understands that one should keep at a safe distance from its tentacles:

> He saw in the Admonition to the Disciples how he was not exempt from the quagmires of life, but how as a seeker of truth he had to pull himself out of all pits where lesser men, especially politicians, would try to throw him. Thus he understood that Malagueta was like a sun which would disappear for a while but would reappear after the rain. (371)

Through this apparently autobiographical character, the author thus reaffirms his ambiguously cyclical world-view, the limited space he envisages for regenerative possibilities in the political realm. A similar view marks Latin American magical realists, for whom time is "frequently presented as cyclical, rather than linear":

> What occurs on one occasion (which is not likely to be the first) is destined to take place on another, perhaps different, plane. [...] Revolution, for instance, appears bound to recur [...] but the promise of a better life in the future made on each occasion of political upheaval is rarely (if ever) realized.[54]

In the above passage, Danow conveys the mood of *One Hundred Years of Solitude*, where revolutions are constantly betrayed and the history of the Buendías is described thus: "a machine with unavoidable repetitions, a turning wheel that would have gone on spilling into eternity were it not for the progressive and irremediable wearing of the axle."[55]

During the launch of *The Last Harmattan* at the Library Board in Freetown, Cheney–Coker declared that "literature is infinitely more superior to the transient relationship between man and politics."[56] The same belief in the primacy of art over political affairs will be evident in Okri and Laing's works, too, as if magical-realist authors wanted to offer a picture of human society that served as an alternative not only to naturalistic depictions but also to committed ones, consciously shorn of any ambition to serve as a catalyst of immediate political change.

On the other hand, Cheney–Coker vehemently affirms his ideological difference from García Márquez:

---

[54] Danow, *Spirit of Carnival*, 74.

[55] García Márquez, *One Hundred Years of Solitude*, 402.

[56] Smith, "Dreams from the Mind," 632.

> the Latin American situation with the repeated revolutions they had, with the rise and falls of dictators, is very different. Look at the way he [García Márquez] treats [...] Colonel Aureliano Buendia, the revolutionary who starts and loses 17 wars. At the end there's an almost nihilistic acceptance of the hopelessness of life. I don't see it that way. For me in spite of all the sadness and suffering [...] at the end there is hope.[57]

The closing sections of his novel introduce hope through the resilient spirit of the Malaguetans, who are even more oppressed by colonial greed (and by Arab traders) when a rare diamond is discovered, introducing "a new philosophy called individualism." The Arabs' coming is anticipated by a circus caravan "from the Shouf mountains and the markets of Damascus [...] colourful creatures in their outlandish costumes" (373). The circus with its carnivalesque spectacles also introduces a new storytelling tradition – the lore of the *Arabian Nights*; significantly, the chapter recounting the pillage of the country is entitled "Ali Baba and the Forty Thieves.[58] The book's epilogue comes full circle to meet its prologue in another instance – this time structural – of cyclicity, and General Masimiara, former Head of State, is sent to the gallows after his failed coup against the tyrannical Sanka Maru. On his death, lightning, wind and hurricane suddenly rise and Sulaiman appears flying on a magic carpet, another scene reminiscent of the *Arabian Nights*; Cheney–Coker explains this as directly inspired by both García Márquez and his country's history:

> [García] Márquez describes how he had gone out one day and seen a woman hanging her laundry and the wind came and a piece of laundry was being blown out and this is how he decided he was going to send one of his characters to heaven. Remedios the Beauty, she was going to fly. I remember someone saying to me that on the night that a major character in my novel, Tamba Masimiara the general, died (you know he was modeled on someone who really lived in Sierra Leone) the night that the real soldier died, there was such a strong wind. It was just incomprehensible. There hadn't been a wind like that in a long time. So I woke up one morning thinking about it and I said: well, why don't you have Alusine Dunbar flying on a magic carpet and let this wind with its enormous power.[59]

David Lodge notes that "Since defiance of gravity has always been a human dream of the impossible, it is perhaps not surprising that images of flight, levitation and

---

[57] Cooper, "Syl Cheney–Coker," 11.

[58] Pages 369–84. Brenda Cooper rightly notes (*Magical Realism in West African Fiction*, 136) how the depiction of the Arabs is far less complex (more simplistic) than the description of the white European colonialists.

[59] Cooper, "Syl Cheney–Coker," 12. García Márquez's novel explicitly refers to flying carpets as well as to the *Arabian Nights*, which is read by Aureliano Segundo; García Márquez, *One Hundred Years of Solitude*, 31, 189.

free fall often occur in this [magical realist] kind of fiction," and cites García Márquez, Salman Rushdie, Angela Carter, Jeanette Winterson and Milan Kundera.[60] The same is true for West African authors, as this chapter of Cheney–Coker's novel demonstrates. From his carpet, Sulaiman kills Sanka Maru with the light emanating from his testicles and sticks together the traitor Colonel Akongo and the woman he is having sexual intercourse with; the novel closes in an highly metaliterary manner reminiscent of the parchment writings by Melquíades embodying the novelistic enterprise of *One Hundred Years of Solitude*: "he and his concubine would not hope for deliverance from their lust, because they had been condemned to an eternal public disgrace in *The Last Harmattan of Alusine Dunbar*" (398).

By and large, Cheney–Coker's novel is deeply rooted in the colonial and neocolonial contradictions of Sierra Leonean and African history, even though its mystic solution offers no patent way out. Brenda Cooper is right when she writes that the book is "located somewhere between the magical realist cosmopolitans of the Latin American variety and the culturally nationalistic African decolonisers."[61] Nevertheless, she insists on absolving Cheney–Coker's 'ironic distancing' from any kind of ethnic essentialism and myth-making; in her view, the author privileges the myth of the founders of Malagueta, while at the same time deconstructing it by way of his farcical and grotesque perspective. We have already seen how the founders' return is realized through a negotiation of different cultures, thereby dispelling any danger of ethnic essentialism. Cooper brings to the fore the farcical nature of Sulaiman's luminous testicle, the dwarves, and Garbage's name. Bakhtin's carnivalesque, which she often mentions, envisages the coexistence of the comic and serious dimensions. Cooper separates the two, bringing in the concept of 'ironic *distancing*,' which seems to be quite another thing.[62] On the other hand, Cooper appears to hit the target when she hints that the founders' nature as a "benevolent elite [...] a blood elite of innately better" people may account for the ambiguities of Cheney–Coker's political vision.[63]

All in all, *The Last Harmattan*'s greatest import is within the context of the development of the African novel. In 1990, when the novel won the Commonwealth Writers Prize for Africa, the Africanist establishment finally acknowledged the rise of a new mode in the novel genre. Cheney–Coker explains thus the urge to write it:

---

60 Lodge, "Magic Realism," 114.

61 Cooper, "Syl Cheney–Coker," 5.

62 Cooper, *Magical Realism in West African Fiction*, 121, 122, 131, 133, 146, 147.

63 Cooper, *Magical Realism in West African Fiction*, 140.

> It was also this feeling that the novel in Africa has been as if it were cloistered within very prescribed forms. It was either you had a sociological view of the novel within the Achebian definition, or you were a political novelist within the Ngugian concept of it. There were all these perceived notions of what the African novel should be like [...] I felt the need for new kinds of directions.[64]

Ben Okri: The *abiku*'s double vision

Ben Okri's *The Famished Road* – published only a year after *The Last Harmattan* – develops West African magical realism in an altogether different direction, albeit probably originating in a similar rejection of stylistic assumptions:

> One of the strongest impulses which made me write *The Famished Road* is that I got tired of the traditional artifices and realism of the novel. I wanted to cut all that, going directly to the point in a different way, but still in the form of a novel.[65]

Having been awarded the prestigious Booker Prize, the book certainly contributed to the affirmation of the mode in world literature.

Prior to its publication, Ben Okri's literary career could be seen as a slow approach to the style and subject-matter of magical realism. His third and fourth books are collections of short stories, *Incidents at the Shrine* (1986) and *Stars of the New Curfew* (1988), where the author experiments with the oneiric dimension as a potential door to the exploration of other worlds and realities. The protagonist of "The Dream-Vendor's August," for instance, dreams of a midget who becomes the main determinant of his destiny.[66] In both "Worlds that Flourish" and "What the Tapster Saw," a temporary death takes the characters into fantastic worlds peopled by outlandish creatures.[67]

In the case of "Incidents at the Shrine," the unreal dimension is associated with the protagonist's return to his native village.[68] Ato Quayson, the critic who has most thoroughly investigated Okri's inspirational sources, traces a parallel between these short stories and the structure of Tutuola's works: in his view, both writers tend to place the esoteric outside the city. On the other hand, in Okri's stories such a geographical dichotomy also blurs into an urban climate of dispossession "in the form of hallucinatory impingements on the perceptions of the characters." Nevertheless,

---

[64] Cooper, "Syl Cheney–Coker," 10.

[65] Pietro Deandrea, "An Interview with Ben Okri," *Africa America Asia Australia* 16 (1994): 82.

[66] Ben Okri, *Incidents at the Shrine* (1986; London: Flamingo, 1987). 117–18, 134–35.

[67] Ben Okri, *Stars of the New Curfew* (1988; Harmondsworth: Penguin, 1989): 25–33, 185–294.

[68] Okri, *Incidents*, 53–66.

"it seems [to Okri] important not to depart completely from the realist mode because of the need to force a recognition of the contexts which anchor the stories."[69]

Okri's three *abiku* novels – *The Famished Road* (1991), *Songs of Enchantment* (1993) and *Infinite Riches* (1998)[70] – mark a decisive turn in his style and fortunes. Their protagonist is the child Azaro, who narrates in the first person his life in a Nigerian urban ghetto around 1960, the year of independence. The city is never specified, but it is likely to be Lagos, where the author grew up and set his first two novels.

The pivotal novelty of the two books is Azaro's nature: he is an *abiku* – a spirit-child believed by Yoruba lore to be "any child who dies and is reborn several times into the same family."[71] Okri's magical realism, therefore, is rooted in an indigenous belief-system, but it must be noted that this system has non-Yoruba, pan-Nigerian implications. First of all, Okri himself is not Yoruba, but half Urhobo and half Agbor, as he informed me.[72] Furthermore, the myth of the mischievous child cyclically dying in the same family does not belong to Yoruba culture only, but is shared by several Nigerian ethnic groups.[73] Before Okri, some patriarchs of anglophone West African literature – Achebe, Clark, Soyinka – had already treated the subject and its man–spirit ambivalence.[74]

---

[69] Ato Quayson, *Strategic Trasformations*, 53–56, 102–103, 116, 115. This chapter makes abundant use of Quayson's insights into Okri's works. As for the Tutuola / Okri connection, Harry Garuba has remarked on how Okri's short stories came out after his enthusiatic review of Tutuola's *The Witch-Herbalist of the Remote Town*: from this and "from his meetings with other writers in Britain, most notably Salman Rushdie, it seems that Okri's search for new directions and alternative traditions of narrative had started to take shape by the time he published his two collections"; Garuba, "Ben Okri," in Lindfors & Sander, *Dictionary of Literary Biography*, 157, 280.

[70] Ben Okri, *The Famished Road* (London: Jonathan Cape, 1991); *Songs of Enchantment* (London: Jonathan Cape, 1993); *Infinite Riches* (London: Phoenix, 1998). Further page references are in the main text, preceded by FR, SE and IR respectively.

[71] Timothy Mobolade, "The Concept of Abiku," *African Arts* 7.1 (Autumn 1973): 62.

[72] Deandrea, "Interview with Ben Okri," 55. Ato Quayson and Harry Garuba curiously assert that his parents are both Urhobo; Quayson, *Strategic Transformations*, 101; Garuba, "Ben Okri," 277.

[73] According to John C. Hawley, such a widespread notion "says volumes about the heartrending deaths of countless newborns throughout the region's history"; Hawley, "Ben Okri's Spirit-Child: *Abiku* Migration and Postmodernity," *Research in African Literatures* 26.1 (1995): 30.

[74] Chidi T. Maduka, "African Religious Beliefs in Literary Imagination: *Ogbanje* and *Abiku* in Chinua Achebe, J.P. Clark and Wole Soyinka," *Journal of Commonwealth Literature* 23.1 (1987): passim. In his essay, Maduka omits mention of two important books which touch on the *abiku*. In his first autobiographical volume, *Aké* (1981), Soyinka describes the the *abiku* condition of one of his childhood friends, whose fits resemble epilepsy. In the young narrator's mind, the existence of the *abiku* is never doubted. Furthermore, this friend is depicted in words that would be suitable for

Azaro describes the spirit-world he comes from as a place of unbounded joy: "With our spirit companions [...] we were happy most of the time because we floated on the acquamarine air of love" (FR 4). That is the reason why "as we approached another incarnation we made pacts that we would return to the spirit world at the first opportunity" (FR 4).

According to Mobolade, an *abiku* never "pledges to stay put in life, which explains why the abiku is so indifferent to the plight of its mother and her grief,"[75] whereas Bolaji Idowu holds that, "sometimes, the spirit may be made to 'decide' to break the pact with its spirit-companions and remain a human being on earth."[76] Azaro's choice to live through the squalor of the ghetto is motivated by a longing for experience and by the concern denied by Mobolade:

> I wanted to taste of this world, to feel it, suffer it, know it [...] But I sometimes think it was a face that made me want to stay. I wanted to make happy the bruised face of the woman who would become my mother. (FR 5)

Okri's use of the *abiku* differs from his predecessors' inasmuch as he founds his magical-realist style with its coexistence of rational reality and spirit-world on Azaro's first-person narration, since the child's contact with his original place is never severed and his perceptions therefore constantly touch on both dimensions at the same time. As the author said to me:

> One half of him is in the spirit world, the other is in the world of the real. Whenever he looks at reality, he does it through the eyes of a spirit as well as through those of a human being, so everything is both ordinary and transfigured, simultaneously [...] In *The Famished Road* there is this unique point of view because it's a first person narration, if it were a third person I wouldn't do that.[77]

Given this fundamental concept sustaining his three novels, the main point to be investigated is the kind of use Okri makes of this unique point of view – unlike him, Cheney–Coker and Laing always employ third-person narration in their novels. In

---

Okri's Azaro: "She was so rare, this privileged being who, unlike Tinu and me, and even her companions in the other place, *could pass easily from one sphere to another*" (emphasis mine); *Aké: The Years of Childhood* (Ibadan: Spectrum, 1981): 17. The protagonist of Amos Tutuola's *My Life in the Bush of Ghosts* (London: Faber & Faber, 1954), during his otherworldly wanderings, finds himself in a town inhabited by *abikus*. See also the birth of the protagonist in Kole Omotoso's *Memories of Our Recent Boom* (Harlow, Essex: Longman, 1982): 1–3.

[75] Mobolade, "Concept of Abiku," 62.

[76] E. Bolaji Idowu, *African Traditional Religion: A Definition* (1973; Lagos: Fountain, 1991): 175.

[77] Deandrea, "Interview with Ben Okri," 80.

other words, what kind of magical realism is developed in the (almost) twelve hundred pages of Azaro's cycle? What analysis of Nigerian society does it evince?

To start with the latter question, it must be said that, as with several of the magical-realist authors mentioned so far, Okri's *abiku* novels are solidly rooted in Nigerian contemporary social issues and its recent dreadful calamities. The ghetto where Azaro lives with his parents – "mum" and "dad"[78] – is home to the wretched of the earth *par excellence*; besides lacking all kind of hygienic facilities and being constantly flooded during the rainy seasons, it seems to offer few viable alternatives to a life of daily suffering and hard work. In Azaro's house – actually, a room in a compound – regular meals have to be grubbed for day by day through mum's hawking and dad's desultory and humiliating jobs – load-carrier, nightsoil man and the like. After one of his miraculous recoveries from death, Azaro is named after the resuscitated Lazarus; on the other hand, the name could also refer to the other biblical Lazarus, the beggar who fed on the rich man's leftovers (FR 8).[79] The all-pervasive poverty and rawness of environment are perfectly embodied in the following passage:

> Everywhere there was the crudity of wounds, the stark huts, the rusted zinc abodes, the rubbish in the streets, children in rags, the little girls naked on the sand playing with crushed tin-cans, the little boys jumping about uncircumcised, making machine-gun noises, the air vibrating with poisonous heat and evaporating water from the filthy gutters. The sun bared the reality of our lives and everything was so harsh it was a mystery that we could understand and care for one another or for anything at all. (FR 161)

Poverty is paralleled by oppression, brought about by various factors: a harassing landlord who does not hesitate to call policemen to defend his interests and thus ignites the very first riot; the two indigenous political entities created by the forthcoming independence, the Party of the Rich and the Party of the Poor. Initially, the former seem to effect much more evil than the latter, since one of its vans distributes rotten milk in the ghetto; its next visit to the area will cause another clash.[80] Dad openly declares his sympathy for the Party of the Poor, but Azaro's descriptions tend to blur any difference between the two; here is his rendering of one of the clashes between the two factions: "They lashed at one another with long sticks,

---

[78] For the sake of consistency, "mum" and "dad" are spelt here without a capital letter. Strangely enough, Okri (or his editors) chose to use the capital in the first and third volume, whereas *Songs* employs lower case.

[79] John 11:1–44 & Luke 16:19–31.

[80] FR 122, 156. Okri told me that the episode is based on a real event; Deandrea, "Interview with Ben Okri," 82.

clubs, and whips. They all looked alike. They were the interchangeable faces of violence and politics" (FR 192). Both parties end up unleashing mindless violence on their opponents and on the harmless populace, sometimes sending their night-runners into the ghetto in order to spread terror:

> Wild men were wreaking devastation on windows, wooden doors, and human bodies. We rushed out into the haze, into the smell of burning hair, into the acrid yellow smoke from the barber's shop, into the noises of corrupted ritual chants and caterwauling and machetes giving off electric sparks, crying for medicinal war. (FR 178)

In the end, the Party of the Poor resorts to the same methods: "their new strategy was to out-terrorise the Party of the Rich. They had seen just how many converts the other party had won through sheer terror" (SE 247).

In the face of such onslaughts, violence becomes a model of survival and inevitably engenders further violence, as Azaro is asked by dad: "Do you see how they force a man to become an armed robber?" (FR 237). Another author dealing with the theme of widespread violence in today's Nigeria is Festus Iyayi, Okri's contemporary; in his novel *Violence* (1980), he naturalistically describes a society ruled by jungle ethics, hence by injustice of various kinds.

Even though they belong to the same context, Okri's novelistic world-view is not in tune with Iyayi's materialist analysis. Besides the rational goings-on of daily life, the other side of Azaro's vision is peopled with spirits of all kinds, ghosts of dead people and deformed humanoids of whom he can see the real nature, "spirits who had borrowed bits of human beings to partake of human reality" (FR 136).[81] In African traditional religions, supernatural beings "can assume various dimensions whenever they wish to be seen."[82] Another scholar of African religions, J.S. Mbiti, writes that

> whatever science can do to prove the existence or non-existence of the spirits, one thing is undeniable, namely that for African peoples the spirits are a reality [...] which must be reckoned with, whether it is a clear, blurred or confused reality.[83]

The main difference between Iyayi's and Okri's narrative mode is that the latter strives, in the words of Angela Carter, at "establishing, for the European reader, a world based on a different sense of reality from the one current in all the advanced industrialized countries."[84]

---

[81] See also IR 164.

[82] Idowu, *African Traditional Religion*, 174.

[83] John S. Mbiti, *African Religions and Philosophy* (London: Heinemann, 1969): 91.

[84] Angela Carter, "Gaudy Metaphysics," *Sunday Times* (31 March 1991): 8.

The encounters between Azaro and the spirit-world belong to different categories.[85] Spirits can visit Azaro's family suddenly and for no apparent reason, as at the beginning of *Songs*, when a "strange demon" enters dad "in the form of a beautiful girl with green eyes" (SE 10) that will disappear just as mysteriously twenty pages later. Spirits can also reach Azaro as emissaries of his fellow *abikus*, who want him back with them. A couple of albinos put him in a sack, but he escapes thanks to a pen-knife given to him by a mysterious midget (FR 110–13).[86] Then a three-headed spirit appears: "Each of its heads was a different shape. One was red with blue eyes, the other was yellow with red eyes, and the third was blue with yellow eyes. The spirit had about ten eyes in all" (FR 297). Later on, the same spirit almost succeeds in convincing Azaro to die, when the boy, in reaction to his father's beatings, refuses to eat.

The spirit-world is associated with particular geographical spaces such as the marketplace[87] and, above all, the forest near the ghetto, where Azaro often wanders. When he finds a strange mask on the forest floor and puts it on, Azaro sees

> a village of spirits [...] skyscrapers and flying machines and fountains, ruins covered in snails and flowering climbers, grave-stelae, orchards, and a monument of a black sphinx at the gate of the village. (FR 246)

Usually, though, Azaro has such visions without the help of masks. The creatures he encounters or sees are strongly reminiscent of Amos Tutuola's ghosts. As already indicated, the influence exerted by Tutuola on Okri is evident, and once again the latter's departure from his inspirational source is thoroughly examined by Ato Quayson. In Tutuola, the hero's journeys in the lands of ghosts follow a pattern of crossing and re-crossing the boundary between the rational world and the mysterious unknown. This, Quayson infers, is akin to the patterns of initiation rites, divided into the phases of separation, transition and re-absorption into 'everyday'

---

[85] Cf Quayson, "Orality – (Theory) – Textuality: Tutuola, Okri, and the Relationship of Literary Practice to Oral Tradition," in *The Pressures of the Text: Orality, Texts and the Telling of Tales*, ed. Stewart Brown (Birmingham University African Studies Series 4; Birmingham: Centre of West African Studies, 1995): 109.

[86] As mentioned above, a midget determines the protagonist's fortune also in one of Okri's short stories, "The Dream-Vendor's August" (Okri, *Incidents*, 105–13), while in Cheney–Coker's novel a couple of dwarfs help Isatu get pregnant (Cheney–Coker, *Last Harmattan*, 205–206). In Ghana, Akan lore involves belief in the existence of similar small people, called *mmoatia* and comparable to European fairies; see Peggy Appiah, *Gift of the Mmoatia* (1972; Accra: Quick Service Books, 1996).

[87] See FR 15.

reality as we know it. In Okri, thanks to Azaro, who can be considered as liminality incarnate, Tutuola's neat separation between the human and the spirit worlds blurs into a continuum:

> a continuous intercourse is permanently established between the real world and that of spirits [...] these shifts are completely arbitrary. Azaro does not necessarily desire them and is completely at the mercy of the shifts in the narrative.[88]

Boundaries are thus crossed on every page, and Azaro cannot be considered as a hero like Tutuola's protagonists, who accomplish their mission and come back to their fellow human beings. His impotence in the face of intercourse between the two worlds is a conscious state of being: he calls himself "an unwilling adventurer into chaos and sunlight, into the dreams of the living and the dead" (SE 4)[89] and later realizes "that just as I could unintentionally enter the spirit of things, they too could enter into me" (SE 123).

Quayson rightly links the liminal status of Azaro with the border-position of his environment: the ghetto, which grows "at the margin of the city absorbing the rural migrant population," where the "ideas of modernity are absorbed very rapidly, but traditional belief systems are continually activated to make meaning of the ghetto existence and to forge productive alliances."[90] This is the background against which Okri channels Tutuola's traditional lore into the hybridity of contemporary society, and marks the development from outlandish Tutuolan travels to magical realism.

Nevertheless, the great importance of the forest, spreading on the other side of the ghetto, should not be neglected. In Tutuola's narratives it represented the privileged home of the otherworldly, the space beyond the liminal. In Okri's *abiku* novels, it remains one of the main seats of magic energy connected to ancestral powers, steadily decreasing in size but still constituting a solid force against the total dominance of urban and colonial culture; as Frantz Fanon writes,

> Hostile nature, obstinate and fundamentally rebellious, is in fact represented in the colonies by the bush [...] Colonization is a success when all this indocile nature has finally been tamed.[91]

---

[88] Ato Quayson, "Orality – (Theory) – Textuality," in Brown, ed. *The Pressures of the Text*, 109.

[89] An identical definition is used in FR 487. On another occasion, Okri writes: "with no choice, resorting to the freedom of the world of spirits, I began to mutate" (SE 43).

[90] Quayson, "Orality – (Theory) – Textuality," 115.

[91] *The Wretched of the Earth*, preface by Jean–Paul Sartre, tr. Constance Farrington (tr. 1965; Penguin Twentieth-Century Classics; Harmondsworth: Penguin, 1990): 201; "la nature hostile, rétive, foncièrement rebelle est effectivement représentée aux colonies par la brousse [...] La colonisation est réussie quand toute cette nature indocile est enfin matée"; *Les damnés de la terre*

As mentioned above, Azaro's wanderings in the forest plunge him into protracted visions of supernatural beings who invest the whole environment with anthropomorphic features; trees are seen as houses, for example: "I saw people with serene bronze masks emerging from trees" (FR 243). In Okri's words:

> It is an old and ancestral perception of the fact that trees have autonomous existence, as good as I could go back to a time when trees were spirits and houses of beings.[92]

And when a tree is felled, "Red liquid dripped from its stump as if the tree had been a murdered giant whose blood wouldn't stop flowing" (FR 16).

The other location of maximum interpenetration between real and spirit dimensions is undoubtedly that of party politics, where humans clash with ruthless violence throughout the three novels. On one side, the converts of the Party of the Rich – and later of both parties – exploit ancestral supernatural powers for their own purposes; on the other, the inhabitants of the ghetto, with no party connections, desperately try to salvage the wrecked spaces of their existence. When the Party of the Poor resort to the same methods as their opponents by spreading dread in the night, Azaro describes them thus:

> their bodies, solid and quivering and half-naked, were like ancient memories of a mystical time without boundaries when it was possible to enter the consciousness of a cornseed and foretell the harvest to come. But the terror they spread, their breaking of windows, the people that they beat up who were returning home late, and the vehemence of their counter-mythology was a distortion of that mystical time, and it made their night alien. (SE 248)

The development of the character of Madame Koto, a formidable woman running a bar on the edge of the forest, is exemplary inasmuch as it shows the import of politics in the novels and its links with the marvellous. At the beginning of *The Famished Road* Madame Koto behaves benevolently towards Azaro's family and to the ghetto-dwellers, on one occasion saving mum's life. Her aura of power starts to grow when she beats up and humiliates a troublesome customer, but she also reveals certain supernatural connections: Azaro notices that "The spirits encompassed her, talking about her in astonished voices" (FR 47). With the coming of politics into the

---

(Paris: Maspero, 1961): 178. The forest acts as a source of the marvellous in Latin American magical realism, too: "The geographical proximity of the jungle to the city elicits a related omnipresent sense of the closeness of the prehistoric past to modern life, of myth, or primordial thinking, to scientific thought"; Danow, *Spirit of Carnival*, 71.

92 Deandrea, "Interview with Ben Okri," 70. The same image is employed by Okri in one of his short stories (*Stars*, 28).

area, she grabs the chance to increase her influence and fortunes by allying with the Party of the Rich. Little by little, her formidable stature acquires a dreadful aspect, connected with the spreading of terror and violence by the Party.

In Azaro's description of her, it is plain that her links with the world of spirits have not been severed; on the contrary, she merely exploits them for different purposes and against the ghetto-dwellers, in a wicked perversion of ancestral powers. When he surprises her while she is counting money, she is "a person rapt in a secret ritual" (FR 249). Later on, she is depicted as "a great old chief from ancient times, a reincarnation of splendour and power and clannish might" (FR 374). During her celebrations at the end of *Famished*, Azaro finds himself inside the eyes of a magic duiker – he is indeed at the mercy of all otherwordly creatures – and realizes that Madame Koto is pregnant

> with three strange children. Two of them sat upright and the third was upside down in her womb. One of them had a little beard, the second had fully formed teeth, and the third had wicked eyes. They were all mischievous, they kicked and tugged at their cords, they were the worst type of spirit-children, and they had no intention of being born. (FR 464)

In *Songs*; her mythic, uncanny status is magnified to such a point that she sucks people's energy in the night like a vampire-witch, and is rarely seen in public: "all we knew about her were the legends we invented" (SE 36).[93] In one of her last apparitions she is seen by Azaro as "so fat, so enormous, and yet she seemed to be floating, hovering above the ground like a dream-image, with a great peacock in her hand.[...] Servants were fanning her as if in a liquid dream […] a holographic form" (SE 212–13).[94] Her political affiliation marks a change in her clientele, too. Her bar is often crowded with thugs and mutant customers bearing all kinds of deformities. In *Infinite Riches*, she will die just before the birth of the new independent nation, when her lust for power starts being tainted by moral doubt. Her majestic funeral, symbolically heralding the birth of her political creature, occupies the closing pages of the saga.

---

[93] This spiritualization of Madame Koto is seen as perpetuating misogynist paradigms; Cooper, *Magical Realism in West African Fiction*, 112.

[94] Ato Quayson rightly observes that the development of Koto's character unfortunately reaffirms the southern Nigerian stereotype linking commercially successful women with witchcraft; Quayson, *Strategic Transformations*, 45. This may be explained by the general "Manichean morality" present in *Songs of Enchantment*; see Quayson, "Esoteric Webwork as Nervous System: Reading the Fantastic in Ben Okri's Writing," in *Essays on African Writing 2: Contemporary Literature*, ed. Abdulrazak Gurnah (Oxford: Heinemann, 1995): 155.

Another figure that embodies the confluence between contemporary politics and ancestral supernatural forces is the tall red Jackal-Headed Masquerade, situated before Koto's bar in *Songs*. It appears all of a sudden one day, and

> held aloft a shining machete in one hand and a white flag, emblem of their party, in the other [...] had the head of a jackal, with fiercely protruding jaws, and it had the twisted horns of a ram – but it had human eyes. The eyes kept looking at us, turning in their sockets, regarding us with intense hostility. It was when people noticed the eyes that they began to be really mesmerised with horror. (SE 98)

The Masquerade, often surrounded by spirits of all sorts and found with its machete dripping blood after one of the nights of clashes, often seems to be animated by the blind old man, a character in a morally descending but politically ascending parable similar to Madame Koto's. In *Songs* he reveals himself as an evil 'master sorcerer' or 'master transformer'; once Azaro follows him in spirit and discovers that

> he was a demonic spirit-child of the worst kind, the kind that had developed all its potential for malignity to the highest degree, that had re-connected the old forces which ran in the veins of ancient secret societies and cabals, fuelled by an abundance of spirit energies. (SE 146)

All three figures – Madame Koto, the blind old man and the Masquerade – will be finally united in one of Azaro's visions, where he sees the woman being made pregnant by the Masquerade to the accompaniment of the old man's "infernal accordion." This triangle of malignant forces generates three baby masquerades strikingly similar to the three main Nigerian ethnic groups: "children who spent their lives divided, warring against each other, fighting for their mother's milk, savaging her breasts, and tearing her apart in a bizarre, incestuous and greedy rage."[95]

The civil war that Nigeria went through after independence (1967–70) – hence subsequent to the temporal setting of the novels – pervades the three books in the form of more or less explicit references that hint at the impending and inevitable catastrophe. Such omens can be interpreted through the *abiku*'s point of view; as Okri explains, his double vision implies an overlapping not only of spatial dimensions but also of temporal planes:

> Because of the fact that this boy is half spirit and half human, with the doors of death perpetually open inside him, [...] everything he sees is transfigured, even time is different, what we perceive as future consequence for this child is present.[96]

---

[95] SE 142–43. Cf another image for Nigeria's internecine divisions in Femi Osofisan's *Yungba-Yungba and the Dance Contest* (Ibadan: Heinemann Educational, 1993); see pp. 230, 239 below.

[96] Deandrea, "Interview with Ben Okri," 80.

Azaro claims that "on days when my body's light dims" his memory "goes back a thousand years" (SE 117), and feels sometimes overwhelmed by the broad temporal span encompassed by his mind: "I had no idea whether these images belonged to this life, or to a previous one, or to one that was yet to come [...] One lifetime flowed into the others and all of them flowed into my childhood" (FR 7).[97]

When Azaro finds himself in the blind old man's dream, what he sees is evil minds plotting for the Nigerian future:

> I saw soldiers in armoured trucks rolling into the city, I saw coup after coup, till our history became an endless rosary necklace of them, each new bead an assassinated head of state, or the secret numbers of failed coup-plotters, executed at dawn.
>
> I saw history as a madman with a machine gun, a madman eating up the twisting flesh of the innocent and the silent. (SE 89)

Later on, references to the Biafran War become more direct: "The war raged and the blind old man turned into a mosquito, spied on the rebel troops, and reported back to the army chief who had hired him, whose emblem was a white lion" (SE 90).

The Biafran War undoubtedly had a decisive impact on Okri's outlook and artistic motivation. He lived through it as a child, and it is not by chance that both his story collections open with narratives about young protagonists witnessing the cruelties of those terrible years.[98] The looming tragedy of the civil war is likely to account for the changes between *The Famished Road* and *Songs of Enchantment*, sharply outlined by Ato Quayson when he writes that Okri's balance between reality and mythopoeia "is abandoned in *Songs of Enchantment* in which the whole narrative takes a complete turn into mythopoeia."[99] An in-depth reading of *Songs* would reveal the reason behind this shift – the chaos brought about by impending war. Okri once declared of *The Famished Road* that "life in Nigeria is so chaotic that it can only be understood by going beyond reality."[100] In *Songs of Enchantment*, once he has to deal with the brutal climax of Nigerian chaos as embodied in the Biafran War, the mythic and magical dimension inevitably wrests control of the narrative.

---

[97] Margaret Cezair–Thompson argues that the mythic temporal span of Okri's "decolonized fiction [...] asks us, as critics, to look beyond the postcolonial and to recognize a new direction in African literature, one which, while recognizing historic situations, is not limited to a historic perspective"; Cezair–Thompson, "Beyond the Postcolonial Novel: Ben Okri's *The Famished Road* and its Abiku Traveller," *Journal of Commonwealth Literature* 31.2 (1996): 34.

[98] Other autobiographical suggestions are present in *Infinite Riches*, regarding Azaro's adult life in England, the dangers of fame and his future career as a writer; IR 12, 88, 149.

[99] Quayson, "Esoteric Webwork," 154.

[100] Kate Muir, "An Author in Search of Humility," *The Times* (London: 25 October 1991): 15.

The second novel consequently abounds with visions, hallucinations and journeys into otherworldly spheres that occupies large sections of it, sidelining the concrete problems of everyday survival in the ghetto that constituted the other thematic pole of *The Famished Road*. The prophetic first chapter includes a significant sentence: "We didn't see the chaos growing; and when its advancing waves found us we were unprepared for its feverish narratives and wild manifestations" (SE 3). 'Feverish' is a fitting epithet for the whole book, which is mainly concerned with the 'wild manifestations' visited on the helpless inhabitants of the ghetto. What one sees at work is the effects of indiscriminate violence, unhingeing human perceptions of the world, and released not only on the victims but also on the persecutors. When Madame Koto's driver kills Ade by running over him, he goes mad:

> he had entered the world which those who have committed murder wander into – a world of spirits and silences, where chickens become familiar people, where cats are antagonists; a world of unidentified voices, where nightmares drift past the eyes as they stare at the ordinary faces of the earth; a place in which several spheres and realities are all scrambled up. (SE 204)

This violent context is so pervasive that in *Songs*, starting on page 138 and continuing for several chapters, first-person-singular narration is replaced by a plural "we," which indicates all the ghetto inhabitants who have not converted to the Party of the Rich and are consequently subject to its oppression. They go collectively insane, have the weirdest visions, swap one another's features, remain mysteriously transfixed, are invaded by butterflies whose bonfire will liberate spirits seen by everyone, enter one another's dreams and undergo further such experiences. At one point the casualties of this generalized fury are so many that "We ceased to be aware of the number of the dead. We began to live with ghosts and spirits. Our night-spaces began to crawl with other presences" (SE 208).

Ato Quayson considers the impact of Civil War experiences on Okri's writing as an interpretative key not limited to the peculiarities of *Songs* but suitable to his whole magical-realist output: "It can be conjectured that in such conditions stories about spirits and their relationship to the real world would take a greater urgency."[101] Whatever import the Nigerian Civil War may have had on Okri's style, his *abiku* novels appear to share the relationship between history and literature pointed out by David Lodge:

> All these writers [García Márquez, Grass, Rushdie, Kundera] have lived through great historical upheavals which they feel cannot be adequately represented in a discourse of

[101] Quayson, *Strategic Transformations*, 147.

> undisturbed realism. Perhaps Britain's relatively untraumatic modern history has encouraged its writers to persevere with traditional realism.[102]

On another occasion, Azaro's ghetto-dwellers wake up to find their area completely devastated:

> The chaos made us brain shocked: everywhere we looked our stunned brains conjured further devastations. The chaos made us hallucinate. The air had changed. Some people screamed that they saw spirits melting in the air. [...] It became difficult to separate the actual devastations from the strange effects they had on our minds. People kept disappearing from our midst and reappearing somewhere else. (SE 151)

The above quotation is drawn from a chapter entitled "The Invention of Chaos." The necessity to manufacture chaos in order to preserve power is a concept that Okri had already articulated in his short story "Stars of the New Curfew." He repeated it very clearly during our first interview:

> It's really difficult to maintain power if democracy is running exactly the way it should run. Very difficult to do it. The suppression of democracy is always in the interest of those who are in power.[103]

When Azaro gets transported into the Jackal-Headed Masquerade he has a chance to see this phenomenon: "I saw the powers of the Kingdom, how it manufactures reality, how it produces events which will become history, how it creates memory, and silence, and forgetfulness" (SE 115).

From what has been said so far, it is evident that Okri's *abiku* novels are solidly rooted in their Nigerian sociohistorical context. Nevertheless, some critics have attempted to uproot them through a process of affiliation to universal, generalized critical theories. Olatubosun Ogunsanwo, for instance, construes the coexistence in Okri of the rational and the magical as one of parodic intertexts that "arise from its interlocking narrative modes, a distinctive combination of the African and the European which reflects the collective modes of discourse underlying postmodern parody."[104] If we take into consideration the meaning of 'parody' as 'amusing, exaggerated, comic, mocking imitation,' what exactly is being parodied, one wonders? Certainly not the real or marvellous side of the novels, developed by Okri with the utmost respect for their descriptive and prophetic power, verging sometimes on vatic utterance. In his narratological nomenclature, Genette's definition of 'parody' is not applicable to Okri, either, because it is conceived of as a stylistic shift in a

---

[102] Lodge, "Magic Realism," 114.

[103] Deandrea, "Interview with Ben Okri," 59.

[104] Olatubosun Ogunsanwo, "Intertextuality and Postcolonial Literature in Ben Okri's *The Famished Road*," *Research in African Literatures* 26.1 (1995): 41.

playful tone.[105] The matter in question here is once again the primacy of theory over the text, currently dominant in Western critical theory and occasionally superimposed on literary products from other areas of the world. John C. Hawley aptly quotes Linda Hutcheon's theorization of the dismantling and constructive features of the postcolonial;[106] if the latter category is to be employed at all, this definition is the most suitable to the authors examined here. Unfortunately, Hawley produces the generic and objectionable definition of "postcolonial postmodernity" to characterize the way in which Okri's experimental style is coupled with an alternative ontology; he also comes to the conclusion that, given the novels' countless metamorphoses and their "animistic appreciation of a surging and constantly transmogrifying reality," Okri can be seen to be celebrating "the Western dilemma of the dissolution of the subject."[107] Azaro undoubtedly traverses different dimensions, by which he is often overwhelmed, but his decision to live is a strong affirmation of human resilience, and by no means a dissolution, let alone a dissolution of identity.

The ghetto subjects also reaffirm their identity on the sites of resistance that Okri conjures up for them. The reaction to political oppression is often inspired and supported by the same mythic reservoir tapped by the manufacturers of reality. As Okri has said to Jane Wilkinson, when myth "is a living, sustaining thing [...it] is what makes possible for those who suffer and struggle [...] to live and carry on."[108] One of the night-runners' attacks is withstood through the intervention of the spirits of the dead, much like what happens in *The Last Harmattan of Alusine Dunbar*:

> I saw the dead rising, I saw them rising at the same moment that the second wave of havoc started with the chants of the antagonists. The dead joined the innocents, mingled with the thugs, merged with the night, and plundered the antagonists with the cries of the wounded. (FR 180)

The dead and the unborn are constantly present in Okri's *abiku* novels as a force that is part of a more inclusive cycle of reincarnation common to most traditional African cultures. Wole Soyinka describes the form this notion takes in Yoruba culture: "the past is not a mystery and [...] although the future (the unborn) is yet unknown, it is not a mystery to the Yoruba but co-existent in present consciousness."[109]

---

105 Gérard Genette, *Palimpsestes: La littérature au second degré* (Paris: Seuil, 1982): 7–48. See also Cooper, *Magical Realism in West African Fiction*, 111.

106 Hawley, "Ben Okri's Spirit-Child," 33.

107 Hawley, "Ben Okri's Spirit-Child," 35–36.

108 Jane Wilkinson, "Interview with Ben Okri," *Guardian* (24 October 1991): 19.

109 Wole Soyinka, *Myth, Literature and the African World* (Cambridge: Cambridge UP, 1976): 149. Renato Oliva coins the definition "shamanic realism" for such a coexistence of the dead and

When dad decides to become a boxer, he acquires a sort of heroic status for the ghetto-dwellers against the persecutions of the Party of the Rich. Quayson observes that Okri's imagery links dad with the Yoruba deities Shango and Ogun, and rightly notes how his rise to the status of hero "depends on the resources of the real world as well as that of spirits."[110] One of dad's greatest fights is against one of the Party's thugs, Green Leopard.[111] After an unpromising beginning, dad manages to overcome his rival by establishing contact with his first great opponent, Yellow Jaguar, whom he previously beat before realizing that he had died three years before.[112] Yellow Jaguar first appeared in the night as "a bright yellow pair of eyes [...] from over the swamp" (FR 354) and later disappeared mysteriously into the earth. Consequently, when dad finds himself in a critical situation with Green Leopard, he makes the following move:

> Suddenly Dad reappeared. He stepped out from the spectators, a ghastly, horrifying sight, an apparition covered in rubbish. From the waist downwards he was pouring with mud and slime. *For some reason he had gone into the swamp.* He was an ugly sight. He was beyond caring, his eyes were not afraid of dying, he was no longer a defensive animal, and his eyes burned as if he had the sun in them. (FR 399, my emphasis)

As in Cheney–Coker's novel, therefore, readers are left to trace connections among widely spaced episodes. This passage also shows clearly that, aside from the 'evil' characters such as Madame Koto and the blind old man, Azaro is not the only one who enters a supernatural dimension, even though the books are founded on his *abiku* perspective. After his first mythic experiences, dad also fights in his dream – where he visits the Land of the Fighting Ghosts – and during Madame Koto's celebrations he comes to blows with a weird stranger displaying animal features and the "legs of a spiderous animal" (FR 473).[113]

---

the living, and traces some stimulating comparisons between Okri's and W.B. Yeats's spirit-worlds; Oliva, "Re-Dreaming the World: Ben Okri's Shamanic Realism," in *Coterminous Worlds: Magical Realism and Contemporary Post-Colonial Literature in English*, ed. Elsa Linguanti, Francesco Casotti & Carmen Concilio (Cross/Cultures 39; Amsterdam & Atlanta GA: Rodopi, 1999): 171–96.

[110] Quayson, *Strategic Transformations*, 140–41, 143.

[111] FR 395–402.

[112] FR 354–58.

[113] This "spiderous" man will reappear briefly two volumes later, in *Infinite Riches*, as "a man who was half-spirit and half-human. He had the trickster god's smile on his face" (IR 214). Trickster, spider, half-spirit: the description perfectly fits Ananse, the spider-trickster of Akan lore, used in this book as an interpretative matrix for Kojo Laing's novels; see the next part of this chapter, and Chapter 3 below.

Nevertheless, it remains to be asked what significance such feats may yield. In other words, how can these spaces of resistance offered by Okri be turned into values and principles viable in contemporary Nigeria? The author's proposed means for changing the status quo do not go further than generalized benign concepts such as love, light and the hidden potential within human souls and suffering, which one day "will turn into the wonders of the earth" (FR 338). At the end of *The Famished Road*, utterly exhausted by his latest fight, dad "was redreaming the world as he slept. He saw the scheme of things and didn't like it" (FR 492). When he recovers from sleep he utters a series of fine-sounding precepts, such as:

> We must look at the world with new eyes. We must look at ourselves differently. We are freer than we think. [...] We can redream this world and make the dream real. Human beings are gods hidden from themselves. My son, our hunger can change the world, make it better, sweeter. [...] It is more difficult to love than to die. (FR 498)

David Jowitt takes up Okri's hope about social and political justice, stating that "the pre-condition of its ultimately successful outcome is the constant moral renewal of the individuals by whom it is carried on."[114] Unfortunately, as will also be noticed in Chapter 3 with regard to his novel *Astonishing the Gods* (1995), Okri never proceeds beyond statements like those mentioned above. One would like a hint or two about what humans *would do* if they became gods; about what a "better world" would imply; about possible ways of making the dream real.[115] The novel ends on a hopeful yet faint note: "A dream can be the highest point of a life" (FR 500). Just like Cheney–Coker and the next author to be examined next, Kojo Laing, Okri does not seem to lend much importance to immediately practicable solutions to contemporary issues. As Ato Quayson writes:

> In many ways Okri's experiments with narrative form harbour ambiguous meanings for working out the relationship between literature and the real-life conditions which it is meant to be engaging with.[116]

The same enigma also characterizes *Songs of Enchantment*, where supernatural elements invade mum's consciousness and life. Her newly acquired aloof calm is

---

[114] David Jowitt, "Structure and Meaning in Ben Okri's Magic Fiction," *Guardian* (Lagos; 9 October 1993): 20.

[115] With regard to this, John Otu writes that at the ending of *The Famished Road* "Okri overplayed his hand on philosophy"; Otu, "Beyond Okri's Surrealism: A Gestalt Perspective," *Guardian* (Lagos; 10 April 1993): 19. Quayson describes it as "unduly homiletic" (*Strategic Transformations*, 143).

[116] Quayson, "Esoteric Webwork," 153. See also Cooper, *Magical Realism in West African Fiction*, 86.

linked with the novel's main source of resistance to the expanding power of politics, once again located in the forest: "Young girls vanished. At night we heard the haunting threnody of multiplied female voices from the impenetrable screen of trees" (SE 70). These women are sometimes seen in the form of white antelopes or bejewelled women dressed in white, and carry a message of great import for the ghetto-dwellers: "mum surprised me one night by telling me that the women were singing of the forgotten ways of our ancestors" (SE 79). After the umpteenth coming of the night-runners, "three women in white robes with jewels round their neck" are found slaughtered; significantly, the following day, "We noticed with alarm that gore dripped from the machete which it [the Masquerade] clasped in one hand like a conquering and ruthless god" (SE 109, 110).

In the chapter entitled "Fragments of the Original Way," Okri attempts to elaborate on the meaning of the ancestral "forgotten ways" mentioned above. The concept of an African Way (ie, world-view) is undoubtedly inspired by Ayi Kwei Armah's *Two Thousand Seasons* (1973). Armah defines this as a balance between giving to and receiving from other cultures, an immediacy of collective action following thought, and articulates it into practice throughout the action of his novel.[117] Okri, for his part, is often too limited to abstract definitions that possess very vague practical implications:

> The Way of compassion and fire and serenity: The Way of freedom and power and imaginative life; [...] The Way whose centre grows from divine love [...] The Way that preaches attunement with all the higher worlds, that believes in forgiveness and generosity of spirit, always receptive, always listening. (SE 159–60)

Armah's narrator – who firmly believes in reciprocity – would certainly find Okri's generous stance too unilateral. The difference between the two conceptions probably lies in Okri's strands of passivity and acceptance reminiscent of Christianity and Oriental philosophies, strongly evident in his *Astonishing the Gods*:[118] his Way is also "The Way that always, like a river, flows into and flows out of the myriad Ways of the world" (SE 160). Several critics observe that Okri's sources, far from being limited to a Nigerian or African scope, include Western literature ranging from ancient to modern times.[119]

However, *Songs of Enchantment* includes one instance of collective practical solidarity among the ghetto-dwellers that recalls Armah's novel. When dad goes

---

[117] See Chapter 1 (p. 10) above.

[118] See Chapter 3 (p. 88) below.

[119] See, for instance, Derek Wright, "Whither Nigerian Fiction? Into the Nineties," *Journal of Modern African Studies* 33.2 (1995): 328.

blind, his temerity undaunted, he is saved from the thugs by the ghetto-inhabitants, who come to his rescue. His blindness is later transferred to all his neighbours after their refusal to acknowledge the presence of the corpse of Ade's father – a literalization of a metaphorical refusal to recognize the true nature of reality. Dad is the only one who, despite his blindness, ventures out into the forest night to give the corpse a proper burial, defying the edicts of both political parties: at first "the whole community was dreaming him on towards our universal deliverance, urging him towards our restoration" (SE 276), then they all join him physically when dad's solitary move lifts the blindness from everybody's eyes. That is why the sentence that closes *The Famished Road* is expanded to "A dream can be the highest point of a life; action can be its purest manifestation" (SE 275). Once the rites for the dead man have been performed, they all feel ashamed "of what we had allowed our lives to become" (SE 286). Things have not developed in the direction of substantial change, but the novel's ending still leaves room for hope, this time sustained slightly more by facts: "Maybe one day we will see that beyond our chaos there could always be a new sunlight, and serenity" (SE 297).

In this regard, *Infinite Riches* can be considered as an interesting building on the foundations laid by *Songs of Enchantment*. When dad is paradoxically arrested for having allegedly murdered the carpenter, a further knot of collective resistance is organized: in their search for dad, mum and seven other women become the terror of police stations and renew popular interest in active involvement. Significantly, Azaro notes that "the word politics took on a warmer meaning" (IR 136). Such a change seems to encapsulate some peculiarities of *Infinite Riches* as a whole: the novel marks a return to the social preoccupations of *Famished*, together with its otherwordly dimension, thereby constituting an inversion of the pattern indicated by Quayson. At times, *Infinite Riches* tackles head-on the mechanisms and dangers of practical politics: when mum and her seven sisters-in-arms are about to transform their rage into a political project, they are joined by a group of elite women who "distorted the rage of the originals, confused them with orderly plans, with decent processions" (IR 40).[120]

Even during Azaro's numerous trips in and out a variety of characters' thoughts, dreams and situations, Okri tends to focus on the sociopolitical issues that the hallu-

---

120 This link between *The Famished Road* and *Infinite Riches* is implicitly reinforced by the reappearance, in the third novel, of Jeremiah the International Photographer, whose work documents the political upheavals occurring around Azaro; see also Cooper, *Magical Realism in West African Fiction*, 98–108.

cinatory twist of *Songs of Enchantment* had in some ways thwarted. For instance, Azaro often enters the Governor-General's mind, bringing out the tenets of colonialism: "he laid before our eyes the written evidence of our recent awakening into civilization – we who bear within us ancient dreams and future revelations" (IR 127). While the Governor-General's written history disparages Nigerian oral culture, a mysterious old outcast woman living in the forest weaves the tapestry "of our true secret history, a history that was frightening and wondrous," a history foreseeing "a brief nightmare of colonization and an eventual, surprising, renaissance" (IR 128, 130).

The forest, then, once again represents a site of resistance to imposed destinies. The natural world is still under attack,[121] as Azaro witnesses, but it still harbours spirits and sacred statues,[122] along with the old woman. The Governor-General's colonizing vision mellows when he is touched by the wanderings of a flying angel with regenerative powers. On one occasion, the governor even utters a statement almost identical to what the old woman suggested fifty-nine pages earlier: "It is only when the diverse people of the earth meet and learn from and love one another that we can begin to get an inkling of this awesome picture" – that is, the picture of humanity (IR 128, 187).[123]

Infinite Riches oscillates between these typically Okrian philosophical statements and further instances of political narrative. Among the former there is the old woman's dream about the new millennium, "when the ambiguous gift of karmic angels had enfeebled the former world powers and when the salvation of the earth would be in the hands of the righteous people of this world, unknowing custodians of the best secrets of life" (IR 240).[124] The latter is represented by the event that in the previous two novels is announced so many times that it has acquired an unreal aura: the great political rally heralding the first elections of independent Nigeria. Wandering among the crowd, Azaro sees a metaphysically hybrid audience taking control of the event, thanks also to another intervention of the spirits (including the dead carpenter) and of their infectious, grotesque laughter: "the manufacturers of reality had no power over laughter" (IR 281).

---

121 Another threat to the natural world is embodied in the heatwave striking Azaro's city, possibly linked with a distant atomic explosion (IR 146).

122 IR 171, 153, 169, 100–108, 164, 167.

123 See also Robert Fraser, review of Ato Quayson's *Strategic Transformations in Nigerian Writing* and Ben Okri's *Infinite Riches*, *Wasafiri* 29 (Spring 1999): 87.

124 See also IR 5, 389–90.

In the end, the politicians' stage is destroyed and massive riots break out, giving rise to weird transformations. This is another hallucinatory experience to be interpreted as a result of social chaos: "The bad dreams of politicians were wreaking havoc on the earth [...] New realities were being born in the birth-throes of a new nation" (IR 296). It is no surprise that Azaro should end up having doubts about himself: "I didn't know if I was still a human being. Or if I had changed into a butterfly, a bird, a fox, a spirit or a mixed-up song" (IR 298). What should be considered as an utter failure for the political class, though, is described by the newspapers as a success: "We began to wonder if our rage so much as affected a single shadow in that hard world they rewrite as history" (IR 347). The self-perpetuating neocolonial structures are already at work.

Thus Azaro's cycle ends – for the moment? – on the eve of the general elections "whose results had already been decided in advance in all the realms of manipulated reality" (IR 200). All in all, in *Infinite Riches* Okri has not allowed his hallucinated digressions to dominate his narrative, thereby offering an infinitely richer depiction of Nigeria's seemingly inescapable contradictions. As stated already in my Introduction, there is no point in the critic's calling for a novel to stage an armed revolt. "Revolution. It takes time and one second," says dad (IR 231).

Okri's *abiku* novels are founded on two recurrent images that account for both their content and their structure. The first one is the road, which appears at the very start: "In the beginning there was a river. The river became a road and the road branched out to the whole world. And because the road was once a river it was always hungry" (FR 3). This inception epitomizes several facets of Azaro's journeys: the mythic, almost biblical tone;[125] the contemporary setting; and the prevailing atmosphere of destitution, against a background in which the two dimensions overlap.

---

125 The biblical tone of the novels further enriches Okri's diverse sources. Several critics compare that inception with the opening of the Gospel according to John, while Quayson writes that Okri's spirit world has much in common with the Western conception of Paradise (*Strategic Transformations*, 137). More generally, their prophetic and sometimes apocalyptic mood may remind one of the Book of Revelation.

Another case in point is the seven-headed spirit whose coming is often heralded but actually never occurs. This figure further shows the multiplicity of Okri's sources. It is repeatedly announced during the encounters between Azaro and, successively, the three-headed, four-headed and five-headed spirit. This succession builds up suspense, even though the dreaded seven-headed spirit will only be seen by dad during his spell of blindness (SE 224). Suspense is similarly fostered in the Yoruba folktale of the Tortoise and the god Osanyin, where the latter appears first

The image of the road has oral and literary antecedents. A Yoruba prayer goes: "may you never walk when the road waits, famished." Wole Soyinka re-works the symbol from a metaphysical and concrete point of view; similarly, as Ato Quayson points out, "with his title [*The Famished Road*], Okri makes an important ritual gesture towards the literary tradition he is elaborating as well as to the indigenous traditions and beliefs. From the very outset he pays homage to both."[126]

The road image is also intertwined with the unpredictable tortuosity of Okri's writing, its dizzying meandering in long digressions in the shape of visions and journeys into the spirit-world. Harry Garuba employs the same image to describe its narrative progress, "Bumpy as a car on a Nigerian potholed road."[127] The structure is sequential and episodic, further complicated by its occasional contextual incoherence. The reader encounters apparently inconsequential events and symbols, characters lasting the space of one page, tangential twists hard to rechannel into the main story-line. Unlike Cheney–Coker's digressions, these do not appear to belong to an ordered plot. Okri displays a meta-commentary on this when mum criticizes one of dad's narrations to Azaro:

> 'Your story isn't going anywhere,' mum said, in the dark.
>
> 'A story is not a car,' dad replied. 'It is a road, and before it was a river, a river that never ends.'(SE 266)

Some critics have expressed bafflement at the novels' structure.[128] Others convincingly highlight Okri's lack of linearity as characteristic of his cultural background, a

---

with sixteen legs, then with fifteen, and so on, until he has only one; Olayemi, "The Supernatural in the Yoruba Folktale," 962. But this figure is also reminiscent of two written literary works: both the Book of Revelation (12:3, 13:1) and John Pepper Clark's *Ozidi* recurrently feature the number seven and include terrifying seven-headed monsters; Clark, *Ozidi* (London: Oxford UP, 1966): 96–101. The number seven recurs in *Infinite Riches*, too, but similar references abound in West African literature, both anglophone and traditional: the *abiku* protagonist's name in Omotoso, *Memories*, 1–3; the evil bird with seven heads and the seven-headed monster of Ewe lore in Zinta Konrad's *Ewe Comic Heroes: Trickster Tales in Togo* (New York & London: Garland, 1994): 153–54, 226; the devil disguised as a seven-headed monster in Mary Esther Kropp Dakubu's "The Significance of Language, or Why Spider Must Be Punished in Ga Tales," in *Sprache, Symbole und Symbolverwendungen in Ethnologie, Kulturanthropologie, Religion und Recht: Festschrift für Rüdiger Schott zum 65. Geburtstag*, ed. Werner Krawietz, Leopold Pospisil & Sabine Steinbrich (Berlin: Duncker & Humbolt, 1993): 499. Any dictionary of symbols, in any case, testifies to the sacred value of this number in all world cultures.

126 Quayson, *Strategic Transformations*, 122.

127 Harry Garuba, "Ben Okri's Animist Realism and the Famished Genre," *Guardian* (Lagos; (13 March 1993): 23.

128 "Somewhere about page 250, I began to ask myself, where is it going?"; Gabriel Gbadamosi, review of Okri's *The Famished Road*, *Wasafiri* 14 (Autumn 1991): 35. Jacqueline Bardolph

ground-breaking stylistic novelty inseparable from the alternative ontology that *The Famished Road* propounds.[129] After all, digressions are constitutive elements of African oral literature.[130] Linda Grant writes that "readers who cannot cope without linear narrative structure will find the book meandering repetitive, overlong. But Okri makes his point clearly enough: not even the road is linear."[131]

Even when an obscure connection between distant incidents is likely to be traced, its rationale might be rather elusive. To mention only one example, half-way through *The Famished Road* mum addresses Azaro: "'One day I will tell you the story of how Death was conquered,' she said, in the voice of a mysterious priestess" (FR 230). In case a meticulous reader should discover that the same story is narrated by dad three hundred pages later in the next novel (SE 45), is he / she supposed to make any use of this discovery? The overall impression is that Okri could have been slightly less prolix for the sake of conveying his vision, especially considering the arresting lyrical spareness he exhibits in his short stories.

On the other hand, the inconsequentiality of some parts of the novels can be construed through their second master-image, that of the *abiku*. Just as the *abiku* is at the mercy of intrusions from the mythic dimension, the reader is placed in a similar position with respect to Okri's inventiveness; any potential impatience with Okri's digressions could be equated with Azaro's suffering. Why should one expect global coherence from such agents? Okri, then, build his stylistic standpoint by way of a correspondence between his implied reader and his protagonist, his own role as an author and the multidimensional reality of his plots.

The explanation provided by him reinforces this parallel with the *abiku*'s cycles of births and deaths:

> The book [*Famished*] is really intended to be a flow of life. So the divisions would be akin to moments in tidal waves, sea patterns, the way rollers race towards the shore,

---

states that *Famished* "seems static, repetitive, shapeless in its last chapters. It is not only due to an evolution in the story line, but to an apparent lack of inspiration, a loss of narrative intensity and sense of direction." She explains this lack through the "feeling of anomy, of powerlessness" pervading the social environment of the book; Bardolph, "Azaro, Saleccm and Askar: Brothers in Allegory," *Commonwealth: Essays and Studies* 15.1 (1992): 46, 50.

[129] Balzer refutes Bardolph's interpretation: "Okri replaces a teleological trajectory with a mode of development, one into which it is difficult to read any kind of pattern, even in retrospect, not to mention during a first reading"; Cam Balzer, "Mme Bardolph and the Question of (Post-colonial) Art," *Commonwealth: Essays and Studies* 18.2 (Spring 1996): 15.

[130] See Okpewho, *African Oral Literature*, 70–104.

[131] Linda Grant, "Long Walk of Men and Angels," *The Independent* (31 March 1991): 31.

> the way the water beats and then there are lappings and then it retreats. So that within each beginning is an ending, and within each ending a beginning.[132]

The *abiku* image also provides a metaphor for Nigerian history:

> History itself fully demonstrates how things of the world partake of the condition of the spirit-child. [...] Dad found that all nations are children; it shocked him that ours too was an abiku nation, a spirit-child nation, one that keeps being reborn and after each birth comes blood and betrayals, and the child of our will refuse to stay till we have made propitious sacrifice and displayed our serious intent to bear the weight of a unique destiny. (FR 487, 494)[133]

In this light, one can appreciate Henry Louis Gates, Jr.'s words on *The Famished Road*: "Okri, by plumbing the depths of Nigerian mythology, has created a political fable about the crisis of democracy in Africa."[134]

As far as the style of the three novels is concerned, the critic Maja–Pearce passes severe judgment on Okri's use of language, which he sees as limited to fantastic apparitions and events "purely for effect," with "no organic connection between language and event."[135] He contrasts Okri with the Ghanaian Kojo Laing's creative English. Maja–Pearce's observations are relevant in two respects: Laing's disruptive and revolutionary use of language finds no equal in anglophone West African narrative, as demonstrated further on in Chapter 2 and 3; and Okri does make lavish use of these kinds of effect.

On the other hand, Maja-Pearce construes Okri's English too reductively. To start with, Okri's style is as lyrical as Cheney–Coker's. See, for instance, the following passage:

> The songs wounded me with their relentless beauty. Seared by the agony of their melodies, I stumbled across the road and suddenly saw them all, spirits in full bloom on a field of rainbows, bathing in the ecstasy of an everlasting love. Something sharp tore through my brain. I collapsed on the flowering tarmac, with lorries thundering around me. (FR 18)

---

132 Jane Wilkinson, interview with Ben Okri, *Guardian* (24 October 1991): 19.

133 Quayson traces this back to the "cyclicality of political irresponsibility" expressed by Soyinka in *A Dance of the Forests* (*Strategic Transformations*, 132).

134 Henry Louis Gates, Jr., "Between the Living and the Unborn," *New York Times* (6 August 1992): 20.

135 Adewale Maja–Pearce, *A Mask Dancing: Nigerian Novelists of the Eighties* (London: Hans Zell, 1992): 102.

The haunting quality of the three *abiku* novels has been pointed out by several critics; Gates writes that "Plot structure may not be this lengthy novel's [*The Famished Road*'s] main concern, but the fine art of storytelling certainly is."[136] But the rapport between the novels and poetry is even more direct than this: "A great deal of *The Famished Road* was actually written in poetry, metrically," Okri said.[137] Actually, a passage from that novel (338) is nothing more than a prose version of his poem "An African Elegy."[138]

Unlike Cheney–Coker's English, Okri's distinctive use of language is not limited to its lyrical tone. His paragraphs often include stylistic parallelisms among subsequent sentences that echo traditional storytelling.[139] In *The Famished Road*, Okri also composes anonymous dialogue meant to represent a sort of popular voice and public opinion, commenting on the novel's events and characters and resembling Ama Ata Aidoo's use of the same technique. When dad starts training on his own as a boxer, a "pair of wits" comments thus:

> 'While his power increases ....'
> 'His wife's presence decreases.'
> 'While he learns new tricks ....'
> 'His son's legs become like sticks.'[...]
> 'Big man ....'
> 'With no shame.'
> 'Big muscles ....'
> 'With no brain.'(FR 367)

The magical realism of the content is paralled by figures of speech breaking the bonds of rationality, such as synaesthesia and paradox. The former involves expressions such as "green wind" (SE 39), "yellow silence" (SE 212) and "saffron-coloured breeze" (IR 156). The latter are exemplified in the following passage: "Dad was in a frenzy. My head kept spinning. We sat on the forest floor. All around us in the dark everything was still, and yet everything was moving" (SE 24). When the corpse of Ade's father grabs Azaro, the latter describes him as "deafening me with his high-pitched agonised silence" (SE 257).

Paradoxes also point back at the *abiku* as the central image of the novels. Azaro's decision to live, after all, is a way of liberating himself from the excessive

---

136 Gates, "Between the Living and the Unborn," 20.

137 Deandrea, "Interview with Ben Okri," 82.

138 See Okri, *An African Elegy* (London: Jonathan Cape, 1992): 41. With regard to this, *Infinite Riches* is notable in closing with a poem.

139 See Jowitt, "Structure and Meaning," 20; Okpewho, *African Oral Literature*, 78.

freedom of the spirit-world – which is itself a contradiction in terms – and of entering the contradictions of human existence:

> I was a spirit-child rebelling against the spirits, wanting to live the earth's life and contradictions. Ade wanted to leave, to become a spirit again, free in the captivity of freedom. I wanted the liberty of limitations, to have to find or create new roads from this one which is so hungry, this road of our refusal to be. [...] Given the fact of the immortality of spirits, could these be the reason why I wanted to be born – these paradoxes of things, the eternal changes, the riddle of living while one is alive. (FR 487–88)

Breaking fresh ground: Kojo Laing's *Search Sweet Country*

The publication of *Search Sweet Country* (1986), by the Ghanaian writer Kojo Laing (b.1946), preceded the work of both Cheney–Coker and Okri, and could be considered as the real inception of West African magical realism in prose. As said above – and as this chapter attempts to demonstrate – Laing's English is far more imaginative and disruptive about linguistic conventions. Perhaps it is too disruptive, in a way, since most critics have largely ignored the three novels he published between 1986 and 1992. One of the few reviews of his books considers *Major Gentl* "awful" and "silly," closing an avalanche of academic virulence with a "Pfah!"[140] Among the few critics who instantly recognized Kojo Laing's importance is Robert Fraser, who considers *Search Sweet Country* "the finest [novel] ever written in Africa [...] his novelistic venture can perhaps most helpfully be seen as an attempt to break intellectual and literary moulds which set hard 20 years ago."[141]

The novel's title includes all the main facets of the book in its three words. Set in a colourful and multifarious Accra in the period 1975–77, the action is deployed through the evolution or 'search'[142] of a wide range of characters who often cross or

[140] Harold H. Waters, review of *Major Gentl and the Achimota Wars*, *World Literature Today* (Spring 1993): 22.

[141] Robert Fraser, "Kojo Laing: Profile and Extract," *Wasafiri* 3 (Autumn 1985): 9. This critical indifference is even more puzzling in the face of the awards won by *Search*, including the VALCO Award, the Ghana Book Award, the Ghana Association of Writers' Kwame Nkrumah's Prize, and a special mention for the David Higham Prize; see Mary Esther Kropp Dakubu, "Kojo Laing," in *Dictionary of Literary Biography* 157: *Twentieth Century Caribbean and Black African Writers, Third Series*, ed. Bernth Lindfors & Lionel Sander (Detroit MI: Bruccoli Clark Layman / Gale, 1996): 145.

[142] In addition, there is probably a pun on 'search,' which Ghanaian English would pronounce as 'such.'

run into one another. What all of them are after is a meaning to their existence, each in his/her own way, a meaning inextricably linked with the future of Ghanaian society – "a quest," Robert Fraser writes, "for a meaningful and self-renewing Ghanaian identity"[143] right in the middle of the worst years of recent Ghanaian history when Colonel Acheampong's National Redemption Council (later Supreme Military Council) was draining both the nation's coffers and its hopes. The presence of a collective preoccupation pervades the book, even between loving couples. The trader Araba Fynn says to her naive lover Kojo Okay Pol:

> But does your head really live in Ghana? [...] don't speak of love yet, innocent people like you shouldn't speak of it. You have to do something first, you have to find some of that new Ghana you speak of![144]

According to M.E. Kropp–Dakubu, in this novel there can be no retreat from public failure to private concerns.[145]

The pivotal scene of the book takes place at Kotoka Airport, where the principled Okay Pol has been sent to supervise the illegal importation of racehorses, financially supported by government funds for agricultural production. The whole operation falls apart when the boxes break and the horses start galloping through the airport, creating universal havoc. A panic-stricken Okay Pol resorts to threatening the crowd that gathers:

> I must warn you that what you are seeing here is not true [...] the government needs your support [...] you are in the name of law asked to remain here until further notice ... you may continue to look but don't pass water – I mean don't pass judgement. (40–41)

Other main characters are introduced one by one. The daydreamer Kofi Loww, "the man who walked with the sky in his eyes," refuses to be intimidated: "he would not be told when to leave an airport in his own country" (9); he is saved by the timely intervention of the preacher Osofo Ocran, founder of the Church of the Smiling Saint: "Stop stop stop all you gentlemen, three times stop. Remember the trinity, in the name of the Lord, not the law" (42). Pol will eventually manage to silence the crowd by offering them drinks: "Beer is served, all you kind people that don't see what you see, you can have free beer [...] Long live Ghana!" (46).

---

[143] Fraser, "Kojo Laing," 9. For a detailed analysis of each character's search, see Cooper, *Magical Realism in West African Fiction*, 158–86.

[144] Kojo Laing, *Search Sweet Country* (London: Heinemann, 1986): 110, 112. Further page references are in the main text.

[145] Mary Esther Kropp Dakubu, "*Search Sweet Country* and the Language of Authentic Being," *Research in African Literatures* 24.1 (Spring 1993): 27.

The same chapter closes with Beni Baidoo, who arrives just in time to enjoy the beer and whose role in the novel deserves more attention than that of any other character. He seems to be omnipresent in the narrative, opening and closing several chapters with his sudden, sometimes slapstick appearances, linking all the characters together and apparently playing a great variety of roles. He may seem a beggar, to start with, since he is always asking for money to make his personal dream come true – the founding of a village, a search epitomizing that of the other characters, since "The search of a fool touches other lives" (1). He could appear to be a fool, in fact, given his odd behaviour and language, but it would be wrong to interpret him as if he were a living character like the others: he is, rather, a collective thread among them, since "he watched others as he did not watch his own life [...] flowed with his one obsession in and out of the lives he met" (1–2). He seems, in other words, to embody the soul of the town: "Beni Baidoo was Accra, was the bird standing alive by the pot that should receive it, and hoping that, after being de-feathered, it would triumphantly fly out before it was fried" (1).

The sweetness mentioned in the title of the novel is a fairly obvious hint at the boundless lyricism of the language describing the characters' searches, both in their own words and in the omniscient third-person narration: "Araba's smile was a market: it brought in everything and gave out everything, the warmth being at the edges and only for the few" (96). The lyrical dimension of Laing's narrative is also supported by a wide range of typically poetical devices such as rhyme ("Where is the church that began this search?," 136) or alliteration ("his lap was like the sound of the sea in a shell," 216):[146] such devices clearly show how much Laing's writing is affected by oral narrative in general, and by Akan poetic style in particular.[147]

Other cases in point would be Laing's graphic experimentation ("She must Must MUST give me sons!," 163), emphatic exclamation ("All that stagnation around him bogged him down, Ah," 142),[148] onomatopoeia and ideophones ("Gasps and OOOooos varied the air, tilted Pol's fez in consternation," 39). His graphic innovations may be considered as remnants of his poems, later collected and published as *Godhorse*.[149] Lent physical substance, language is returned to its oral dimension, something Tutuola had already tried to achieve by using capital letters.[150] The use of

[146] Note also the pun on 'lap.'

[147] See Okpewho, *Epic in Africa*, 220–26; Dakubu, "Language of Authentic Being," 23–25.

[148] Note another pun here on 'bog.'

[149] Kojo Laing, *Godhorse* (Oxford: Heinemann, 1989). See Chapter 5.

[150] Tutuola, *Palm-Wine Drinkard*, 21, 118; see also Laura Lasagna, "The Logos of the African Trickster," *Africa America Asia Australia* 16 (1994): 33–34.

exclamations, too, seems to be affected by oral influences: the reader feels compelled to ask him/herself whether the "Ah" quoted above comes from the character or the narrator. I think that such a distinction would not provide an answer, though; that "Ah," in fact, can be traced back to what Isidore Okpewho calls the "climactic alerts" of the oral bard, when he communicates to the crowd the "momentous points" of his narration. It is common for the artist in oral literature "to weave his personality into that of his characters [... so] that it is difficult to tell where narration ends and dialogue resumes." Such authorial empathy, according to Okpewho, would be unacceptable in written literature "for its failure to make the right distinction between its characters" – an analysis that would not apply to Laing's writing.[151]

All those oral stylistic influences in *Search Sweet Country* give striking evidence of how Laing may be located in a specific tendency of modern anglophone Ghanaian literature which has been deeply affected by ancestral patterns, as seen in Chapter 1 with Armah, Aidoo and Awoonor: all tradition-influenced attempts to blur the boundaries between literary genres and to recover that continuum of verbal discourse in which traditional performances were anchored. The distinction between traditional narrative and traditional poetry, after all, is "based more on the circumstances of the performances than on any formal elements."[152] Laing started as a poet, in fact, and later moved to the novel, but not wholly:

> I wrote the novel partly in the same way I would write the poems. Sometimes you will find whole lines within the novels which have come direct from the poems, they're quotations. (Laing, Accra, 15 December 1993)

It is notable that the same method of novelistic composition has been used by Okri.

In addition, the richness of Laing's English is increased by the insertion of a lot of Ghanaian words and cultural references, a constant feature in his novels, all of which have an appended glossary – a way of looking for an "authentic" language, as Dakubu would say, which does not neglect the employment of other sources, such as (as befits his dual heritage) Scots words or a Steinbeckian intertextuality ("but the third generation *of men of mice* had come to Araba," emphasis mine, 99). Laing's Ghanaian English is 'authentic' in betraying all the Ghanaian cultural influences,[153]

---

[151] Okpewho, *Epic in Africa*, 211–14, 238.

[152] B.W. Andrzejewski, *Literatures in African Languages: Theoretical Issues and Sample Surveys* (Warsaw: Wiedza Powzechna; Cambridge: Cambridge UP, 1985): 141. See also Cooper, *Magical Realism in West African Fiction*, 160, 187–88.

[153] A.A. Amoako cites an example of Laing's Ghanaian English: 'to take seed,' meaning 'to conceive a child,' literal translation of the Akan '*fa aba*'; Amoako, "*Search Sweet Country*: B. Kojo Laing," *Legon Journal of the Humanities* (University of Ghana) 4 (1988): 105. See also

besides containing highly realistic dialogue; Accra, after all, has been a thoroughly multilingual town for centuries.[154]

Laing's sensitivity to the multiplicity of his heritage is probably the main drive behind his constant creative effort to up-end the clichés of language: "There's a gap between written history and oral history," he said. "That gap should be the source of an original thrust in ideas, in inventions, in creation."[155] His own exploitation of that gap is palpable in his prolific coinage of neologisms (such as 'logologo' for genitals or 'zagazogo' for wild man) and in the abundance of puns, the latter already present in several quotations above. See also the following passage:

> Sally Soon [...] was an English witch sent over on a secret assignment against Ghana, but she had now fallen in love with Ghanaians, and had almost neutralised her own powers: the weaker she became the more she became Sally Sooner, the weakest she became the more she became Sally Soonest. She usually travelled the degrees of her surname. (124)

The humour of *Search Sweet Country* is often raw and popular, sometimes almost gross – another affinity with traditional oral performance.[156] Beni Baidoo appears to embody this feature:

> And let me tell you a secret: when I get money, I intend to sneak toward Libo and pay for a touch of woman's softness. I will pay for softness to exercise my own hardness. I will pay for a resurrection of the past, for a little exercise for my popylonkwe [penis]! (131)

The definition of Beni Baidoo's role becomes more and more complex: why does this character take all the features of Laing's language to their extreme? The African trickster figure and the Ghanaian spider-trickster Ananse come easily to mind, because of their wicked humour and penchant for pranks and taboo-breaking, which Baidoo certainly shares.[157] When he suddenly materializes in the back of Professor Sackey's car and then steals its keys (150–51), he really seems to assume a

---

Dakubu, "Language of Authentic Being," 25; Kofi A. Sey, *Ghanaian English* (London: Macmillan, 1973): 84.

[154] See Mary Esther Kropp Dakubu, *Language and Community: The View from Accra* (Accra: Ghana Universities P, 1996): 12–13. More recently, Ghanaian educational policies promoted multilingualism in local languages through the 1987 reform; see Kevin Shillington, *Ghana and the Rawlings Factor* (London: Macmillan, 1992): 119. For the novel's multiplicity of languages, see Michael Lim, "Written Communication: Ghana and the Fiction of Kojo Laing," *New Literatures Review: Factions and Fictions* 28–29 (Winter 1994–Summer 1995): 49.

[155] Adewale Maja-Pearce, "Interview with Kojo Laing," *Wasafiri* 6–7 (Spring–Autumn 1987): 28.

[156] See Okpewho, *Epic in Africa*, 202–208.

[157] See Robert D. Pelton, *The Trickster in West Africa: A Study of Mythic Irony and Sacred Delight* (Berkeley: U of California P, 1980): 31–36.

supernatural dimension. Moreover, he acts as a diviner, an explainer of others' lives, since he often knows the subject of their streams of thought and what their future will be like. Trickster – or perhaps Shakespearian fool – could be valid terms of comparison, also given the implicitness and ambiguity of his language:

> If I say herbs herbs herbs herbs herbs herbs herbs herbs herbs; then I say Lord lord lord lord lord lord lord lord lord; then I divide this ten-ten draw with very fresh palm-wine, equally, what chance would I have of being thought a holy Ghanaian? (218)

The West African trickster – and Ananse in particular – is said to act against the rigidity of tradition, continuously redrawing its boundaries "not so much in defiance as in a new ordering of their limits."[158] In *Search Sweet Country* tradition is also synonymous with the supernatural, thanks to the presence of the witches Adwoa Adde and Sally Soon, to Allotey's contacts with the spirits of his village and to the presence – once again – of the dead among the living. When Kofi Loww walks through the crowd of Accra's Makola Market,

> He stood still caught in perfect African time – time that existed in any dimension – and blocking the paths of other sellers with this same time that brought ancestors to the market, that touched the eyes of sellers and buyers now that moved beyond those yet to be born [...] he saw all sorts of dead faces moving among the living. (117)

As for the two witches – one Ghanaian, the other English – they benevolently fly over the heads of their spiritual children (26–34, 124–34); Beni Baidoo's ability to see Adwoa's transformations (28) says a lot for his special role in the novel.

On the one hand, the magic is not so widespread as it is in Okri's *abiku* novels; on the other, it influences – albeit theoretically – other characters who are not directly touched by it. Even the academic Professor Sackey does not limit his search to rational enquiry: "There is no territory between the supernatural and the purely factual," he says (240). In any case, nothing, not even the supernatural dimension, is immune to change. Allotey has to leave his village "because of his impudence, his constant questions, and his own idea about the rituals" (199).[159]

The author's idea of a new society, then, betrays the same multicultural characteristics as the language on which it is built: a middle way between "narrow eurocentrism" (235) and "the weight of our past" (241). As Laing has said,

---

[158] See Pelton, *Trickster in West Africa*, 35. Baidoo is also compared to the African–American figure of the Signifying Monkey; Cooper, *Magical Realism in West African Fiction*, 190.

[159] "Any supposed purity of traditional ways cannot, therefore, be the true object of the search for wholeness and authenticity with which the book is concerned," writes Dakubu ("Language of Authentic Being," 20).

> To suggest that there should be a change in the way that libation is poured is something which the average Ghanaian would be shocked at. But the point is being made [in *Search*] that change must come even there, just at that point where the Ghanaian feels no change is possible.[160]

In the novel, Professor Sackey, Allotey and Kofi Loww embody different attempts to overcome an apparently inescapable dichotomy: "you either live fragmented and half yourself, half your heart, or you keep slow, and whole, and die!" complains Sackey (79–80). Laing's fear of fragmentation involves both the coveted multiculturalism and the separation of ideal and real life, spirit and body, the latter facet shared with Armah's *Two Thousand Seasons*.[161]

Laing's new wholeness is far from being easily attainable on a collective level, and his disillusionment with the present state of Ghanaian political structures is quite evident in *Search Sweet Country*. That is probably the reason why the only political enterprise in the novel is led by the preacher Osofo Ocran, whose ideas of church community are another way of combining different cultures: "near his knees the herbs of the fetish priest appeared without warning, and joined Jesus Christ in giving his life meaning" (47). Osofo decides to lead a miles-long procession to the centre of town, and it becomes a joyous, musical, overwhelmingly massive march fuelled by Baidoo's endless witticisms. Osofo's intentions are overtly political, because he wants to march to the seat of the government, and the huge crowd seems to stand by him at first: "ONE WHOLE COUNTRY CANNOT FIT UNDER A SOLDIER'S CAP! [...] 'Ampara!' [true] was the refrain. [...] Ghana was a photocopy country, and they wanted the original truth!" (222). But the whole spirit of the enterprise is channelled elsewhere by a group of policemen offering food to everybody: Osofo's search, being too mystical and not down-to-earth enough, has no chance of succeeding politically – "he's one of those zagazogos who can't discuss God without going off into a spiritual fury. He can't last in Ghana!" (226).

What is left to do, then, after the march's failure? Rejecting any immediate political solution – just as Cheney–Coker and Okri do – Laing brings to the fore the power of individuals: "All the ordinary people were real people: they lived beyond the slogans, outlasted the politicians" (244). That is where the author's hope resides – in the creativity of the ordinary:

---

160 Maja–Pearce, "Interview with Kojo Laing," 28.

161 Dakubu finds a source for this preoccupation in the Scottish psychiatrist R.D. Laing's existential phenomenology; Mary Esther Kropp Dakubu, "Kojo Laing," 142–43. See also Chapter 5 below (p. 169), on Kojo Laing's poetry.

> It looked as if each space given to each person to walk in was a source of art: the movement of people was nothing less than a series of abandoned dances controlled marvellously in the most ordinary, most triumphant ways [...] Thus the universe was danced in all the walking of Ghana. (16)

After the novel's publication, Laing declared that

> It's almost a paradox but the more self-sufficient literature is the more effect it will have on other sectors, including the political [...] I am fundamentally committed to literature and I consider it an end in itself.[162]

The Nigerian critic and playwright Femi Osofisan thoroughly examines the qualities of Laing and other 'new' (francophone) African authors with respect to the politically committed generation who started producing literature in the 1970s:

> Mythopoiesy, fabulation, polyphony – or according to some, cacophony – these are the narrative goals, and grammar, realism the sacrificial elements. [...] High preference is given to syntactic and semantic idiosyncrasies, such as the use of sudden phrasal inversions, verbal inflation, ideophones, eccentric punctuation and neologisms.[...] Clearly the new writers have turned away from our own burning concern to mobilise the society for political goals.

Osofisan then quotes an interesting parallel drawn by the critic Xavier Garnier:

> What they seem to be aiming at, instead, is fabulation for its own sake, the endless (re)creation of myth by weaning out of resistant language its allusive acoustic and suggestive power. [...] what the new writers appear to be after is no longer 'commitment', but 'possession', comparable in a sense to the current spread of religious fundamentalism in the social realm.[163]

Even though the ending of *Search Sweet Country* is politically despondent, it cannot be said to be in tune with the inescapable corruption and decay in Armah's *The Beautyful Ones Are Not Yet Born:* "I felt that his exposition of the Ghanaians' and Africans' world didn't do enough justice to their humanity. My first novel was partly a reaction against that" (Laing, Accra, 15 December 1993). In her comparison of Armah and Laing, Dakubu correctly argues that "Laing's interest is not in nationalism as a political idea or force, but in 'national development' as a moral and spiritual endeavour"; this is why she defines Laing's works as "post-nationalist."[164]

---

[162] Maja–Pearce, "Interview with Kojo Laing," 28.

[163] Osofisan, "Warriors of a Failed Utopia?," 26–27.

[164] Mary Esther Kropp Dakubu, "The Trope of the Nation in Kojo Laing's Poetry," in *English in Ghana*, ed. Kropp–Dakubu (Accra: Black Masks / Ghana English Studies Association, 1997): 275, 283.

Despite the fact that the reader is bound to be stimulated by the magical dimension of the novel, the characters' diverse searches achieve no fulfilment within the magical-realist coexistence of the two 'belief systems'; this coexistence looks like something of an impasse, as exemplified by the autobiographical sociologist, Professor Sackey, who complains that "the weight of our past seems to be crushing the present… and the future will not be born!" The "new worlds, new wholes" (241) still waiting to be created in contemporary Ghana should be based on a higher plane of fluidity between supernatural and factual spheres, "a fairly easy flow between abstract, symbol, action and thing" (234). A more dynamic magical-symbolic realm, then, one more likely to affect the daily tempo of life and less congealed in its own force-fields. As Ato Quayson notices, in *Search Sweet Country* the dichotomy is resolved only on a linguistic level, whereas the characters cannot negotiate the contrast between the traditional and the modern world.[165]

This may help in interpreting his later novels (examined in Chapter 3), which go well beyond the notions of magical realism outlined earlier, and where the dead-end seems to have been avoided by shifting the action to other worlds, to other dimensions resting on linguistic foundations and therefore offering the dynamism that the realistic setting of *Search* could not provide.

---

[165] Quayson, "Esoteric Webwork," 147–48. See also Cooper, *Magical Realism in West African Fiction*, 158.

3 Beyond Magical Realism

THIS CHAPTER DEALS WITH NOVELS which abandon the magical-realist environment where rational and supernatural dimension are interlaced in a contemporary context. In terms of setting, these books belong to fantasy, being completely located in fictional worlds totally different from our own.

Approaching the subject of fantasy in Western literature, Kathryn Hume remarks:

> In Orwell's *1984*, one of the creators of Newspeak gloats that the rapidly narrowing vocabulary of the language will soon make thoughtcrime impossible because there will be no words to express subversive ideas. Trying to talk about fantasy is practically as difficult as wordless thoughtcrime. We do not have the analytic vocabulary to frame our enquiries.[1]

In a province such as anglophone African prose, where realism still constitutes a dominant stylistic mode, any attempt by critics to analyse literary works set in other worlds than our own similarly meets with a formidable aphasic wall. As implied above, the emergence of magical realist narratives – and their critical interpretations – can throw little light on the subject.

The main aim of this chapter is to emphasize the connections between these alien settings and the social issues of contemporary Africa. In other words, is it literarily possible and effective to tackle the aftermath of imperialism – "an act of geographical violence," writes Edward Said[2] – through a radical geographical displacement? Once again, Kathryn Hume provides a useful standpoint, grounded on a concept of literature as a varying blend between the mimetic and the fantastic

---

[1] Kathryn Hume, *Fantasy and Mimesis: Responses to Reality in Western Literature* (New York: Methuen, 1984): xii.

[2] Edward W. Said, "Yeats and Decolonization," in *Nationalism, Colonialism, and Literature*, ed. Terry Eagleton, Fredric Jameson & Edward W. Said (Minneapolis: U of Minnesota P, 1990): 77.

impulse. Her "inclusive definition" holds that "departure from reality does not preclude comment upon it: indeed, this is one of fantasy's primary functions."[3]

Throughout her *Fantasy: The Literature of Subversion*, the way in which Rosemary Jackson employs the rebellious facet of fantasy is comparable to Hume's thought-crime image. Jackson's theoretical paradigm will sometimes prove useful to the present chapter, in spite of the explicitly Western orientation of her targets: "In a secular culture, fantasy has a different function. It doesn't invent supernatural regions, but presents a natural world inverted into something strange, something 'other'."[4] This is what she focuses on, without leaving much room for the purely marvellous. Furthermore, her Western scope is supported by a critical frame which includes, among its pivotal points, the Freudian evolutionist and Négritudinist equivalence between animism and childhood, "when primitive man and the young child have no sense of difference between self and other, subject and object world."[5] The need to correct similar eurocentric biases through a process of contextualization further challenges this chapter.

An etherized invisibility: Ben Okri's *Astonishing the Gods*

> Be astonished, O ye heavens, at this,
> and be you very desolate, saith the Lord.
> [Jeremiah 2:12]

The opening of Ben Okri's *Astonishing the Gods* (1995) looks somewhat promising. Displaying his usual enchanting lyricism, the author begins with two pages of covert hints at African history. The unnamed protagonist comes from an invisible people whose culture is described as oral:

> Their lives stretched back into the invisible centuries and all that had come down from those differently coloured ages were legends and rich traditions, unwritten and therefore remembered. They were remembered because they were lived.[6]

The encounter with the written culture from another land – inevitably reminding one of the colonial experience – is decisive:

---

[3] Hume, *Fantasy and Mimesis*, xii, 20–25.

[4] Rosemary Jackson, *Fantasy: The Literature of Subversion* (London: Methuen, 1981): 17.

[5] Jackson, *Fantasy*, 72.

[6] Ben Okri, *Astonishing the Gods* (London: Phoenix House, 1995): 3. Further page references are in the main text.

> It was in books that he first learnt of his invisibility. He searched for himself and his people in all the history books he read and discovered to his youthful astonishment that he didn't exist. This troubled him so much that he resolved, as soon as he was old enough, to leave his land and find the people who did exist, to see what they looked like. (3)

The connections between the trope of invisibility and 'postcolonial' issues (ie, the colonial subject reduced to voicelessness in Western histories) are pointed out in Amit Chauduri's and Abdulrazak Gurnah's reviews of the novel.[7] Gurnah quite rightly traces this back to Ralph Ellison's *Invisible Man*, a novel impelled by the urge to lay bare US racism:

> Being invisible and without a substance, a disembodied voice, as it were, what else could I do? What else but try to tell you what was really happening when your eyes were looking through?[8]

As Alessandro Portelli remarks, Ellison's book opens with an "I" and closes with a "you," and its dialogue between the author and the readership who are supposed to take up his denunciation cannot be overlooked.[9] In the present case, for whom and to whom does *Astonishing the Gods* speak?

The protagonist's voyage represents the promise of the book's inception: "My quest is for the secret of visibility" (4). One page later he arrives in the town / island where the rest of the narrative unravels, and readers are faced with otherworldliness and lack of geographical and historical references, two constant features of the whole book that are by now familiar features in Okri. After the Nigerian-ghetto magical realism of his first two *abiku* novels, a shift to poetical allegory would appear to be a natural creative development, in accordance with his frequent stylistic transitions. "Creating a separate reality and calling attention to it is one characteristic of great, as opposed to merely competent, fiction," writes Hume.[10] A further question that should be posed here, therefore, regarding the reality of *Astonishing the Gods*, the way it works and what it consists of.

The physical location of this timeless setting is impressive, with buildings that

> seemed to hang in mid-space. They appeared to rest on nothing, suspended. Even the great churches, with their golden domes and their moody spires, seemed to be made of an ethereal substance. The buildings, in their perfection, looked like some kind of

---

[7] Amit Chauduri, "Immoral, Invisible, God Only Wise," *Spectator* (1 April 1995): 33; Abdulrazak Gurnah, "The Accidental Tourist," *Sunday Times* (12 March 1995): 21.

[8] Ralph Ellison, *Invisible Man* (New York: Random House, 1947): 439.

[9] Alessandro Portelli, *Il testo e la voce* (Rome: Manifestolibri, 1992): 93.

[10] Hume, *Fantasy and Mimesis*, 82.

> dream-created illusion. He was puzzled by the monumentality of things and their apparent lightness. (8–9)

"A trip into a De Chirico landscape," in David Profumo's words.[11] Such ethereal beauty resembles one of Italo Calvino's *Invisible Cities* (1972), the much-acclaimed masterpiece of world fantasy where the Venetian traveller Marco Polo describes to the Tartar emperor Kublai Khan the cities he has seen. Among them, Lalage allows the moon to rest on its pinnacles, in exchange for the capability of growing in lightness.[12]

The lightness of Okri's city has an illustrious precursor in anglophone West African prose as well: Joseph Ephraim Casely Hayford's *Ethiopia Unbound: Studies in Race Emancipation* (1911), "the first known Ghanaian creative work in English."[13] Casely Hayford is renowned for his impressive range of activities: nationalist leader, journalist, legal practitioner and, above all, "the first African on the African continent to stress the idea of pan-Africanism and the African way of life which some call the African personality."[14] His novel constitutes another example of the mixing of genres which perfectly fits the theme of this book; its episodic plot frames a series of reflections and conversations on issues like the need to support native institutions instead of aping European customs, the lack of a locally inspired educational system based on native languages, the potentially regenerative power that African religions – faithful to the true spirit of Christ's message – can offer to the spiritual crisis of the West, and so on. The porosity of genres in Casely Hayford, then, goes well beyond imaginative literature, encompassing politics, educational and religious studies, and linguistics. This novelistic enterprise is an exception to the Enlightenment separation of the aesthetic from other departments of *écriture*.[15]

---

[11] David Profumo, "From Sublime Dreaminess to Radical Chic," *Daily Telegraph* (11 March 1995): 27.

[12] Italo Calvino, *Invisible Cities*, tr. William Weaver (San Diego CA: Harcourt, Brace, 1972): 73–74.

[13] Angmor, *Contemporary Literature in Ghana*, 18.

[14] L.H. Ofosu–Appiah, *Joseph Ephraim Casely Hayford: The Man of Vision and Faith* (J.B. Danquah Memorial Lectures, Series 8; Accra: Academy of Arts and Sciences, 1975): 25.

[15] "Literature was ideologically, if not actually, confined to the realm of sense, intuition and imagination, where previously it had comprehended virtually everything written"; John Bender, "Eighteenth Century Studies," in *Redrawing the Boundaries: The Transformation of English and American Literary Studies*, ed. Stephen Greenblatt & Giles Gunn (New York: Modern Language Association of America, 1992): 87. Curiously, this precept was likewise ignored by the pioneering *The Interesting Narrative of the Life of Olaudah Equiano*, published in 1789; see David Dabydeen, "Freedom's Slave," *Observer* (8 August 1999): 23.

These cultural and historical topics are interrupted by an oneiric chapter in which the autobiographical protagonist Kwamankra dreams of meeting his deceased wife and daughter in "Nanamu-krome," the city of ancestors, "the city of immortals, [...] simple, yet majestic, ethereal yet earthly,"[16] full of gardens and temples, a paradise similar to Okri's island. Both writers end up promising a sort of heaven on earth for mankind's future, but Casely Hayford's standpoint rests on the practical needs of his age, unlike Okri's preoccupations.

Ethereality and semblance are undoubtedly two reigning features in Okri's town, teeming with "invisible enchantments" (5). Like all things around him, the 'he' is dissolved when walking down an avenue completely made of mirrors: "As he went along, shivering in the silver façades, he felt himself becoming more insubstantial, less real. He seemed to be losing his identity to the mirrors." The loss is outlined in positive terms: "He felt as if the heaviest and less important parts of him were dissolving in effulgent lights [...] he felt himself becoming more peaceful, less questing, and freer from anxieties" (10). Accordingly, there is a bodiless voice guiding him, coming "out of the fragrant air" (6), who says: "The next stage of our evolution is to be free of our visible things. Then we will become sublime forces in the universe" (54).

In order for it to lead him "into the city of the Invisibles" (31), he has to cross a bridge suspended over an abyss: "a dazzling construct, composed entirely of mist [...] It too seemed to be made of light, of air, of feelings" (16). The bridge is held up by the person crossing it, as the guiding voice says. The decision whether to cross it or not is of no small moment for the protagonist, as if it implied the discarding of his previous existence, an entry into a higher level of consciousness and especially the reversal of his initial objective, namely the secret of visibility. At the foot of the bridge, "Time howled from the abyss as the creeping emptiness slowly enveloped the visible world" (19).[17] Threatened by dissolution into the same nothingness, he crosses the bridge, which changes into fire, water, air and dreams, later becoming solid again: "He thought of it as the bridge of self-discovery" (30). During the

---

[16] Joseph Ephraim Casely Hayford, *Ethiopia Unbound: Studies in Race Emancipation* (1911; London: Frank Cass, 1969): 54.

[17] In the course of his discoveries, the protagonist is often overwhelmed with terror and horror at what he sees or feels, sensations associated with the holy, the beautiful and the sublime (13, 59, 128). This further blending of opposites has illustrious precursors in British literature: consider, for instance, the "terror be in love and beauty" of Milton's serpent, and W.B. Yeats's "A terrible beauty is born," about the 1916 Irish uprising; Milton, *Paradise Lost* ix.490 (1667; London: Longman, 1971): 468; Yeats, *Collected Poems* (London: Macmillan, 1978): 203.

crossing he meets with a whole people rising from the waters, possibly an obscure echo of the African people described in Ayi Kwei Armah's *Two Thousand Seasons*:

> He saw them building a great new future in an invisible space. They built quietly for a thousand years. They built a new world of beauty and wisdom and protection and joy to compensate for their five hundred years of suffering and oblivion beneath the ocean. (27)[18]

Words and the weight of language are touched by the general insubstantiality. He finds some monoliths inscribed with words in "a language no longer spoken" (35), anticipating a later situation in which he is unable to decipher the motto on the great gate of the city (59–60). Actually, the problem is not so much one of translation, since the philosophy of the Invisibles explicitly disregards the actualization of concepts into sounds or printed letters: "We don't believe in names [...] Names have a way of making things disappear" (6). Later he is touched by a breeze carrying "unspoken words" (119), until "he became aware that silence was speaking to him" (147).

In his essay "Beyond Words," Okri similarly writes: "We began before words, and we will end beyond them." The fact that "the highest things are beyond words" is linked with a desire to shed the physical substance of human existence: "When things fall into words they usually descend. Words have an earthly gravity. But the best things in us are those that escape the gravity of our deaths." The same view is applied to creativity: "Any artist will tell you that ideas are happier in the heaven of their conception than on the earth of their realization."[19]

This is the key to explaining the shortcomings of *Astonishing the Gods*. The urgency in Okri to seek release from such gravity is successful, contrary to the needs holding down another famous invisible man of literature, that of H.G. Wells, who says: "I am just a human being – solid, needing food and drink, needing covering too – But I'm invisible. You see? Invisible. Simple idea. Invisible." Unfortunately Okri severs himself and his own book from any possibility of establishing contact with his readers' lives, an effect similar to the consequences of Wells's character's dream of founding a Reign of Terror: "He has cut himself off from his kind."[20]

In *Astonishing the Gods*, Okri's scepticism about the power of language is paralleled by an analogous attitude towards reason. As the voice teaches, "Don't try to understand [...] Understanding comes beyond trying [...] Understanding often

---

[18] Okri also refers to Armah's book in *Songs of Enchantment*; see Chapter 2.

[19] Ben Okri, *A Way of Being Free* (London: Phoenix House, 1997): 88, 89, 94.

[20] H.G. Wells, *The Invisible Man* (1897; New York: Dover, 1992): 32, 94.

leads to ignorance" (15, 30). Consequently, the proper approach to attain the Invisibles' higher state is one of passivity:

> he felt the world was telling him to stop looking, for then he would see beyond; to stop thinking, for then he would comprehend; to stop trying to make sense of things, for then he would find the truest grace. (39)

All these precepts resemble certain Oriental philosophies and their championing of desirelessness, non-agitation and futility of worldly struggles. Readers are, in any case, not told much about what Okri's "truest grace" might consist of. His disbelief in language and reason leads him to limit his own writing to shallow truisms ("Things are what they are," 11). Another significant notion could be the following: "It suddenly appeared odd to him, but the solid things of the city seemed like ideas. And ideas, which were alive in the air, seemed to him like solid things" (40). Once again, what kind of ideas does he mean? Being told that "what you think is what becomes real" (46) and that the city can be seen as "a vast network of thoughts" (66) does not help us find an answer. In Alev Adil's words, the protagonist's journey looks like

> a pompous and obscurantist expedition which continually assure us that hidden behind each elliptical fog of hyperbole there lies the most perfectly constructed vision of harmony. The trouble with Okri's castles in the air is that he writes air well but he doesn't seem moved to write the castles.[21]

Adil's complaint is well-founded, yet Okri's favourite figures of speech, rather than being hyperbole, seem to be paradox and synaesthesis, just as in the *abiku* novels;[22] in this case, though, the absence of a real-life background prevents reading these figures beyond their face-value.

Such stylistic devices in Okri's novel are suggestive and inspiring at first, but their repetition as the only discernible element can produce annoyance as one gets further into the book. David Buckley notes how "the language refuses to come off the page or images to become concrete."[23] David Robson compares the novel's island to Prospero's, "full of noises, sounds and sweet airs," but laments its lack of variety.[24]

Cultural allusions are not deepened, either, and like the *abiku* novels they reveal multicultural sources. Sometimes they sound classical, like the "sea-god [...] with

---

[21] Alev Adil, "More Narnian than Olympian," *Times Literary Supplement* (10 March 1995): 23.

[22] See Chapter 2.

[23] David Buckley, "Full Diddly Delirium," *Observer* (16 March 1995): 19.

[24] David Robson, "Keep Off the Spirits," *Sunday Telegraph* (19 March 1995): 25.

his mighty beard and glistening trident" associated with the aforementioned people rising from the oceans (89). At other times the presences seem to be Christian – angels, demons,[25] and "the gentle master who had been visible to his followers for only three days before ascending into invisibility" (92).

The ethical / spiritual principles on which Okri's fabulous island rests are equally perplexing, being made of facile definitions that have no contextual support, and therefore run dry in the space of a sentence: the Basilica of Truth, to mention only one (11). Or, to add another that had already surfaced in the *abiku* novels:

> Love was the most important subject in the universities. Entire faculties were devoted to the art of living. The civilization was dedicated to a simple goal, the perfection of the spirit and the mastery of life. (66–67)

Sadly, *Astonishing the Gods* is a sequence of similar utterances, as David Robson states: "Individually, such pieties would be harmless; cumulatively, their effect is irritating."[26] On the whole, reviewers attempt to detect similarities with some corresponding ethos ("Zen-like aphorisms," Emerson's transcendentalism, the Christian logic of the Narnia books of C.S. Lewis)[27] when they do not resort to harsh judgements as Ed Porter does: "such doctrines [...] would also not be out of place in a self-help manual by some quack American psychology guru."[28] In "Beyond Words," too, similar generalizations are offered as an alternative to the much-despised language: "I think we need more of the wordless in our lives [...] We need more love, more silence, more deep listening, more deep giving."[29]

Given Okri's background and literary history, the 'slogan' I find most telling comes on page 54, where the guide declares that the attainment of invisibility "would be a victory, an eternal victory of Light." In his previous books, Okri employed the image of electricity by working on the connections between electric and manipulative power in pre- and post-Independence Nigeria.[30] In that extract from *Astonishing the Gods* – as was already the case in the *abiku* novels and particularly in *Songs of Enchantment* – the concept is consciously capitalized and decontextualized, in order to convey an idea of abstract spiritual illumination strangely close

[25] See 11, 26, 131.

[26] Robson, "Keep Off the Spirits," 25.

[27] See Buckley, "Full Diddly Delirium," 19; Gurnah, "Accidental Tourist," 21; Adil, "More Narnian than Olympian," 23.

[28] Ed Porter, "Invisible Men Lost in a Fog," *Evening Standard* (6 March 1995): 15.

[29] Okri, *Way of Being Free*, 90.

[30] See the short story "When the Lights Return," in *Stars*, and also *The Famished Road*, 10, 78, 123, 223, 277–78, 293, 349, 373.

to the 'Light' colonialists claimed to be bringing to Africa, but in perfect agreement with the overall purport of the novel.

Okri's full awareness of what such an abstraction from history and society might imply, in any case, is demonstrated when he gives voice to the contradictions highlighted here so far. First, the protagonist meets a woman, "the first visible being he had seen since his disembarkation," who shows a craving for life: "Too much beauty is bad for the soul [...] I want illusion. I want some ugliness. I want some suffering. I want to be visible" (76–77). Later on, a dwarf-like figure advises him to leave the island, otherwise "in the end you'd scream for visibility and you'd flee this island, crying out for places where people have names and where you can participate in some useful struggle." Here is the dwarf's description of the island:

> a hell made out of beauty. Can you think of anything more stultifying, more suffocating, than a nightmare composed entirely of beautiful things, of flowers, of pure lights, and mirrors? (108)

The protagonist's resolution towards invisibility, though, remains unswerving, without the slightest trace of vacillation or self-irony: after refusing the love of a beautiful woman, he notices in a mirror that his features are fading (122). This marks his involvement with another, even more ethereal, state. He is purified with a bath, then subjected to a ceremony in a hall "crowded with invisible presences" (135), including "the tender presence of a great mother, protectress of the island and its secret ways" (142), until the great hall seems to be "spiralling into the soaring sublimity of the great mother" (143). In the interstices left by an endless series of further unspeakable sensations and sublime illuminations, the first of three unspecified masters fashions a landscape

> filled with peaceful spirits, with a faun playing a pan-pipe, and a white horse galloping up the first mountain, and the leaves of the trees glistening under a heavenly light. [...] he listened to the ritual music, to [...] its soaring pastoral mood. (137)

As in the escapism of *Astonishing the Gods*, the pastoral mode has often been a way "to disengage us from its [reality's] grey unpleasantness and to enfold us in comforting illusions."[31] Okri's fascination with the pastoral recently concentrated on Arcadia, thanks to the BBC project "London to Arcadia with Ben Okri." In his account of his travels to Greece, he recalls that the Arcadian ideal dates back to Theocritus and Virgil.[32] Raymond Williams's seminal book *The Country and the City*, though, avoids making generalizations on the subject: Theocritus and Virgil

---

[31] Hume, *Fantasy and Mimesis*, 55.

[32] Ben Okri, "A Poet in Search of Arcadia," *European* 346 (26 December 1996), Magazine: 17.

include the social disturbances of their times, whereas in Renaissance adaptations of the pastoral "living tensions are excised, until there is nothing countervailing, and selected images stand in themselves: not in a living but in an enamelled world."[33]

In Okri's novel, the protagonist undergoes a final ceremony where he answers the voices' questions with further universal statements, such as: "WHAT IS THE DREAM OF THE INVISIBLES? [...] TO CREATE THE FIRST UNIVERSAL CIVILIZATION OF JUSTICE AND LOVE." At the end, "flooded with a supernatural intelligence" (155–56), he becomes one of them: "It seems odd and beautiful that he who had left home in search of visibility should have found a higher invisibility, the invisibility of the blessed" (159).

The route followed by the protagonist is worth further reflection. If its direction were to be traced, it would doubtless be upward. Or heavenward, to be precise. Far from employing his enchanted island to cast light on contemporary issues, and a far cry from Rosemary Jackson's definition of fantasy – "to make visible the invisible, and to discover absence"[34] – Okri would appear to consider the gods of the title as the exclusive focus of his novel. To astonish them through "our self-overcoming" (148) is taken to be the primary human goal.

When the protagonist mysteriously finds himself among "the earliest heroes of the Invisibles [...] rising from the sea-bed," for instance, he realizes that "They saw themselves mirrored in heaven. They saw the shining double of themselves, clothed in the miraculous light of perfection." Their aim is to "realize a little of heaven on earth" (132). Like Plato's epistemology, then, Okri seems to place his emphasis exclusively on pure Ideas. Rawdon Wilson affirms that, contrary to the 'dirty realism' of minimalist writing, fantasy tends to be maximalist,[35] but Okri's version never goes beyond such abstract principles.

Unfortunately, his Universals lead him to neglect other fundamental facets of existence, and in this regard one of Calvino's invisible cities, Beersheba, once again offers an interesting comparison. In Beersheba, there is a general belief that,

> suspended in heavens, there exists another Beersheba, where the city's most elevated sentiments and virtues are poised, and that if the terrestrial Beersheba will take the celestial one as its model the two cities will become one.

---

33 Raymond Williams, *The Country and the City* (1973; London: Hogarth, 1993): 18.

34 Jackson, *Fantasy*, 4.

35 Rawdon Wilson, "The Metamorphoses of Fictional Space: Magical Realism," in *Magical Realism: Theory, History, Community*, ed. Lois Parkinson Zamora & Wendy B. Faris (Durham NC: Duke UP, 1995): 54.

The image of the celestial city is strikingly similar to Okri's island, but in Calvino's book another Beersheba is believed to exist underground, "the receptacle of everything base and unworthy that happens to them [...] prolonging the route of the human bowels, from black hole to black hole [...] a fecal city." Nevertheless, readers are told that Beersheba's scale of values is to be turned upside-down: its hellish, underground model is made of the really precious materials:

> the empty vessel of itself [...] a treasury of cast-off things [...] fingernail-cuttings and pared calluses, eggshells. This is the celestial city, and in its heavens long-tailed comets fly past, released to rotate in space from the only free and happy action of the citizens of Beersheba, a city which, only when it shits, is not miserly, calculating, greedy.[36]

Calvino's warning about the importance of the basest aspects of life is perfectly in tune with the scatological revels of Kojo Laing's otherworlds,[37] rather than with Okri's etherized realm of the Invisibles.

This is what has frustrated reviewers most: "One awaits, from Okri, gods who are less God-like";[38] "the best fairy-tales [...] are anchored in human experience, and by denying his story specificity [...] he has denied his story life."[39] A partial exception to this rejecting chorus of rejection can be found in Derek Wright's essay on Nigerian novels of the 1990s. His detailed analysis of Okri's first two *abiku* novels reflects upon whether, "after eight hundred or so pages of phantasmagoric apocalypse sweetened by romantic utopian effusions," Okri has reached "a formal cul-de-sac." To him, *Astonishing the Gods* shows a new course, despite its "meaningless mystical word-mongering [...] clichéd preciosity." Wright appreciates the novel's metaphysical enquiry, its "Barthean *jouissance* in the probing of the limits of language [...] it marks at least an interesting turning point, if no major change of direction."[40] Nevertheless, one can hardly see readers feeling any *jouissance*; rather than being a diversion, it seems to me that, if this novel must be compared with his previous ones, Okri's writing has started spinning dangerously round and round. In addition, a specific comparison with a single passage from *Songs of Enchantment* may show a sort of self-contradiction in Okri's thought: when Azaro sees the Jackal-Headed Masquerade's evil kingdom, he is surprised by its "uncanny sense of order [...] There was no chaos, no confusion, no alternatives, no dialectic, no disturbances.

---

[36] Calvino, *Invisible Cities*, 111–13.

[37] See p.106 below.

[38] Chauduri, "Immoral," 33.

[39] Kathy O'Shaughnessy, "A Real Nowhere Man," *Independent on Sunday* (23 April 1995): 12.

[40] Wright, "Whither Nigerian Fiction?," 330–32.

It was almost peaceful, almost – paradisial. It was a strange kind of utopia" (SE 115). Could not this sentence be suitable for the island in *Astonishing the Gods*? And could not *Infinite Riches*, written three years after *Astonishing* and marking a return to social preoccupations, signify Okri's awareness of this impasse and his desire to escape it?

The realm of contemporary utopias has become mainly "a study of the future" by intellectuals, producing such dark dystopias as *1984* and *Brave New World*. For such positive utopias as Okri's chimerical island of the Invisibles, Negley and Patrick's definition sounds appropriate: "contemporary utopian fantasies are more likely to reflect literary skill than profound social or political significance."[41]

Kojo Laing's folktale realism

In his second and third novels, *Woman of the Aeroplanes* (1988) and *Major Gentl and the Achimota Wars* (1992), the Ghanaian Kojo Laing continues the linguistic project he started with *Search Sweet Country*.[42] The connections between his poetry and his novels are again far-reaching: the unknown world he constructs in *Woman of the Aeroplanes* (1988) resurfaces in one of his poems, "Twenty Years Flying":

> This fine forest morning beyond Kumasi
> tries to hide in mist, both a small town
> and the idea that a philosophy
>   seen in the breast of a dove hiding the rising sun,
>   seen in proverbs or systems,
> can REALLY fit into
>   wisely scrubbed genitalia.[43]

Tukwan, the place in question, is an invisible town, banished – and still persecuted – by the real Ghanaian town of Kumasi. Its location is unclear:

> this town was near enough Kumasi to be far enough away never to be seen by residents of that city, except rarely; and if it had not been situated over one hundred miles from Accra but was nearer Koforidua than Ho, you would not have seen how far it was from Bolgatanga.[44]

---

[41] David Bleich, *Utopia: The Psychology of a Cultural Fantasy* (Studies in Speculative Fiction 5; Ann Arbor MI: UMI Research, 1970): 35.

[42] See Chapter 2 (pp. 71–80) above.

[43] Laing, *Godhorse*, 41.

[44] Kojo Laing, *Woman of the Aeroplanes* (London: Pan / Picador, 1989): 8. Further page references are in the main text.

These are all Ghanaian towns, but a map of the country would not help much. The same is valid for the Scottish town of Levensvale,[45] later to become Tukwan's twin. The inhabitants of both towns, constituting once again a great number of characters, have been kidnapped to live there, and are all immortals: a "far-flung vision" which, writes Chris Dunton, "has no parallel I can think of."[46] Their hopes and aspirations are basically human, but their lives defeat any kind of realistic expectation, creating a series of perceptival displacements in the mind of the reader. In Tukwan, laughter can be collected by tractors, people can photograph dreams and meet one another when dreaming; Kwame Atta "was so agitated that when he inadvertently picked up a piece of rubbish on the clean streets of Tukwan, he threw himself in the bin instead, with the rubbish motionless in his left footprint" (1). Pokuaa, the woman of the title, is

> the mistress of two small aeroplanes which both stood at the level of her lips: one at her upper lip and the other at her lower lip. She perfumed her aeroplanes every morning with frangipani lavender. (6)

Such planes will carry people to Scotland later on: they are not a metaphor, but the actual world of the novel, inexplicable to our ordinary physical perceptions, as Laing himself confirms:

> That is the whole impetus behind my language; cubism, expressionism and other aspects of modern art seem to be propounding a world that I feel already exists for me on a day-to-day basis. (Laing, Accra, 15 December 1993)

The influence of African art on Cubism is well-documented. In both, objects are not painted as seen, but as thought, and Laing feels the need to translate this into literature:

> I believe we already have the basis from which one can start. Our own art is non-representational, isn't it? Our drawings and masks are non-representational and they form part of the basis of Western modern art: so what are we Ghanaians doing with this basis? If it doesn't constitute the root of our own creativity, if it doen't help us make works that don't fit into the artistic moulds we were imposed, then what are we doing? Nothing! (Laing, Accra, 15 December 1993)

---

[45] Laing lived in Scotland from 1957 to 1968. The Vale of Leven Academy was the name of the secondary school he attended in Alexandria, Dumbartonshire; see Dakubu, "Kojo Laing," 141. The Vale of Leven is also quoted in his poem "Jaw," *Lines Review* (Edinburgh) 24 (1968), repr. in *Scottish Poetry* 4, ed. George Bruce, Maurice Lindsay & Edwin Morgan (Edinburgh: Edinburgh UP, 1969): 65.

[46] Chris Dunton, "Far-Flung Vision," *West Africa* 3783 (26 February–4 March 1990): 317.

Woman of the Aeroplanes teems with similar warps: a movable lake, pens writing on their own, rains falling upwards, aeroplanes with sentient noses, to cite only a few. These instances, too, should not be taken as merely metaphoric constructions, be they symbols or hyperboles, because they really exist and occur in the action of the novel. Eliot wrote "I have measured out my life in coffee spoons" in his "Love Song of J. Alfred Prufrock";[47] in Levensvale, Margaret Mackie is "going round the sitting room at exactly the same speed as her husband was stirring his tea [...] he gave his wife a rest by reducing the speed of his controlling teaspoon" (64). This is Laing's description of marital harmony.

Tukwan's sage, Kofi Senya, is found "perched on his own pipe with his vulture, while he was still smoking it" (185); sometimes he

> could blow words out of his pipe, as others blew smoke rings. This was when he did not want to talk. The words would rise up blue in elegant short sentences, and then disappear when the vulture flapped his wings. (13)

The latter image is highly significant for the whole book, since *Woman* could be described as a cartoon world, with the same taste for absurd comicality reaching its apex when the characters start swapping parts of their bodies.[48]

The same rules apply to space and time:

> Much to everyone's surprise in the town, the same year somewhere in the 1950s had shown itself for the last three weeks, during which the sun had been saved from the sweat of running in and out of different decades in the same week. (49)

The temporal dimension is wholly disrupted: Tukwan is called a "happy renegade of history" (17), living as it does simultaneously in every year yet none, since "History never walks here, it runs in any direction" (1). Tukwan and Levensvale "are both towns out of time" (153), sharing a "manoeuvrability of time" (66) so wide-ranging that, when it comes to business deals, they have to choose in what year these are supposed to occur: "How can we calculate in the same economic year when we are children of eternity?" (95) Temporality and spatiality occasionally identify with each other as well: "The time of the meeting was in the running of the stream beyond the disused townhall" (28).

The Akan spider-figure Ananse is once again a key image in the interpretation of the book's transgressiveness. In the first chapter of *The Trickster in West Africa*, Robert Pelton delves into the folktales from the Ashanti area of Ghana, where

[47] T.S. Eliot, "The Love Song of J. Alfred Prufrock" (1917), in Eliot, *Collected Poems 1909–1962* (London: Faber & Faber, 1963): 12 (l.90).

[48] See 22, 86–87, 193.

Tukwan is situated. Their protagonist is the spider Ananse, a figure that survived the Middle Passage experience and still appears in Caribbean folktales. In the Akan language, all folktales are called *anasesem* – 'Ananse's stories' – even when this trickster is not present in the narrative. One of his principal features is the violation of biological rules, including the modification and removal of his and others' bodily parts.[49] Pelton locates Ananse's subversion and renewal in "another dimension":

> In the first lines of nearly all the *anansesem* given by Rattray there appears the word *ho*, which he usually translates as 'once' or 'once upon a time'. In other contexts the word ordinarily means 'there'.

Having to choose between "the mythic time of life's beginning" and "some other form of sacred time," Pelton opts for the latter: according to him, Ananse folk stories announce "a dislocation in ordinary life"

> so that the listener can expect to suspend his everyday knowledge of physical causality and appearance, of social relationships [...] The very telling of tales thus proclaim that both teller and listener are now in a different place, another world, whose relationship to the daily world is strange, ambiguous and mysterious. [...] The mythic time, then, which *ho* signifies, is more truly understood as a mythic space.[50]

Laing's *ho*, Tukwan could therefore be considered as an answer to the complaint lodged by a character in his first magical-realist, Accra-based novel, *Search Sweet Country*: "The contours of the mind's geography are rather tired here" (241).

The Scottish historian Tom McCaskie further interprets this *ho* by linking it to Ananse's regenerative qualities: "h*o* is a referent to an Ananse that *never* existed but that *always* existed in terms of the capacity of the *Asantefoo* [Asante people] for re-definition and renewal."[51]

This *ho* from folktales constitutes the setting of an earlier novel, *The Children of Ananse* (1968), by the British writer Peggy Appiah, married to the Ghanaian statesman Joe Appiah, mother of the philosopher Kwame Anthony Appiah, and author of several books set in Ghana, most of them for children. In this novel, the teacher Yao Bonsu, living in the Ashanti region of Ghana, discovers by chance the village of

---

[49] See Pelton, *The Trickster in West Africa*, 35. This particular characteristic also appears in Konrad, *Ewe Comic Heroes*, 156, and Paul Radin, *The Trickster: A Study in American Indian Mythology* (London: Routledge & Kegan Paul, 1956): 105.

[50] Pelton, *Trickster in West Africa*, 68–70.

[51] Tom McCaskie, "Komfo Anokye of Asante: Meaning, History and Philosophy in an African Society," *Journal of African History* 27 (1986): 337. See also McCaskie, "Asantesem: Reflections on Discourse and Text in Africa," in *Discourse and Its Disguises: The Interpretation of African Oral Texts*, ed. Karin Barber & P.F. de Moraes Farias (Birmingham University African Studies Series 1; Centre of West African Studies, University of Birmingham, 1989): 81.

Nananomkrom,[52] where he meets one Kweku Ananse, who is a descendant of the folktale hero. Nananomkrom has many characteristics in common with Laing's Tukwan: it is close to the rest of Ghana, but "hard to find" because enveloped in forest mist and by a "bamboo thicket," the latter reminiscent of the maze built by Tukwanians to defend themselves from the mortals' invasion.[53] The inhabitants of both Appiah's Nananomkrom and Laing's Tukwan live in a state of "timelessness,"[54] and Yao Bonsu recognizes the world of Nananomkrom – where people talk to animals and storytelling is a constant pastime – as the dimension of Ashanti folktales. Peggy Appiah's simple narrative is a far cry from Laing's innovative English, but the two novels share this otherwordly setting, which does not prevent them from looking for an exchange with the real world, beyond their immortality: the need "to bring back ideas" is felt by Kweku Ananse, who sends his son to Bonsu's school.[55]

In *Search Sweet Country*, the trickster role was performed by a single character (Beni Baidoo), whereas in *Woman of the Aeroplanes* it is unfurled by the language and the incidents of the whole narrative, thanks to an increasingly ingenious style studded with neologisms[56] and an innovative graphic layout. The language contains the same rich variety of formal devices as *Search Sweet Country* – alliteration, rhyme, multifarious vocabulary, puns, humour, emphatic authorial exclamation. It is still rendered physically on the page, with graphic devices ranging from the fractional line ("meet / meat me there!" says Dogo the khebab seller, 20) to a whole page of words and numbers arranged in mathematical formulae (196). Tukwan's writer–historian–*griot* Kwaku de Babo even accuses native speakers of English of becoming "too soft and self-indulgent" with their own language (62), a momentous assertion in the context of contemporary anglophone literature.

Nevertheless, one character proves to be unequalled in trickster-like transgression: Kwame Atta, the historian's twin brother, whose impudence, dishonesty and vulgarity are balanced by a creative spirit. He is capable of taking off on the propulsion of his own flatulence,[57] but also of saving the town through his inventions

[52] 'The village of ancestors' in Akan. Note that a very similar name is employed by Casely Hayford for his heavenly realm; see Chapter 3 above.

[53] Peggy Appiah, *The Children of Ananse* (London: Evans, 1968): 7, 25, 33.

[54] Appiah, *Children of Ananse*, 114.

[55] Appiah, *Children of Ananse*, 30.

[56] The coinage of new words is a feature of the trickster's language; see Lasagna, "Logos of the African Trickster," 35.

[57] See 42–43. Notably, a similar occurrence was described by Radin in his study of two North American Indian trickster cycles (*Trickster*, 102, 139).

(155), to the point where he threatens to "stop thinking very soon so that they all rotted in their stagnation" (21). Atta is the mischievous critical spirit who is often scorned: "He would say to the scorners: know me! For if they wanted him to lead them from the back, then some of the values too would come from the back" (39).

Such a dual aspect induces one to make another comparison with Ananse: in Pelton's view, his animal coarseness, sexual exuberance, selfishness and the laughter he provokes are means of highlighting the social and moral workings of Ashanti society. Ananse's insolence in the face of any law, taboo and even divinity is not inspired by a Promethean instinct or an urge to chaos, but is to be seen as a way of laying bare Ashanti religious and ethical mechanisms, and eventually to regenerate them in new shapes.[58]

Ananse's disruptions have a creative nature, then, just like Laing's writing, where the fantastic setting is not severed from the social issues of present-day Ghana: "History is there and its brutality acknowledged," Dunton states.[59] Adewale Maja–Pearce would not agree with this: "This was fantasy for its own sake, as if the author had simply fallen into a mannerism."[60] Behind all Laing's fireworks, though, his characters share human hopes and aspirations; like those in *Search Sweet Country*, they are seeking a new Ghanaian society, for better or for worse.

Woman of the Aeroplanes, therefore, needs to be considered neither as magical realism nor as pure fantasy. With the usual reservations attached to the theoretical ambiguity of any critical label, some new definitions could be proposed: fantastic realism, social fantasy or, in the light of Laing's connection with the folktale world outlined above, folktale realism.

That ideal Ghanaian society longed for by most of the characters in *Woman of the Aeroplanes* is, as in *Search*, an inevitable combination of ancestral and Western

---

[58] Pelton, *Trickster in West Africa*, 35, 60. Kwawisi Tekpetey stresses the cathartic function of *ananseseṃ* as "tension-relieving aesthetic devices. The members of the audience purge themselves of tensions built up by social restrictions and thus of their latent desires to become involved in Ananse-like adventures"; Tekpetey, "The Trickster in Akan–Asante Oral Literature," *Asemka: A Bilingual Literary Journal of the University of Cape Coast* 5 (September 1979): 81.

On both sides of the Atlantic, Ananse's relevance remains strong. In his collection of tales *Anancy's Score* (1973), the Jamaican writer Andrew Salkey shows the spider's connections with contemporary issues. Karin Barber ("Popular Arts," 40) describes (as an example of cultural syncretism) some Ghanaian mimeographed comics from the mid-1970s where folktale and Marvel Comics heroes join forces to defeat military and political corruption, with Spiderman and Ananse making use of their superhuman powers or organizing popular uprisings.

[59] Dunton, "Far-Flung Vision," 317.

[60] Adewale Maja–Pearce, review of Laing's *Woman of the Aeroplanes*, *Wasafiri* 10 (Summer 1989): 23.

values: "new things were as wise as the old in Tukwan, and [...] the opposition between the two was welcome and controllable" (36). When they meet in Levensvale, Ghanaians and Scots face a similar world-view; David Mackie is convinced of the worth of exchanging ideas: "they take some of ours and we take some of theirs, that's the way to the new toughness of the world" (130), while Tukwan has been banished from Ghana "for refusing to listen to *all* the songs of the ancestors" (1–2, italics in the text). Traditional structures must therefore undergo readjustment, as confirmed by the already quoted poem:

> High above the remaining trees,
> the hawk flew some ancestors away,
> especially those that could not bear the edge of time.[61]

This syncretist philosophy accounts for Tukwan's twinship with the immortal Scottish town of Levensvale, seen by both populations as a way of attaining a spiritual and economic growth. Incidentally '*tu kwan*', in Akan, means 'to travel'. On their arrival in Scotland, the Ghanaian group has to dispute with a couple of Immigration Officers before a compromise can be reached:

> every living thing on the two aeroplanes was to be classed as a human being for the next three months, after which, if there was any evidence that anyone or anything had become a spirit, or that any animal wished to become a human being and could prove that this was a possibility, all applications of an ontological or supernatural nature should be presented anew. If the soul was to be kept in a form, the form too could be kept in the soul [...] Officer and officette marched down the valleys with one shrug between them. (82–83)

In spite of its fantastic events and location, the novel evidently does not avoid issues of contemporary and traditional political structures: "Like any other text, a literary fantasy is produced within, and determined by, its social context."[62] Laing deals with the theme of political power, a subject he will further develop in his third novel. Actually, Tukwan has a traditional chief, Nana Bontox, who is stubbornly fond of traditional ways, but his lack of cultural flexibility makes him appear "unwiser than anyone else [...] Nana did not disappoint his people: he continued to make a fool of himself as often as possible" (10). Sometimes Laing's parody of the uselessness of frozen ancestral customs shakes the pillars of Akan history: Bontox, for instance, owns a golden ring he claims belonged to Okomfo Anokye, the legendary divine messenger who gave the Asante people the Golden Stool which is still

---

[61] Laing, *Godhorse*, 41.

[62] Jackson, *Fantasy*, 3.

believed to contain the soul of the Asante nation.[63] On the other hand, the rest of Tukwan seem to strive after a different kind of political decision-making. Apart from Bontox, there are three more recognized 'bosses': Kofi Senya, the town's spiritual guide, Pokuaa with her beauty and down-to-earth entrepreneurship, and the lake (probably a reference to Lake Bosomtwe, sacred to the Akan because it embodies one of their twelve patrilinear groups),[64] which can be moved closer to a public meeting by pulling its ripples. Resolutions are quite often made collectively, the meeting about the journey to Scotland narrated in "Class Two" (the second chapter) being a case in point.

As regards hybridity in contemporary Africa, the Anglo-Ghanaian philosopher Kwame Anthony Appiah writes that "if you postulate an either–or choice between Africa and the West [...] your home must be the otherworldly, the monastic retreat."[65] Such a seclusion could clearly apply to the unknown dimension of *Woman of the Aeroplanes*, but Tukwanians try determinedly to regain their mortality in the most diverse ways – breaking the barrier of ninety-nine houses that is a god-imposed limit, flying abroad for profit and change "so that the gods were giving Tukwan a final choice: the more change it made, the more mortal it became" (41); mortality is at last attained when someone dies without resurrecting, Pokuaa becomes pregnant, more houses are built, and profits are made:

> True, mortality was toffee.[66] It was a dance of glee at the edge of the highest neon-cross hill, for the knowledge of the drop, the death, seemed to add sweetness to the movement of the dance. (229)

Tukwan's utopian society is taken back into reality. The new society must therefore be lived concretely on earth, trying to employ elements of both dimensions: mortal-

---

63 See Max Assimeng, *Social Structure of Ghana* (Tema: Ghana Publishing Corporation, 1981): 111; McCaskie, "Komfo Anokye," 318–19. Oral histories hold that Okomfo Anokye made the Golden Stool descend from the sky, as one can verify by reading Michael Dei–Anang's play mentioned in Chapter 6; Dei–Anang, *Okomfo Anokye's Golden Stool* (Accra: Waterville, 1963): 59. In Laing's only published short story to date, a lorry which has "golden wood, and many seedless guavas for the hungry" is similarly lowered from the sky; Kojo Laing, "Vacancy for the Post of Jesus Christ," in *The Heinemann Book of Contemporary African Short Stories*, ed. Chinua Achebe & C.L. Innes (Oxford: Heinemann, 1992): 185.

64 See R.S. Rattray, *Ashanti* (New York: Negro UP, 1923): 54–76; Kofi Asare Opoku, *West African Traditional Religion* (Accra: FEP, 1978): 98.

65 Kwame Anthony Appiah, *In My Father's House* (London: Methuen, 1992): 251.

66 In Ghanaian English, 'toffee' can mean all kinds of sweets apart from chocolate; see Sey, *Ghanaian English*, 111.

ity, in a way similar to Azaro's choice in Okri's novels, means to "substitute one freedom for another, hoping that both would prevail" (230).

The choice between immortality and mortality (present throughout the book) is simply another way of facing the dilemma which opposes the "monastic retreat" mentioned by Appiah to a new multicultural society. Nevertheless, the contact with real life ends up being dangerous, carrying within it all the implications of neocolonialism: "the first invasion [by Kumasi] was physical and it failed; this second one [...] is more subtle [...] it is a phantom: ignore it and you look a fool, fight it and you look outdated" (234–35). Taken aback by the threat of having one's consciousness narrowed, Tukwan makes a final effort to obtain fifty years more of immortality:

> another fifty years in which to be fine and original, in which to watch the joy of forests and the joy of machines; and this watching was not to be done as mere spectating: it was and was to be a joy of multicentred dimension, a joy that did not necessarily take knowledge far beyond the knower. (249)

As in *Search Sweet Country*, the new society is not yet ready to be built in our world. From her characteristically Bhabhian perspective, Brenda Cooper considers this ending an unfortunate embracing of tradition (in the guise of the shrinemaster Kofi Senya) with a corresponding decrease of authorial ironic distance: an "elite solution," a "monolithic pronouncement" which moves the novel "away from the embrace of open borders."[67]

What is left, in any case, is once again the creativity of individuals. Having been their chronicler, Kwaku de Babo is well aware of the dangers looming ahead:

> if you allow the experience and memory of the ordinary person to disappear before the dead-end of politics or stagnation or both, then you are left with a mind that may retain its anatomical size, but it will be a mind that will either grab at straws of meaning, or create an easy spiritual mush over everything. (239–40)

In the year 2020 AD, the Ghanaian town of Achimota has incorporated the neighbouring Accra and Tema, while the rest of the nation has mysteriously vanished. Achimota City has just won the first War of Existence against Torro the Terrible, thanks to the kindness of Major aMofa Gentl, who owns two rooms on the moon, and to the craft of Nana Mai the Grandmother Bomb, who can sew up the sky and lives in a satellite "which had a sexy booster tail to charm the galaxies with."[68]

---

[67] Cooper, *Magical Realism in West African Fiction*, 205, 212.

[68] Kojo Laing, *Major Gentl and the Achimota Wars* (London: Heinemann, 1992): 44. Further page references are in the main text.

In *Major Gentl and the Achimota Wars* (1992),[69] as in his previous novel, Laing re′-creates the world by dismantling any expected connection between things, a "self-conscious violence to time, space and the English language."[70] Here is the how the book begins:

> Major aMofa Gentl was feared in Achimota City for his gentleness, since it was this quality that won the first war for the golden cockroach, the emblem of the city. And this emblem, accompanied by his friend the silver mosquito, would shed its symbolic nature and become a real city cockroach crawling about looking for truth.
>
> The war was won against Torro the Terrible Roman, the only man in the universe who could stand frontally and sideways at the same time. (1)

This passage is not a metaphoric or symbolic rendering of a familiar reality – it is *the very reality* of the book, the foundations on which the actual plot is built: kindness wins a war, a symbol materializes to become one of the main characters, another character is ubiquitous. In Laing's own words: "I've always believed that the metaphor or symbol sometimes cheats, in terms of concentrating more on the message than on the components making the image" (Laing, Accra, 15 December 1993). From among the distinctive marks of magical realism, Wendy B. Faris singles out

> images that take on lives of their own [...] a closing of the gap between words and the world, or a demonstration of what we might call the linguistic nature of experience. This magic happens when a metaphor is made real.[71]

Moreover, the author assumes the tone of a bard-like narrator, especially when he establishes a relation with his readership saying "*I swear*" (44) when facts become too unreal, emphatically enjoining some characters to act or addressing the reader indirectly, as here: "And would you be so kind as to hold your page while one elder went to the toilet, thought the troublesome rabbit" (66).

Laing's disruptions are well-grounded in the Ghanaian cultural context. The rationale behind the choice, for instance, of Achimota as the city where the novel's language is developed in all its richness could be a reaction against its original Ga meaning, 'speak no name', having been a place where runaway slaves took refuge.[72] See also the subsequent image of the three trains rolling "among the people":

---

[69] Winner of the VALCO Award in 1993.

[70] Odia Ofeimun, "Surrealistic Power-Play," *West Africa* 3918 (19–25 October 1992): 1794.

[71] Faris, "Scheherazade's Children," 164, 176.

[72] See Larweh Therson–Cofie, "Life Is War in Achimota City," *People's Daily Graphic* 9 (September 1993): 4. Two of the poets examined in Chapter 4 and 5 write about the origin of Achimota's name; see Atukwei Okai, *The Oath of the Fontomfrom and other poems* (New York: Simon & Schuster, 1971): 111; Abena Pokua Adompim Busia, *Testimonies of Exile* (Accra: Woeli, 1990): 30.

> They were the type of trains that automatically laid out their own tracks as they moved, and then picked them up from behind to reuse in the front again. Train, train, train the duellists, for the engines gave an atmosphere of past and present that brightened the future immeasurably. (116)

Such trains cannot but bring to mind the Akan ancestral image called *Sankofa*, the bird walking on while picking food from behind, signifying a double concern for one's heritage and present needs.[73]

In Achimota City, Gentl's shadow is promoted to the rank of sergeant, a sax can play on its own, a bike acts as the talking referee of a football match, and a man is killed by being put *inside* a bullet. Rather than experiencing a world made of flesh and blood, the reader may sometimes feel as if s / he were – once again – witnessing an animated cartoon where everything is possible, "disestablishmentarianism" being the law. When the two opposing leaders happen to dream the same dream at once, it is consequently impossible to tell this from their waking. This time, though, Laing does not employ a different dimension; his plot develops on our very planet, in a Ghanaian town of the future.

Achimota city in itself also reflects a new relationship between metaphorical and concrete realms, because it has

> devoured Accra almost completely while at the same time most of the rest of the country had inexplicably vanished, land and all. Thus, by the year 2020 Achimota was a truncated city bursting to survive and to find the rest of its country soon. (3)

The disappeared land is to be interpreted as the actualization of the Western ideological and economic assault that has led many Africans to leave their country. Similarly, the Wars of Existence are to be considered as a narrative rendering of a Western neocolonial attempt to impose itself on the rest of the world. On the other hand, Brenda Cooper complains about such a vision of European culture in "Achimoto [sic] City," which she sees as "generalized and stereotypical." One is inevitably reminded of the critical argument concerning Armah's *Two Thousand Seasons*, mentioned in Chapter 1; Cooper herself links her point on *Gentl* with "Armah's classic of exclusivist cultural nationalism."[74] Once again, we are probably grappling with a simple question of points of view: like Armah's traditional *griot*, Laing's bard-like authorial posture should not be constrained by notions of objectivity and psychological depth.

---

[73] See Albert W. Kayper–Mensah, *Sankofa: Adinkra Poems* (Tema: Ghana Publishing Corporation, 1976): 4.

[74] Cooper, *Magical Realism in West African Fiction*, 213–14.

Torro's invisible bosses are after something different from conventional warfare ("Direct wars were too out of date with the bosses abroad, subtle extinction being preferred," 7), trying to control Africa's resources and viewing its people as expendable. Even Torro seems to be a victim of this attitude. He is said to love Achimota, but the ideology within which he has been fostered (he has a touch of Italian Mafia and South African apartheid, being born in both places) drives him to subjugate Gentl's people. His 'spaghetti English', by the way, adds a further nuance to Laing's linguistic palette:

> Mama mia, dear Major, I'm losing my Roman accent, I do not comprehendo. My dear belly is shaped just like one of the eastern hills in your dear city, and I do nothing but let wind escape in any direction. Diavolo! I theenk I have the serious ulcers, noo! (9–10)

Torro's bosses have literally taken most of the Ghanaian land away with them, and the second War of Existence is a way of winning it back. One of the first successful signs in the conflict is the return of fragments of the lost land: "There, miles off beyond Achimota City, a rectangular piece of land slowly crawled through the void, and joined the land of the city!" (104). When a piece of the national soil suddenly reappears from the sea there is only one man on it, a moping individual who would like to support Torro: "A tiny house had been made for him, and they almost built it on his back because he had refused to move from the appropriate spot for it. His favourite occupation was refusing" (123). This 'been-to', then, seems to recoil from the external world like Melville's Bartleby, paralyzed by "the sterility of a spiritless society."[75] It is notable that Melville describes his character as "absolutely alone in the universe. A bit of wreck in the mid-Atlantic."[76] Laing's "tiny house," too, inevitably reminds the reader of the screen that Bartleby's employer puts around him.

In the case of *Major Gentl*, the classification 'science fiction' could be added to the three proposed earlier for *Woman*, but not in its most common sense of being an extrapolation of scientific theories and discoveries. On the contrary, the book includes an open polemic against Western scientific ideology, seen as the main force supporting the neocolonial onslaught, as Laing himself has said: "The march of technology probably has already made it possible for us here to be controlled from abroad. It is not being paranoid: you look at what is being made, and realize that it is possible to recolonize us from a distance" (Laing, Accra, 15 December 1993). One of Torro's army's objectives is to help virtual reality to swallow up all sensorial and

---

[75] Mordecai Marcus, "Melville's Bartleby as a Psychological Double," in *Bartleby the Inscrutable*, ed. M.T. Inge (Hamden CT: Archon, 1979): 123.

[76] Herman Melville, "Bartleby, the Scrivener" (1856), in *The Portable Melville* (New York: Viking, 1952): 493, 475.

physical activities: "The most advanced thing they want to do is turn thought into a sense, diiirectly!" he says (41). Moreover,

> [Torro] had recently become so suspicious that he used a computer to map the route of food from his fork or his hands to his mouth: he couldn't trust what could happen in that tiny interval of oral travel. (116)

The critic Derek Wright aptly argues that "Laing's satiric point is, of course, that Africa for Europe has always existed in a state of virtual reality."[77] The author's accusation reminds one of Guy Debord's theories on postmodern culture as a "society of spectacle" where lived experience has moved across into representation, and of Jean Baudrillard's "desert of the real," an image borrowed from Borges.[78] In the light of this, the destiny awaiting Africa is brutally expressed in Torro's words: "We have decided that conceptually there is no difference between existence and nonexistence, hence we do not consider anything wrong when you no longer exist" (166).

Major Gentl's 'science fiction' does not support conventional scientific theories, but suggests, in addition to a multicultural society and political power based on broad popular participation, an epistemology respectful of nature and the concreteness of human experience. Curiously, such a view is the complete opposite of what Okri propounds in *Astonishing the Gods*, where the supreme aim is "to be free of all visible things."[79] Laing's idea of science is embodied in the "computers of the African kind which were soft to touch" (16). A credible alternative vision of con-

---

[77] Wright, "Returning Voyagers," 187.

[78] See Larry McCaffery, ed. *Storming the Reality Studio: A Casebook of Cyberpunk and Postmodern Science Fiction* (Durham NC: Duke UP, 1991): 6, 20, 25. The disconcerting feeling of losing touch with reality – palpable in Western societies – does not seem limited to intellectual theories and virtual fantasies; see, for instance, Mike Leigh's prize-winner film *Naked* (1993), where the picaresque protagonist Johnny wanders around a dreary and cynical London speculating on the doom of mankind; in a futuristic but empty building, he has a long conversation with its night-watchman:

> JOHNNY: By the very definition of Apocalypse, Mankind must cease to exist, at least in a material form.
>
> *(Brian stops in another doorway).*
>
> BRIAN: What d'you mean, in a material form?
>
> JOHNNY: Well, 'e'll evolve.
>
> BRIAN: What into?
>
> JOHNNY: Into something that transcends matter. Into a species of pure thought.

Mike Leigh, *Naked and other screenplays* (London: Faber & Faber, 1995): 48.

[79] Okri, *Astonishing*, 54.

temporary Africa, in fact, would necessarily imply the establishment of indigenous research structures, as recommended by the scholars who took part in the 1987 Beyond Hunger Project: their vision included a "capitalism [...] with a 'humane face' " based on a "locally derived science and technology."[80]

Laing concentrates, among other things, on the city's architecture: the "fruity columns" (101), Gentl's house of bamboo, "who had taken root and was growing heartily" (137), and termites

> [that] just continued to change the architecture of Government House when they wanted, with their inspired saliva plus earthen engineering. And wasn't it the cheapest way of building strong mansions, using termites intelligently? And the way the biting combined the different forms of red, grey, and brown was beautiful to behold. (66)

In other words, a rapport between nature and culture – already present in *Woman* – where political power is shared with animals. In regard to this issue, Laing's creative route is traceable through a natural metaphor or, rather, to guavas, a fruit recurrent in his work. In *Search Sweet Country* they first appear as a symbol of an object of desire, as Kofi Loww ponders:

> All the stones of a guava pointed in different directions, and each stone could be subversive of love and action. And any love or power that did not have this infinite direction of seeds, this patterned way of variety, could neither fit into his heart, nor his head. Yet what did he in his withdrawn openness, in his slow explorations, have to give towards this very same variousness that he wished for? (152)

The same variousness is feared by politicians in one of Laing's poems:

> Minister likes guavas,
> but considers that each stone inside
> may one day sabotage the skin.[81]

In *Woman of the Aeroplanes*, the novel representing a first step towards the literary concretization of that variousness, the reference to the same fruit is more figurative and idiomatic: "it looks as if the lawyer has already swallowed the guava of truth" (29). In *Gentl*'s Achimota, where "Fruit was law: [...] there was fruit in the toilets, fruit in the halls, and fruit in the aeroplanes, so that you could eat the city," it becomes a simple adjective: one of the elders "enjoyed the joy of ruling in very difficult times that needed much fruit and calm in equal quantities ... O you guava government" (3, 17).

---

[80] *Beyond Hunger in Africa: Conventional Wisdom and a Vision of Africa in 2057*, ed. Chinua Achebe et al. (London: James Currey; Nairobi & Portsmouth NH: Heinemann, 1990): 94, 89.

[81] Laing, *Godhorse*, 27.

The scatological dimension is another point comparable to the trickster Ananse, because in Laing's third novel his characters rejoice in anything connected with excrement. This confirms the atypical direction of Laing's writing among anglophone African authors, for whom fecal images are generally associated with moral decay and corruption, particularly in certain works by Armah, Soyinka and Okri. According to Pelton, Ananse

> discloses how the human mind and heart are themselves epiphanies of a calmly transcendent sacredness so boldly engaged with this world that it encompasses both nobility and messiness – feces, lies and even death.[82]

Pelton avails himself of Victor Turner's studies on shamanism, where ritual immersion in nature leads to a sort of regeneration of culture and society.[83] When Major Gentl has to make a decision, he similarly "had to crawl to think, sharing the grounds with frogs, lizards, crow dung, cricket droppings, the shit of wise sparrows, and worm tunnels" (144). Ananse's unruliness, like Laing's violation of all codes, is instrumental in shaping human society; his theriomorphism makes him break "through the boundaries separating nature and culture in such a way that human life is seen to transform perpetually what is given from both above and below."[84]

Another suitable instrument for interpreting Laing's writing is based on Mikhail Bakhtin's concept of carnivalesque and on his study of Rabelais.[85] The joyful atmosphere of carnival and medieval popular culture share several characteristics with Laing's works and with the function of Ananse: an urge to overturn imposed hierarchies through a dynamic and ever-changing language, and through a refusal of logic that does not amount to pure denial but ambivalently contains both death and life, burial and resurrection:

> la parodie carnavalesque est très eloignée de la parodie moderne purement négative et formelle; en effet, tout en niant, la première ressuscite et renouvelle tout à la fois. La négation pure et simple est de manière générale totalement étrangère à la culture populaire [...] Dans le système des images de la fête populaire, la négation pure et abstraite n'existe pas. Les images visent à englober les deux pôles du devenir dans leur unité contradictoire. Le battu (ou tué).est paré; la bastonnade est joyeuse; elle débute et se termine au milieu des rires.[86]

---

[82] Pelton, *Trickster in West Africa*, 4.

[83] See Pelton, *Trickster in West Africa*, 33–35.

[84] Pelton, *Trickster in West Africa*, 36.

[85] A similar analogy between the trickster and the carnivalesque is traced by C.G. Jung in Radin, *Trickster*, 195.

[86] Bakhtin, *L'Oeuvre de François Rabelais et la culture populaire au Moyen Age et sous le Re-*

The scatological element is one of the main sites of this double phenomenon, appearing to debase the spiritual but actually planting the seeds for a new growth:

> le caractère ambivalent des excréments, leur lien avec la résurrection et la rénovation et son rôle particulier dans la victoire sur la peur [...] Pour lui [Rabelais..] les excréments étaient en outre une matière joyeuse et dégrisante, à la fois rabaissante et gentille, réunissant la tombe et la naissance dans leur forme la moins tragique, une forme comique, nullement effrayante. (178)[87]

Bakhtin, moreover, mentions the popular novel *Aucassin et Nicolette*, a medieval combination of sung lyric and recited narrative featuring a carnivalesque war similar to that in *Major Gentl*: the two protagonists arrive in a country where the king is pregnant and a battle is "fought with rotten crab-apples, eggs and fresh cheeses." When Aucassin draws his sword and slays some of the enemy, the king stops him: "It is not our custom to kill each other."[88]

Compare this with *Gentl*'s children's war, where both sides "laid down their guns and decided to sell hard toffee [...] The sun was hidden with hundreds of toffees thrown in jubilation" (54), and with the football match between the two armies (122–26). Even carnage is described farcically:

> hundreds of his [Torro's] men perished when the branches opened fire, with the perching crows joining in and shooting with the small guns hidden in their beaks. Two dead men propped each other upright. (141)

In spite of its bellicose plot, the general mood is gay and sparkling, unlike the epic gravity and solemnity of Okri's and Cheney–Coker's novels. Nevertheless, Faris raises a general point about magical-realist novels that may account for this list of diverse references: "A carnivalesque spirit is common in this group of novels. Language is used extravagantly, expending its resources beyond its referential needs."[89]

---

naissance (Paris: Gallimard, 1965): 19–20, 204; "The Carnivalesque parody is a far cry from the purely negative and formal modern parody; actually, by negating everything, the former resurrects and renews at the same time. Negation pure and simple, generally speaking, has nothing to do with popular culture [...] In the imagery of popular celebrations, the pure and abstract negation does not exist. Images aim at enveloping the two poles of becoming in their contradictory unity. The beaten (or killed) are adorned; the blow is joyous, it starts and ends amid laughter" (my tr.).

[87] "The ambivalent character of excrement, its link with resurrection and renewal and its particular role in the victory against fear [...] To him [Rabelais] excrement was also a joyous and disenchanting matter, disparaging and kind at the same time, uniting birth and grave in their least tragic form, a comic form, not frightening at all" (my tr.).

[88] Anne Elizabeth Cobby, ed. *Aucassin et Nicolette with The Pilgrimage of Charlemagne*, tr. & intro. Glyn S. Burgess (Library of Medieval Literature A47; New York: Garland, 1988): 160, 162.

[89] Faris, "Scheherazade's Children," 184.

Laing's Achimota is a sort of utopia, a harmonious place that has "achieved something harder that the ancestors could offer at that time. But the ancestors too were learning, were changing" (160). It is doubtful whether a comparison with New World utopias and their inhabitants' solitary retreat into nature could be sustained, though, given the urban and collective atmosphere of *Major Gentl*. At the same time, European dystopias and their state-dominated individuals do not resemble Laing's either: "You could speak your mind koraa [completely] in Achimota City, and even talk to the Government while sitting on the toilet" (74). Such Government is constituted by three extravagant Elders who used to confer power to citizens in rotation until Pogo Alonka Forr, the carrot millionaire, refused to continue the tradition. This character's view on power clashes with the general opinion: Pogo loves and desires power for its own glamour and, in fact, to emulate Gentl's lunar rooms,

> he had faithfully cultivated the sun to see whether an arrangement could be worked out there in a serious and solar manner; bamboozle the sun with attention and you could even end up having a hotel in it, burning ambition, he said. (12)

But in Achimota blind adulation cannot be tolerated.[90] The political project suggested by Laing's narrative, then, seems to follow the paradigms set by those African intellectuals deeply dissatisfied with the democratic model imposed by the colonizers.[91]

The final victory of Achimota, to which armies of diverse animals play a crucial role, leaves Major Gentl jobless yet satisfied:

> it was seen clearly that Achimota City was the standard they all had to follow, a place where power was the last resort, and humanity and invention allowed even the smallest human being to open out into the trees and into the universe, to see the whole, to touch the inner. (180)

Before closing this chapter, one final observation is necessary. Unlike Homi Bhabha, who states that "Magical Realism, after the Latin American boom, becomes the literary language of the emergent postcolonial world,"[92] this chapter does not set up any such literary yardstick. Actually, the novels examined constitute isolated ac-

[90] Its political structure appears to be based on a principle of "decentralised centralism" much like Max Assimeng's definition of the complex traditional Ashanti system (*Social Structure of Ghana*, 98).

[91] See also Cooper, *Magical Realism in West African Fiction*, 201.

[92] Homi Bhabha, Introduction to *Nation and Narration*, ed. Bhabha (London: Routledge, 1990): 6.

complishments in the panorama of anglophone West African prose, which is still dominated by the realist mode.

Given their departure from realistic narratives – which have for decades been the model for West Africa – the impact of Cheney–Coker, Okri and Laing on their West African readership appears to be troublesome and contentious. If the public for the novel as a genre is limited, compared to Western taste, the reception encountered by these experimental books must be even poorer.

The Nigerian critic and novelist Tolu Ajayi argues that Okri "won the Booker Prize by feeding the whites with their own vapid prey – a scandalous picture of Africa."[93] Significantly, the same accusation was levelled against Tutuola by several Nigerian critics some thirty years earlier.[94] As for *Major Gentl*, the Ghanaian reviewer Larweh Therson–Cofie finds it "simple and quick-reading,"[95] whereas Dakubu states that Ghanaians "find [Laing] hard to read. The real problem seems to lie in his highly original poetic syntax and the intense concentration of images."[96]

The novels analysed here doubtless require considerable effort from the reader, given their complex plot and language. If they have all been published abroad,[97] it might also be because British publishers intend to follow in the wake of Latin American magical realism; moreover, the dire straits in which African publishing finds itself do not allow any risky enterprise. This situation may have led to a sort of vicious circle, since being published abroad has further widened the gap between these authors and their West African readers on the grounds of the consequent high prices of the books.[98]

The most balanced view on this new wave of West African novelists is expressed by Femi Osofisan, who appreciates their peculiar relationship to politics, their indigenization of European languages and their new perspective on reality, at the same time calling for renewed attitudes by readers. To him, such books

> are aiming at ridding us of the constraining bonds of habit and dead routines, of our entrapment in the clichés of a too literal, too material relationship with the environment and hence with cognosis. [...] rather than condemn these texts outrightly as being

---

[93] Otu, "Beyond Okri's Surrealism," 19.

[94] See Lindfors, *Comparative Approaches*, 3.

[95] Therson-Cofie, "Life Is War," 4.

[96] Dakubu, "Kojo Laing," 145–46. "Almost unreadable," writes Brenda Cooper on *Gentl*, in her *Magical Realism in West African Fiction*, 213.

[97] Just as the works by their francophone counterparts were all published in France; see Osofisan, "Warriors of a Failed Utopia?," 25, 28.

[98] See Jowitt, "Structure and Meaning," 20. On Laing, see Cooper, *Magical Realism in West African Fiction*, 191.

> irrelevant to our needs [...] it is we readers who must renew ourselves and our relationship with texts and the world. We must become adventurous, like the new writers, and cast our nets for wider waters [...] Okri and others are already embarked: we must hasten to catch up. And in the end, in response to our enthusiasm perhaps, they will learn to tame their extravagant passions.[99]

During our interview, Osofisan emphasized the critics' task in the matter, the same task that this chapter attempts to perform: "In Nigeria it is not catching on, it's as if people didn't like it at all. I've been trying to tell my students to be a little more sympathetic, because the critics also have the responsibility of getting sympathy for this new kind of writing" (Osofisan, Ibadan, 2 August 1997).

[99] Osofisan, "Warriors of a Failed Utopia?," 30–31.

Poetry: Between Page and Stage

4 Individual Voices

> Every revolution in poetry is apt to be,
> and sometimes to announce itself to be,
> a return to common speech.
> (T.S. Eliot)

IF A CLEAR TREND in anglophone West African novels has been explored up to now – a trend that witnesses a shift from prose towards a highly metaphoric, poetic form – the intention of this second part is to find out where exactly written poetry has been going for the last thirty years. The answer provided is: theatre or, rather, the voice: the spoken, shouted, recited, chanted, and / or performed word.

Temporally, the point of departure is the early 1970s. Much has been published on the beginnings of contemporary West African poetry, on its efforts to liberate itself from the Anglo-Saxon tradition. In this regard, Fraser's *West African Poetry* is certainly to be considered a seminal work, not least because it focuses explicitly on the written / oral relationship:

> My principal contention is that the inception of written verse initially marked a sharp break with the tradition of oral verse, after which occurred a slow flirtatious reconciliation. To a large extent this then is a history of a hasty indignant divorce followed by a considered and fruitful remarriage.[1]

In a way, Chapters 4–5 here could be viewed as a modest complement to Fraser's book, which traces exhaustively the most important steps in the 'slow reconciliation' between the written and oral dimensions: Senghor's musicality, the influence of Modernism, Christopher Okigbo's fusion of various traditions, Kwesi Brew's fresh simplicity, all the way to Okai and Anyidoho.

Geographically, Ghana forms the focus of this chapter for a number of reasons. First of all, too much space would be required to treat in depth the development of

---

[1] Robert Fraser, *West African Poetry: A Critical History* (Cambridge: Cambridge UP, 1986): 2.

the Nigerian AlterNative tradition, its break with the Modernist tendencies of the first generation, its rapport with orality and in particular the creative genius of its finest exponent, Niyi Osundare.[2] The poetry of the Sierra Leonean Syl Cheney–Coker deserve proper analysis as well.

Secondly, it is worth dedicating a whole chapter to Ghana because the resurgence in Ghanaian poetry has assumed more general, national proportions. Its size – much smaller than Nigeria – may partly account for this, but it would not be a satisfactory reason in itself. My first chapter similarly argued for how Ghanaian novelists of the first generation all experimented with poetical prose and oral sources, each in his / her own way. According to Fraser, if compared to Nigeria's diversity of talents, Ghana has witnessed

> a cohesiveness of the national mood which has led to a recognizable national literary personality [...] less prone to gather into opposing cabals or groups [...] Ghanaian writers have from the early 50s felt able to turn to an abiding heritage of poetry and song which has fed their work with unifying strength.[3]

Fraser sees the similarity between the Akan and the Ewe funeral dirges as an example of this common heritage. If he is right, it is not surprising that a predominance of poetry developed; in 1973, around the beginning of the period considered in the present chapter, the literary magazine *Growth* declared: "Ghana, as literary statistics show at the moment, has more poets than novelists and playwrights put together."[4] What follows here also contends that Nkrumah's progressive policy on educational and cultural matters helped Ghanaian authors tap their ancestral roots successfully, and stimulated their "active willingness to sit at the feet of the elders."[5]

Kofi Awoonor must necessarily be quoted as a precursor, given his poetic efforts to revive Ewe traditional treasures with their highly proverbial and metaphoric imagery as well as their oral and performance-oriented context. But he is not examined here, partly because he played a marginal role in the actual process of

---

[2] On the subject of Nigerian poetry and oral features, see Ezenwa–Ohaeto, *Contemporary Nigerian Poetry and the Poetics of Orality* (Bayreuth African Studies Series 45; Bayreuth: Eckhard Breitinger, 1998). On Osundare's poetry, see Stewart Brown, "Daring the Beast: Contemporary Nigerian Poetry," in *Essays on African Writing 2: Contemporary Literature*, ed. Abdulrazak Gurnah (Oxford: Heinemann, 1995): 58–72.

[3] Fraser, *West African Poetry*, 139.

[4] Kodzo Tom Dorkenoo, "Ayi Kwei Armah, Winner of Ghana's Highest and First Literary Prize," *Growth: Literary Magazine for Young Writers* (Accra: Arts Council of Ghana / Young Africans Writers' Club) 3 (September 1973): 71.

[5] Fraser, *West African Poetry*, 140.

stage enactments, and partly in the light of the several studies already dedicated to him.[6] He will nevertheless be mentioned in passing, as a touchstone for the poets analysed.[7]

Another of the attitudes for which Awonoor paved the way is the renewed bardic role of the contemporary poet[8] – the same priestly function that Christopher Okigbo envisaged for himself – probably in tune with the Ewe singer's role in oral tradition:

> To have the ability to create songs, the Ewe believes, is a gift from the gods. So in the Ewe pantheon there is a god of songs, or Hadzivodu. He is the inspirer and the creator of songs. The poet, or Heno, is only an instrument in the god's hands.[9]

This consideration does not imply wholesale identification between traditional singers and anglophone poets: if the former were to aim at peace, harmony, order and continuity in their political dissent, the coercive times the latter live through render moderation useless, and therefore require a more aggressive stance.[10] In this regard, Atukwei Okai has declared that, in addition to the praise-singing tradition he is influenced by, "I have come to the point where I'm basically critical of the realities."[11]

In any case, all the poets included in this chapter show a keen urge to maintain that sense of the sacred surrounding the word, and still believe, as Kofi Anyidoho states about the Ewe world-order, in the "ontological value of *the word*, not merely as a semiotic fact, but, above all, as a natural cosmic force with a potential for creative and destructive ends." The shift from literacy back to orality should enhance this value: after all, in the Ewe language the "verb *dzi* means both 'to give birth to a child' and 'to sing'."[12]

---

[6] See Fraser, *West African Poetry*, 9, 158–67, 290–95; Angmor, *Contemporary Literature in Ghana*, 102–23; Adjei, "Tradition and Continuity," 151–81. The latter work offers, among other things, an original insight into the significance of the Ewe language in Awoonor's poetry.

[7] Regretfully, two Ghanaian poets are omitted here: Ama Ata Aidoo and Kwadjo Opoku–Agyemang, whose compelling works do not fall within the thematic range of this chapter.

[8] On ritual, see Adjei, "Tradition and Continuity," 126–50.

[9] Awoonor, *Breast of the Earth*, 115.

[10] See Kofi Agovi, "The Poet's Politics in African Society," *Legon Journal of Humanities* 4 (1988): 3–9.

[11] Theo Vincent, *Seventeen Black and African Writers on Literature and Life* (Lagos: Centre for Black African Arts and Civilization / Cross Continent, 1980): 81.

[12] Kofi Anyidoho, "Oral Poetics and Traditions of Verbal Art in Africa" (doctoral dissertation, University of Texas at Austin, 1983): 99, 340.

Chapter 4, therefore, concentrates on the recovery of the oral dimension in Ghanaian poetry since the 1970s, a socioliterary phenomenon acknowledged by most critics: Jawa Apronti defines it as "the institutionalization of the poetry recital as a popular theatrical event."[13] In this kind of poetry, words and lines are a mere framework around which a composite ensemble gathers, made up of musical instruments, dance, acting, audience response and so on. Hopefully this chapter will maintain a balance between the oral features inherent in the texts and their actual readings / performances I have witnessed or read about.

Atukwei Okai and the resurgence of the voice

Atukwei Okai (b. 1941) is undoubtedly the poet who inspired this new trend, searching for the expression and transmission of a true African poetics. In the words of Charles Angmor, Okai's "art – his writing and public rendition – was a virtual revolution in the scene and brought Ghanaian poetry out from its sequestered quarters."[14] As Okai said to me in our interview,

> I came to the craft of my poetry in a very serious, fundamentally dedicated way. After a lot of research I realized that my people were not listening to the poetry written by Ghanaian authors, if read at all. That was because the latter were writing according to British models. (Okai, Accra, 22 November 1993)

He studied literature at the Gorky Institute in Moscow in the 1960s, the decade when the Beat Generation's fame was spreading all over the world. There, immersed in the renaissance of Russian poetry after decades of Stalinist gagging, he was able to experience a conception of poetry as a live event, much akin to the traditional medium he knew from his Ghanaian childhood. Back in Ghana, he started reading his poems in public and published his two major collections to date, *The Oath of the Fontomfrom* (1971) and *Lorgorligi Logarithms* (1974).[15] Okai is not sure whether a line can be traced between the ancestral and the Soviet influence:

> Basically we needed to change the formalistic mould within which poetry was created and composed, because we were fixed in the classic Western European mould. I broke

---

[13] Jawa Apronti, "Ghanaian Poetry in the 1970s," in *New West African Literature*, ed. Kolawole Ogungbesan (London: Heinemann, 1979): 31.

[14] Angmor, *Contemporary Literature in Ghana*, 163.

[15] Atukwei Okai, *The Oath of the Fontomfrom and other poems* (as "John Okai"; New York: Simon & Schuster, 1971); *Lorgorligi Logarithms and other poems* (Tema: Ghana Publishing Corporation, 1974). Page references are in the main text, preceded by OF and LL respectively.

> it by creating some poetry that has its roots in our experience. Its formalistic aspect comes from the African cultural heritage.
>
> The Soviet influence was a big contribution, too. You know that poetry is read aloud, there. It's a cultural tradition which is very beautiful, inspiring and popular; people fill a stadium to listen to poetry, even in cold winter. We, of the Gorky Literary Institute, were called from place to place, were invited for readings on TV and radio, in farms, factories, stadiums, everywhere. I had readings with authors like Yevtushenko.
>
> But we must say, I have my African origins. I was born in Accra, but I grew up in Northern Ghana for eight years. Ghana is replete with the cultural practice of drumming and dancing and singing and praise-singing. I enjoyed the works of Northern Ghana griots, and I had all this in mind when I went to Moscow. I remembered our own poetry, you know.
>
> Before I came back there were already readings at the Drama Studio, by poets such as Kofi Awoonor and Kwesi Brew, but with a completely different approach to recitation and sound. The real first literary evening happened in 1967, after my return from the Soviet Union. Brew and Awoonor were all there in the programme. I read six poems, including "Odododiodio Concerto," and from then on things could never be the same again: it was a new dawn, for our poetry. (Okai, Accra, 22 November 1993 and Legon, 19 August 1997)

After the twisted logic of the Cold War had compelled Okai to resume his studies in London (1968–71) because the new post-Nkrumah regime would not recognize his Soviet degree, the practice of poetry recitals eventually started spreading in the 1970s. As Okai said to Theo Vincent: "I went round to most of the schools reading my poetry to many, and we organised literary evenings in the main capitals, Accra and Kumasi. Then the Ghana Association of Writers came in and took it on a regular basis."[16] His poem "Lorgorligi Logarithms," for instance, was 'outdoored' at the Great Hall of the University of Ghana campus[17] and performed again at the Accra Community Centre.[18] Its namesake collection was outdoored at the Great Hall again in 1974;[19] all three events benefitted greatly from the organization and support of the Ghana Association of Writers. Okai has also attended countless international poetry festivals.

Nevertheless, trying to track down audio or video recordings of his recitals is a hopeless enterprise nowadays.[20] My present research has utilized mostly indirect

---

[16] Vincent, *Seventeen Black and African Writers*, 80.

[17] 25 February 1972, chaired by Jawa Apronti.

[18] 3 October 1972, "An evening with Efua Sutherland."

[19] Chaired by Nii Amon Kotei.

[20] In his book, Angmor mentions a film on Okai's stay in Britain (*Contemporary Literature in*

sources – Robert Fraser describes his recitals as "electrifying"[21] – and the poet's enthusiastic readings during our two interviews.

Witnessing one of Okai's public readings must certainly mean being overwhelmed by waves of words constantly bubbling with formal devices:

I
 lip
  your nose,
And the land lynches a
Rose –
I
 suck
  your stare,
And my bones are bombed all
Bare –
("Nocturnal Prelude," LL 103)

Okai's relationship with language has always been as acrobatic as in the lines quoted above, thanks to constant recourse to puns, neologisms, assonance, rhyme and, most of all, alliteration, the latter characterizing all his works since his very early poems, such as "Fugue for Waterfrogs":

A silence as silent as the silence
Of the tomb tears at my teeth,
Talks to me and tells me of termites
Taught to stand still at the touch
Of tottering tears tinted with toil.[22]

The listener's ear cannot help being tickled by such a wealth of sounds. The author clearly identifies his linguistic creativity with the search for a rhythm:

> Yes, I use alliteration, but it's not alliteration as such. What you have to talk about in my poetry is the very clear belief, understanding and practice that poetry is half music. In my mother language, Ga, the word 'poetry' means 'songspeech'. Once I was in a Secondary School, talking to students about my poetry because their exam contains one of my poems, "Rosimaya." So I told them that when you have poetry, you must read it aloud because it's music, and I told them that poetry didn't start on the written

---

Ghana, 165), but is unable to be more precise about its particulars; nor can Okai.

21 Fraser, *West African Poetry*, 325.

22 Atukwei Okai, "Fugue for Waterfrogs," *Okyeame* 4.2 (1969): 27. See also Okai, "Freedom Symphony," *Atlantic Monthly* (May 1969): 60; repr. in *African Voices*, ed. Howard Sergeant (London: Evans, 1973): 21 & *West Africa* (19 January 1987): 115.

page but through the mouth, the spoken word. I asked them to try to imagine and imitate how the Stone Age man would behave when he was angry, happy, or in love. Take the ending of "Rosimaya," for instance:

> "You foul
> my Fridays
> You starve
> my Saturdays
> And mess up
> my Mondays
> In the mud;
> You shun
> my Saturdays
> You maim
> my Mondays
> And heap heavy sorrow
> Onto my soul."
> (Okai, Accra, 22 November 1993; quotation from LL 111)

Some critics have objected to what they considered to be an excessive use of these techniques, on the grounds that the message sometimes ends up being submerged by such flamboyant aural effects. Jawa Apronti, in a generally balanced essay, complains that Okai over-indulges this trait, whereas K.K. Dei–Anang pushes judgement too far by defining some easily understandable lines as "mere verbiage": "Preserve my passions from the / pressures of pomposity / delay my homage to / the deities of the day."[23] Anyidoho recalls how the same criticism was levelled at Christopher Okigbo, but in his opinion the Nigerian poet managed to exercise greater control over his writing.[24] Surprisingly, Kofi Awoonor reached the stage of judging Okai's verse to be "screaming hysteria."[25]

This is one of the most debated points about his poetry, and one needing some clarifying analysis. When reading some of his lines, one may wonder whether something is hiding behind the pleasant sounds. Take this, for instance:

> Liberty rebels in an anarchist's
> Bell ... the hangman haughtily hangs
> in hell ... the cricket cries,

---

[23] Jawa Apronti, "John Atukwei Okai: the Growth of a Poet," *Universitas* 2.1 (October 1972): 121; K.K. Dei–Anang, "Discipline in the Making of Poetry," *Universitas* 2.1 (October 1972): 113.

[24] Kofi Anyidoho, "Atukwei Okai and His Poetic Territory," in *New West African Literature*, ed. Kolawole Ogungbesan (London: Heinemann, 1979): 49.

[25] Kofi Awoonor, "The Poem, the Poet, the Human Condition," *Asemka: A Bilingual Literary Journal of the University of Cape Coast* 5 (September 1979): 8.

crouches in a thicket, with a
temporary ping-pong ticket.
("Aayalolo Concerto," OF 110)

On the other hand, a balanced judgement must take into account two fundamental factors: Okai's penchant for surreal images; and, once again, the oral delivery of his lines. As far as the first point is concerned, the author explains his creative process very clearly in the long poem "Aayalolo Concerto":

The dream-reader in my veins

Deserts
The
Beanstalk
Of
Sense

For the tossing canoe of intuition.[...]
We sleep, but a center somewhere
Within us refuses to go to sleep .... (OF 109–10)

Okai's sporadic fusions of apparently unrelated images spring from an attempt to raid the innermost recesses of the human psyche, "to reflect the unconscious, inner working of human life and its relationship with the reality of life," as Angmor writes. The same critic sees Okai's "grotesque images [...] in the light of the twentieth century European artistic principle of surrealism,"[26] a comparison which seems to fit the two passages quoted above. In some instances, though, I consider the paradigm of magical realism to provide a more suitable interpretative approach. See, for example, the following lines, curiously devoid of Okai's usual oral effects:

Do not let us be too particular
About the color of goat or sheep
About
Someone's father or grandfather –
For if you dig and dig too deep
Your fingers may only end up
Among the very pale bones

Of your own grandmother –
For things have come to such
A pass
In this world that I'm not even

[26] Angmor, *Contemporary Literature in Ghana*, 165.

Sure
That it is not with someone's
Else's
Mouth I stand here talking.
("Aayalolo Concerto," OF 108)

Behind the final irony readers encounter parts of different bodies being exchanged, an image similar to the one culled from Kojo Laing's *Woman of the Aeroplanes*, mentioned in the previous chapter. Both writers, who are among the most representative writers in West African anglophone prose and poetry, tend to employ such images to deal with serious social or psychological topics, not as mere linguistic exercises. In this case, the obvious subject is the meeting of different cultures and races. In his introduction to *Lorgorligi Logarithms*, Amanor Dseagu combines the two interpretations: Okai is, and African poetry should be, "surrealist because that is how African poetics works" (LL viii). This is similar to the reason given by Laing himself for his own style: "Our own art is non-representational, isn't it?" (Laing, Accra, 15 December 1993).[27]

The second reason for his extreme fondness for sound-play concerns his public shows, where sound does play a central role:

> People would make a mistake in seeing only the sound, anyway, because I'm doing something with it, it carries the message. This is what I call 'total art': within the poem

[27] See also Chapter 3. Okai also applied this principle to his collection of verses for children, *The Anthill in the Sea* (1988). Most of its poems are structured on puns and rhymes, whereas about one-sixth of the collection also turns on such unrealistic images as "The teacup talks of the tall hawk, / The teacup talks, / The teacup talks. / The sea mocks all who like to walk, / The sea mocks all, / The sea mocks all. / Like pirate ships that cannot dock / Because the rainbow has lost her sock" ("The Peacock") and "I do want to go to sea / For all the fish I must see. / I do want to sting the bee / Like an anthill in the sea" ("I do want to go to sea"); Okai, *The Anthill in the Sea: Verses and Chants for Children* (Tema: Ghana Publishing Corporation, 1988): 18, 1.

In his review of the book, Enimil Ashon recognizes a philosophy based in the children's "world of make-believe in which everything is possible [... the style] refuses to accept a system that literally talks down to the children"; Ashon, "Atukwei Drops a Seed into Young Fertile Minds," *Weekly Spectator* (23 March 1989): 7. Even though Kofi Anyidoho's essay on the quality of Ghanaian children literature does not mention *The Anthill*, its focus seems appropriate, bringing to the fore again the concept of magical realism. Starting from Nancy Schmidt's observations on the importance of fantasy in children's literature lest their imagination might become frozen, "especially along the various boundaries adult rationality imposes on time and space," Anyidoho states that "if we are to keep the essential nature of the child, we must be wary of drawing hard boundaries between *fact* and *fantasy*," and later on theorizes a precept that perfectly becomes Okai's collection: "Our children's literature must seek to expand the child's horizons rather than make them shrink"; Anyidoho, "The Complex Simplicity of Children's Literature: A Reading of *Ghana Motion* and *The Brassman's Secret*," *Legon Journal of the Humanities* 6 (1992): 54–55.

> there is image, rhythm, sound, symbolism, all sorts of things. (Okai, Accra, 22 November 1993)

From a live audience's point of view, if compared to the public of readers, it cannot be so very important if shades of meaning are missed here and there. See, for instance, what this reviewer thinks about one of Okai's US readings sponsored by the University of Iowa International Writing Program on 1 February 1979:

> Listening to sound, rhythm, forgetting the sense for a minute, you can't sit still for the energy, each verse has a refrain like a good strong tune, that sense-less language lifts you, it's English like Dylan Thomas rumbling Welsh & alliteration but with Africa beneath it all.[28]

Okai's verse can be linked with music in many senses. In the following bitter reflections on the fate of the downtrodden, for instance, it is not hard to imagine that the short lines should be read as a percussive, repetitive rhythm:

> Now I am going to start walking–
> Come hell!
> Now I am going to stop crawling–
> Come hell!
> How long should I go on starving–
> No well
> Around here and I am thirsting–
> Go tell
> It upstairs where they are feasting–
> Go tell
> That here downstairs I'm rising–
> Go tell! ("Walewale Chorus," OF 29)

In the title poem of his first collection, "The Oath of the Fontomfrom," the Ghanaian talking drums are described as the soul of the people, ever ready to incite reaction in times of crisis:

> My brothers,
>   my people,
>   my brothers,
> I am sought,
>   I am sought because
> When you want to starve
>   the ocean,

[28] Jeanne Finley & Cynde Gregory, "Okai Mixes Africanisms with Street Lingo in Skidmore Reading," *Kite* (14 February 1979): 4.

You paralyze
its source,
the river. (OF 17)

Formally, the Fontomfrom performs his call through lines where the accents follow regular patterns, just like a repeated beat:

The Fontomfrom keeps on
Wailing
and weeping
and wailing!
The Fontomfrom
keeps on
Booming
and moaning
and booming! (OF 15)

The form of the poem, therefore, is in perfect accord with the expression of its content. This is why to many critics Okai has rightly become synonymous with 'the drum poet'. Angmor writes that "From the indigenous drum culture has come much of his explosive and rumbling sound effects,"[29] while Femi Osofisan asserts that

> Okai was the first to try to take African poetry back to one of its primal origins in percussion, by deliberately violating the syntax and lexicon of English, creating his own rhythm through startling phonetic innovations.[30]

Okai himself recalls how, in that first poetry reading in 1967 mentioned earlier, his "Odododiodio Concerto" was accompanied by the drumbeat of Saka Acquaye, an all-rounder of Ghanaian arts (who will appear again in Chapter 6 below).

It is thus not surprising that the deepest critical analyses of his poetry seem based on the rhythmic nature of such formal devices, not to speak of the syncopation between lyrics and accompanying instruments as a fundamental tenet of oral poetry.[31]

---

[29] Angmor, *Contemporary Literature in Ghana*, 175–76.

[30] Osofisan, "Warriors of a Failed Utopia?," 18. Okai's search for a distinctive African poetics through drum rhythms has been compared to the works of the Caribbean poet Kamau Brathwaite, who lived in Ghana for about eight years. Brathwaite echoes Okai's words when trying to develop theoretically his concept of 'nation language' in West Indian poetry, affirming that it is also based on sound: "if you ignore the noise, [...] then you lose part of the meaning"; Edward Kamau Brathwaite, *History of the Voice: The Development of Nation Language in Anglophone Caribbean Poetry* (London & Port of Spain: New Beacon, 1984): 17.

[31] See Fraser, *West African Poetry*, 325–30, where musical scores are used to interpret Okai's and Anyidoho's poems. See also J. Bekunuru Kubayanda, "Polyrhythmics and African Print Poetics:

In other cases, the connections between his poems and music are even more evident, ranging from the frequent use of musical terms in the titles[32] and of refrains, to the singing of parts of the poems themselves, as I was able to witness when he read and sang "Dreamdom Communique to Valerieville" (LL 120–29) during our second interview.

However, Okai's poetry is not limited to its formal innovations. Social matters always reside at its core,[33] as he writes in "Aayalolo Concerto":

> Reality is responsible for my subconscious ....
> your songs are responsible for my dreams .... (OF 75)

In another poem, "Adikanfo," he complains:

> the quantum physics of existential
> inequality
>
> sweeps my soul's hamlet with the hammer
> of hunger
>
> rake my granaries of reason with the
> cudgel of poverty. (LL 13)

When asked about this, Okai considered it a general phenomenon in African arts:

> Well, I thought poets were living in human society. The West has come this far that it can afford to play games with everything, but in Africa everything has a role to play. An African painter is always throwing stones at something, even when he paints a flower. Here, where we are so beleaguered, every artist must echo, to some extent, the realest essence of our reality. (Okai, Accra, 22 November 1993)

K.K. Dei–Anang wrongly denies any content-value to Okai's poetry, generalizing some of their sporadic traits:

> the printed page never reveals the treasure of sheer theatricality inevitably fossilised by printing, and no amount of reading will give this "poem" life. You ought to have *seen* John Okai, and, one thinks with some anxiety, John Okai alone, reading it. And when he has finished, the poem fails this simple test: Ask any listener what John Okai *said*.[34]

Guillén, Césaire and Atukwei Okai," in *Interdisciplinary Dimensions of African Literature*, ed. Kofi Anyidoho et al. (Washington DC: Three Continents, 1985): 162; Isidore Okpewho, "African Poetry: The Modern Writer and the Oral Tradition," *African Literature Today* 16 (1988): 19.

[32] See Angmor, *Contemporary Literature in Ghana*, 166.

[33] Okai is socially and politically engaged in several ways. Among other things, he is the founder and Secretary-General of the Pan-African Writers' Association.

[34] Dei–Anang, "Discipline," 107.

Such unjustly harsh criticism, verging on the unnecessarily acrimonious, does precious little justice to Okai's talent and to his engagement with society. In his long poem in twenty-one movements, "Aayalolo Concerto" (OF 67–123), one of the main points is the need for the nurturing of ancestral values as a necessary means of overcoming the contemporary crisis. The following lines, for instance, seem to affirm a belief in a cyclical concept of time, and function as one of the refrains for the whole poem:

> The world is too round for me
> To know where to stop for breath;
> Life still progresses in a spiral–
> We shall meet here once again,
> Along these walks of the squirrel,
> Along this free home of the grain. (OF 90–91 et al)

Further fundamental topics of his poems are love, nature and religious feelings, which fuse in these lines:

> I seek a seven-seas multi-seasonal visa
> into the totemic territories of your tenderness
> into the joy jungles of your warmth.
> ("Dreamdom Communique to Valerieville," LL 124)

The poet's deeply religious conscience inevitably connects with his conception of himself – and of poets in general – as performers of a role which is close to that of the ancestral bard or *griot*, receptacle of collective values and beliefs:

> I, Oshamraku Atukwei, standing
>   before your shrine declare
>   myself by appointment the
>   organ-grinder to god and man.
> ("Aayalolo Concerto," OF 75)

Although the matters in question tend to reveal a certain gravity, Okai does not always allow seriousness to predominate in the mood in his compositions. His biting sense of humour, in my view, is a characteristic he shares with very few of the Ghanaian poets studied in this chapter. The following lines contain both a case in point and the theorization of its value:

> Next time I see you sitting upon
> One of the fruit trees in the garden,
> I shall twist your neck Full stop.
> No comma, no colon, no semicolon–
> I shall twist your neck. Full stop.

> a man that sleeps and laughs in his sleep
> carries a soul that shall refuse to creep ....
> ("Aayalolo Concerto," OF 109).

Another feature of his poems is their polyglot constitution. Against a background of English, the linguistic sources of Okai's lines are diverse, including Ghanaian and African languages, Russian and Arabic. Once again, a comparison with Kojo Laing is inevitable, given the similar linguistic tendency of the two authors and the way they can both create literature by mixing different tongues.[35] About Okai, too, one wonders whether it is a matter of Ghanaian environment, personal experience (as Okai's biodata might suggest) or personal talent, but the author would rather concentrate on the conscious effort behind it:

> There is an ideological and aesthetic underpinning to that. First of all those words are beautiful, powerful, just the way they should be used. You see, I could have said 'zig-zag', but 'lorgorligi' is native [Ga], beautiful and carries the meaning at the same time. (Okai, Accra, 22 November 1993)

Could one blame him, after all? Could "lorgorligi logarithms" be replaced by "zig-zag logarithms," or "I'm a shapkaless soul in Siberia" ("Aayalolo Concerto," OF 70) by "I'm a hatless soul in Siberia"? The idea of poetry as primarily sound resurfaces:

> So the challenge lies in the ability to find these two similarly different things and bring them together to form a new whole. It is the artist's task to find the materials, just like the architect's.
>
> Then, the ideological. It is a way to promote tolerance, too. With the use of African languages, I'm trying to show my people that you can be born in one room of the house but you use all the rooms, you can be born in one so-called ethnic group but you embrace all the cultures. (Okai, Accra, 22 November 1993)

Okai's polyglot propensity reaches its pitch in the poem "Chain Gang – Soul Autopsy" (LL 63–81), concerning the death in exile of Ghana's first president Kwame Nkrumah.[36] Perhaps it was the best way to describe Nkrumah's pan-African ideals:

---

[35] See Chapters 2, 3 and 5.

[36] After being ousted in the 1966 coup, Nkrumah lived in Guinea and later died in Rumania in April 1972. The second civilian president, Kofi A. Busia (1969–1972), one of the political opponents formerly persecuted by Nkrumah, created much debate around his "refusal to allow the ailing Nkrumah to return home to die." The next government, led by I.K. Acheampong and parading a return to Nkrumahism and social justice after Busia's "neo-colonial sell out," "ordered the return of his body to Ghana and awarded him a full state funeral in Accra"; Shillington, *Ghana*, 18–20.

> You are right, not just to describe, but to symbolize. The things used to carry the symbol also have an aesthetic function, a so-called 'multi-dimensional functionalism'. That poem could reach all the people in Ghana, because all its various languages were employed. When Nkrumah's body was returned from Guinea, I read the poem on TV: I understand some women were weeping, and I don't think they could speak or understand English. (Okai, Accra, 22 November 1993)

The title poem of Okai's second collection, "Lorgorligi Logarithms" (LL 10–52), also evokes several pan-African figures. Nkrumah's pan-African orientation has profoundly marked Ghanaian culture,[37] as the other poets examined in this chapter – notably Anyidoho and Acquah – will show. The value of Nkrumahist ideals can be felt quite easily today. What went wrong with his regime, then?

> His ideas are alive here, but also beyond Ghana, and into all Africa they are being vindicated. Day in, day out, events show how prophetic, how right, how crucial, how urgent his message was. It is clear that African countries can never really and sensibly survive in the 21st century on their own, as they are doing now – it is the nature of world economy. To have the strength to play ball with this harsh market reality, you must be one single force, a global African community that could prevent all these evil wars from happening at all.
>
> It's true, people were happy when he was overthrown. All great leaderships in human history have their shortcomings, being made of human beings. But now people are understanding, because what you see here now is Nkrumah. Me, and all the educated people you see, are the products of his free and composite educational policy. (Okai, Accra, 22 November 1993)

He is referring to Kwame Nkrumah's efforts to eradicate illiteracy in Ghana. When Nkrumah came back from England in 1947 only twn percent of his fellow countrymen could read, and this was certainly the most effective excuse for the colonial power to maintain its presence. Nkrumah realized that education was a necessary step towards the formation of collective political awareness, and established week-end schools all over the country, along with a National College and a National Education Movement.[38] After independence, he strove to make all education free with a mass literacy campaign that made Ghana the most literate nation in Africa.[39] This process, together with his policy of revaluing traditional cultures as part of a general

---

[37] See Shillington, *Ghana*, 4–5.

[38] See C.L.R. James, *Nkrumah and the Ghana Revolution* (London: Allison & Busby, 1977): 48, 51, 81, 88.

[39] See Kofi Buenor Hadjor, *Nkrumah and Ghana: The Dilemma of Postcolonial Power* (London & New York: Kegan Paul International, 1988): 76; Shillington, *Ghana*, 6.

emphasis on self-reliance and on the concept of African personality,[40] might account for the 'national spirit' in Ghanaian arts pointed out by Fraser.[41] Okai, Anyidoho and Acquah more or less agree on this, whereas Kojo Kyei argues that all of the merit is to be ascribed to the strength of traditional cultures. The critic and poet Kofi Agovi opts for a more convincing middle way:

> This situation is a consequence of both our traditions and of Nkrumah's ideals; after all it's human beings who create – and perpetuate – culture.
>
> It is true, people were happy when Nkrumah was overthrown, but that was because we had never experienced a situation like that, a national independent regime like the one he ran, and his state was based on a continental as well as a world racial nationalism. And when you have never had such an experience, it's difficult to make a judgement about a situation. Before that, Africans were not even considered human beings, you know. If he hadn't been revalued, it wouldn't have been possible for his tradition to continue.
>
> The nation state transcends Nkrumah, but his merits are great. All these people you're meeting, writers and scholars, they all got an education thanks to him, they all came from villages benefiting from the sense of direction of the founder of Ghana. To that extent I am very much committed to Nkrumah. Look at the so-called tribalism, too: it doesn't really happen here in Ghana, also because of Nkrumah's policy. (Agovi, Legon, 18 December 1993)

There are still two facets of Okai's art that have usually been overlooked or ignored by most critics. His fascinating public recitals and his tendency to play with sounds

---

[40] See David Birmingham, *Kwame Nkrumah* (London: Cardinal, 1990): 113.

[41] On the other hand, he seems to have employed traditional structures to support his own power; he had himself called "Osagyefo" ('Saviour-at War') instead of "President," and employed an *okyeame* from a royal court, Boafo Akuffo, whose task was to preface his speeches with an appellation performance always suiting the topic of the day. As Kwesi Yankah writes in his two compelling essays, Nkrumah used ancestral channels to strengthen his charisma over the people; Yankah, "The Making and Breaking of Kwame Nkrumah: The Role of Oral Poetry," in *African Literature in Its Social and Political Dimensions*, ed. Eileen Julien et al. (Annual Selected Papers of the ALA; Washington DC: African Literature Association / Three Continents, 1986): 15–17; Yankah, "Creativity and Traditional Rhetoric: Nkrumah's Personal Poet and His Son," in *Literature and National Consciousness*, ed. Ernest N. Emenyonu (Calabar Studies in African Literature 4; Ibadan: Heinemann Educational, 1989): 78–84. Oral poets, though, can change from mythmaking to mythbreaking, when myths are in conflict with collective goals; Kofi Anyidoho, "Mythmaker and Mythbreaker: The Oral Poet as Earwitness," in Julien et al., ed. *African Literature in its Social and Political Dimensions*, 7. Nkrumah's linguist is no exception, since the attributes he applies to the leader's ruthless home policy only augment the fear he has already instilled; as Yankah writes, praise poetry can be a "double-pronged tool"; Yankah, "Making and Breaking," 18.

have, in a way, been stereotypically identified with the whole of his poetry, regardless of its less conspicuous traits and of his artistic development.

First, Okai is capable of creating stunning images without the help of too many formal resources:

> Dawn is a tightrope walker
> Sunset is a greedy fire-eater.
> ("Aayalolo Concerto," OF 69)

> with the politeness of a sunrise I knock
> upon your door.
> ("Lorgorligi Logarithms," LL 29)

> But the truth
> Is now like the rain;
> He who sees not,
> Feels it on his skin.
> ("Rosimaya," LL 110)

Secondly, a stereotypical treatment of Okai's poems implies the risk of depicting him as a frozen artist, as if his first publication *Flowerfall* (1969) and his most recent unpublished or uncollected poems bore the same qualities.

The end of "Aayalolo Concerto" carries a repeated sentence, "the line is not straight" (OF 123), anticipating the title of his next collection, *Lorgorligi Logarithms*. When compared to "Aayalolo," the main theme of "Lorgorligi Logarithms" is more easily identifiable, and easier to follow: an exhortation to react in the face of world injustices, exemplified by seventeen-year-old Seth Solomon Asare Bonsu, who died in 1971 of a heart disease which could not be cured in Ghanaian hospitals. In the first two movements of the poem, the figure of Asare functions as a point of reference for the reader, then the focus shifts slowly to other related topics, starting with the author's misfortunes due to the Cold War.

The Accra area of Nima is taken again as an instance of squalor and injustice,[42] linked with other recurrent themes of the poem – the loss of traditional values, the mimicking of Western culture:

> my motherland's nose, TAFLATSE[43], is running
>
> etcetera

[42] On Nima's recurrent presence in Ghanaian literature, see also Awoonor's *This Earth, My Brother* and ben Abdallah's *Land of a Million Magicians*.

[43] An apology in both Ga and Ewe.

and god where are you, etcetera
our tap-root TAFLATSE is all rotten
and all we do is follow TAFLATSE any fool. (LL 24)

In the end, after some compelling digressions on, among other subjects, American society and the rape of Africa perpetuated by apartheid, there is a reaffirmation of faith in both popular revolution (probably akin to populism at some points) and Ghanaian religion:

though our dialectic has been arrested
and frozen in mid-season
yet the algebra of the revolution
is being worked out ....
[...]
le peuple, oui! the masses, yes!

and god bless the 77 gods of cape coast
and long live the 77 gods of ghana

hallelujah!
hallelujah! (LL 51–52)

Each movement of "Lorgorligi Logarithms" opens with the invocation of a series of pan-African personalities, who should supposedly work as inspirational models for African resurgence. The second one, "Taflatse," goes:

raphael armattoe, ARE YOU THERE?!
antoine guillaume amo, WHERE ARE YOU?!
willie abraham, ARE YOU THERE?!

NANAMUMPUO, GRANT US THE SPIRIT ....
PATRICE LUMUMBA, GRANT US THE
SPIRIT ....

kakalika kakunankakai dr. malan
– EWOE MEWO NE!
ataa ayitey tutankhamen
– WE ARE COMING!
asafoatsenkpa of bukom square
– OOBOTOI?! (LL 21)[44]

[44] Armattoe: Ghanaian scientist; Amo and Abrahams: Ghanaian philosophers; *Nanamumpuo*: ancient grove in the Fanti area where leaders were buried; *kakalika*: cockroach (Ga); *kukunan-kakai*: all and sundry (Ga); Malan: South African Prime Minister of Apartheid; *ewoe mewo ne*!: I'm talking to you! (Ewe); *ataa*: breadwinner (Ga); *ayitey*: first son of Ayi (Ga); *asafoatsenkpa*:

Just like "Chain Gang – Soul Autopsy," included in the same book, the linguistic medley evidently mirrors a political orientation. On the other hand, the passage above also exemplifies a feature of Okai's poetry from this collection on: the tendency to include in his lines long series of world personalities, mostly pan-African. At times, one has the feeling that this helps neither the understanding nor the enjoyment of the poem, even though Fraser connects it with the traditional practice of pouring libations.[45] Too many notes are needed to lift the veil of the readers' ignorance about history. To give Okai his due, his notes in the appendix are exhaustive; but doesn't this hinder the flow of reading? When it comes to linguistic obscurities, at least one can still appreciate the way they sound: there is, after all, no need for notes to follow the phonetic patterns of "kakalika kakunankakai" on a page or from a stage. It seems clear that Okai considers his didactic purposes to be more important than anything else, but if exaggerated this can work to the detriment of its poetic effectiveness. Besides, grappling with the topic of pan-Africanism in this way seems a little too easy.

Unfortunately, this propensity for cataloguing persists in some of the later poems, and was also meant to be the pivotal concept behind his collection *Rhododendrons in Donkeydom* (often announced as forthcoming but never actually published), as he said when asked if he considered the beautyful ones as already born:

> Well, Armah was talking about the correct political leadership, whereas I was talking about the flowers of humanity, saying that very often they end in kingdoms of donkeys. When you check out the lives of great men like saints, discoverers, social revolutionaries, those who want to change society for the better, they do suffer a lot. (Okai, Accra, 22 November 1993)

One 'rhododendron' often mentioned by Okai is Joern Utzon,[46] the much-discussed architect of the Sydney Opera House. In "Sakumo Concerto" (1980), one of the few published parts of the planned collection, the poet deploys all his gifts for language to describe Utzon's creative genius in the first person:

> 'I am that I am
> I am your omar khayam
> and I come as I am
>
> into your chameleonic zone
> of cosmic chromosomes ....

supreme commander (Ga); *oobotoi*?: are you listening? (Ga).

[45] Fraser, *West African Poetry*, 328.

[46] Utzon reappears in Okai's "In the Stool Room of the Soul: A Concerto for the Black Satellites," *Weekly Spectator* (1 May 1993): 5.

> I zoom
> on the imagination's
> kangarooyan
> ozone!'

But the list of fellow geniuses that follows adds little attractive power to the poem:

> pharaoh tutankhamen's gold funeral mask,
> bennelong point taking a drink at the harbour,
> adja gorback's paintings and sculptures
> in the oxford fields at wheatley.[47]

The same patchy result could be regarded as characterizing "Watu Wazuri" (1986), another part of the collection, which opens with an astonishing image:

> When all the blue is gone
> out of the sky
> and the remaining hue is nothing
> to fly a kite by,

but closes with a rhetorical, barricadero tone and the sentence "Rhododendrons in donkeydom."[48] Another tendency developed in his most recent production is the elegiac, thanks to three compositions written as tributes to deceased persons.[49]

All in all, from *Lorgorligi Logarithms* on, Okai appears to have placed a limit on his ebullient linguistic somersaults. His "All the Suicides in Heaven," for instance, combines his mastery of language with a touchingly introspective mood. The sad feeling of loneliness in London is described thus:

> Suddenly for a second, I think of all the suicides
> In heaven,
> Of all the bodies at the bottom of the sea.
> London
> Is alive and well and living in winter
> Young couples huddle together. They come and go.
> Like lovers, fulfilled and spent after loving,

---

[47] Okai, "Sakumo Concerto," *Callaloo* 3.1–3 (February–October 1980): 140, 144.

[48] Okai, "Watu Wazuri," *West Africa* (15 December 1986): 2612. Unfortunately, the historical and geographical enumerations can be detected again in "Mandela the Spear," *West Africa* (26 March–1 April 1990): 495, and in "The Rosetta Stone in the Meantime of Eternity," *Ghana Association of Writers Commemorative Brochure* (23 November 1991): 42–45.

[49] Atukwei Okai, "A Pharaonic Fandango for Ataa Odartey Lamptey," unspecified newspaper (15 June 1996): 18; "The Calabash Elegy for Lady Victoria Opoku–Ware" and "To the Chlorophyll of Hope: An Elegy for Ayikaikai (Mrs. Regina Ayikaikai Annan)," undated typescripts.

Autumn leaves lies around; I see no sign of snow.[50]

Another interesting work is "Fanfare for Oduduwa" (1981), intended as part of *Rhododendrons in Donkeydom*, where Okai pays homage to Yoruba culture by adding Yoruba to the list of languages he has been employing in his poetry, and by describing the act of creation by the divinity Oduduwa as a sexual encounter generating life:

Oduduwa's desire
Detonates
The ocean
And the water-world is a woman.[51]

The last poem worth mentioning is "And Now to End the World News: Agegeyan Gethsemane" (1980), where the dreadful living conditions of Ghana at the end of the 1970s are depicted with straightforward and realistic images such as

I SEE
the peasant farmer lose his family farm
to the octopus-tentacled
seedy cedi-soiled city creditor.

alternating with cries of desperate irony:

just what, please,
is the correct revised address
of God?

In the same spirit, section IX of the poem lists actual historical news alongside grotesque items:

And now to end the world news,
here are the main points again:

1971 – Ghana has expelled all
aliens; it is reported that
most of them were from
neighbouring Nigeria.[52]

---

[50] Atukwei Okai, "All the Suicides in Heaven," undated typescript.

[51] Atukwei Okai, "Fanfare for Oduduwa," *Pacific Quarterly Moana* (special issue on "African Writing Today," ed. Peter Nazareth) 6.3–4 (July–October 1981): 39.

[52] Reference to Busia's government's "Aliens Compliance Order which expelled from the country, without right of appeal, those not born in Ghana, apart from a few selected individuals such as foreign businessmen [...] over one million Africans were expelled to the neighbouring countries"; Shillington, *Ghana*, 18.

1972 – It has been announced
that the Ministry
of Air of Ghana has directed
that with immediate effect
people whose income is
below 400 cedis a month
should use cotton wool
to block one of the nostrils
to help the conservation of air
which is in short supply.[53]

<>

Atukwei Okai's pioneering efforts have resulted in the emergence of the poetry recital as a mainstream medium of artistic communication. The literary journal *Growth* wrote in 1973 that:

> The Ghana Writers' Association organised an evening of Poetry at the Arts Centre, Accra, in honour of a fellow writer, Mustapher from Nigeria. It was one of many writers' evenings organised during the year by the association to either introduce visiting writers or to get to the public new works by the members of the association.

and, in the same issue:

> KUMASI – THE 12TH ANNUAL NATIONAL FESTIVAL OF ARTS organised in collaboration with the Ashanti Cultural Centre, Kumasi, took place in Kumasi between Aug 25 and Sept 7, 1973. The two-week long festival featured groups representing the various fields of theatrical entertainment, namely, Drama, Music, Drumming, and Dancing and Poetry Recitals. Performing groups were from the nine regions of Ghana. The Festival of Arts is an annual event.[54]

In the following decade, written poetry on stage developed more complex theatrical forms. The Ghanaian poets who worked mostly in this field are Kofi Anyidoho and Kobena Eyi Acquah.

---

[53] Atukwei Okai, "And Now to End the World News: Agegeyan Gethsemane," typescript, 1980.

[54] *Growth: Literary Magazine for Young Writers* (Accra: Arts Council of Ghana / Young Africans Writers' Club) 3 (September 1973): 77, 78.

Kofi Anyidoho and his contemporary dirges

Kofi Anyidoho (b. 1947) comes from Wheta, a town in the Volta Region of Ghana inhabited by the Ewe people. His origins clearly affect both his poetic and his critical works. Anyidoho, in fact, grew up in a family of cantors: his mother and two of his uncles were practising poets.[55] He also happens to be related to Kofi Awoonor, the poet who re-created in English the mood of Ewe dirges. In Anyidoho's poems, the elegiac atmosphere of Ewe funeral dirges is pervasive, and Awoonor himself seems to be aware of this: "It's like Kofi Anyidoho is the one who is taking over from me."[56] Compared to Okai's polyglot outburst, Anyidoho's sources of inspiration appear more monoethnic.[57]

His ethnic oral literature background[58] is the first influence one finds at work in his earlier collection *Brain Surgery*, written in the early 1970s, winner of the Valco Fund Literary Award for Poetry in 1976, but published only later in *Earthchild with Brain Surgery* (1985).[59] The first poem of the collection, "My Song," is described in a footnote by the author as "in part a translation of, and in part an elaboration on, an original Ewe song by one of the poet cantors of the Haikotu Drum of my birthplace, Wheta." The singing voice – "a typical figure from the Ewe song of sorrow"[60] – laments his torn clothes and those of his fellow dispossessed, while his lyrics are densely proverbial:

> I sell My Song for those with ears to buy
> It is to a tree that a bull is tied
> You do not bypass the palm's branches
> to tap its wine. (EC 47)

---

[55] See A.N. Mensah, "Kofi Anyidoho," *Dictionary of Literary Biography* 157: *Twentieth Century Caribbean and Black African Writers, Third Series*, ed. Lindfors & Sander (Detroit MI: Bruccoli Clark Layman / Gale, 1996): 5. In 1997 Anyidoho told me that a CD and audiotape of Ewe songs and poems by his mother and him would be released soon, followed by two collections of poems in Ewe.

[56] Jane Wilkinson, "Kofi Anyidoho: An Ewe Poet between Tradition and Change," *Africa* (Rome: Bulzoni) 43 (December 1988): 30.

[57] See Fraser, *West African Poetry*, 333.

[58] Jane Wilkinson ("Kofi Anyidoho," passim) offers an analysis of Anyidoho's poetry and of its connections with Ewe culture.

[59] Page references to Anyidoho's collections are in the main text, preceded by HD for *A Harvest of our Dreams with Elegy for the Revolution* (1984; London: Heinemann; Accra: Woeli, 1985), EC for *Earthchild with Brain Surgery* (Accra: Woeli, 1985), and AC for *AncestralLogic and CaribbeanBlues* (Trenton NJ: Africa World Press, 1993).

[60] A.N. Mensah, "Kofi Anyidoho," 7.

Anyidoho enriches his English rendition with repeated assonances in "I," "My," "buy," "tied," "bypass" and "wine," in part re-invoking the phonetic resonances the original version must contain.

Brain Surgery shows the limits of a young creative spirit still striving to attain full control of his craft. By and large, though, the poem just quoted displays most of the main features of Anyidoho's poetry in embryo: oral roots, social commitment, controlled sound effects which are never pushed to their furthest extremes as Okai's sometimes are, the ability to build compelling lines on well-hewn imagery that is often precisely symbolic and therefore easy to capture in its main thread of thought. In "A Dirge for Christmas" Anyidoho sees the impossibility, for voices like his, of not confronting the ills of his people:

> With
>   these blood-shot eyes what do we see in flowers
>   but the succulence of our crops sucked by the Sun
>   even while we starve to build our barns? (EC 62)

Some poems from *Brain Surgery* reveal that Anyidoho was already envisaging the stage representations that will occur in later years. In two poems there is a presence of multiple voices requiring theatrical representation of the lines. The long poem "In the High Court of Cosmic Justice" has a Chorus introducing a High Priest who invokes various West African deities:

> The voice you hear is mine
> but the words are not my own
> I am but a child with an egglike mind
> too brittle to grapple with
> slippery truths of Earth and Death and Life. (EC 77)

Therefore he only calls seven witnesses to testify in favour of or against the burial of Kwame Nkrumah in his native land. This involvement in specific Ghanaian political issue will be a constant trait of Anyidoho's poetry; as does Okai, the author highlights Nkrumah's achievements, rather than condemning him outright for his undeniable mistakes.[61] Since each witness represents a different social, age or gender group of Ghanaian society, different characters are certainly needed to transpose this poem onto the stage, in order to transform a poetic divine trial into a play in verse.

The same could be said about "Agbayiza," where the poet alternates what "they" did with what he and Agbayiza should do:

[61] Nkrumah did not display much tolerance for his political opponents: according to Shillington, his fatal mistake was the move to the one-party state in 1964 (*Ghana*, 11–13).

They who went before
There they come
with bloodshot eyes

... *Let us unpack our things* ....

They sold their farms
and went away
to fight for higher things

... *And guard our land* .... (EC 50–51)

When only one voice is declaiming, musical instruments can be inserted, as in "The Inevitable":

Tin ... gon ... gon ... gon ... tin ... gon ...
My enemy-friends   I call you
Tin ... gon ... gon ... gon ... tin ... gon ...
The reverend keepers of the oracles   I call you
Tin ... gon ... gon ... gon ... tin ... gon ...
Dying members of the ancient Asafo company   I call you
Tin ... gon ... gon ... gon ... tin ... gon ...
The venerable Omankrado
and his conclave of mystic makers   I call you. (EC 69)[62]

Since his very poetical beginnings, Anyidoho has shown where his major aesthetic preoccupations lie – in the transformation of the printed word into performed poetry. In his doctoral study, when writing about Ewe oral literature and the activities of the many musical-poetic clubs, he underlines the idea that "the talent of the individual poet–cantor achieves full realization only in the communal participation of the ensemble of singers, drummers, dancers and their audience." Such a formal frame implies an obvious ideological stance, being based "on the intricate patterns of interdependence between the individual creative talent and the communal ethos of Ewe artistic tradition."[63] As a consequence, he recognizes the potential power of oral literature over its audience when compared to the sterile seclusion of the printed word.

In the two collections that followed, the poet increasingly masters his craft and continues this process of modernizing the social role of the oral cantor to lament the wounds dealt to the society he lives in. This is the quality he sees in oral literature, too: "a great deal of the vitality of oral literature in performance," he writes, "is due

---

[62] Here the instrument is the *gankogui*, the double hand-bell that often functions as the main rhythmic regulator in oral performances; see Anyidoho, "Oral Poetics," 312.

[63] Anyidoho, "Oral Poetics," 232.

to its ability to update the past, to make the past alive and relevant to the present, and its ability to project the present into the future."[64] His greatest gift as a poet resides precisely in his ability to bend his people's traditional poetry to the needs of current affairs, extending the genre "into a field of political commentary not previously undertaken."[65]

Elegy for the Revolution, published first on its own in 1977 and later with *A Harvest of Our Dreams* (1984), centres on a very specific historical theme: the disillusionment over the military administration of General I.K. Acheampong, which lasted from 1972 to 1979 and brought the country to its knees; the same period that is setting for Kojo Laing's *Search Sweet Country*.[66] During our interview, Anyidoho described this disillusionment as wide-reaching, touching more than one period of Ghanaian history:

> In those poems I was talking about the military coup against Nkrumah: the people involved in that claimed they were engaged in a revolution. That gave way to the civilian regime that was also overthrown, the Busia one. The second military rule also claimed it was a revolution, but personally I didn't think it was a real one. (Anyidoho, Legon, 19 November 1993)

"Long leave the revolution," in this connection, is a significant statement by the author ("Radio Revolution," HD 65).

In the following lines from "Ghosts," Anyidoho, while lamenting the whole situation, demonstrates increased ease with the subtleties of language:

> watch revolution of worlds
> load guts of goats with power of
> bulls, the fools we were
> we would seek refuge on wings of their visions
> deserting the dream we placed among the thorns. (HD 68)

---

[64] Anyidoho, "Mythmaker and Mythbreaker," 5.

[65] Fraser, *West African Poetry*, 9.

[66] See Chapter 2. After all, Anyidoho grew up in the midst of Ghanaian politics: his literary beginnings were fostered by the Creative Writing Programme sponsored by the Ministry of Education in the 1960s (see Wilkinson, *Talking with African Writers*, 8). Regarding this mood of disillusionment, A.N. Mensah writes: "It was fashionable initially for young and radical Ghanaians to see the Acheampong government as representing a revolutionary and populist dispensation that contrasted to the supposedly pro-Western and élitist regime it had overthrown" (Mensah, "Kofi Anyidoho," 5). Angmor recounts that "with his colleagues, he [Anyidoho] supported and participated in the development projects of the era of the National Redemption Council, such as the Dawhenya Irrigation Project, voluntary work camp projects, and the projects of the international Operation Crossroads"; Angmor, *Contemporary Literature in Ghana*, 177.

Yet the same poem ends with an excessively rhetorical tone that sometimes still surfaces in *Elegy*:

> My voice my voice they seek after my voice!
> Do not put to sleep my people. (HD 69)

The unfortunate political failure is paralleled by a longing for a lost organic community that, apparently, cannot possibly be recovered in its fullness, and that is often represented through agricultural and natural images. This desired ancestral spirituality is sometimes symbolized by lands of passage, images like "milky way," "twilight zone" or the shore, which he shares with Awoonor, both of them being from the Ewe coastal area:

> I would rebuild our laughter
> with echoes of the past
> sleep at noon on remembered shores
> dream of
> doves perched on clouds across your milky-way.

In the same poem the image of the mermaid, pivotal to Awoonor's novel *This Earth, My Brother*,[67] is the carrier of that very hope:

> The dolphins came riding the waves
> a mermaid on their shoulders
> She was casting your name upon the seas
> whispering your laughter to the winds
> They sat in the sand
> purged my heart with a dirge, gave me
> a piece of hope.
> ("A Piece of Hope," HD 87)

Anyidoho, though, was adamant in insisting that these realities are still enjoying a full existence:

> I believe that you are right, but it's not that I long for these things in a kind of nostalgic way. Those remain the basic realities of large numbers of population in this and in many other countries. Those who are entrusted to run them often tend to lose sight of that, to not recognize them well enough. It is not a simple question of nostalgia for something imaginary, or long gone. Many of our people have a deeply spiritual life without denying themselves the need for material prosperity. (Anyidoho, Legon, 19 November 1993)

---

[67] See Chapter 1 (pp. 23–24).

In his next collection, *A Harvest of Our Dreams* (1984), such mood and images are still predominant:

> Somehow we know the carnival days
> cannot be gone too soon
> We may gather again those
> unfinished harvests of our soul.
> ("A Harvest of Our Dreams," HD 7)

This collection betokens the author's intensified use of a precise and recurrent system of symbols that will continue in his later works: the Panther represents Acheampong's clique, colonialists are "moonchildren"[68] or, in his latest *AncestralLogic*, associated with the polar bear,[69] and traditional society is often described as a beehive.[70] The last image bears autobiographical origins. In his doctoral dissertation, when explaining the varieties and uses of Ewe praise-names, he mentions his family's name as well: "Anyidoho, menya tatam o: Bees have formed a hive; it is not easy getting at the honey."[71]

Ancestral values are obviously thrown into sharp contrast with the colonialist onslaught and, above all, by the coming of Christianity, which is depicted in a wholly negative way throughout his collections:

> *Chukwu* has grown impatient with the unlimited
> patience of *Jehovah*, and can no longer
> await the pleasure of Jesus.
> ("Oath of Destiny," HD 60)

The author sees in Christianity one of the main obstacles to a real liberation for African people all over the world: "Above all, there are powerful usurper gods to depose, gods that preach self-denial and suffering as necessary conditions for a doubtful future bliss."[72] In our interview he also brought out this radical difference – an ideologically convenient one in the colonial process – between Christianity and traditional African beliefs:

---

68 Strangely enough, in Awoonor the moon symbolizes the ancestors; see Angmor, *Contemporary Literature in Ghana*, 116.

69 See AC 84.

70 See "Our Fortune's Dance," HD 47.

71 Anyidoho, "Oral Poetics," 127.

72 Kofi Anyidoho, *The Pan African Ideal in Literatures of the Black World* (Accra: Ghana Universities P, 1989): 10.

For me that seems obvious. I remain convinced that that was really where things began to go wrong. Any group of people who are persuaded to completely forget about whatever they have historically developed, throwing all aside to embrace what other people have developed for themselves, they would remain lost for a long long time.

One of my quarrels with Christianity is that I have no business with that religion that should come and tell me that poverty is good for my soul: poverty is not good for anybody. That is deception plain and simple, inspired by people who are fully provided for, materially. I wouldn't say that Christianity has been totally negative, but in many ways it was. The kind of education I received in the Mission Schools, while at the same time it was giving me something useful, it was also oppressing me in a way I find very regrettable. When you have a religion that, because of its doctrine, would beat me up if I got to singing my mother and my father's songs, then there is something terribly wrong, something fundamentally vicious with that. (Anyidoho, Legon, 19 November 1993)

Mensah connects the poems indicting the effects of Christianity, such as the one quoted above, with another traditional genre: the *halo* or song of abuse, successfully deployed by Anyidoho against various targets.[73] Further, the poem mentioned above closes with a mocking remark strikingly similar to what we read in Atukwei Okai's "And Now to End the World News" about God's address:[74]

We the little great-great-grand-children of
   Oduduwa and *Obatala*
   We charge you
   charge you with innumerable counts of
   despoiling our virgins and killing our little joys
   we challenge you

By all the thunders of *Xebieso*
By all the incurable infirmities of *Sakpana*
We swear
We swear to post copies of the Judgement
   to your God, who is in Heaven
   Whose address we shall look up
   in the opening chapters of the
   Holy Bible, Unrevised Version.

A Harvest of Our Dreams marks Anyidoho's full maturity as a poet, and constitutes the peak of his creative output. Its images are carefully interwoven, as in these lines:

---

73 Mensah, "Kofi Anyidoho," 11.

74 See Okai, "And Now," 5.

> They say our thoughts are threads, crossing
> and criss-crossing into new cobwebs of life
> And
> I shall spin a handful of hopes
> against this cutback in our dreams
> against this wild backlash of screams
> even against these lingering doubts
> at testing time for our faith in Gods.
> ("Seedtime," HD 4)

The most successful compositions of the collection are in its second section, "Akofa," including scenes of ancestral setting with memories of childhood and adolescence, and the following "Food for Ghosts":

> And they gathered our souls
> into massive metal mortars and
> with tall truncheon for pounding sticks
> they are crunching our bones into sacrificial
> food for their outraged ghosts
> playing dirges on martial drums
> to lend rhythms to the violence of their lust .... (HD 28)

A Harvest, if compared to *Elegy*, is also more varied in theme, tone and linguistic register, and contains intimate lyrics and an epistolary section.

> *Elegy for the Revolution* was written when I was a young student, here (1975–76). You could say there's an increasing degree of complexity in *A Harvest of Our Dreams*. (Anyidoho, Legon, 19 November 1993)

Nevertheless, the political crisis in Ghana still plays a prominent role. His poem "From ChristianBorg to UssherFort (From UssherFort to ChristianBorg)," to start with, records one of the paradoxes of Ghanaian politics:

> That's part of the political history of this country, once again. My poetry often records my reaction to it, and that was a period when people who had been imprisoned for political reasons during the time of the military regime, they were now likely to be the ones in government. They had been in prison because they had tried to criticize the previous government, obviously expecting to do better. ChristianBorg is the seat of our government, whereas UssherFort is one of the main prisons of this country, often employed to lock up political detainees. So we have a curious situation here, where people move from the first place to the second and vice versa. (Anyidoho, Legon, 19 November 1993)

The collection sweeps chronologically through Acheampong's last period in power and the coup staged by Jerry Rawlings on 4 June 1979, days whose atmosphere Anyidoho poignantly conveys. "Food for Ghosts," quoted whole above, renders the general frustration in the face of the continued shameless exploitation of the nation's riches. The outraged reaction of the populace led to an historic call for violence and executions of the corrupt leadership:

> They who eat the feast of war and beat
> war drums for a joke, must pay with blood
> in the peace time of their soul harvest.
> ("My Mailman Friend Was Here," HD 36)

In those days public opinion was angrily demanding public retribution against the corrupt élite that had flourished under Acheampong; on 12 June, for instance,

> a large body of students from the University of Ghana marched from Legon to Burma Camp waving posters which demanded: 'Firing Squad for Nation Wreckers!' and 'Let the Blood Flow!'[75]

Apparently the latter slogan had a profound echo, and even Acheampong ended up being executed. This call for seemingly inevitable and cleansing violence is reminiscent of Christopher Okigbo's *Path of Thunder*, concerned about the situation after the Nigerian 1966 coup and prophesying the civil war to come: "The smell of blood already floats in the lavender mist of the afternoon. / The death sentence lies in ambush along the corridors of power."[76]

The rise to power of Rawlings was recorded by Anyidoho's pen very soon, in 1979, as a sign of hope for the country, reflecting the general mood of the period:

> For Rawlings, the greatest achievement of the June 4th Revolution was the awakening of the spirit of the people. [...] Ghanaians faced the new era of the Third Republic with a far greater sense of hope and expectation for the future than they had felt for many years.[77]

Anyidoho said to me:

> I have to be optimistic on this country, I don't intend to give up with it. People have been talking a lot about J. J. Rawlings's regime: I would say he did a great job, because when I came back to this country from the States things were really hard. (Anyidoho, Legon, 19 November 1993)

---

[75] Shillington, *Ghana*, 52.

[76] Christopher Okigbo, *Labyrinths* (London: Heinemann, 1965): 66.

[77] Shillington, *Ghana*, 59–60. The same hope is registered at the end of Okai's "And Now to End the World News," 10.

The beginning of "Our Fortune's Dance" evidently plays on the new leader's name:

> The raw energy of a certain rolling stone
> came rumbling through our well-carved dreams. (HD 47)

On the other hand, the greed and craze for power that seized past regimes is still seen as a possible danger that inspires more than one warning:

> You who made a name sharpening your tongue
> splitting open the wrapped-up shame of false deities
> beware the slippery stairs to heavens gate [...]
> But if you too should leave ungathered
> all the bounties of our dreams
> We would hang a thousand curses round your neck.
> ("From ChristianBorg to UssherFort," HD 49)

A Harvest of our Dreams, just like *Brain Surgery*, diplays oral features pointing at potential public renditions. There are lines made of single-word proclamations, such as "Revolution!... Devolution!... Resolution!" ("Radio Revolution," HD 64), and:

> revolutions
> subversions
> tribunals
> confessions.
> ("Final for Evil Ones," HD 69)

This, in turn, is reminiscent of the beginning of Okai's "Elavanyo Concerto":

> Cross. Banner. Swastika. Sickle.
> Dross. Hammer. Floodfire. Spittle.[78]

In the invocation poem "Fertility Game" (the last piece of the section "Akofa"), Anyidoho informs his readers that the refrain line "Come back home Agbenoxevi come back home" should be repeated by the audience throughout the poem in a public performance, as if he wanted to create an incantatory musical background (HD 19). The reprinting of this poem at the start of his next collection, *Earthchild* (1985), is indicative of an increasingly keen interest in the production on stage of his creative works.

Anyidoho studied the phenomenon theoretically, too, and his essay "Poetry as Dramatic Performance: The Ghana Experience" (1991) must be considered a seminal work on the subject of writing poetry for stage presentation. Against the marginalization of the artist's role and the absence of publishing facilities, he considers poetry recitals as a way to make oneself known and recover the traditional combina-

[78] Okai, *Lorgorligi Logarithms*, 114.

tion of poetry and music, embodied in the Ewe terms '*ha*' ('song/poem') and '*heno*' ('singer/poet'). "In the actual public performance of his role the picture becomes even more complex, for the poet–singer performs as part of an ensemble of drummers, dancers, and singers."[79]

The greatest merit of this essay of his is the much-needed categorization of different kinds of poetic renditions. The basic starting point is defined as 'Level One Performance – Dramatic Reading', where the written text is enriched by the poet's "dramatic use of body language, voice, pause, tempo, gesture, and other paralinguistic techniques." According to him, even Ghanaian poets who have not reached popularity through publication – such as Kwabena Asiedu Aboagye and Abeiku Sagoe – have built their own audience thanks to their public readings. Anyidoho praises Okai's talent and the Caribbean Edward Kamau Brathwaite's compelling readings during his stays in Ghana; he also describes the programme "Drum & Voices: A Performance Dialogue" held at the Ghana Drama Studio on 4 February 1987, which was presented by the W.E.B. Du Bois Memorial Centre for Pan-African Culture, Accra.[80] The participants in the event were the Ghana Dance Ensemble and the oral poet Okyeame Akuffo (all playing drums), plus Brathwaite and several Ghanaian writer–performers: Kwabena Asiedu Aboagye, Kobena Eyi Acquah, Kofi Anyidoho and Kofi Awoonor.

Although this multimedia poetry event was video-recorded, I could not find a tape of it in the Du Bois Centre video archive during my research sojourns in Ghana. Nevertheless, I managed to watch other tapes of the same kind, and realized that the practice of recital has touched occasions other than poetry evenings *tout court*. They have entered the realms of the intellectual and the religious.

The fifth Du Bois–Padmore–Nkrumah Memorial Lecture is one instance of this: it was held by Ayi Kwei Armah at the Centre on 18 and 20 September 1996, a momentous return to the motherland of a world-famous Ghanaian novelist renowned for his reserved attitude. The lecture concerned the subject of Africa as a dismembered continent, with several references to Ancient Egypt's culture being also made in connection with his then latest novel, *Osiris Rising*.[81] Armah's speech

[79] Kofi Anyidoho, "Poetry as Dramatic Performance: The Ghana Experience," *Research in African Literatures* 22.2 (Summer 1991): 42.

[80] Anyidoho, "Poetry as Dramatic Performance," 44–46. The centre was opened in 1985, and Anyidoho also acted as its chairman. For data regarding the Centre's history and characteristics, see John Collins, *Highlife Time* (Accra: Anansesem, 1994): 153–54.

[81] See Emmanuel Gawuga, "Remembering the Dismembered Continent: Ayi Kwei Armah," *Pan African Capital of the World: Newsletter of the W.E.B. Du Bois Memorial Centre for Pan African Culture* 1.1 (January–March 1997): 1, 11.

was prefaced by a brief performance by the actress Ama Boabeng, a speech on pan-Africanism read by Kobena Eyi Acquah, who interspersed it with poems by Du Bois and Okai, and a few closing words by Anyidoho. The lecture was followed by a prayer in English and Akan delivered by Acquah.

Another, earlier example of recorded performance is the poetry evening (28 August 1986) held during the ceremonies for the re-interment of the great scholar W.E.B. Du Bois in the Centre, which

> turned out to be a huge event. Thousands of people lined the route from the Castle to Circular Road while a special detachment of the Ghana Armed Forces carried the remains of DuBois and his wife on a gun carriage.[82]

This tribute ceremony, entitled "Du Bois Night at the Drama Studio," involved the most diverse interventions. A group of women in mourning garments from Kumasi sang, danced and poured a libation; messages about Du Bois and his heritage, sent from all over the world, were read, along with a letter sent by Du Bois to Nkrumah. A brief appellation performance in Du Bois's honour was recited by Kwasi Akuffo, son of the *ọkyeame* Boafo Akuffo, who was Nkrumah's traditional poet, as mentioned in Chapter 2 above.[83] Anglophone poetry was another of the main features of the ceremony: Du Bois's "Children of the Moon" was read, while some poems were presented by their own authors: the African–American Maya Angelou, Kobena Eyi Acquah, Kwesi Brew, and Kofi Anyidoho himself. One main difference among them was soon evident: all the writers had different kinds of approach to the reading of their own poems, ranging from Brew's admittedly plain reading, through Anyidoho and Acquah's inspired declamation, to the charming, enthralling recitation by Maya Angelou, who deployed her theatrical talents and experience to the utmost.

With regard to this, in his essay Anyidoho seems to associate the same difference with the boundary between Level One and "Level Two Performance – Fusion of Poetry, Music and Action," where

> even though the poet may still be holding the text, he performs with little or no reference to it. The ideal situation exists when the text has been memorized, or rather assimilated into an artistic design that makes for spontaneity of performance reinforced by a more elaborate use of body language and paralinguistic devices.[84]

[82] Collins, *Highlife Time*, 153.

[83] Kwasi Akuffo, in turn, was appointed to special presidential duties by the governments of Hilla Limann (1979–81) and Jerry Rawlings (1981–): "both governments have used him essentially as the state practitioner of traditional rhetoric and libation poetry on occasions of national significance"; Yankah, "Creativity and Traditional Rhetoric," 83.

[84] Anyidoho, "Poetry as Dramatic Performance," 46–47.

"Level Two" is akin to the breakthrough brought about by Okai's performances. Before then, apparently, texts were mostly read. Moreover, this definition perfectly suits the poems recited by Maya Angelou on the occasion mentioned above, especially her use of body language during "Phenomenal Woman." Another delightful videotape from the same archive is "Maya Angelou in Performance with the Ghana Dance Ensemble," held at the National Theatre, Accra.[85] Introduced and accompanied by dances and music of the Ensemble in a traditional royal court set design, Angelou speaks, sings and recites poems by some African–American authors including herself, dressed as a traditional Queenmother and holding the stage like one.

The importance Anyidoho gives to this Level Two as a higher ground of creative communication is also evident in his report on the sixth Ibadan Annual African Literature Conference, where he relates how the poetry reading on the second night disappointed those who expected the poets to make an effort and perform:

> At least one fact was underscored by the noisy argument generated by this remark: the fact that oral literature in performance has vibrancy all its own, and written tradition can only make a sometimes pathetic attempt at animating an audience.[86]

Anyidoho includes in his Level Two the use of music, simultaneous mimed enactments and audience participation. This is why he mentions his poem "Fertility Game," quoted earlier, including the line that the public is supposed to repeat.

What is most interesting in Anyidoho's essay – and in the phenomenon of poetry on stage – is "Level Three Performance – Total Art," where the author relinquishes control of the performance in favour of other artists: actors, singers, mime artists, musicians and so on; "the transformation of the poem as written / printed text into a full-scale stage production or drama." The barriers between the genres of poetry and theatre are definitely crumbling down at this point. The original lines are reduced to a pre-text – in Anyidoho's words, "waiting to be brought to its full realization in a face-to-face dramatic encounter with a live audience through the enriched form and meaning helped by directors and performers."[87] Atsu Dekutsey states that, "in cinematic language, the poem becomes the shooting script."[88]

As an example of Level Three, Anyidoho describes, among other things, a dramatization of selected poems from *Earthchild with Brain Surgery* staged by the Abibigromma, the Resident Theatre Company of the School of Performing Arts at

---

[85] Date and occasion unspecified.

[86] Kofi Anyidoho, "The 6th Ibadan Annual African Literature Conference: The Oral Performance in Africa," *Research in African Literatures* 13.2 (Summer 1982): 225–26.

[87] Anyidoho, "Poetry as Dramatic Performance," 47, 53.

[88] Atsu Dekutsey, "Poetry as Theatre," *West Africa* (24 March 1986): 618.

the University of Ghana in Legon.[89] On the one hand, this collection does not equal the compelling imagery of *A Harvest of Our Dreams*; on the other, it is certainly suitable for live performance.

The title poem has a sort of refrain evoking the resilience of the earthchildren, the black race, opposed to the Western "moonchildren." In between the refrains the lines are studded with echoing repetitions, verbal parallelisms such as anaphora, alliteration, single repeated words creating a suggestive effect, chiasmus, inversion and explicit references to pan-African musicians:

And still we stand so tall among the cannonades
We smell of mist and of powdered memories ....

Born to Earth and of the Earth
we grew like infant corn among the Locust Clan
we gathered our dawn in armfuls of dust
we blew brainstorms in the night of our birth [...]

And still we stand so tall among the fields of thorn
We smell of mists and of scented memories .... [...]
Sinaj Seyam Seyam Sinaj Sinaj Seyam
Earthchild Earthchild Earthchild
Seyam Sinaj Sinaj Seyam Seyam Sinaj

I am you are my Song our dream my love our Hope
You sought my Soul I sought your Soul so long
in cross-rhythms of Jazz in polyrhythmic miles of Jazz
till Miles our Davis led us through the rumbling weight of drums

I found I lost you again to wails of saxophone
lost found you again in booming hopes of God's trombones[...]

And those who took away our Voice
Are now surprised

They couldn't take away our Song. (EC 39–42)

Comparing Senghor's and Anyidoho's studies of two different oral traditions, Fraser notices that they share the inclusion of verbal repetitions as a fundamental trait of vernacular performance, "as a basis for incidental departure and variation."[90] No wonder A.N. Mensah writes that the poem above "is supremely musical."[91] In its

[89] Premiere performance at the Ghana Drama Studio, 1 February 1986.

[90] Fraser, *West African Poetry*, 315.

[91] Mensah, "Kofi Anyidoho," 13.

performance, the piece was introduced by a chain-gang and the music of some Negro spirituals. The other poems staged by Abibigromma were those highly oral / theatrical compositions from *Brain Surgery* mentioned earlier: the oral cantor's dirge "My Song," with the tape-recording of the original song in the background; "The Inevitable," with the town-crier beating on his gong; the double-voiced "Agba-yiza" and the theatrical "In the High Court of Cosmic Justice," with all its characters / witnesses. Furthermore, the poem "Shattered Dreams" is dramatized with the help of a ladder on stage, surrounded by a downtrodden people and with a corrupt leader on top:

> You promised us rooftops
> Where we could sit and feel like Gods
> We helped to build the roof
> You offered to teach us how to climb
> We pushed you to tops
> Now   you won't come down to let us go
> The ladder too you've taken with you
> We cannot reach you with a leap [...]
>
> Patapaa   we are watching you
> Baba   we are watching you
> We say   we are watching you
> and the Gods   are watching too ....(EC 97)[92]

In his review, Atsu Dekutsey wrote that "The occasion was a unique experience [...we] came away overwhelmed that we had experienced something new and total." As for the audience response, the reviewer leaves very little doubt: after the singing of "We Shall Overcome," "the cast merged into the audience only to filter back onto the stage for the final curtain-call amidst thunderous applause."[93] The role of the theatre company Abibigromma, whom we will encounter again later in connection with Mohammed ben Abdallah's plays, was not restricted to a particular interpretation of the author's lines, since they added a musical invocation at the beginning and a dance-drama interlude.[94] Moreover, one of the actresses, Dzifa Glikpoe, insisted that Anyidoho create another female witness to close "In the High Court of Cosmic Justice," on the grounds that "given the dominant role women played in Nkrumah's political career, it was a serious blunder to have no more than

---

92 See Anyidoho, "Poetry as Dramatic Performance," 48–49; Dekutsey, "Poetry as Theatre," 618–19.

93 Dekutsey, "Poetry as Theatre," 618, 619.

94 See Anyidoho, "Poetry as Dramatic Performance," 49.

one female witness at his trial."[95] The resulting addition, "Lolita Jones," was later inserted in his latest collection, *AncestralLogic and CaribbeanBlues* (1993). In her outspoken African–American English, Lolita defends Nkrumah's efforts to restore the dignity of the black race:

> And aint nobody like this Brother
> Who gave me back ma Soul
>
> But you   you kicked hem out
>   you pushed him off
>   you segregated him from his SoilSoul. (AC 28)

This collection includes the old poems "Earthchild," "The Song of a Twin Brother" and "Fertility Game" as interludes, but its new compositions do not represent Anyidoho's poetic talent at its best; on the contrary, they appear to lack that gift for stunning images his readers were used to. On the other hand, he seems to enjoy creating neologisms through the blending of terms ("SoilSoul," 28) or inversions, as in "Queendom Gone" (AC 50).

Written in the course of journeys to the Caribbean, Britain and the USA, the book is informed by an inescapable pan-African focus, and needs to be interpreted alongside his critical work *The Pan-African Ideal in Literatures of the Black World* (1989). Coming to terms with the Caribbean world and history means, for the poet, a painful voyage to recover a long-lost coherence:

> Across infinite sadness
> Of plantations
> Of sorrow grown to harvest point.
> ("San Pedro De Macoris," AC 6)

But the search cannot be escaped:

> AncestralLogic reclaims
> lost dimensions of the Soul.
> ("Republica Dominicana," AC 9)

Indeed, the sorrow involved must be accepted as a necessary component of the process:

> I've been in Sorrow's cooking place
> licking clean the pots and pans and floors
> getting high on sad delight

[95] Anyidoho, "Poetry as Dramatic Performance," 53.

> celebrating Life in spite and because of Death.
> ("For Zora," AC 30)

After all, the quest for wholeness in a pan-African ideal implies that

> There are bridges to build, even if most of these can be no more than mental bridges reconnecting one psyche to ancestral time despite irreversible physical separation. There are wounds to heal, even though some of these wounds lie so deep and so close to the heart.[96]

As in Okai's work, unfortunately, the pan-African focus also seems to encourage him merely to list the names of places and personalities:

> Ao! Amigo Los Amigos
>
> Adios Domingo
> Adios Santo Domingo
>
> Hispaniola Hispaniola Hispaniola
> Lost Land of the Taino
>
> Christoph Colomb Christoph Colomb
> Duarte Sanchez Mella
> Imperial Statues in a Sea of Blood.
> ("The Taino in 1992," AC 3)

The same trait can be noted in the long poem "Children of the Land – A Sequence for African Liberation," written for the Ghana Commission on Children as a "literary-dramatic program for children from selected schools in Accra as part of a flag-raising ceremony at the O.A.U. Monument in 1984," and constituting another instance of "Level Three – Total Art."[97] Each child represents an African state with its appropriate costumes, flag, dance-steps and music. The young actors, divided into five regions, would introduce their area all together, in one voice. In section III:

> WE are the Children of the Western lands.
> the lands of the Falling Sun.
>
> Once so long the Children of the Polar Bear
> set upon our Dream and tore it into shreds.
>
> But by the cunning of our warriors of our Elders
> by the Divine intervention of the Mosquito
> Today our hopes rise higher than the Eagle's pride. (AC 36)

---

[96] Anyidoho, *Pan African Ideal*, 10.

[97] See Anyidoho, "Poetry as Dramatic Performance," 48.

Then every child/country would introduce itself, stating name and capital. Given its specific target, the text in itself cannot be blamed for its excessive simplicity, but it is hard to understand why it is followed by a second version of the same poem that is composed by the mere suppression of the lists of states that introduce themselves. The first version was probably too performance-oriented.

In any case, watching the videotape of one of its productions[98] suggests that it must have been a very instructive show for both the performing children and those in the audience, in terms of both their pan-African vision of the continent and of geography at large. Anyidoho thus confirms here his interest in children's literature, a concern also conveyed by the essay by him quoted above and in his books for children in Ewe. This is part of a broader urge, deeply felt by Ghanaian writers, to produce creative literature for the younger generations.

Kobena Eyi Acquah and the Living Echoes

Another poet who presented his works by directing "Level Three" performances, together with Kofi Anyidoho, is Kobena Eyi Acquah,[99] who openly acknowledges Okai's guiding influence:

> I first met Atukwei Okai in 1971, and he entirely influenced me. He trained in the Soviet Union, and there the public, the format, was the same as here. When I came into the Ghana Association of Writers – he was the president, then[100] – I was at the crossroads of my own writing. In Ghana the older poets were writing out of the British and the American tradition but Okai, with his poetry that must be proclaimed and declared, showed me exactly the African poetry I knew from home! My mother's mother was a cantor, a song-leader playing with music and lyrics, while the group would come in and respond. It was public performances, just like drummers' speaking, libation pouring or linguists' talking. So for us it was a natural thing to do, to put our poetry on stage, and a sort of school developed. Virtually every Ghanaian poet is an oral poet, in the sense that you write to be heard. Thus Okai has influenced not only me, but a whole generation of writers who reaffirmed their own nature. (Acquah, Accra, 13 December 1993)

---

[98] University of Ghana Primary School, 11 July 1987.

[99] Page references to Acquah's collections are in the main text, preceded by MWD for *The Man Who Died* (Accra: Asempa, 1984), MDD for *Music for a Dream Dance* (Accra: Asempa, 1989), and NTM for *No Time for a Masterpiece* (Accra: Woeli, 1995).

[100] At the time of our first meeting, in December 1993, Acquah was acting as president.

His first collection, *The Man Who Died* (1984), contains a poem entitled "Anti-Lorgor Logarithms" written after the reading of Okai's *Lorgorligi* and modelled on his mentor's peculiar style. It concentrates on the subject of evil rule:

> What is your desecrated stool
> so bespattered with guilty blood,
> What joy is it to rule
> upon your filthy flood? (MWD 81)

This hints at some of Okai's favourite topics and artistry. When reading the following lines, for instance –

> You are coining consciousness
> and faking fate
> I am drowning drowsiness
> and startling state. (MWD 80)

– one cannot but recall this stanza from Okai's poems:

> They are buying names
> And laundering lakes,
> They are sunning suns
> And slaughtering songs.[101]

Nevertheless, *The Man Who Died* is not a collection teeming with sound-play or startling images. In this regard, Acquah generally appears to lack the depth and complexity of Okai and Anyidoho's language and imagery. The dominant trait in the book is, rather, a delicate and well-balanced lyricism:

> They seem the very last to go,
> forming a reef of islands to
> resist the swelling sea of love.
>
> Yet from somewhere within their camp
> comes call on call for liberation,
> before they become alienated
> strangers to surrender
> refugees from love.
> ("Unsurrendered Isles," MWD 19)

The example above is indicative of his style – easy to follow and maybe at times bordering on the excessively sentimental, like the captivating ballad "I Want to Go to Keta," about the coastal Ewe town eroded by the advancing sea:[102]

---

[101] Okai, *Oath*, 36.

[102] Poems on Keta's impending disappearance were also written by Kwesi Brew and Kofi

I want to go to Keta
before it's washed away,
before the palm trees wither
and drown outside the bay.

I want to go to Keta
where boys drum all the day
and the girls dance *agbadza*
to keep the tears away. (MWD 47)

The sections of *The Man Who Died* tackle love, experiences in Hungary and, once again, the inescapable topic *par excellence*: the vicissitudes of Ghanaian and African politics. The title of the collection, to start with, is a reference to Wole Soyinka's prison memoirs *The Man Died.* The poem "Where We Are Going Is Long," the title of which is a direct translation of an Akan and Ga expression,[103] alludes to the disillusionment felt about the failures of the Nkrumah, Busia and Acheampong administrations:

We have walked and walked and got nowhere–
It is like losing your way in Tema,
Each street, each block, like the last, the next.
We have gone three full-cycles and ended each time
Where we began, or a few yards back. (MWD 90)

In his latest published collection, *No Time for a Masterpiece* (1995), Acquah concentrates again on the topics of *The Man* – love and politics, but with a higher, more mature control of his talent. The following lines display a smooth fusion of irony, moral indictment and well-built imagery:

In the navel of the soul
the midwives of the spirit say
they can hear a heart-throb

The experts, of course
disagree
The urine test they ordered
said, Negative
confirming their palpation results
Our fundal height is at an
all time low

Awoonor; see Fraser, *West African Poetry*, 157–58.

[103] In Akan it goes: 'Nea yerek*o* no ware.'

> our breasts bear no
> tell-tale tints upon their tits.
> ("In the Navel of the Soul," NTM 13)

Acquah, contemporaneously with Anyidoho and following the example of Okai, started reading his poems in public. The already mentioned videotape of the 1986 Du Bois Night includes an instance of this: Acquah reads his "The Man Who Died" with the book in his hand and an inspired voice. The same is true of Armah's lecture, introduced by Acquah's readings. Following Anyidoho's useful classification, these are typical "Level One" performances.

His development in the direction of "Level Three Performance" was guided decisively by an encounter with the theatre group The Living Echoes:

> The Living Echoes had been working on Ghanaian poetry performance, starting by putting up performances for schools, of set-books required for their examination. They did the set plays and also performed the set poems. Once they invited me to one of their performances which featured some of my poetry. I was overwhelmed by it. Amateurish, yes, but genuine! You could see real life in that. And this tiny, tiny girl that the wind could blow away from the stage, doing "I Want to Go to Keta" with meaning and with dance.
>
> So when the book won the Africa Area Award of the Commonwealth Poetry Prize, in 1985, and we had to celebrate it, I said "Look, let me bring these people and let them perform poetry, instead of I standing there and reading it all." So we put up this performance with music and dance, people performing in costumes, all those things. (Acquah, Accra, 13 December 1993)

Therefore the group, under Acquah's supervision, dramatized a selection of poems from *The Man Who Died*. Later they staged another production called "Birth and Rebirth"; the event was held at the Du Bois Centre (27 January 1988), and its video recording shows a performance alternating speeches, poems by West African authors (performed by The Living Echoes accompanied by music), dancing and sound effects. After a few words by Kofi Anyidoho, Acquah starts introducing the various compositions: a translation of the traditional Akan poem "The Awakening" introduced and closed by drumming, "Gently" from Acquah's *The Man Who Died*, a speech by Acquah himself on the importance of Atukwei Okai for Ghanaian poetry, a rendition of Okai's "Afadzato" conveying the full force of its surreal humour and musical orientation, J.P. Clark's "Casualties," Kofi Awoonor's "Song of War," Acquah narrating how he came to know The Living Echoes, Anyidoho's "Song of a Twin Brother" and so on, with more poems by Okigbo and Joe DeGraft, among others. The chorus functions as a constant support for the progress of the performance, singing interludes between its various parts and sometimes singing along with the reciting actors.

Such an experience inevitably inspired the writing of Acquah's next collection, *Music for a Dream Dance* (1989):

> When I came to work on it, I was greatly influenced by the success I had had in "Birth and Rebirth." I was thinking of seeing these people on the stage actually working it out, of hearing the drums as they spoke, the background music, the dances. So it was obvious to me that the only way the poem could get its fullest exposure was in that type of performance. Once you've structured your poetry that way, it becomes part of you, and whatever you write you do it with the voice in your ear, knowing that it's going to be heard rather than just read. (Acquah, Accra, 13 December 1993)

Music is an ambitious volume – and successfully so: a long poem in five movements on pan-Africanism, touching again on a recurrent theme central to Okai and Anyidoho's poetics. The title is inspired by one of Amiri Baraka's poems, but the book seethes with quotations or indirect references culled from the works of the most influential pan-African personalities: W.E.B. Du Bois, Martin Luther King, Jr., Malcolm X, Harriet Tubman, Gwendolyn Brooks, to mention a few.[104] As Anyidoho writes in his introduction to the volume,

> Acquah's *Music* is an intricate tapestry of echoes from a wide range of African and African-heritage poetic and musical voices [...] The challenge – and triumph – of the poet is the drawing of all these voices into one coherent discourse without sounding derivative. (MDD 12–13)

One example of Acquah's intertextual relationship with his sources is his poetic interpretation and rewriting of Langston Hughes's "Harlem," quoted also as one of the introductory epigraphs to the collection; the second poem of Movement Two, "A Dream Deferred" is worth quoting in full:

What happens to a dream deferred?
You ain't got no idea, man
You just ain't got no idea

Dry up?
Yeah, so it might become
Tighter, sweeter

---

[104] For a detailed analysis of how Acquah explores and reinforces these sources, see J.Y. Sekyi–Baidoo, "A Study of Kobena Eyi Acquah's Use of Antecedents to *Music for a Dream Dance*," in *English in Ghana*, ed. Mary Esther Kropp Dakubu (Accra: Black Masks / Ghana English Studies Association, 1997): 248–62.

The flabbiness expelled from its ranks

Fester and *run*?
Why not?
Let those who butcher for pleasure
Live with the stench of rotting meat

Crusting, sugaring over–
But don't be fooled
Beneath the calm surface of the
Gulf of Guinea
Currents are sweeping
Back and forth
And back and forth
Across the Atlantic

Sags–
Just like a catapult
Before it unleashes its load
At the battlements of bitterness
And the towers of hatred
Before it explodes
And engulfs us all in love. (MDD 44; italics in the original)

In his reinterpretation of Hughes's poem, Acquah makes a triumphant declaration about the future of the pan-African dream by steering all the pessimism implied in the original lines towards a positive future. Sekyi–Baidoo rightly observes that

> he defines the themes and style of his work in the framework of the works he refers to, and again, his message seems to be a continuation, a reinforcement of what these earlier works, events and personalities stand for. It is in this context that we consider his references not as mere allusions but as a way of contributing to and harnessing these works in order to complement the thematic and artistic visions they represent.[105]

Hughes's significance for the pan-African arts and for the development of an authentic pan-African poetics is also confirmed by one of Awoonor's poems, "To Langston Hughes when He Walked Among Us in Kampala, 1962," which states: "you heard the sweep of ancient rivers / and daddy-o you died in Harlem."[106] Further, among the foundations of his Caribbean 'nation language' Brathwaite ac-

[105] Sekyi–Baidoo, "Study of Kobena Eyi Acquah," 248.

[106] Kofi Awoonor, *Until the Morning After: Collected Poems 1963–1985* (Accra: Woeli, 1987): 99–100.

knowledges Hughes's role in eroding the authority of the pentameter.[107] In this regard, Hughes may constitute a linguistic model for most of the poets examined in Chapters 4 and 5, who similarly ground their poems in musical and immediately accessible language. In their renowned and much-criticized rejection of Western influences on African literature, Chinweizu, Jemie and Madubuike extol Hughes and call for a discarding of poetic obscurity: "In their search for models, our writers and critics would do well to look at the best of Afro-American writing. Langston Hughes, for instance. His is writing that attain surface lucidity, yet can carry an abundance of rich meaning."[108]

Music for a Dream Dance, by contrast, is built on a strongly Ghanaian skeleton. It is opened by "Invocation: Atumpan Prelude," from the name of the traditional talking drums, representing an invocation to the divinity:

> Before the atumpan I am poised
> Ready to point out
> By its peals
> The paths my people must pursue
> Ready to speak in oracles
> A word of wisdom as from you
>
> And lest I also mislead them
> Lest I confuse them or dismay
> Show me the way and
> Hold my hand
> For I am only a child, Lord
> Only a beginner–
>
> I am learning
> Please let me know
>
> I am learning
> Please let me know. (MDD 24)

The final, repeated sentence is a reminder of the way the Akan drummer closes his preludes: "I am learning, let me succeed."[109] The above quotation is significant in

---

107 Brathwaite, *History of the Voice*, 41.

108 Chinweizu, Onwuchewka Jemie & Ihechukwu Madubuike, *Toward the Decolonization of African Literature*, 1: *African Fiction and Poetry and Their Critics* (Enugu: Fourth Dimension, 1980): 228–29.

109 See Kwabena J.H. Nketia, "Akan Poetry," in *Introduction to African Literature: An Anthology of Critical Writing from 'Black Orpheus'*, ed. Ulli Beier (London: Longmans, 1967): 29–30. Acquah appears to be quite fond of the Atumpan Prelude, having quoted it in his previous collec-

highlighting three features of this collection: the increased attention to formal devices, as the alliteration show; the traditional concept of poet as bard and link between sacred and profane life, in an appropriate continuation of Okai's and Anyidoho's work;[110] and, finally, the syncretic nature of his deeply religious vision. In contrast to Anyidoho's rejection of Christianity, Acquah easily embraces both traditional and Western creeds, as the biblical references in his works show:

> This is not difficult for me, to fuse the two things in their basic sense. Christianity is different from ancestral religion, but mine is a religious being, and once you accept your religious commitment then you can express it in the most diverse terms. I'm a Bible-believing Christian, but I grew up close to the earth, I understand drum language: why shouldn't I use drums to praise?
>
> There are quite a few instances of religious mix here. In Winneba, my hometown, there is a building of the African Methodist Episcopal Zion Church (it's one of the mainstream churches in Ghana), where over the altar they have adinkra symbols (Akan religious symbols) craftily selected. You must note the difference between the nut and the husk. For me the African lyric in praise of God, as a Christian worship experience, is as powerful as any hymn, and I really don't have any personal problem. I've resolved the basic issues of the God I believe in, I switch from mould to mould. I'm a practising lawyer, but when I put on my agbada it's the same thing, there's no dichotomy at all, it's an expression of the totality of my cultural heritage. True, Anyidoho believes differently from what I do because of some atrocities committed by Christianity, but I know that idiot things can also happen in traditional African religions. That is why I consider this proliferation of new churches as healthy: there are some false prophets, of course, as it has always been, but on the whole it's exciting that many people are finding genuine outlets for their religious expression. (Acquah, Accra, 13 December 1993)

To come back to *Music*: it must be noted that its ancestral framework is also composed of a "Meditation: Atenteben Interlude" and a final "Celebration: Fontomfrom Fanfare," recalling Okai's Fontomfrom lines:

Drumming
    Fontomfrom
Dancing
    Fontomfrom
Our song
    Fontomfrom

---

tion (MWD 66, 67) and having had it recited in the performance "Birth and Rebirth." This prelude is mainly used in ceremonies involving royalty, as a standard procedure for the Ashanti chief, to recite eulogies of kings and distinguished ancestors; see Okpewho, *African Oral Literature*, 258.

110 See also Kobena Eyi Acquah, "'Na My Mouth Be Gun?'," *West Africa* (12 May 1986): 23.

Swelling
Fontomfrom. (MDD 93)

In Sekyi–Baidoo's view, "Structurally, the use of short lines or short sentence-structures [...is] typical of drum poetry."[111] Acquah also seems to have borrowed from Okai's style his use of expressions and songs from different Ghanaian languages. Furthermore, his ongoing dialogue with his contemporaries (alongside historical figures) is enhanced by his quotations and reinterpretations of Anyidoho's "Earthchild," such as

That is why we stand, Kofi
So tall
Confounding, confusing the cannonade
With music springing from our soul
And with dance springing in our hoe. ("Tell Freedom," MDD 35)

It may sound bizarre that, in a long poem on pan-Africanism with Ghanaian foundations, Kwame Nkrumah is not mentioned at all:

> The Pan-African heritage, for me, is mainly summed up by W.E.B. DuBois and Martin Luther King. I grew up in Nkrumah's era, I was a young pioneer. I got free education because of him, and I share Nkrumahism and Nkrumah's vision – I'm a Nkrumahist, in fact. Perhaps I don't mention him because his personality is so steeped in my thinking that it's almost impossible to put myself outside him. I firmly believe in Pan-Africanism, I believe that is the only way forward not only for Africans, but for the world. So I didn't quote him because for me he's granted, no need to quote him specifically because his thinking permeates my work.
>
> I agree with Okai: people have understood his value, today. He did wrong things, of course, after a while things fell apart and the centre could not hold. But we ran the risk of throwing both the baby and the dirty water! And people are realizing more and more that it was not personal ambition that was driving him, but a clear vision of what Africa must be. I remember that the Nkrumahist Constitution of 1960 specifically provided that Ghana's sovereignity should be given up in the event of African unity. We do need a united African continent. I am optimistic about it now, with the optimism of faith, the optimism of someone who knows that it is the only way out, and people will come in due course to realize it. That is why Europe is coming together, when only fifty years ago they killed one another wildly: when two fighting squirrels see a bigger animal, they both run into the same hole. (Acquah, Accra, 13 December 1993)

From the point of view of the content, *Music* displays a few weaknesses, as when the author sounds too anxious to find a role for African–Americans in the American

[111] Sekyi–Baidoo, "Study of Kobena Eyi Acquah," 249–50.

Dream, at the cost of justifying or avoid commenting on wars like Vietnam and Korea so long as "we could also root / Our dream / Deep in the American dream" (MDD 67). Fortunately, penetrating passages abound. Acquah is capable of linking the two shores of the Atlantic in the most diverse ways, from the simply thematic –

> And lest the contact should be lost
> Before they were out of mind's reach
> We tied a knot in the atmosphere
> Coupling their souls to
> The hearth at home
> A link that would live in their loins
> Till we found them
> Or they found home
> ("Kromantse," MDD 28)

– to the subtler employment of imagery:

> Most of it is plain jazz –
> Some of the things
> I have heard my brothers say –
> Most of it is just jazz
>
> But you know
> Jazz too has its place
>
> The art of survival for the
> Porcelain pot
> Caught sandwiched in a system
> Of steel kettles
> Is to live each day, each minute
> Just as it comes –
>
> Flexibly, unpredictably
> On the spur of every moment
> Improvising
>
> Here is no rigid martial formation
> The idea is to pop up
> From nowhere –
> Or so it must be made to seem
> To the uninitiated –
> Hit hard – as hard as you can
> Then disappear before they even
> *Think*

> Of hitting you back.
> ("In Jazz Mood," MDD 51)

Acquah weaves together the techniques of an African–American musical style and the tactics of guerrilla war, united in the common thread of improvisation. Moreover, both of them are fused in the metaphor of the pot, an object belonging to the traditional setting and commonly associated with ancestral wisdom.[112]

The predominant role of music in this collection becomes even more evident when watching its live performance or the videotape of the event, premièred at the Du Bois Centre on 29 July 1988. The poem "In Jazz Mood," for instance, is accompanied throughout in the background by keyboards. As for the quotations of Negro Spirituals in "Tell Freedom" (MDD 35–37), the experience of reading them on the page is a far cry from listening to the chorus taking them up. Singing sometimes introduces and closes individual poems, with a solo and / or chorus accompanied by drums as in "One Story Is Good" and "Menanom Adzewafo" (MD 45–46, 50). Singing voices may be used for interludes during single poems ("Nnwonkoro," MDD 53) or for creating a humming background for the reciting voice ("Soweto," MDD 55–57).

The variety of instruments used further signifies the pan-African orientation of the performance, as noted in the concert brochure:

> we find a structural and historical balance between the *atumpan* [...] and the saxophone, symbol of the New World African's musical definition of a harmony forged from an experience of alienation and discord.[113]

Generally, Acquah's poems have fewer theatrical characteristics than Anyidoho's: the performances of his works discussed so far have implied that single members of the Living Echoes recite at a time, with no room for dialogue such as we find in Anyidoho's "In the High Court of Cosmic Justice." Acquah and The Echoes have, in any case, also accepted the challenge of working on the latter text, performing it for the stage and for television. They also put on Level Three performances of the whole sequence of "Aayalolo Concerto" by Atukwei Okai, in venues such as the Du Bois Centre, the British Council and the Arts Centre in Accra, apart from other performances in Kumasi and Cape Coast.

---

[112] Not when it is made of porcelain, of course. See also, on the image of the pot, MDD 49; Anyidoho, *Harvest of Our Dreams*, 15, and the traditional folktale on Ananse and the pot of wisdom in Appiah, *Children of Ananse*, 55–56.

[113] Quoted in Anyidoho, "Poetry as Dramatic Performance," 51.

5 Orality and Performance

Poetry performances: A possible precursor

DURING OUR SECOND INTERVIEW, Kobena Eyi Acquah confidently claimed to be the father – or one of the fathers – of Level Three Performances. According to most of the available data, he and Anyidoho started at roughly the same time, in the mid-1980s. To establish who was the very first, after all, is of little significance. What might sound curious is a small notice published by the journal *Growth*, an Accra-based "literary magazine for the young writers," in 1973:

> An amalgam of poetry, drama, dance and music was performed at the Accra Arts Centre by the Adwinasa Theatre Company directed by Adelaide Amagatcher of the Arts Council. The production was based on Kwadjo Gyinaye Kyei's collection of poetry entitled *The Lone Voice*.[1]

Isolated cases of Level Three Performances were thus already being staged in the 1970s, – and not so isolated, either, since the same issue of the journal also states:

> THE BLACK EXPERIENCE was the title of a collection of poetry by various African writers with intermittent African drumming and dancing, performed by the Koforidua Students Drama Group. It was produced by Kwadwo Osafu Adu-Amankwa and directed by Martina Quarcoo of the Arts Council, Koforidua.[2]

Along with Efua Sutherland, Kojo Gyinaye Kyei (b. 1932) was one of the editors of *Okyeame*, the first Ghanaian literary magazine launched in 1961 by the Ghana Society of Writers and printed until the early 1970s by the Institute of African Studies, University of Ghana at Legon. In traditional Akan power structures, the

---

[1] *Growth: Literary Magazine for Young Writers* (Accra: Arts Council of Ghana / Young Africans Writers' Club) 3 (September 1973): 76.

[2] *Growth* 3, 78.

'Okyeame' is the linguist or spokesman, the one who acts as a link between popular sentiment and those in power. The editors' choice of name was another sign of the intense affinities between ancestral culture and contemporary written literature, of the continuity existing between oral bards and storytellers and modern writers. As the foreword to issue 1 says, *Okyeame* was meant to be "a channel of communication for Ghanaian creative writers." And that is what it turned out to be, since the magazine published the first works of people who today are renowned novelists, poets, playwrights and critics, like Kofi Awoonor (George Awoonor–Williams at the time) and Ayi Kwei Armah, to mention only two.

Kyei is first of all an architect and then a poet, but, above all, he is a chief: Nana Ankoanna Apoma Kyekyeku III, chief of Gyedu, of the Brong–Ahafo region. To his regret, this has hindered his participation in poetry recitals:

> I used to be invited to public readings, but since I've become a chief I've been very busy, I have to go to so many places .... (Kyei, Accra, 17 December 1993)

The Lone Voice (1969), staged at the Arts Council, is his first collection of poems, and is composed of simple, unsophisticated, stark and straightforward poems that point to Langston Hughes (indeed a recurrent figure for contemporary Ghanaian poetry) as a literary model for "his life-long effort to integrate his poetry with music."[3] In his preface to the collection, Kyei admits admiring Hughes's "richly pithy simplicity,"[4] and in our interview he added:

> I studied in the USA, University of Kansas. Hughes had studied there, too, so they invited him to come and read some poetry. I met him, and later in New York he had a look at my poems, making some remarks. That way he gave me some perspective, because all along I was writing on my own. His observations helped me to see my poems in another light, so that some of them were rewritten. (Kyei, Accra, 17 December 1993)

Kyei's best-known collection, though, is the photographic *No Time to Die* (1975), already reprinted several times, in which his poems are inspired by the Bedford mammy-lorries, known as 'tro-tros', the most common means of transportation in Ghana for decades. In his history of the Ghana Revolution, C.L.R. James writes that these lorries "did more to prepare Ghana for independence than all the graduates produced in Achimota during the same period. They reunited the common people."[5]

[3] Onwuchewka Jemie, "Hughes's Black Esthetic," in *Critical Essays on Langston Hughes* (Boston MA: G.K. Hall, 1986): 111.

[4] Kɔjo Gyinaye Kyei, *The Lone Voice* (Accra: Ghana Universities P, 1969): vii.

[5] James, *Nkrumah*, 57.

Kyei went around talking to the drivers about the painted slogans on their lorries, and interpreted them through his lines while Hannah Schreckenback was taking pictures of them. Kyei's poems are once again extremely oral, quite song-like, but *No Time to Die* is also a piece of social history, re-creating the atmosphere of that world through a fascinating blend of popular wisdom in English, pidgin and local languages:

> Though you hear noise coming
>   from my *songron songron* body
>   and from connections to my muffler
>   and from my bonnet
>   and from my wobbly wheels,
> Still 'trong dey for my inside o!
>   proper!
>
> Ei, me, *Tro-tro* the great,
> What, nobody!
>   *moko moko bee* !
> I 'trong pass Hercules self.
> Me, SEA NEVER DRY!
> ("Sea Never Dry")[6]

When the book was launched the drivers of the mammy-lorries were not present, and a critic wrote: "it is unrealistic to presume that there is such an audience waiting for the poets to write for them."[7] Be that as it may, Kyei's poetry clearly shows a sustained effort to recapture the spoken dimension of Ghanaian English, and is easily suited to theatrical transposition.

Poetry performances into the 1990s

In 1991 Kofi Anyidoho stated:

> *re*-presentation of written poetry as a full dramatic performance has gone beyond the experimental stage; in fact it has become a fully established tradition on the contemporary scene in Ghana. Of special significance is the fact that these productions are being broadcast by the media.[8]

---

[6] Kojo Gyinaye Kyei (with Hannah Schreckenbach) *No Time to Die* (privately printed, 1975): 17.

[7] Donatus Nwoga, "Modern African Poetry: The Domestication of a Tradition," *African Literature Today* 10 (1979): 48.

[8] Anyidoho, "Poetry as Dramatic Performance," 50.

Nevertheless, before this tradition – on all its three levels– could take even firmer roots in the Ghanaian cultural soil, with the coming of the next decade the whole phenomenon appeared to wane slightly. The main and manifest reason for this was the expanding market for home videos, nibbling at a potentially broad audience for poetry performances through the offer of an 'easier' kind of cultural consumption, perhaps more suitable to the TV medium than broadcasting a performance originally meant for a live audience. After all, the popularity of poetry recitals affirmed itself when, at the beginning of the 1970s, the country's economy was going through such travails that poets were led to search for alternatives to publishing.[9] The improvement of living conditions in recent years might well have generated the inverse process.

Atukwei Okai does not really agree with this:

> Yes, recently the phenomenon has slowed down; TV and videos might have contributed. But I think it is the economic difficulties that must be blamed more than anything else: they nearly wreaked havoc on the overall cultural situation, prevented the ambience of this phenomenon to progress and increase. To attend a literary reading or a theatre performance I would first have to find the money, get transportation. So you can see that if people opt for the screen, it's not because they really made a choice. Lots of them would want to go to the theatre or to poetry reading, but the hassle and the financial burden is too much.
>
> When all this was going on, with the markedly modest presence of the screen at the time, you could feel a love for the real arts in the masses. You would see people from all walks of life coming to the theatre to attend poetry readings. (Okai, Legon, 19 August 1997)

Anyidoho agrees with Okai's interpretation:

> Too many economic pressures, indeed. It may have slowed down officially, but not stopped altogether. I have recently been invited to read some of my poems in an Accra school, for instance. (Anyidoho, Legon, 30 May 1997)

Kobena Eyi Acquah, though, has described the whole process with an economic analysis closer to the perspective I outlined at the beginning:

> I must say that poetry readings and performances haven't really picked up, they have slowed down slightly. I think it's temporary. As the economy has picked up, inputs have become more and more available, through media and so on. Today it is easier to

[9] See Fraser, *West African Poetry*, 314 (see also 152: "material progress and cultural rigour flourished in inverse ratio. Ghana's economic ruin was her artistic salvation").

have a collection published, too, and that might not incite someone to read his or her poems in public.

Let us be honest: part of that impetus was linked to the fact that if after 10-15 years of writing there was no way your thing was going to get published, even if you had written momentous poems concerning the times you were passing through, then you wanted to take onto the stage. So, when things began to ease and it became possible to get published more easily, the tendency steered towards the written word, even for us.

Because it is also a matter of generations: those of us who, ten years ago, were younger or middle-age writers, have now become virtually the older generation. Younger writers now keep sending you things to look at, there are so many of them. So we have become less able to go around reading, and more able to ask a publisher to issue our work.

As for me, The Living Echoes have changed their cast, but they are still working. Apart from the poetry, they also put on plays, especially at the Arts Centre or during the National Theatre Festival. And they stage set books for schools, too. We were thinking of putting on something at the National Theatre but the cost of hiring it is such that, unless you get a comprehensive sponsorship [...] Unfortunately I am a sort of conscientious objector to the 'richer' sponsors such as alcoholic beverages and tobacco companies. I hope I can manage by the end of this year.

On January 21st, 1997, we put on *Music for a Dream Dance* again at the DuBois Centre. A similar version to the one you watched on tape, but with new players, actually only two from the original cast. Honestly it was a wow, and people asked me to do it again for PANAFEST '97 (Cape Coast, August–September). We were preparing it, but the whole thing was cut down drastically. There were fifty applications from Ghana alone, and Accra was cut as a venue: seven nights of performances only in Elmina and Cape Coast. So many things were left out, together with ours.

Now I've been asked to read portions of it, unfortunately without The Living Echoes, as part of a poetry night during the festival together with Okai and Anyidoho. In any case, there could not be a whole week of performances in Ghana without a poetry event: it has certainly become an institutional genre, whatever may have recently happened. (Acquah, Accra, 13 August 1997)

Has the 'crisis' affected mainly the younger generations, then? Acquah did not agree with this, holding that younger writers were at least still reading their poetry in public to make themselves known. Unfortunately, despite Anyidoho's reliance on modern technology for audio-visual recordings,[10] such testimonies are still very hard to get hold of for research purposes, the Du Bois archive being a happy exception.

As a consequence, written testimonies are still the principal source of information. In the preface to his first collection *Eté: A Woman of Africa* (1995), Ladé

[10] See Anyidoho, "Poetry as Dramatic Performance," 54.

Wosornu recounts "an evening of poetry and music"[11] in Accra, September 1994, also attended by Atukwei Okai and Kofi Anyidoho. This may confirm what Acquah says about beginners using public readings to launch their works. Unfortunately, the author's handling of his own poetry is still too immature to warrant detailed analysis. The title poem is a composition in three voices (chorus, narrator and Eté) that could arguably be performed on stage, although there is an excess of *faux-naïveté*, moralism and out-of-place archaic forms in the expression as a whole.

The language of orality in Kojo Laing, Abena Busia and Kwabena Osei–Boahene

There are three more Ghanaian poets worth discussing here, given their evident performance-oriented styles, each in his / her different way. Kojo Laing's novelistic output has already been examined in Chapter 2 and 3, with particular reference to the close connections between his novels and his poetry and to his magical / folktale realism. The latter cannot but constitute a recurrent feature of his poems, also shared with Atukwei Okai. In the works of both, the pendulum swings between surrealism and magical realism, but in the case of the poetry a certain lack of realistically reconstructed fictive context tends to indicate the former category. Laing explained to me thus the rationale behind its use:

> In my case, anyway, I don't believe it is advisable or literarily true to say in a simple manner what can easily be said in ordinary talking and communication. When you come to literary prose or poetry, I believe it should say something which is both intrinsic to the language and goes beyond the language. Let me give you an example: in one poem I started by describing a woman's breast, where its nipple is a pencil that draws the shape of the breast and then comes back to the point of departure. You must try to push the boundaries of sense, of words, of meanings, and when you reach such a boundary you meet words and inspirations which don't reflect in the ordinary day-to-day communication. (Laing, Accra, 15 December 1993)

This image is contained in his first published poem, "Jaw":

> And the curve on the hill travels & reaches its own size,
>   without moving. [...]
> And the breast fills and draws and reaches its own curve
> with the short pencils of the nipples,
>   without moving.[12]

---

[11] Ladé Wosornu, *Eté: A Woman of Africa & other poems* (Accra: Woeli, 1995): ix.

[12] Laing, "Jaw," 62. The works considered here are the long poems "Jaw" and "Resurrection"

In terms of meaning, readers' expectations are constantly unsettled by his lines:

> Can you really believe
> that one day, on a purple morning,
>   I nearly sat
>   on my own lap?
> ("I Can't Sit on Chairs," GH 14)

As Stewart Brown writes in his review of *Godhorse*, his poems "demand that their reader enter into the game (there's a lot of fun in Laing's poems) of finding and continually adjusting the linkages between lines, images and the very idea of 'meaning'."[13] As for his first two long poems, they are not particularly endowed with humour, probably because they describe the author's racially based suffering and alienation during his years in Scotland: "I am the man resting in the shade of the word hunted," he writes (R 27). According to Kropp Dakubu, who has written extensively on Laing's poetry,

> "Jaw" and "Resurrection" can be said to deal specifically with the feelings af alienation, and the alienation of feeling, resulting from culture shock, experienced on many levels by a young African in Europe.[14]

Such feelings open up a chasm between the concrete and the abstract, outer and inner, the object and the thought, a divide that Dakubu associates with the Scottish psychiatrist R.D. Laing's studies on schizophrenia. The following lines by his Ghanaian namesake are to the point:

> I am only sitting here passing and repassing myself,
> overtaking myself at dangerous corners,
> leaving myself and collecting myself later in strange places. (R 26)

The finding of a means of communion between the two poles – and its description – is the poet's aim, and will be the basis of Laing's Ghanaian social quest in *Godhorse* and in his three novels, where such a new harmony between the physical and the spiritual is the premise of any political, social and collective project. The definition "new wholes" (*Search Sweet Country*) was already employed in "Resurrection":

>   Thus the inner, Yes,
> will provide great suffering and suppleness for the outer,

(*Okyeame* 5 [November 1972]), plus his only collection of poems published so far, *Godhorse*; page references are in the main text, preceded by J, R and GH respectively.

13 Stewart Brown, "Dreams, Godhorses and Vultures," *Planet: The Welsh Internationalist* (June–July 1990): 97.

14 Mary Esther Kropp Dakubu, "The Language of Being in the Poetry of B. Kojo Laing," *Legon Journal of the Humanities* 5 (1991): 77.

so that when we rise, we take every presence with us,
in new wholes. (R 29–30)

Just as in his novels, Laing carries out his search by means of language – or, rather, of linguistic experimentation. Even though he has never taken part in live poetry events, his lines fully exploit the oral characteristics of Ghanaian English. He often has recourse to exclamations and single repeated words that concentrate pathos:

Hey! I Hey! Hey! I Hey! I
hate hate hate hate
shape density, colour and texture height, I hate width! (R 28)

He also alternates such lines with long, loose, narrative passages:

[...] What can we say of men who are
more moved by small inconveniences and small events,
than by thunder made with blood and with sound? [...]
Quickly!
They are invading the TOWN to see its failures in the drains
present your weapons and dance over the drains! (R 32)

M.E. Kropp Dakubu compares Laing to Whitman, and identifies the root of this feature in Akan orature: "Akan thus show a tendency to ignore the distinction between oral poetry and oratory, that Laing picks up."[15] Once again, the blurring of genres seems to spring from traditional literature.

Yet the one feature that makes his poetry stand out among the Ghanaian authors studied so far is his physical treatment of language: words cease to be a mere medium of expression and acquire a concrete dimension, like an object of research. See, for instance,

And I ride the horse of the word The all through the poem.
And I hold hard onto the two Rs of inner presences,
for I am the hunted man. (R 23)

I am the letter T joined onto an H while E looks on
unwillingly. (J 65)

The weaver bird dappling its flight in yellow light
has no needle in the sky but my words, [...]
I see the mist
weave the bird in and out of its own skin,

[15] Dakubu, "The Language of Being," 90.

> weave the vowels out of my words
> because this hill has no photogenic dusts,
> and every rock is a consonant.
> ("No Needle in the Sky," GH 12)

Kropp Dakubu states that the definite article is one of Laing's favourite indices, "as a symbol of the reality of language and also of the things it represents."[16] The poet breaks all kinds of conventions concerning the representational value of language:

> Gods have mercy on all the full-stops of the world,
> for they stop nothing. For any word can jump over a full-stop
> and run. (R 36–37)

In both his poetry and his fiction, such a physical conception of language is expressed in graphic terms. The space of the page is physically occupied by his creativity just as a voice would occupy the time at its disposal:

> And every moment of true surrender and openness,
> Will be used partly as stars, partly as children.
> I will listen quietly to your woes in the next four blank lines.
> ....…
> ....
> ....
> .... (R 36)

Possibilities of visual patternings, then, are explored as expressive devices. Kamau Brathwaite's poetry once again offers a useful point of comparison: experimenting with spacing and layout through the use of a word processor, he has recently developed a visually striking new language that he calls "Sycorax Video Style."[17] Bearing in mind the years Laing spent in Scotland, Dakubu writes:

> The highly concrete typographical device notwithstanding, it is presumably only an accident of terminology that the existential striving for 'concrete' experience is echoed in the name of the 'concrete poetry' movement. Even so, the resonance set up by the homonymy is interesting. A striking characteristic of the Scottish concrete movement, as well as of its French antecedent, is a fascination with language as a material phenomenon [...] with language made visible, in print, so that poems are not only intellectual objects but also physical things constructed of paper, ink, letters and the spaces between them, made by pens or typewriters.[18]

---

[16] Dakubu, "The Language of Being," 86.

[17] See Stewart Brown, "Writing in Light: Orality-through-typography; Kamau Brathwaite's Sycorax Video Style," in *The Pressures of the Text*, ed. Brown (Birmingham University African Studies Series 4; Birmingham: Centre of West African Studies, 1995): 125–36.

[18] Dakubu, "Language of Being," 84–85.

Laing continues his visual experiments in the collection *Godhorse*:

Gently church door wants to grow moustaches.	P
My Almighty	E
Lord, all transferred priests take time	P
to get used to church doors.	P
Some doors unfriendly,	E
some belong to more than one church,	R!
some are Muslims in Anglican churches.	
("Godsdoor," GH 15)	

Dakubu defines this device of naming fruit and spices a "choric system," and sees its function as a "direct affirmation of physical, organic outer life that must feed the inner life to make it whole."[19] Other typographical expedients in the collection are one-word lines in capital letters and interlinear commentary, as in "More Hope, More Dust."[20] As for the more strictly oral qualities of his English, Laing employs ideophones and prolonged consonants with great gusto.

Laing's physical conception of language is to be considered a fundamental part of his attempt to harmonize the spiritual and the material. In her collection of picture-texts from very ancient times to the International Concrete Poetry movement, B.B. Bowler notes:

> many of these early picture-texts were in some way connected with magic, ritual, religion or superstition, and that they had an urgency evocative of the LOGOS itself – the incarnated word.[21]

In the historically shifting function of such texts from amulet to prayer and later to poem, Bowler identifies a common trait defined as "means of arriving at the sense of unity, integration, the all-embracing synthesis"; as a contemporary term of comparison she chooses a phenomenon reminiscent of the topic being discussed here:

> large poetry gatherings where masses of people are led by sound poets into reciting random words and parts of words, occasionally going so far to stimulate the trancelike power of speaking a holy mantra. The spectator is thus once again engaged in a vast communal ritual experience.[22]

---

[19] Mary Esther Kropp Dakubu, "Kojo Laing's Poetry and the Struggle for God," in *FonTomFrom: Contemporary Ghanaian Literature, Theatre and Film*, ed. Kofi Anyidoho & James Gibbs (*Matatu* 21–22; Amsterdam & Atlanta GA: Rodopi, 2000): 235–41.

[20] See GH 38–40.

[21] Berjouhi Barsamian Bowler, *The Word as Image* (London: Studio Vista, 1983): 5.

[22] Bowler, *Word as Image*, 11–12.

Godhorse is a richer, more mature and diversified work, adding to the fragmented poet's self of the two long poems the new dimensions surfacing in his novels. First, the delicate lyric:

> The rain slants like the thighs
> of a tall woman dancing
> by the bending sea with its whys
> whose rolling corners have at last
> moved together in nudges of white
> so that love rolls in between
> and makes the songs of shells high.
> ("The Rain Slants," GH 6)

Secondly, the humorously saucy:

> Dede, don't let them push my hearse so fast, have
> a little posthumous consideration
> for my erection of the after-life:
> a dead man can't go to God with his popylonkwe at attention.
> God forgive your speed
> for you want to disgrace me before the ancestors!
> Hurrying to bury me ....
> ("I Am the Freshly Dead Husband," GH 35)

Thirdly, a preoccupation with the state of the Ghanaian nation, still informed by the same search for harmony between the material and the spiritual. Laing often associates Ghana with food, his recurrent – and usually positive – image:

> the loaf of the maps of ghana had many bites missing, and
> the bad and bitter biter was never seen.
> ("Tatale Swine," GH 32)

According to Dakubu, "the name of the country is not capitalized, and again this symbolizes its undefined, unrealized condition."[23]

Another recurrent symbol for Ghana (also present in the novels and in "Resurrection," 24), is the horse, as the title poem may suggest.[24]

---

23 Dakubu, "Trope of the Nation," 281. See the same essay for a detailed study of the national quest in Laing's poetry.

24 The equine metaphor used to symbolize Ghana is also present in one of the most famous highlife tunes from the 1960s, by E.K. Nyame: "*'Oponka abo dam a, ne wura no dze ommbo dam bi'* (If the horse is mad, its owner cannot also be mad at the same time), a dark suggestion that a regime may lose control of itself but that the country and the people remain steadfast in their sanity"; Kofi Agovi, "The Political Relevance of Ghanaian Highlife Songs since 1957," *Research in African Literatures* 20.2 (Summer 1989): 197.

> I think "Godhorse" is both what you are saying and also a symbol of the universe which goes on its own way, aside from human frailties and desires, because it throws off the old man. In other words, we must try not to make the same mistake that the West has made, creating a dichotomy between the external world and the inner self, regarding the external dimension as something to be controlled and manipulated, whereas with the African-Ghanaian way it's an extension of the spirit of man. (Laing, Accra, 15 December 1993)

Laing's poetry shares such a regular correspondence between symbol and concept[25] with Anyidoho's. Another common particularity is a penchant for graphic experimentation, already noticeable in Anyidoho's first two collections. After an initial sortie in *Brain Surgery* (103), Anyidoho finally hit the mark in *Elegy for the Revolution* with two effective passages. The first is a visual depictions of a sacrifice:

> the thunder god demands a ram
> with
>
>   dangling
>   testicles.
> ("Upon the Harvest Moon")[26]

The second is a river separating two people:

> Upon opposing banks
>   we squat,
>   our backs
>   upon
>   the smouldering wastelands of our heritage
> mourning each other
>   across
>   the turbulence of flooded passions.
> ("The Passion-Gulf")[27]

Another writer who models some of her poems graphically is Abena Pokua Adompim Busia, in her sole collection to date, *Testimonies of Exile* (1990).[28] The titular condition is a real, autobiographical one: the daughter of the former Ghanaian Prime Minister Kofi Abrefa Busia, who ruled between 1969 and 1972, she had to live through exile twice with her family, in 1959 and 1972, first in order to escape

---

25 See his recurrent image of the guava in Chapter 3.

26 Anyidoho, *Harvest*, 75.

27 Anyidoho, *Harvest*, 79.

28 Abena Pokua Adompim Busia, *Testimonies of Exile* (Accra: Woeli, 1990). Page references are given in the main text.

Nkrumah's, then Acheampong's regime. She presently lives and teaches in the USA. The vicissitudes of contemporary Ghanaian politics thus once again enter mainstream Ghanaian poetry in English.

The experience of forced expatriation dominates the first section of her book, called "Exiles," and more generally informs all of her poetry and outlook. As she said in an interview:

> It gets to a point that those of us who have been out get this sort of terror about whether or not there is a home to come back to anyway, rather than the wonderful ideas of one's childhood.[29]

The lack of a solid 'home' results in feelings of displacement and a fragmentation of self, which she attempts to articulate in visual terms:

I am a passion of disharmonies
axing my dismembered self
splitting my body among continents.
At my death re/collect me. [...]
Let's   not   twi-
                    st down
                              or ré lé vé
o   ver my r-
                 o-
                    ving ra ging bones.
("At Last Rites," 22)

The same phenomenon involves her creative processes, as in "Annotations," which is designed to be read as a curve:

Something shattering happened.

We can't re   the fra
            as se   le   gme
                  mb   nts. (43)

Phyllis Pollard criticizes Busia for the distance she keeps from her native culture, for not being able to reassemble her own self, "to regain contact with a lost cultural heritage and to speak on behalf of black women."[30] Even if she were right, it does not make much sense to expect any artist to express something he / she does not feel. In any case, the author's introspective depth and linguistic skill convey a penetrating sense of multiple loss:

---

[29] Ivor Agyemang–Duah, *Some African Voices of Our Time* (Accra: Anansesem, 1995): 72.

[30] Phyllis Pollard, "Meditations on Time and Exile," *CRNLE Reviews Journal* 2 (1994): 128.

I see piles of dirty coffee cups
which mark
the many beginnings of this one work.

The smell of sweaty paper possess
this space
and haunts the thoughts I try to find.
("A Sense of Writing," 42)

It is hard to see how, to quote from Pollard's review again, Busia's poetry "too often [...] remains simply ordinary, lacking both context and wider horizons and indicating more than anything else what happens to creativity when it is denied its roots."[31] Besides the fact that being confessional and private does not – must not – imply a negative judgement, one wonders whether the following "Mawu of the Waters," possibly the best piece in the collection, would pass Pollard's test:

I am Mawu of the Waters.
With mountains as my footstool
and stars in my curls
I reach down to reap the waters with my fingers
and look!, I cup lakes in my palms.
I fling oceans around me like a shawl
and am transformed
into a waterfall.
Springs flow through me
and spill rivers at my feet
as fresh streams surge
to make seas. (39)

Another interesting poem from the collection, "Mawu / Mawo" (67–68), is centred on a linguistic pun: Mawu is a name for the supreme creator in Ga (Busia's maternal ethnic group) and, with slight variations of tone and stress and spelling, can carry several meanings in Asante (her father's group), as the author's detailed explanation makes clear. Playing on such similarities, the resulting poem, opened and closed by ideophones, should be read by a great performer: "there is aural play evident when the poem is chanted," she writes (69).

The last poet examined here, Kwabena Osei–Boahene, has performed his compositions several times in Holland, accompanying himself on a drum. In the introduction to Osei–Boahene's very promising first collection, *The Day of the Dancing*

[31] Pollard, "Meditations," 128–29.

Gods (1995),[32] Charles McGeehan writes that "this activity culminated in the Talking Drums Poetry Festival in June 1983" and in the award of the 1994 Rotterdam Arts Council Poetry Prize. The poems of his collection are marked by a strong sense of rhythm. Osei–Boahene is a musical poet who lavishly displays refrains and oral constructions from Akan tradition.

The first poem, "I Am a Poet," reminds one of the way the Nigerian Niyi Osundare introduced himself and stated his artistic intentions in his renowned first collection: "Poetry / is / man / meaning / to / man."[33] Osei–Boahene makes a similar pledge to reject poetical obscurity:

> See what I do with my
> ABCs; not a chore
> but my first love:
> COME, GO, LOVE, DIE!
> EAT, SHIT, LIVE, ABOA [stupid]! (1)

On the other hand, he simultaneously claims to be complex:

> I spin words like the spider
> the webs I weave are not
> simple, like the enigmatic spider's–
> the mischief-maker himself. (1)

Not only does he describe his art by using the image of Ananse, but he also draws on the Akan term for 'poetry,' '*anwonsem*,' meaning 'stories woven together.' The author often uses similar borrowings and half-borrowings, as when he writes:

> If you allow thousands to die
> thousands will rise with warrior spirit.
> ("Mother Africa, Good Day," 3)

This echoes the Asante appellation '*Asante Kotoko, kum apem a, apem beba*' ('Asante Porcupine, when thousands are killed, thousands come'), which Okai had repeatedly used in his "Tinkongkong! Ayawaso!"[34] Another instance of this is the poem "Where We're Going Is Long" (34), which translates the Akan expression as Kobena Eyi Acquah did before him. This oral, proverbial density, akin to Awoonor's recovery of Ewe imagery,[35] reaches its peak in "The Gifted Linguist," written in praise of an *okyeame*:

[32] Kwabena Osei–Boahene, *The Day of the Dancing Gods* (Accra: Woeli, 1995). Page references are in the main text.

[33] Niyi Osundare, *Songs of the Marketplace* (Ibadan: New Horn, 1983): 4.

[34] See Okai, *Lorgorligi*, 54–81.

[35] See Adjei, "Tradition and Continuity," chapter 6.

O, Opanyin Agyaaku!
the most gifted orator,
the wisdom that dwarfs a thousand men
from the surrounding villages
the chief's chief linguist. [...]
the foolish chief can take refuge
under your barrage of intricate
questions. (9)

This hints at the *okyeame*'s function of taking the blame in the chief's place, according to the proverb '*Ohene bone nni ho, na mmom okyeame bone wo ho*' ('The bad chief does not exist, but the bad linguist does'). The poem is full of this kind of imagery:

You're hunter by profession and even braver
than the bravest hunter, yet you maintain
a low profile, for you believe that the most
beautiful beads never claim beauty. (10)

– referring to the proverb '*Ahwene pa nkasa*' ('precious beads make no noise');[36] and:

A new broom may sweep well
but an old broom knows better
the corners of the room. (10)

Osei–Boahene's style sometimes recalls Okai's flourishing alliteration:

What a bandit country we ya
living in
In this bandit country
they con the contractors
dock the doctors for the
    flimsiest
Trailing after traders
robbing them of their profits
They pry into the privacy
of the priest.
("Bandit Country," 36)

---

[36] Florence Abena Dolphyne, *A Comprehensive Course in Twi (Asante)* (Accra: Ghana Universities P, 1996): 127.

The following quotation instantly reminds one of Okai's word-play on day-names in "Rosimaya":[37]

> So as a boy I could spew any
> amount of heresy on Mondays
> One could till the land on Tuesdays
> Wed your boyhood sweetheart on Wednesdays.
> ("The River Has Drowned a Man," 6)

The author's talent, though, is far from being simply derivative, because his collection offers riveting moments, particularly in his poems on his difficult years in London and Holland; the sense of alienation conveyed by Kojo Laing is deepened here by economic privation and the lack of a visa:

> It is not a race to the finish line
> Unlike the marathoner who races to the finish
> however long the distance may be
> I am forever on the run with not a soul
> in sight I am the running man
> The mouse flees from the cat
> The chick from the merciless hawk
> and I from mortal man
> I am forever on the run from
> the long arm of the law.
> ("The Running Man," 12)

The fundamental question now should concern the relationship between the written and the oral medium, in order to formulate a new poetics capable of being more 'African' and less Western-oriented. Isidore Okpewho's standpoint, for instance, refuses those oral devices which do not take into account "the cold privacy of the printed word."[38] Nevertheless, the exchange between page and stage should work both ways; in Kofi Anyidoho's belief, "new developments in poetic practice have radical implications for the impact of written poetry in Africa." Working in both directions, the link between orality and literacy should be considered as having circular characteristics, as opposed to the linear concept of publication as the final act in a series of public readings. "How do we account," writes Anyidoho in the

[37] Okai, *Lorgorligi*, 107.

[38] Okpewho, "African Poetry," 24.

same essay, "for the fact that even poets whose work is already in print nevertheless insist on publicizing their poetry through continued public performances?"[39]

The reality behind these theoretical queries, though, is represented by a considerable number of West African poets in English who have not yet had a chance to show their talent on the written page. Robert Fraser accordingly defines his own book as "a study of the exposed tip of an impressively large iceberg."[40]

<>

[39] Anyidoho, "Poetry as Dramatic Performance," 42, 44–45.

[40] Fraser, *West African Poetry*, 8.

DRAMA: FROM A DIFFERENT DIMENSION

6 The Paths of the Pioneers

WHILE PARTS ONE AND TWO above examined the shifts, respectively, of prose towards poetry and of poetry towards the stage, this final chapter will prove much less monodirectional in its attempt to deal with some trends in contemporary West African drama. The general phenomenon described here could be defined as multiple incorporation, or multifaceted contamination.

During the earlier years of Independence, anglophone playwrights had to relieve their own mentality of the decades-long burden of colonial drama[1] in order to seek a more immediate mode of expression capable of conveying their peculiar experience:

> there is a marked difference in dramatic quality between the plays written before and those written after Independence. Since the early playwrights' aim was strongly literary, their attention was mostly on the content of their works rather than the possibilities of presentation on stage.[2]

The dominant figure in this search is Efua Sutherland, who guided her generation towards two dramatic models not previously associated with literary drama: the first one is traditional theatre, thus repeating the pattern of borrowings and inspiration from pre-colonial aesthetics as practised in prose and poetry.[3]

> in the area of incorporating traditional oral forms, of building a direct bridge to the audience by addressing their immediate concerns, the theatre is of course advantaged, since it deals with performance.[4]

---

[1] See Kofi Agovi, "The Origin of Literary Theatre in Colonial Ghana, 1920–1957," *Research Review* (Institute of African Studies, University of Ghana at Legon) 6.1 (1990): 1.

[2] Angmor, *Contemporary Literature in Ghana*, 194.

[3] "In West Africa, perhaps more than in Eastern, Central and Southern Africa, there is a whole tradition of modern dramatisations of old narratives"; Mineke Schipper, *Theatre and Society in Africa* (Johannesburg: Ravan, 1982): 72.

[4] Femi Osofisan, "Warriors of a Failed Utopia?," 22.

The second model is represented by contemporary unwritten popular theatre such as the Ghanaian Concert Party and the Yoruba Travelling Theatre, thus widening the scope of this book to include performance theory and cultural studies. Interestingly, the syncreticity of their features and historical origins makes the notion of 'authenticity' an extremely elusive one. This chapter has benefitted immensely from a recent and much needed publication, *West African Popular Theatre* (1997) by Karin Barber, John Collins and Alain Ricard, which is extremely detailed and exhaustive in its geographical distinctions and generic categorizations. An earlier study by Kwabena Bame, *Come to Laugh* (1981) tended to blur the boundary between traditional and popular, as its subtitle indicates: "A Study of African Traditional Theatre in Ghana." By and large, the present chapter is structured on a perspective reminiscent of Chris Dunton's seminal *Make Men Talk True* (1992), focused on Nigeria, where English language drama is seen as

> being surrounded by [...] a multiplicity of other kinds of theatre; and of there being an increasing willingness amongst English-medium theatre practitioners to take advantage of this diversity, to work across different kinds of theatre projects.[5]

These two models, followed by Sutherland and other West African authors of her generation, invitte some inevitable implications regarding stage configuration and genre contamination.

Chapter 6 closes by considering the absence of themes relevant to contemporary social issues and introduces Chapter 7, which is centred on Mohammed ben Abdallah's plays. His works take up the legacy of Sutherland's efforts and offer a tentative, variedly successful fusion of African-based techniques and thematic depth. Among the West African dramatists of Abdallah's generation, the Nigerian Femi Osofisan is given well-deserved prominence thanks to the undeniable achievement of his huge creative output. Among other things, Chapter 7 attempts to highlight the connection between Abdallah's generation and the practice of Theatre for Development and the anti-naturalistic techniques of certain Western playwrights.

A few clarifications need to be made. First, unlike the case in Part Two above, Ghana is not the exclusive subject here, but still constitutes the backbone as in Part One. In particular, the decision to highlight the work of Mohammed ben Abdallah is also due to the unjust critical neglect of his work to date. Secondly, among the works employed as points of comparison for the main authors, a few unpublished plays deserving of attention have also been taken into consideration. In a sense, the

---

[5] Chris Dunton, *Make Men Talk True: Nigerian Drama in English since 1970* (London: Hans Zell, 1992): 2.

choice almost becomes a necessity, given the enormous difficulties with publishing plays in Ghana. In Abdallah's words: "The problem is that publishing houses have a limited interest in African writing and then plays don't sell nearly as well as novels, so they're not interested in publishing plays."[6] The Ghanaian situation is especially dreadful: during my second research stay in Ghana in 1997, I realized with amazement that not a single Ghanaian play had been published since my first visit in 1993! A four-year-long void is certainly something to think about.

Finally, Chapter 7 includes two instances of contemporary plays expressly inspired by two of the West African novelists examined above: Bode Sowande's version of Tutuola's *My Life in the Bush of Ghosts* and Abdallah's link with Armah's *Two Thousand Seasons* in his *The Fall of Kumbi*. In the light of the pattern followed by this book, such correspondences may partially suggest a return to the beginning, a phenomenon of generic metamorphoses coming full circle.

The ancestral pool

Efua Theodora Sutherland (1924–96) was undoubtedly the writer who paved the way for the Ghanaian renaissance of drama. Her innumerable achievements, as Agovi writes, point to "possibilities of liberating the African theater from its fixation in European form."[7] In the midst of the cultural renaissance ideologically supported by Nkrumah's government, she assumed a leading role in the search for new modes of expression in the arts. Her 'institutional' creations include the founding of the Ghana Experimental Theatre (1958), which culminated in the birth of the historic Ghana Drama Studio (1960). Officially inaugurated by Nkrumah in October 1961, the studio later became part of the Institute of African Studies, University of Ghana.

The main thrust behind Efua Sutherland's efforts was aimed at a fusion between literary theatre and traditional forms. Together with other authors, she began "to look at the traditional material again in the hope that they will be able to make indigenous forms of dramatic expression the foundation for contemporary drama."[8] In this sense, her most representative product is the play *The Marriage of Anansewa* (1975), which enjoyed great success and aroused wide interest. The publication of this book should be considered as the outcome of her long research into the per-

[6] Wilkinson, *Talking with African Writers*, 42.

[7] Kofi Agovi, "Towards an Authentic African Theatre," *Ufahamu* 19.2–3 (Spring–Fall 1991): 73.

[8] J.H. Kwabena Nketia, *Ghana: Music, Dance and Drama; A Review of the Performing Arts of Ghana* (Tema: Ghana Publishing Corporation, 1965): 46.

formance of traditional *anansesem*, the folk stories of the Akans, which she undertook with her theatrical companies. As she writes in the foreword to the play:

> Although this storytelling is usually a domestic activity, there are in existence some specialist groups who have given it a full theatrical expression with established conventions. It is this system of traditional theatre which I have developed and classified as *Anansegoro*.[9]

In other words, the *anansegoro* ('spider plays') she ccreated are a literary continuation of the traditional form that Nketia defines as narrative drama, "a composite of speech (narrative and dialogue), music, dance and mime."[10] Martin Owusu offers a detailed instance of a partly-narrated, partly-acted *anansesem*, where "actors play the parts of characters in the story at various points, the narrator taking the position of 'observer' at times."[11]

As testimony to Sutherland's research prior to the publication of the play, it might be interesting to mention a report in which she describes the staging of an *anansegoro* by her Ghana Experimental Theatre Players in the Twi-speaking town of Akropong, on 27 March 1959.[12] The performance is composed of music, a storyteller dictating the flow of the action, actors' recitation and, above all,

> the CHORUS of men and women representing people gathering for a story session, [who] made their appearances in friendly groups of twos or threes. Some shook hands in greeting each other across the stage in Ghanaian fashion. Some even shook hands in greeting with the audience nearest the wings! [...] The Chorus in ANANSEGORO can draw the theatre audience into participation. That day Akropong demonstrated this.[13]

As S.D. Lokko writes, this is a constant feature of traditional Ghanaian drama:

> During a performance, there might be an exchange between actors and spectators – an exchange more prominent in the storytelling form than in others. If an actor or protagonist is unskilled in repartee – whether he is a chief, a priest, an office-holder, or otherwise – he can jeopardise the success and effectiveness of such an exchange.[14]

---

[9] Efua Sutherland, *The Marriage of Anansewa* (Harlow, Essex: Longman, 1975): v.

[10] Nketia, *Ghana: Music, Dance and Drama*, 29.

[11] Martin Owusu, *Drama of the Gods: A Study of Seven African Plays* (Roxbury MA: Omenana, 1983): 4.

[12] The article's importance is heightened by the fact that it appeared in issue 1 of the historic journal *Okyeame*, one of Sutherland's accomplishments, mentioned in Chapter 5. See also Amma Kyerewaa–Gyapon, "Drama and Theatre in Post-Independent Ghana" (BA thesis, Institute of African Studies, University of Ghana, nd): 12.

[13] Efua Sutherland, "Venture into Theatre," *Okyeame* 1 (1961): 47–48.

[14] Sonia Lokko, "Theatre Space: A Historical Overview of the Theatre Movement in Ghana," *Modern Drama* 23 (1980): 311.

The Marriage of Anansewa recounts Ananse's wiles in betrothing his daughter to more than one suitor in order to collect money as gifts from all of them; in the end, he has to simulate Anansewa's death as a way out of this sad pickle. The trickster–protagonist shows some of his familiar traditional traits: he speaks with a nasal tone – only when afraid, in the play[15] – and, when he realizes the mess he has got himself into, the solicitous Property Man screens him from view with a spider's web.[16] His character exemplifies the humorous tone of the play, and its recitation certainly requires at times the skills of a practised comedian. In the end, for instance, after having wailed incessantly in fake mourning, he must pretend to be in a state of spiritual possession when the desired suitor is the only one left:

> Ancestors, I am pleading with you,
> If it is your desire
> As it is ours
> That Chief-Who-Is-Chief
> Should marry Anansewa,
> See to it that she returns to life!
> Wake her!
> See to it that Anansewa awakes
> And returns to become a bride!
> [*He falls into the arms of PROPERTY MAN as though he is overcome by contact with the spirits. He sings like a man in a trance.*][17]

The work displays the same features as that of the performance in Akropong, along with all the formal elements of traditional theatre that several other West African playwrights have made use of until very recently, as this chapter will attempt to show.

First of all, this is a theatre close to the conception of 'total art', including music, singing, dance and mime, following the ancestral performance aesthetic based on "a communication strategy which focuses on an integrated perception of visual, kinetic, aural and auditory elements."[18] This feature asserted its presence from the very beginnings of anglophone West African drama. The songs in *The Marriage* belong to the '*mboguo*' ('interlude') type, with a varying degree of relevance to the

15 Sutherland, *Marriage*, 14, 42, 44.

16 Sutherland, *Marriage*, 32, 44. On the characteristics of the spider Ananse in Akan folklore, see Chapters 2 and 3 above (pp. 76, 95–97).

17 Sutherland, *Marriage*, 79.

18 Agovi, "Authentic African Theatre," 67.

plot, or are straightforward tunes meant to express a character's feelings or to be sung during Anasewa's outdooring ceremony.[19]

The second point is audience involvement, which constitutes a main feature of traditional theatre:

> Many observations and comments made by members of the audience have the tendency to force the narrator to expand the text of the story by incorporating their ideas and even their phrases; the story told under such circumstances is a sum total of the narrator's descriptions and the audience observations, in the sense that the entire performance is a *collaborative activity*.[20]

In *The Marriage*, songs and dances are designed to invite public participation:

> Anansesem is a community art. All the people present are performers in one way or another, either actively or potentially. Though the specialists control the main flow of the action, their performance requires the participation of the audience.[21]

To facilitate the intended integration, Sutherland devised a group of players acting on stage as the audience of a storytelling session.

The third, fundamental point is the presence of the storyteller, who is invested with an intermediary function between play and audience while at the same time interacting with the players.[22] His presence breaks the fourth wall typical of naturalistic theatre, and he is meant to accompany the audience continuously back and forth between the two dimensions of fiction and reality. It is worth noting, however, that the storyteller is not the only one who speaks to the public: Ananse does this as well, so that no one has the exclusive right to cross the barrier. Actually, the storyteller appears only after Ananse has already explained his situation extensively. Another significant character is Property Man, who distributes props and prompts: in theory he starts out as a non-naturalistic character, but in the end he will show an pronounced involvement in Ananse's troubles. In this story, the boundary between meta-fiction and naturalism is indeed imperceptible.[23]

Such fluidity is enhanced by the highly dynamic integration of all the elements just described, so much so that the play appears to be a display of sophisticated

---

[19] Sutherland, *Marriage*, 37–42.

[20] Isidore Okpewho, *African Oral Literature*, 62.

[21] Sutherland, *Marriage*, vii.

[22] It is not by chance that he holds an *Okyeame*'s staff.

[23] See Helen Gilbert & Joanne Tompkins, *Postcolonial Drama: Theory, Practice, Politics* (London & New York: Routledge, 1996): 132–33.

theatricalities where roles are assumed and dropped with the greatest of ease and interludes blur into the main plot. At the start of Act Two, for instance, we find:

> STORYTELLER: So then, Ananse didn't toil in vain?
>
> PLAYERS: No.
>
> STORYTELLER: Still, isn't this the first sign of trouble?
>
> PLAYERS: Well, we shall see.
>
> STORYTELLER: All right, whatever the case may be, we may as well wish him luck. *[To the gong-player:]* Calling!
>
> *[Gong rhythm. Two women rise, one starting off the song for the Mboguo]*
>
> MBOGUO
>
> *[The two women share the song with the PLAYERS. They dance to it in a matronly way. STORYTELLER leads them in the dance to PROPERTY MAN who hands to one of them a girdle with money tied in a huge knot in it. She ties it round her waist. STORYTELLER accompanies them back to sit in their places.]*
>
> [... After they have sung and danced]
>
> *[PROPERTY MAN sets a chair and a side table when the dance ends. ANANSE, dressed in brand-new cloth, enters in good spirits and sits.]*
>
> ANANSE: Serve my gin here.
>
> *[PROPERTY MAN obliges. While ANANSE is sipping his gin the song ceases. Promptly, the two women rise in haste and keeping step with each other they move towards ANANSE. They are SAPAASE MESSENGERS now.]*

The message is delivered, and the two women will pick the same Mboguo up again while dancing back to their places.[24]

Etherton writes that *The Marriage* "is part of a much wider Ghanaian concern to make a very thorough formalistic reorganization of traditional performing arts into modern theatre."[25] Another Ghanaian author who has made use of the *Anansewa* plot is Patience Henaku Addo, a poet, playwright and teacher, whose works have been strangely ignored by most critics.[26] Her biography sounds exemplary with regard to the search for new forms of theatrical expression in the years around independence and to the resistant colonial mentality felt at that time:

---

24 Sutherland, *Marriage*, 21–23.

25 Michael Etherton, "Trends in African Theatre," *African Literature Today* 10 (1979): 78. In 1968, Sutherland formed the New Studio Players to bring the Drama Studio back to life (since the 1966 coup against Nkrumah, it had been almost abandoned). The company's inaugural plays were Sutherland's *Tweedledum and Tweedledee* and the children's play *Ananse and the Dwarf Brigade*; see Kyerewaa–Gyapon, "Drama and Theatre," 33.

26 Naana Jane Opoku–Agyemang's essay "Lest We Forget" (1995) introduced me to this and other rewarding works by Ghanaian women writers.

> Theatre has always been part of my education. In primary school we had end-of-the-year performances; we didn't do plays, but dances and games. In Achimota Secondary School we did little plays, entertainments called 'girls at home' or 'boys at home'. In the former, for instance, girls did short plays and they invited the boys to come to their house to see, with some dancing too.
>
> As for dancing, I was doing it in the public arena even before I went to school. But when I started schooling I was told that it was wrong to dance Ghanaian dances. Therefore, I was part of a group doing things like Scottish dancing. I continued being involved in performances at Training College, where I played in Goldsmith's *She Stoops to Conquer*.
>
> Later on, together with Mr. Opoku, I started the Ghana Dance Ensemble, sent by the Ministry of Education. It was the first of September, 1962. Paradoxically, I had to polish up my Ghanaian dances, because I had grown better in ballroom dancing – I had also represented Ghana for an international tango formation in 1960. A month later we had our first students; I was helping with drilling them. (Addo, Madina, 18 August 1997)

Her career also testifies to the easy flow among different artistic expressions, symptomatic of the conception of total art mentioned above and of the holistic approach of theatre workers:

> I didn't stay there for long. By the end of the first term, April 1963, I had switched on to Drama, as a member of the Drama Studio, taking part in their plays and also working as wardrobe mistress for several productions. I was in the first production of Efua Sutherland's *Edufa*, playing Chorus Two. Then, while I was working as assistant to the director Joe De Graft, I decided to be a student, acting in students' productions. For my final year I did playwriting as an optional subject, I think I was the first female student doing that. Later I moved to Britain to do my post-graduate course, and there I also did dancing, playwriting and directing in schools. (Addo, Madina, 18 August 1997)

In 1971 she put on an unpublished play called *Anansewa*, which prompts one to wonder what kind of connection might exist with Efua Sutherland's work:

> When I was in Bristol I wanted to do a short production with students. Not a European play, but something original. So I took the popular Ananse story. Back home in Ghana we had used the same story to improvise in class with Efua, and years after *Anansewa* came out of that. The plot was practically the same as Efua's: at a loss about what to do after having promised his daughter to several wealthy chiefs, Ananse pretends the girl is dead. In my case I got a fetish priest to intervene, performed by myself.
>
> Basically, it's the same popular Ananse story. We had improvised this in class with Efua, under the bamboo tree of the Institute, during my first year. Ananse's

> daughter has different names among the ethnic groups. I think the name 'Anansewa' was probably coined by Efua. She put on her version much later. (Addo, Madina, 18 August 1997)

The format of the two performances, though, was different:

> My show was a dance drama with a mixed group of students, to whom I taught Ghanaian dances. It was only narration and dancing, with no dialogue: the dancers performed what the narrator said. I got my husband [the British critic James Gibbs] to play Ananse. Culturally, for Anansewa's suitors I selected chiefs from different parts of Ghana, and dressed everybody in costumes. It went very well, at the end the whole audience was on the floor dancing.
>
> I don't know whether she knew about my version when she put on hers, but I don't think that was important, was it? I met her again in 1993, and a lot of times before then, but the issue never came up. (Addo, Madina, 18 August 1997)

If one keeps the traditional dramatic forms outlined by Nketia as points of reference, Addo's *Anansewa* seems to occupy a middle position between narrative and dance drama, the latter "expressed through music, poetry, mime and movements of the dance," where "speech is relatively less important."[27]

Other Ghanaian authors apart from Sutherland and Addo drew inspiration from ancestral dramatic lore in the wake of the 1956 National Theatre Movement, when a "national cultural policy document [...] had the mandate to refashion indigenous Ghanaian traditions to suit our modern theatre through creative experimentation."[28] As far as Ghana is concerned, this also chapter examines works by Asiedu Yirenkyi, Martin Owusu, Joe DeGraft and Michael Dei–Anang.

Asiedu Yirenkyi's *Amma Pranaa*, to start with, is based on a well-known folk story about a stubborn girl who marries a stranger and meets a terrible end.[29] In this case, the stranger turns out to be a lion, but Amma is saved by a hunter whom she will marry. Traditional elements abound in this spoken, narrated, danced and mimed play: at the beginning a Master Drummer, similar to Sutherland's Property Man, prepares the stage and sings a formulaic introduction; this is taken up again near the

---

27 In Nketia's nomenclature, the third and last form is "ceremonial drama [… A] dramatic expression associated with social ritual and ceremonial occasions"; Nketia, *Ghana*, 29.

28 Agovi, "Origin of Literary Theatre," 3.

29 For the various versions of the tale, which seems to be ubiquitous in West Africa, see Naana Jane Opoku–Agyemang, " 'A Girl Marries a Monkey': The Folktale as an Expression of Value and Change in Society," *Asemka: A Literary Journal of the University of Cape Coast* 7 (September 1992): 5–12. Amos Tutuola incorporates this story in the adventures of his *Palm-Wine Drinkard*, 17–34.

end, to close the play.[30] Next it is the players' turn to sing the 'Entrance song', in order to announce the presentation of the Ananse story. The appearance of the Storyteller marks the beginning of the re-created folktale session:

> 1st CHORUS: What story are you telling us today?
>
> STORYTELLER: What story do you want me to tell you?
>
> 1st AUDIENCE: Tell us the story about Ananse and the ten thousand giants.
>
> 2nd AUDIENCE: No, tell us ... eh ... yes; tell us the story about Kwaku Ananse and Nana Nyankpong, the Creator.
>
> 2nd CHORUS: Ohh ... you all leave him alone; let him tell us any story.
>
> STORYTELLER: You want me to tell any story?
>
> 3rd CHORUS: No, why should you tell us just any story. We are not here just to laugh and forget .... We are here to laugh and learn. So you'll tell us the story about that proud but pretty girl [...] that pretty but insolent girl who rejected the man her parents wanted her to marry and nearly met her death. The ever rebellious youth of today need it. They all need some talking to .... in proverbs.[31]

Some players are to be positioned in the audience and some of them join the chorus on stage during the play; Yirenkyi thus takes a further step here towards that collective involvement envisioned by Efua Sutherland.[32] The choice of subject is accordingly presented to give an impression of casualness, through an apparent improvisation that nevertheless allows the storyteller to hint at other works by the same author. After a digressive dialogue between two men, one blind and the other deaf, the storyteller asks:

> everyone is useful in his own way. Have you heard about the fool who saved his father from death after all his wise brothers had failed in their attempt to save him?
>
> CHORUS: No.
>
> STORYTELLER: Would you like to hear it?
>
> CHORUS: Yes, yes, of course.
>
> STORYTELLER: All right. Join us here again tomorrow night. I will be here again with another interesting story .... and bring your friends.[33]

A footnote by the author mentions his play *Piesie*, still unpublished. During our interview, he said:

---

30 Asiedu Yirenkyi, *Kivuli and other plays* (London: Heinemann, 1980): 100, 120.

31 Yirenkyi, *Kivuli*, 102.

32 A further similarity is the *O*kyeame's staff held by the storytellers in both plays.

33 Yirenkyi, *Kivuli*, 115.

> I wrote a number of plays like that, *Amma Pranaa* was the first of the series. My intention there was to create a group that seems to be going around telling stories, selecting the theme according to the situation. As for that interlude between the deaf and the blind, in storytelling session you often have these asides, in the form of dialogue or songs not strictly related to the theme. (Yirenkyi, Legon, 23 November 1993)[34]

Sutherland's *mboguo* in *The Marriage*, in fact, can take the form of a dialogue, too. And, as in Sutherland's play, the divide between naturalistic acting and presentational style is practically non-existent here: when the storyteller is asked for advice by Amma's desperate mother, he invites her to choose a husband from among *all* the men present, including the male chorus and the male members of the audience.[35]

Martin Owusu likewise adapted *anansesẹm* in three of his plays: *The Story Ananse Told* (1971), *The Pot of Okro Soup* (1973) and *A Bird Called 'Go-Back-for-the-Answer'* (1973). In all of these, Ananse plays the rọle of storyteller and sly character at the same time. In the first, the audience is drawn into the plot at several points, disrupting any pretence to naturalism: "No, I didn't. Ask the audience," replies Ananse when suspected by the Queen of having caused trouble.[36] Other characters perform the same function. When the antelope's head turns into a beautiful woman, it makes a hunter promise not to reveal its secret nature:

> HUNTER: But I'm not the only person who knows. A lot of people do.
>
> WOMAN [previously antelope]: What? Where are they?
>
> HUNTER: Look ahead of you ....
>
> WOMAN: The audience? As for the audience they can know. I mean people in this world created by Kweku Ananse.[37]

In the same play, the author manages to show the spider's comic potentialities to their fullest extent, just as *The Marriage of Anansewa* does. When trying to confuse the linguist, Ananse shows his true nature, that of comedian trickster:

---

[34] In 1975, during the years of Acheampong's military rule, Yirenkyi wrote *Dasebre*, a play about the bloody internecine wars in a traditional setting, heavily relying on ritual and folklore. He told me that he researched deeply into local festivals before writing the play, which was intended as a criticism of the excesses of illegitimate military governments in Ghana. *Dasebre* was first performed at the School of Performing Arts, University of Ghana, 15 March 1990.

[35] Yirenkyi, *Kivuli*, 106.

[36] Martin Owusu, *The Story Ananse Told* (London: Heinemann, 1971): 22. *The Story Ananse Told* was first presented by the St Augustine's College Staff in the college assembly hall, Cape Coast, on 1 December 1967, and also broadcast by Ghana Television on 24 December.

[37] Owusu, *Story*, 6. The folktale of the hunter marrying an antelope-woman is another narrative found throughout West African oral literature. In anglophone writing, it is elaborated in Tutuola's *My Life in the Bush of Ghosts* and Ben Okri's *Songs of Enchantment*, 265–70.

ANANSE: Yet I seek nothing but the welfare of fellow beings.

OKYEAME: That's why I thank you even before I seek your help.

ANANSE: I almost feel like weeping.

OKYEAME: Please, don't; don't.

ANANSE: [*Weeping*] *Agya ee – agya ee – agya ee – mawu oo* ....

OKYEAME: Oh, Kweku, don't weep like that.

ANANSE: *Mawu oo – mawu oo – agya ee – agya ee* ....

OKYEAME: Kweku, when I hear you weep like that it arouses my feelings. I also feel like weeping.

BOTH: *Agya ee – agya ee – mawu oo – mawu oo* ....

ANANSE: [*Stops suddenly and looks at Okyeame who is still weeping*] What are you weeping for? Anything the matter?[38]

Joe De Graft (1924–78), once director of the Ghana Drama Studio and of the School of Performing Arts, wrote a play called *Ananse and the Gum Man* (staged 1961). In this work the trickster plays dead in order to consume all his family harvest on his own. The funeral rites are complex and well-structured, but the storyteller's role is limited to the introduction and the connecting up of different situations, and he never actually interacts with the flow of the action.

Michael Dei–Anang is one of the many intellectuals who responded early to the the appeal of Kwame Nkrumah's Convention People's Party for cultural revival. His *Okomfo Anokye's Golden Stool* (1963), an historical play on the wars between the Denkyira and the Ashanti peoples,[39] is an example of total theatre in which a linguist occasionally performs the function of storyteller and a storytelling session among children is effectively re-created.[40]

The Nigerian theatre scene did not witness such a general movement towards the recovery of precolonial modes of expression, as I have already indicated, but more isolated individuals and groups worked in the same direction as their Ghanaian colleagues. The tendency to include a wide range of different forms of expression in one's plays was present from the very beginning. Dapo Adelugba, one of the fathers

[38] Owusu, *Story*, 31.

[39] The legendary figure of Anokye is satirized in Kojo Laing' *Woman of the Aeroplanes*, see Chapter 3 (p. 98) above.

[40] Dei–Anang, *Okomfo Anokye*, 22–24, 27, 43. With respect to total theatre and storytelling, another Ghanaian author worth mentioning is Yaw Asare, particularly his unpublished plays *Ananse in the Land of Idiots* and *The Secret of the Ancient Well*, performed respectively in December 1993 (Drama Studio, School of Performing Arts, University of Ghana at Legon) and July 1997 (National Theatre, Accra).

of Nigerian theatre, sees it as a continental phenomenon: "This often lauded version of [traditional] total art (some would even call it 'total theatre') has fired the imagination of modern African creative artists and theatre-makers."[41]

Traditional forms offer a great variety of exploitable creative ideas. The Alarinjo Travelling Theatre of the Yorubas, for instance, after starting with masquerading for ancestor worship, has gone on to stage a more diversified programme:

> profane topics from low life to satirical sketches [...] operatic in nature, each consisting of a series of brief dramatic sketches and acrobatic displays linked together by *bata* drum music and choral chanting, with little dialogue or storytelling within sketches.

Another experience of total theatre is provided by the Kwagh–Hir Puppet Theatre of the Tivs, which involves "puppetry, narrative summaries, song, dance, and dialogue between the prompter / narrator and the audience."[42]

The Apidan of the Yorubas similarly implies a conception of theatre beyond simple dramatic mimesis, where the use of paralinguistic techniques goes hand in hand with a narrator and constant dialogic flow between actors and audience:

> [it] includes enactments that are at the same time presentational and representational [...] conceived of as a duality by the appropriate spectators, comprising reality and fiction simultaneously.[43]

Kacke Götrick has pointed to formal continuities between this traditional genre and modern anglophone Yoruba playwrights, and one of the writers she analyses most extensively is the 1986 Nobel Laureate for Literature Wole Soyinka (b. 1934). In his *The Trials of Brother Jero* (1964), the eponymous protagonist acts and recounts to the audience his trickster-like adventures, "to show you one rather eventful day in my life," he says jokingly.[44] Jero introduces the other characters and comments on

[41] Dapo Adelugba, *Towards a Theory and Criticism of Theatre Arts* (Discourse 3; lecture delivered in the Postgraduate School Forum for Interdisciplinary Discourse, University of Ibadan, 25 July 1991; University of Ibadan, 1991): 12.

[42] Okpewho, *African Oral Literature*, 270, 274. Okpewho quotes Joel A. Adedeji, "The Alarinjo Theatre: The Study of a Yoruba Theatrical Art from Its Earliest Beginnings to the Present Times" (doctoral dissertation, University of Ibadan, 1969), and Iyoruese O. Hagher, "The Kwagh Hir: An Analysis of a Contemporary Indigenous Puppet Theatre and Its Social and Cultural Significance in Tivland in the 1960s and 1970s" (doctoral dissertation, Ahmadu Bello University, Zaria, 1981), for the Alarinjo and Kwagh-Hir theatre respectively.

[43] Kacke Götrick, *Apidan Theatre and Modern Drama* (Stockholm: Almqvist & Wiksell, 1984): 130–31.

[44] Wole Soyinka, *The Trials of Brother Jero* (1964), in *The Jero Plays* (Ibadan: Spectrum, 1973): 10.

what is happening to him, creating an overall comic effect which has made this work one of Soyinka's most successful.[45]

Among the champions of dramatic continuity along the traditional–contemporary anglophone axis, Götrick also mentions Ola Rotimi (b.1938) and the abundant use of music and dance characterizing his *Ovonramwen Nogbaisi* (1974), an historical play on the defeat of the Chief of Benin by the British army.[46] Rotimi has inspired "widespread admiration for [...his] mastery of stagecraft,"[47] and he also developed a close link with his audience, who are often brought into the dramatic action. In *Ovonramwen Nogbaisi*, for instance, a stage direction suggests that, during the ceremony of the Oba's surrender, "some chiefs and commonalty move into the auditorium and share seats with the members of the audience or simply crouch whenever possible in the aisles, so that the audience now becomes a living part of the action in that scene."[48] In the prologue to another of his plays, Rotimi writes: "the African audience is a *polaroid audience*. [...] If you're good, the African audience lets you know *in the instant* of your acting, by its reaction. If you're bad, it lets you know as well. You don't have to wait, as in Europe or America, till the following day or days later, for a *critic* arrogating to himself the perception of the majority."[49]

Another play worth mentioning written in English by a first-generation Nigerian author is certainly John Pepper Clark's *Ozidi* (1966), a rendition of an Ijaw saga that traditionally could be enacted in two forms:

> as a story narrated by a storyteller who assumes all the roles and who may or may not be accompanied by musicians; as a community performance, in Orua, in which certain members of the community take certain roles in the saga.

In his play, Etherton continues, Clark (b. 1935) uses both versions, accomplishing "a modern work of art."[50] Full of music and dancing, *Ozidi* features a storyteller

---

[45] The same author displays his gift for total theatre in plays such as *A Dance of the Forests* (1963), where dances and dirges are linked with ancestral rituals, and *Kongi's Harvest* (1967), including traditional dances and music but also anthems of the fictional dictatorship of Isma.

[46] At the beginning of Ola Rotimi's *The Gods Are Not to Blame* (London: Oxford UP, 1971), a much-discussed version of Sophocles' *Oedipus*, the actors dance, mime and chant what the Narrator (instead of the Greek chorus) is explaining to the audience.

[47] Dunton, *Make Men Talk True*, 12.

[48] Ola Rotimi, *Ovonramwen Nogbaisi* (Benin City: Ethiope; Oxford: Oxford UP, 1974): 51.

[49] Ola Rotimi, *Hopes of the Living Dead* (Ibadan: Spectrum, 1988): ix (emphasis in original).

[50] Michael Etherton, *The Development of African Drama* (Hutchinson University Library for Africa; London: Hutchinson, 1982): 69, 70.

who introduces the plot and sometimes reappears to narrate it, while playing major and minor roles. About the protagonist, he says:

> I know him well; why, I am the fellow himself when I am not the plain narrator of our story; in the actual drama I play brother to the King as well as father to, and in fact your hero himself. Quite some intricate and interesting relationship that, isn't it?[51]

After this introductory speech, a rite is performed "to placate our hosts from the sea," and the storyteller, as a stage direction prescribes, "*assumes the powers and postures of a priest.*"[52]

The last Nigerian author to be mentioned here is Wale Ogunyemi (b. 1939), who has never concealed "his preference for a 'total theater' in which non verbal elements play a crucial signifying role," and whose substantial output constitutes "an important reference point for other artists."[53] See, for instance, his historical *Kírìjì* (1976) and *Langbodo* (1979). During our interview, Ogunyemi elaborated on the widespread presence of total theatre in Nigeria:

> Total theatre is common here, but it is not a rule as such. We just thought that these works could appeal to the audience. A Nigerian audience would be bored by something like *Waiting for Godot*. Here they want to identify with whatever they are used to seeing everyday. So if you spice your plays with dance, music and mime, apart from dialogue, they will enjoy it. That is why they always like to watch dance dramas. If you are not careful, the message might get lost into all this. Amateur playwrights will fall into that mistake, but with some craft the dance and the music will communicate the message. (Ogunyemi, Ibadan, 1 August 1997)

The pull towards the popular and the language question

The traditional approach to theatre was not the only model investigated and tapped by the first generation of contemporary anglophone playwrights. Alongside a literary theatre dominated by Western paradigms and by the indigenous taste of the élites,[54] different kinds of popular drama increasingly thrived in West Africa, starting in the early decades of the twentieth century.

In Ghana, the whole process began with vaudeville for the affluent performed by Teacher Yalley. In his one-man shows he sang, danced and joked to the accompani-

---

51 John Pepper Clark, *Ozidi* (London: Oxford UP, 1966): 2.

52 Clark, *Ozidi*, 1, 3.

53 Dunton, *Make Men Talk True*, 252.

54 See Agovi, "Origin of Literary Theatre," 1.

ment of jazz music: "he dressed in wigs and false moustaches, and wore black-face make-up for several of his acts. His eyes and mouth were thickly rimmed with white."[55] Inspired by his shows, Ishmael Johnson (with Ansah and Hutton) set up his company, The Two Bobs, which emerged in the 1930s and established the historic mould of the Concert Party genre: a fusion of comic sketches (between the two jokers, known as 'Bobs') and a play featuring a Gentleman, a Lady Impersonator and a Servant making trouble between them. Ishmael rose to popularity as 'Bob Johnson', probably because the affordable prices of his 'Concerts'[56] did away with any pretence to exclusivity. His Two Bobs (later Axim Trio) toured Ghana and Nigeria extensively.

Efua Sutherland's research into the Concert Party includes a seminal book on Johnson, *The Original Bob* (1970). He became part of the Workers' Brigade No.1 Drama Group at the Drama Studio, and there she was able to interview him at length, assessing his fundamental work in establishing the genre. *The Original Bob*, like other volumes on the subject, lists four inspirational sources for the genre: the African–American vaudeville artists who toured West Africa in the 1920s,[57] the Charlie Chaplin films which were very popular at the time, the religious musical plays known as 'Cantatas' performed by church groups, and traditional storytelling sessions. The outcome of these manifold influences was a composite of jokes and plays: "He took ordinary life stories and with them composed plays by the method of 'Kasa-ndwom. Kasa-ndwom' (Speech and song)."[58]

On the one hand, continuity with traditional forms is evident in the presence of trickster characters cast in the many-faceted mould of Ananse, such as "a comic servant or hanger-on who cracked jokes and indulged in horse-play and buffoonery, but who often remained loyal and told the truth when others did not."[59] On the other, the presentational form of the genre must be traced back to its vaudeville origin as well as to traditional storytelling. In their exhaustive and engrossing work on the subject, *West African Popular Theatre* (1997), Karin Barber, John Collins and Alain Ricard write that "The presentational style is strikingly direct: characters simply

---

[55] Efua Sutherland, *The Original Bob: The Story of Bob Johnson, Ghana's Ace Comedian* (Accra: Anowuo Educational, 1970): 6–7.

[56] "At that time the word 'Concert' had become a common name for performances on Empire Day, and Teacher Yalley's shows were also called Concerts"; Sutherland, *Original Bob*, 7.

[57] The duo Glass and Grant seem to be the most famous; see Barber et al., *West African Popular Theatre*, 18.

[58] Sutherland, *Original Bob*, 12.

[59] Barber et al., *West African Popular Theatre*, 15.

announce themselves to the audience and tell them the essential features of their character and situation."[60] Interaction with the audience necessarily follows suit.

The origins of this itinerant popular theatre, therefore, bear traces of a syncretism of the Western with the traditional: "The hybridity that characterizes all modern popular culture in West Africa is exhibited in peculiarly concentrated form in concert party." The African–American contribution is defined as a "transatlantic feedback cycle,"[61] a process we have already observed (in Chapter 2) with regard to the magical-realist novel.

During later decades, up to a boom period in the 1950s, Concert Parties underwent a gradual process of indigenization, or 'Akanization'. First of all, highlife music, a peculiarly West African genre, replaced jazz and became an increasingly integral part of the show – so much that, starting with E.K. Nyame's Akan Trio in 1952, several Concert groups were founded by guitar bands: "Since then concert acting and highlife music have become inseparable."[62] This involved further, linguistic indigenization:

> Highlifes were already being sung in Akan languages, and E.K. Nyame's second decisive innovation was to carry the use of the indigenous language over into the dialogue of the play. For the first time, audiences who spoke no English could watch an entire play in Akan language. The highlife-and-Akan recipe was an instant success.[63]

The slapstick caricatures, moral pathos, musical entertainment and easily recognizable set of characters and plots in the Concert Parties account for their immense popularity, both in urban and in rural areas. Although these plays are rarely political, in the 1950s some companies supported Nkrumah's fight for independence; later on, confirming its flair for utilizing successful forms of art, "Nkrumah's government itself began to set up guitar bands and concert parties to act as organs of CPP propaganda, such as the Workers' Brigade band and concert party."[64]

A similar interest was expressed by the National Theatre Movement's playwrights, as I have already indicated, and should be construed in the light of their intention to establish channels of creative communication that westernized literary drama could not even dream of. The Concert Party genre could not be properly considered 'traditional', but its development and consolidation are further proof of the

60 Barber et al., *West African Popular Theatre*, 16.

61 Barber et al., *West African Popular Theatre*, 16, 21. For the syncretic features characterizing popular arts in the whole African continent, see Barber, "Popular Arts in Africa," 10.

62 Barber et al., *West African Popular Theatre*, 12.

63 Barber et al., *West African Popular Theatre*, 33.

64 Barber et al., *West African Popular Theatre*, 23.

highly syncretic and incorporative dynamic of West African art-forms, which in turn validates the holistic rationale behind this work. Anglophone drama, it must be assumed, naturally utilized the same healthy outlook.

Once again, Efua Sutherland's personal interests became allied with governmental policies on culture and education. Since she was determined to "take the theatre to both urban and rural areas,"[65] the Concert Party model was the most suitable example for inspiration, as her book on Bob Johnson shows. The company she founded, Kusum Agromma, became

> the resident group of the Drama Studio [...] they modeled themselves exactly on concert party, except for two deviations: they used actresses for the female parts, and they sometimes staged propaganda plays with government-sponsored messages, for instance on family planning.[66]

In other words, they endeavoured to effect a marriage between Concert Party techniques and structure and topics of pressing social concern and a politically correct approach to gender matters.[67] Thematically, though, Ghanaian popular theatre (and its offshoot in Togo) appears to lack a significant message, relying on stereotyped, predictable moral lessons.[68] Sandy Arkhurst,[69] one of the leaders of the company, confirms how hard this could be:

> It was not always easy to broach such subjects to crowds of theatre-goers used to different things altogether. On a few occasions we met with a very hostile reception; I remember a very tense show in the Ashanti Region, for instance. (Arkhurst, Legon, 8 May 1997)[70]

---

[65] Chikwenye Okonjo Ogunyemi, "Efua Theodora Sutherland," in *Dictionary of Literary Biography*, 117: *Twentieth Century Caribbean and Black African Writers, First Series* (Detroit MI: Bruccoli Clark Layman / Gale, 1991): 285.

[66] Barber et al., *West African Popular Theatre*, 20. See also Kyerewaa–Gyapon, "Drama and Theatre," 35–36. A further deviation is financial: Kusum Agromma were not economically self-sufficient as Concert Party troupes used to be.

[67] In this regard, see also Kwabena N. Bamé, *The Concert Party in a Birth Control Campaign Programme: A 1975 Report Project* (a paper prepared for the 4th International Conference on Popular Music Studies at Accra Arts Centre, 12–19 August 1987; Institute of African Studies, University of Ghana at Legon, 1988): passim.

[68] See Barber et al., *West African Popular Theatre*, 116.

[69] Among other things, Arkhurst directed Kusum Agromma in a very successful version of the late medieval play *Everyman* devised by Efua Sutherland under the title of *Odasani*; see Etherton, *Development of African Drama*, 116.

[70] Arkhurst also reports that several members of Kusum Agromma have recently formed the Adehyman Company, which has toured rural areas on behalf of the Ministry of Education.

The figure of Patience Henaku Addo also played an important role in the relationship between literary and popular theatre. Her radio play in English, *Company Pot* (1973), is in tune with the policy of Kusum Agromma in vindicating women's rights: the protagonist Akyebi, a woman trying to gain financial independence by working as a bar-girl in a Ghanaian town, manages to elude several passes made at her by various sorts of men: "let any cheat of a man come to make me a company pot!" she concludes.[71] In the author's own words:

> 'Company Pot' means any man can come and use me, like the male characters in the play. This is a woman who says: "Look, I'm going to start a trade, and if I manage to do my own thing, let any man who thinks he can take advantage of me, try." (Addo, Madina, 18 August 1997)

The initials of the title could be seen as taken from "Concert Party":

> I wasn't aware of that. It never crossed my mind. "Company Pot" comes from an Akan expression, "abusua kuruwa," which literally means "family pot." I used "Company" because the whole community seems to want to come and use her. (Addo, Madina, 18 August 1997)

The stage directions envisage sound effects typical of a Concert Party format: a bell ringer advertising the show in a street atmosphere,[72] along with highlife music at various moments.[73] Further, the hypothetical audience is addressed by the actors, and some of them introduce themselves; after having done so, Akyebi explains her dire financial straits and directs an embarrassing appeal to the crowd: "If... er... if any man could employ me in his house... permanently... keep me comfortably. But usefully... yes, usefully... happily... that would be best. Meanwhile I am a bar girl."[74] The author has given the following explanation for her choice:

> I chose to draw on Concert Parties because nobody had done it before, with a written play in English. I wrote *Company Pot* as one of my two plays for my final in Legon. I had worked on Concert Parties and transcribed a lot of them, eight actually, on Efua Sutherland's request. Scholars like Kwabena Bame used them for their research.
>
> You know, it is not easy to make Ghanaian theatre practitioners appreciate and respect this genre. If the play hadn't been done by BBC World Service on March the

[71] Patience Henaku Addo, *Company Pot*, in *Nine African Plays for Radio*, ed. Gwyneth Henderson & Cosmo Pieterse (London: Heinemann, 1973): 185.

[72] "The most popular method of publicity," writes Efua Sutherland, "was by a bell ringer. Costumed in tail-coat and mask and made to look comic with a big belly, the bell ringer carried a bill-board round the town. Children loved his antics and trailed after him on his rounds and relayed the news to other people"; Sutherland, *Original Bob*, 16.

[73] Addo, *Company Pot*, 164, 179, 185.

[74] Addo, *Company Pot*, 164.

> 2nd, 1972, it wouldn't have caught the attention of Ghanaians. Since its publication it was done by Ibadan TV, Lagos TV, taken onto the stage by the Tricycle Theatre in London (1975) and performed by Michael Etherton somewhere in Central or Northern Nigeria. (Addo, Madina, 18 August 1997)

There is an additional form of drama which, in the early 1960s, strove to recover the appeal of traditional and popular theatrical patterns: the folk opera. Its inventor, Saka Acquaye, is another eclectic figure in Ghanaian arts: traditional and highlife musician,[75] art teacher, designer, decorator and sculptor – a 1997 Ghanaian magazine has defined him as "the greatest sculptor of our time."[76] His works include the popular musical plays *Obadzeng* and *The Lost Fishermen*, the latter based on Ga folktales.[77] The kind of music to be played and sung in his folk operas was both highlife and traditional, and the generic description provided by the author suggests another way of realizing a form of total theatre:

> a dramatic art employing folk music, folk dance and folklore with a view to preserving and fostering the highest values in the civilization of our people, and we present it as a treat for eye, ear emotion and the intellect.[78]

Unfortunately, the scripts of his plays are very hard to find. As for their language, Acquaye has always proved highly sensitive to the age-old controversy about the relationship between anglophone drama and heterogeneous African audiences. Once he proposed a predominance of mime over dialogue as a solution to the problem,[79] but in another essay he supported the usefulness of English in crossing ethnic boundaries, this conclusion being the fruit of personal experience:

---

[75] Atukwei Okai told me: "Saka Acquaye added drumbeat to my 1967 reading of 'Odododiodio Concerto'. He's a great man, a modern renaissance figure." (Okai, Legon, 19-8-1997)

Acquaye formed historic bands such as The Black Beats with King Bruce in 1952, Saka Acquaye and His African Ensemble during his studies in the USA, and the band Wulomey (playing indigenous Ga music) with Nii Ashitey in 1973; see W.B. Hagan, "Profile: Saka Acquaye Blends the Arts in Ghana," *Africa Report* (January 1971): 34; Collins, *Highlife Time*, 59, 128.

[76] Ablade Glover, "Contemporary Art in Ghana," *Sunday Herald* (6–12 July 1997), Living: 7.

[77] See Hagan, "Profile," 34; Angmor, *Contemporary Literature in Ghana*, 188–89; Kyerewaa-Gyapon, "Drama and Theatre," 28–30.

[78] Saka Acquaye, "Folk Opera in Ghana and Nigeria," paper delivered at the Symposium on African and Afro-American Music (March 1–6 1972), Institute of African Studies, University of Ghana: 2. Kwame Cumale and Batilloy Warritay report that contemporary Sierra Leonean drama in Krio employs the traditional techniques of total theatre, too; Cumale & Warritay, "Theatre for the People," *West Africa* (16 December 1985): 2642.

[79] Saka Acquaye, "The Problems of Language in the Development of the African Theatre," *Okyeame* 4.2 (1969): passim.

> if a production from a minority area goes to another area it faces an empty hall. We tried this in different places and decided to change the dialogue into English. The result is that we get far more audiences in those previously unsuccessful areas than we get within the language area.[80]

Efua Sutherland often had recourse to Akan – which is a sort of lingua franca in most areas of Southern Ghana – in order to touch Ghanaians more widely and deeply, and probably in an attempt to bridge the broad gap between traditional theatre and Concert Parties on the one side and literary drama in English on the other. Her plays *Foriwa* and *The Marriage of Anansewa* were first performed in Akan. Her companies Ghana Experimental Theatre Players and Kusum Agromma accordingly toured the country with plays in that language.[81] The issue came up again when she was asked about the predominance of poetry in Ghana:

> Our normal people, our laymen, are very poetic; it's not conscious, it's our nature, our use of language. That's why I'm happy about the introduction of local languages in the schools:[82] when you put a Ghanaian on stage, with the English he's half himself, he doesn't wear that language, half of his potential is lost. (Sutherland, Accra, 17 December 1993)

In this connection, in *Okyeame*, the literary journal she edited for years, she published and translated into English some poems in Akan by Patience Addo and a traditional poem she translated with J.H. Nketia.[83]

In the Nigerian theatrical panorama, the flourishing Yoruba Travelling Theatres were likewise an effective model, especially with regard to their rapport with the audience (as witness the immense popularity enjoyed by, among others, the pioneering Hubert Ogunde, who started producing his plays in the 1940s[84]). This Yoruba popular theatre evolved from church performances called Cantatas, staged from the

---

[80] Acquaye, "Folk Opera," 15.

[81] Actually, she often worked first in Akan. Her works "were 'put to the highest test' in Ghanaian language performances before a mixed audience [...] Works that passed such tests were then made available in English translations as well"; Kofi Anyidoho, "National Identity and the Language of Metaphor," in *FonTomFrom: Contemporary Ghanaian Literature, Theatre and Film*, ed. Anyidoho & James Gibbs (*Matatu* 21–22; Amsterdam & Atlanta GA: Rodopi, 2000): 1–22. Another historically significant group performing in Akan were the Anokye Players, the resident theatre company of the National Cultural Centre in Kumasi, founded in 1963.

[82] See Shillington, *Ghana*, 119.

[83] Patience Henaku Addo, "Nyankonkra" and "Nea Ohwehwe Annya," *Okyeame* 4.1 (1968): 16–19; J.H. Kwabena Nketia, "A Poem in Praise of Osei Tutu: from Traditional Apaee," *Okyeame* 2.1 (1964): 21.

[84] For a detailed description of Ogunde's career, see Etherton, *Development of African Drama*, 43–48.

beginning of the century, and exploded with the oil boom between the late 1960s and early 1970s. It gradually included improvised dialogue between the songs, though the present-day musical element has been reduced radically and is now limited to an "Opening Glee."[85]

The Yoruba Travelling Theatre developed its very own style, quite different from the Concert Party: a greater variety of modes, such as political criticism, topical satire, folkloric tales, and crime thrillers in Ogunde's work, Kola Ogunmola's realistic depictions of contemporary life, Duro Ladipo's Yoruba myths, to mention only a few;[86] a more varied audience, cutting across social classes as in Greek or Elizabethan drama;[87] a more representational and naturalistic performance mode, marked by less interaction between audience and performers as well as the use of platform stages: "The acting space was distinct and segregated from the audience space [...] They would not consider performing in the round."[88]

As early as the 1960s, the School of Drama at the University of Ibadan founded a university travelling theatre which "indicates an early awareness of the stultifying effect of allowing performance to be restricted to campus."[89] In the following decade, during the 1971–72 tour of the already mentioned *Kírìjì* by Wale Ogunyemi, a direct link was established with a Yoruba travelling theatre company, the Oluyole Theatre. Dapo Adelugba, the director of this production, describes this experiment as a fruitful cooperative venture which paved the way for a sort of linguistic contamination, thereby calling into question any pretence to a hierarchy of value among dramatic forms:

> For the Oluyole Theatre, *Kírìjì* served as a theatre workshop (and they were allowed to use the Theatre Arts Departrment facilities for rehearsals of plays in their own repertoire when they were not required for *Kírìjì*). Their uninhibited acting style helped to loosen up our students at the early stage of rehearsals. They were not given any major speaking parts as they were not fluent in the use of English, but their dancing, singing and acting as soldiers and townspeople helped to invigorate the entire performance [...] One of the significant issues raised by this production is the question of language. While the bulk of *Kírìjì* is in English, two vernacular languages (Yoruba and Hausa, more of the former than the latter) are also used freely when the situation demands

85 See Barber et al., *West African Popular Theatre*, 42.

86 See Barber et al., *West African Popular Theatre*, 40–41.

87 See Biodun Jeyifo, *The Truthful Lie: Essays in a Sociology of African Drama* (London & Port of Spain: New Beacon, 1985): 107; Barber et al., *West African Popular Theatre*, 42.

88 See Barber et al., *West African Popular Theatre*, 45.

89 Dunton, *Make Men Talk True*, 4.

> them [...] The kind of English used was what one might call a Nigerian brogue. Thus *Kíríjì* followed the philosophy of our Laboratory Theatre – language as a vehicular rather than a vernacular means of communication. We do not agree with those theorists who see English as the language of an exclusive, élitist, academic theatre, and Yoruba (and often Nigerian languages) as the true language of popular theatre in Nigeria.[90]

Wale Ogunyemi, the author of the play, was adamant about the central importance of that experience:

> We had to bring the Oluyole Theatre in because most of the the people we used were students. Niyi Osundare was an actor in it, too, and others like Femi Fatoba choreographed the dance. We brought the Yoruba group in as singers and dancers, and to form the crowd of warriors and hunters. That enhanced the play, because we couldn't start teaching the students how to do the traditional dances, we also had students from other Nigerian states, whose culture was not Yoruba.
>
> In general, the contribution of Yoruba popular theatre to English-speaking theatre has been substantial. When Hubert Ogunde started his company in 1944, he became the doyen of this country's theatre. If he hadn't started at that time, we probably would not have any drama group, or they would have come much later.
>
> There have been other instances of collaboration between those two kinds of theatre. In 1969, during the OUA Festival of Arts in Algiers, I was in Kola Ogunmola's adaptation of Amos Tutuola's *The Palm-Wine Drinkard*, with students of drama from here, and it was in Yoruba. (Ogunyemi, Ibadan, 1 August 1997)

Acting spaces

The search for authentic and 'rootsy' forms of dramatic expression could not help involving the physical shape of theatrical space. Needless to say, a westernized building with its proscenium-arch stage could not effect the desired organic integration of performers and audience. Traditional performances, after all, did not make use of such structures but of circular dispositions, which Arit Essien Essien compares with "the earliest theatre practices from the Greek era with some vestiges of ritual."[91] The same is sometimes valid for popular theatres. According to John Djisenu, "Concert parties [...] still use courtyards in most places in the country-

---

[90] Dapo Adelugba, "Kíríjì: the Concept of Theatre as Exploration," *African Notes* (Institute of African Studies, University of Ibadan) 7.1 (1971): 108–109.

[91] Arit Essien Essien, "Symbiotic Unity in Oral Performance," in *Literature and National Consciousness*, ed. Ernest N. Emenyonu (Calabar Studies in African Literature 4; Ibadan: Heinemann Educational, 1989): 93.

side."[92] Generally speaking, in Ghana "there has been a commitment since the days of Nkrumah to place both traditional and contemporary performances where they belong, namely, in the very midst of the people."[93]

Consequently, the Drama Studio in Accra was built on the design of a traditional Ghanaian household as an open-air space which "embodied the flexible features of the early courtyard performance spaces for both proscenium and circular staging."[94] Kofi Awoonor praised it because it encouraged participation: "In an age in which Africa is starting to build, to reproduce an English theatre in the tropics is mere stupidity. An eye must be kept [...] on the content of the drama itself."[95]

With respect to this, another landmark by Efua Sutherland is the Kodzi Dan ('Story House') theatre in the village of Atwia, in the Central Region of Ghana, built with the help of the village chief Nana Okoampa VI. Its most detailed description is probably provided by James Gibbs:

> The shape of the structure was inspired by the compound of an existing clan house, which had a rectangular depression in the concrete floor – a sort of 'orchestra' or performance area, around which people could sit. The Kodzidan is built on a larger scale and has more levels for members of the audience to sit on; on one side of the 'orchestra' is a 'stage' backed by a curve, concrete cyclorama. The roof is supported in such a way that the sides are almost entirely open, and the central portion of the roof is covered by opaque roofing sheets. All this means that the structure is shaded, well ventilated and well-lit – by natural light.[96]

The Kodzi Dan marks Sutherland's endeavour to have a drama which may work according to the life-rhythms of a community and at the same time revive Atwia's life; as E. Ofori Akyea writes, "to inject some new life into the village."[97] The project is still alive today, and one can see why Sutherland described it with such pride:

> The whole thing started in June 1965. Since then I've been keeping up my relationship with the village. I think it is an example of an approach to community life and development; someone should document it. The work in Atwia throws light on my writing:

---

92 John Djisenu, "Performing Spaces and Institutional Organisation in Ghana," *Journal of Performing Arts* (School of Performing Arts, University of Ghana at Legon) 2.1 (1996): 22.

93 Etherton, "Trends," 71.

94 Djisenu, "Performing Spaces," 23. On the Studio's architecture, see Kyerewaa–Gyapon, "Drama and Theatre," 14–15.

95 Awoonor, *Breast of the Earth*, 330.

96 James Gibbs, "Theatre of the Villages," *West Africa* (19–25 February 1996): 278.

97 E. Ofori Akyea, "The Atwia–Ekumfi Kodzidan: An Experimental African Theatre," *Okyeame* 4.1 (1968): 83.

> I don't know whether I'm a writer or a social worker, because writing is a way of thinking aloud about my society.[98] After 28 years, the village has developed. One of my happiest thoughts is that I have seen it develop. Without the proper attention, villages would just go more and more down. Part of my project regarded economic development, too. Now the young people are there, they're back! In Atwia, the youth of 1965 are now the elders. (Sutherland, Accra, 17 December 1993)

Asiedu Yirenkyi has revealed how much his generation owes to the Atwia project: "this is where the storytelling form as a stage play evolved" (Yirenkyi, Legon, 23 November 1993). Sutherland aside, the project involved another theatre pioneer of the time, Patience Addo, who later exported to Bristol this urge to work out more effective arrangements when she staged her dance-drama *Anansewa*:[99]

> That was the first time that what is now called Wickham Theatre [formerly Vandyke] was arranged so that the audience sat on three sides. A U-shaped audience, with one side as backstage. It was impressive. Since then, I have been to several departmental plays, and they used the same arrangement! I can say I was the very first. (Addo, Madina, 18 August 1997)

In Nigeria, the same dissatisfaction with proscenium-arch theatres was expressed by some critics and practitioners. In 1981, Meki Nzewi lamented the use of the Western proscenium structures: "the modern physical stage in Nigeria is an unimaginative transfer of the Euro-American stage but devoid of the facilities of the latter."[100] Efiok B. Uwatt subscribes to this view and criticizes Soyinka, who complains about this borrowed frame but does not reject it, whereas he praises Ola Rotimi's experiments, such as his employment in his companies of the 'theatre-in-the-round' structure, the Ori–Olokun Theatre at the University of Ife (1968–76) and the Crab Theatre from 1981 onwards.[101] In the former, unlettered and university-trained performers alike converted a hotel courtyard into a theatre-in-the-round. Uwatt links Rotimi's form with Eastern ones:

> By adapting this theatre formation to the modern stage, Rotimi shows that the African theatre can demonstrate fidelity to traditional African dramatic models in much the same manner as the Kabuki, Noah and Chinese Opera stages are faithful to their origins, by using dance, music, acrobatics, song and the open space [...] in the oriental theatre the audience was not rejected, but integrated with the acting area, usually from three, and sometimes from four sides.

---

[98] Her play *Foriwa* is about bringing new life to a dying village; see below, this chapter.

[99] See above in this chapter.

[100] Meki Nzewi, "Music, Dance, Drama and the Stage in Nigeria," in *Drama and Theatre in Nigeria: A Critical Source Book*, ed. Y. Ogunbiyi (Lagos: Nigeria Magazine, 1981): 437.

[101] See also Dunton, *Make Men Talk True*, 12.

In his interview with Uwatt, Rotimi himself associates such stage configurations with the need for the audience participation he tries to attain in his performances; therefore, he accordingly terms the Western proscenium "technical apartheid."[102] Another Nigerian play mentioned earlier, *Ozidi* by J.P. Clark, envisages a similar structure in its very first stage direction: "As spectators are settling down all around, a man walks into the open area of play."[103]

The Ahmadu Bello University at Zaria has also incorporated local architectural styles, since its drama studio is built of mud – "mud walls, mud arches, mud domes – in the style of a traditional Hausa public building."[104]

Generic contaminations: The case of Sutherland's *Foriwa*

Efua Sutherland proved to be an exemplary artist for Ghanaian and West African letters by embodying the main concept of this book: the intense incorporativeness of the three main genres – prose, poetry and drama. The prime example is her short story "New Life at Kyerefaso" (1960), which she later turned into a play, *Foriwa* (1967).[105] The inception of the short story displays a highly lyrical and rhythmic English, reminiscent of the novels and short stories of Ama Ata Aidoo:

> Shall we say
> Shall we put it this way
> Shall we say that the maid of Kyerefaso, Foruwa, daughter of the Queenmother, was a young deer, graceful in limb? Such was she, with head held high, eyes soft and wide with wonder. And she was light of foot, light in all her moving.
> Stepping springily along the water path like a deer that had strayed from the thicket, springily stepping along the water path, she was a picture to give the eye a feast. And nobody passed her by but turned to look at her again.[106]

---

[102] Efiok B. Uwatt, "Towards a New Form of African Theatre: Theatre-in-the-Round Performance in Ola Rotimi's Drama," in *Literature and Black Aesthetics*, ed. Ernest N. Emenyonu (Calabar Studies in African Literature 5; Ibadan: Heinemann Educational, 1990): 180, 181.

[103] Clark, *Ozidi*, 1.

[104] Uwatt, "Towards a New Form," 171.

[105] The short story was originally written in 1953; Kyerefaso is a town in the Ashanti region.

[106] Efua Theodora Sutherland, "New Life at Kyerefaso" (1960), in *Unwinding Threads: Writing by Women in Africa*, ed. Charlotte H. Bruner (London: Heinemann, 1994): 18. These lines are caustically parodied by Ayi Kwei Armah in his second novel, *Fragments* (1969; London: Heinemann Educational, 1974): 112–14.

Some poetic features are immediately evident to the reader: the initial anaphora with 'shall we' written in verse – lines that will reappear five times in the five-page story, as a sort of musical refrain; the alliteration of 'h' and 'w'; the echoing repetition of 'light'; the repetition-cum-inversion in the second paragraph.

The rest of the story contains further groups of verses designed to convey ritual oral poetry, such as the songs of the Asafo (warriors) Companies' festival:

> 'Osee!' rang the cry. 'Osee!' to the manly men of old. They crouched like leopards upon the branches.
> Before the drums beat
> Before the danger drums beat, beware!
> Before the horns moaned
> Before the wailing horns moaned, beware!
> They were upright, they sprang. They sprang. They sprang upon the enemy. But now, blood no more! No more thundershot on thundershot.[107]

or the sung folktale with which the village mocks Foruwa's supposed pride:

> There was a woman long ago,
> Tell that maid, tell that maid,
> There was a woman long ago,
> She would not marry Kwesi,
> She would not marry Kwaw,
> She would not, would not, would not.
> One day she came home with hurrying feet,
> I've found the man, the man, the man,
> Tell that maid, tell that maid,
> Her man looked like a chief,
> Tell that maid, tell that maid,
> Her man looked like a chief,
> Most splendid to see,
> But he turned into a python,
> He turned into a python
> *And swallowed her up.*[108]

In spite of the folktale's predicaments, the stranger chosen by Foruwa brings new enthusiasm to a village where idleness has long reigned. The play derived from this poetic short story confirms how Sutherland "exemplifies in her work the unity of

---

[107] Sutherland, "New Life," 19.

[108] Sutherland, "New Life," 20–21.

artistic expression in West African life."[109] According to C.O. Ogunyemi, the author expanded the story into a play "as if bothered by the limited impact that a short story could have in an analphabetic population,"[110] touching on the subject of the limited readership of prose in West Africa (mentioned here at the end of Chapter 3).

In *Foriwa* – a much less experimental play than *The Marriage of Anansewa* – the stranger Labaran conquers the protagonist's heart thanks to his industriousness. Beside displaying the author's eclectism with literary genres, both works contain strong thematic implications: the folktale mentioned above about the proud girl marrying an evil outsider is turned into a decisive choice for the improvement of society at large. Gay Wilentz writes: "The folktale has been reworked by numerous West African writers, yet Sutherland is unique in that the moral of the folktale in *Foriwa* is a positive one."[111] In doing so, the author follows Mineke Schipper's advice on the use of traditional themes and techniques, where "the artist is to give the material a new contemporary reference."[112]

Such a new regard was also geared to conveying a feminist orientation. The critic Naana Jane Opoku–Agyemang, always alert to the male-chauvinist background of both traditional and contemporary literature, comments on a series of African folktales based on that plot, and concludes that "the structures which inhibit the sense of initiative on the part of the heroines are sexist in thrust."[113] On the other hand, she also recognizes the potentiality inherent in folktales for counteracting the ills of society, but strangely does not mention either "New Life at Kyerefaso" or *Foriwa*. In the latter, the gender divide seems quite prominent, since the commitment to change shown by Foriwa and her mother, the village's Queenmother, stands in sharp contrast to the men's laziness and chauvinism. Sutherland, though, believes that the play should be interpreted more broadly:

> Foriwa wants to realize her potential, get an independent position. I'm very interested in the progress of the whole of our society, and I don't want to be distracted into femi-

---

[109] Charlotte H. Bruner, introduction to *Unwinding Threads: Writing by Women in Africa* (London: Heinemann, 1994): 17.

[110] C.O. Ogunyemi, "Efua Theodora Sutherland," 285.

[111] Gay Wilentz, "Writing for the Children: Orature, Tradition and Community in Efua Sutherland's *Foriwa*," *Research in African Literatures* 19.2 (Summer 1988): 183. The critic mentions, among the authors compared, Ama Ata Aidoo, John Pepper Clark, Flora Nwapa, and Amos Tutuola, but omits Yirenkyi's *Amma Pranaa* (discussed in this chapter). See also Syl Cheney–Coker, *Last Harmattan*, 56–58, and its story of Gustavius and Isatu, 87–208.

[112] Mineke Schipper, *Beyond the Boundaries* (Chicago: Ivan R. Dee, 1989): 85.

[113] N.J. Opoku–Agyemang, "Girl Marries a Monkey," 10.

> nine arguments. If a traditional attitude is suppressing me, I must stand up. It's not gender, but society. (Sutherland, Accra, 17 December 1993)

This could be linked with her declaration, quoted above, about feeling like a social worker and an artist at the same time; according to C.O. Ogunyemi, "The core of the play emanated from Sutherland's experimental theater the Kodzidan, in the village of Atwia – an attempt to inject a fresh spirit into the community."[114] The playthus also symbolizes the need for independent Ghana to rally all its ethnic groups towards the creation of an organic society: the stranger Labaran is a Hausa from Northern Ghana.[115]

Unresolved questions

The generation of West African writers publishing around and after the years of Independence was not wholly successful in its endeavours. Efua Sutherland, one of its leading members, behaved as one of its most pungent critics as well. In her pamphlet "The Second Phase: A Review of the National Theatre Movement in Ghana" (1965) she lamented a slow-down in creative output, not enough touring outside Accra by dramatic companies, and the absence of any plan to promote a drama programme for the educational system.[116] According to Kofi Agovi, the final point to be considered is crucial:

> Although the expression 'colonial mentality' was bandied about as an unfortunate tag on those who refused to move with the times or change their allegiance and tastes for African things, no one quite anticipated the subtleties of neo-colonialism and its implications for education and cultural development [...] Merely creating new and more institutions of culture, including a corps of élite writers and artists with their own specialized journals and magazines (that essentially entered into dialogue with an outside audience) without taking effective steps to integrate them into the educational system from primary school to the university level was one of the fundamental mistakes of the New Theatre Movement in Ghana.[117]

The efforts of several West African authors included in this volume to write literary texts for children, and their marked interest in children's literature, testifies to a

---

[114] See also Wilentz, "Writing for the Children," 186.

[115] C.O. Ogunyemi also identifies wider influences, touching on the autobiographical: "The outsider's interest and involvement reflect Ghana's ideological contacts, especially with African–Americans (Labaran could represent Sutherland's husband)"; Ogunyemi, "Efua Theodora Sutherland," 285–86.

[116] See Agovi, "Origin of Literary Theatre," 4.

[117] Agovi, "Origin of Literary Theatre," 4, 17.

widespread urge on their part to fill this institutional gap creatively.[118] The poet Atukwei Okai describes this general tendency thus:

> I think it is a collective awareness of the need for African writers to write books specifically for our children. Because inasmuch as we are making an effort through the works we write for normal adults, we think it's necessary and more reasonable to try to reach out to the sensibility of our young people at the time of their lives when they are most fertile for good seeds, when they are least thwarted, when their beings are certainly more receptive.
>
> It's a conscious attempt to create relevantly beautiful and beautifully relevant material for children of that age, especially because they've mostly been aware of what is coming from outside, so far. This does not help the self-sufficiency and self-confidence of our people and children. It came to a point that I decided that instead of going round and complain as a writer about the books that are not too correct for our children, I should try and do something about it. If they hear only Western nursery rhymes like the one about the Pussycat and the Queen, then, at an early age, their minds are being taken away. That's why I tried to create verses that would mirror our African, fantastic, beautiful, gorgeous, colourful world. (Okai, Accra, 22 November 1993)[119]

Sutherland occupies a pioneering position in the West African anglophone arts as far as children's literature is concerned as well. Gay Wilentz quotes her as saying: "I've heard a lot of people discussing at conferences the role of the [African] writer – all this rigmarole, well if there's any role, they should write for the children."[120] In our interview, she added that the children were not getting what she called "a propelling influence" (Sutherland, Accra, 17 December 1993). Besides inaugurating such institutions as the Children's Drama Development Project and the Mmofra Foundation,[121] she composed plays for children. Both *Vulture! Vulture!* and *Tahinta* (1968) are meant to be sung by a chorus acting with the protagonists: "The music that accompanies [the play] is deliberately employed to lighten and entertain and make general participation possible."[122]

The unresolved questions do not end with the lack of educational application of the principles outlined so far. The tapping of both traditional and popular theatre does not appear to have worked out completely. One could hardly say, for instance,

---

[118] Armah's *Fragments* bitterly disparages such a urge. A scene in the novel depicts a pathetic (and dishonest) workshop set in the drama studio, where the fictional figure of Akosua Russell betrays a strong resemblance to Efua Sutherland; Armah, *Fragments*, 105–17.

[119] See Okai's *The Anthill in the Sea* (1988), briefly discussed in Chapter 4.

[120] Wilentz, "Writing for the Children," 182.

[121] In Akan, 'mmofra' means 'children.'

[122] C.O. Ogunyemi, "Efua Theodora Sutherland," 288–89.

that the recovery of traditional techniques by literary dramatists has been harnessed to topics of contemporary relevance. Let us take the much-studied and much-enjoyed *The Marriage of Anansewa*: what is the theme of the work, apart from its being a commentary on human behaviour at large? The issue is discussed at length by Michael Etherton:

> it is hard to find any specific satire or finely-honed criticism of a particular society [...] Perhaps the dramatic sophistication of the play is more important than any 'contrived' profundity: tight control in the writing, a precise ironical tone, well-regulated comedy and excitement, embellishment and inventiveness – in short, high art.[123]

In our interview, Sutherland herself did not seem to aspire to anything more than a satire on human nature, and was somewhat vague about the play's specific targets:

> For me Ananse is not a crook, but an amalgam of all sorts of anti-social strands in our society; at the same time he is a full human being, in full command of his intelligence. His main role is not to be bad, but to reflect all the wickedness in our society and expose it. Like a spider, he weaves his web and catches his prey. It's a deep observation of human nature into which I weave present-day problems like poverty. I'm trying to show what makes people corrupt. (Sutherland, Accra, 17 December 1993)

Etherton would object to both 'poverty' and 'corruption' in their realistic sense – and his detailed analysis of the plot proves him right – but would endorse her general interpretation:

> The credibility of *The Marriage of Anansewa* obviously does not lie in its approximation to the reality of the daily lives of people in a specific social stratum, but rather in its essential meaning.[124]

The same incomplete fusion of form and content can be detected in the other plays mentioned in this chapter: Martin Owusu's and Joe De Graft's plays featuring Ananse, to start with, do not go beyond the trickster's traditional features, while Michael Dei–Anang's *Okomfo Anokye* enacts the legacy of oral histories on the rise of the Ashanti kingdom. It is as if the broad didactic thrust inherent in folktales thwarted any movement towards more focused concerns.[125] If this is the case, there-

---

[123] Etherton, *Development of African Drama*, 225.

[124] Etherton, *Development of African Drama*, 218–27, 225.

[125] Kofi Anyidoho similarly complains about "the tendency of some practitioners and scholars to treat all traditional forms as sacred and unchanging models of excellence that must be carefully, almost religiously preserved, memorized and reproduced with absolute fidelity to a presumably pure and original form"; Anyidoho, "National Identity and the Language of Metaphor," in *FonTomFrom: Contemporary Ghanaian Literature, Theatre and Film* ed. Anyidoho & James Gibbs (*Matatu* 21–22: Amsterdam & Atlanta GA: Rodopi, 2000): 1–22.

fore, the adoption of traditional features has ended up stifling contemporary relevance. Symptomatic of this is Yirenkyi's *Amma Pranaa*, which, as outlined above, takes up the African folktale of the girl marrying a stranger with no active authorial intervention in its content. The author has frankly admitted that "My main concern there was the form, trying to find out how I could fix it on stage" (Yirenkyi, Legon, 23 November 1993).

Perhaps another Ghanaian playwright belonging to the first generation, Ama Ata Aidoo, has proved to be less formally daring but more concerned with thematic depth. Her play *Anowa* (1970) employs the same folktale as a point of departure for the treatment of a burning issue – the slave trade practised by native Africans. Her earlier play *The Dilemma of a Ghost* (1965) tackles the difficult integration of an African–American woman among her Ghanaian in-laws.[126]

The Nigerian scenario presents different problems. Ola Rotimi's *Ovonramwen Nogbaisi* has been much criticized for its idealization of a historical bloody tyrant. Generally speaking, Chris Dunton mentions a widespread critical "scepticism about the ideological function of his [Rotimi's] drama." This is especially directed at his early plays, where the élite "is viewed almost the exclusion of the relationship that exists between them and the other sectors of society."[127]

This phenomenon is sometimes described as being widespread in Nigerian theatre. In this regard, the renowned poet and critic Niyi Osundare published an essay in 1988, "Theatre of the Beaded Curtain," where he complains about what he defines the "Kabiyesi Syndrome." The term 'Kabiyesi', meaning 'to ask him is not possible,' is the title given to the Yoruba Oba (Chief). Osundare equates the survival of traditional Yoruba rulers with the defeat of human progress: "Monarchy, like other forms of political oppression, is a maggot which breeds most comfortably in the putrefying carcasse of ignorance." Unfortunately, he continues, the syndrome has infected Nigerian arts such as popular music and, in particular, the theatre: "Seeing a Nigerian play today, whether on stage or on the screen, is like witnessing a sickly courtyard ritual." The author regrets that he cannot discern a great deal of social vision and critical thinking about monarchy in playwrights such as Hubert

[126] Formally speaking, though, in *Anowa* Aidoo embodies in the old couple called "The-Mouth-That-Eats-Salt-And-Pepper" a feature which is also present in her prose: characters who do not belong to the plot and whose role is to comment on the plot itself. The same is true for the characters First Woman and Second Woman in *The Dilemma of a Ghost*. On Aidoo's "choric storytellers," see Gilbert & Tompkins, *Postcolonial Drama*, 131, and Schipper, *Theatre and Society*, 70.

[127] Dunton, *Make Men Talk True*, 12, 20.

Ogunde and Duro Ladipo. Some of Soyinka's plays are similarly criticized, whereas his views on Rotimi differ: *Ovonramwen Nogbaisi* is worth praising for its analysis of royal contradictions, but *Kurunmi* depicts the common people as "merely serving as mute cannon-fodder."[128]

The phenomenon diagnosed by Osundare surfaces again in some works by Wale Ogunyemi. His *Ijaye War* (concerning the same Kurunmi that featured in Rotimi's play) and *Kiriji* are two historical plays on the bloody internecine wars (1860–65 and 1877–86) among different Yoruba groups clashing for power. In both scripts litres of blood are spilt in an unabated fury of victory-propitiating human sacrifices and severed heads carried as trophies, so much so that accustomed readers are unlikely to wonder at exclamation such as "No slaves, kill all of them!"[129] For better or for worse, the spotlight is constantly directed on kings of various political colours and moral standards; the scenes, once again, seem to revolve around whichever *kabiyesi* happens to be on stage.[130] In *Ijaye*, for example, the wicked Kurunmi is described fearsomely: "*His eyes are ember red, his features that of a lion,*" reads the stage direction. The same character is invested with awesome praise-names worthy of a Tutuolan spirit world: "the mighty, triumphant arc of the city gate who borrows with the violence of robbery; the phantom spirit of the night, [...] The skull-eating imp, roving masquerade of the forest."[131]

---

[128] Niyi Osundare, "Theatre of the Beaded Curtain: Nigerian Drama and the Kabiyesi Syndrome," *Okikè* 27–28 (March 1988): 103, 105, 109. On the controversy over the play and Rotimi's ideological shift in his successive works, see Dunton, *Make Men Talk True*, 17–20, 28–31. In the case of Soyinka, it must be said that his preoccupations sometimes touch the core of Nigerian social ills. *The Trials of Brother Jero*, for instance, concentrates on the commercialization of religion. Also worth mentioning are the author's experiments with guerrilla theatre in 1964–65 and 1978–82, which had social and political satire as their thematic core; see Ahmed Yerimah, "The Guerrilla Theatre as a Tool for National Re-Awakening: A Study of the Soyinka Experiments," in *Literature and National Consciousness*, ed. Ernest N. Emenyonu (Calabar Studies in African Literature 4; Ibadan: Heinemann Educational, 1989): 181–204 passim. In his later works, Soyinka's has moved right into the centre of contemporary political oppression; see, for instance, *From Zia, with Love* (1992).

[129] Wale Ogunyemi, *Ijaye War (in the nineteenth century): A Historical Drama* (Ibadan: Orisun Acting, 1970): 53.

[130] In his essay on Ogunyemi's works and career, Chris Dunton similarly points out the author's "imaginative absorption in the role of leadership figures"; Dunton, "Wale Ogunyemi," in *Dictionary of Literary Biography*, 157: *Twentieth Century Caribbean and Black African Writers, Third Series*, ed. Bernth Lindfors & Reinhard Sander (Detroit MI: Bruccoli Clark Layman / Gale, 1996): 252. Among other things, the essay discusses exhaustively his uncritical approach towards Yoruba myth and his seminal contribution to the development of total theatre in Nigeria.

[131] Ogunyemi, *Ijaye War*, 14, 51.

During our interview, Ogunyemi described the Kabiyesi Syndrome as deeply rooted in Yoruba performing arts, without sharing Osundare's view of it as something problematical:

> African traditional theatre also started with the rituals performed in palaces by Sango worshippers, for example. They sort of staged mock battles, with music and dances, fighting until the final settlement. I can see Osundare's point, but I don't agree with him. We've always had plays full of kings and chiefs. In a way, they are the grassroot people, the people you need to go to when you arrive in a town. Together with the elders, they are very important: that's why they play a prominent role in some of the plays we write. Nowadays, people are not putting things in their place as they used to. (Ogunyemi, Ibadan, 1 August 1997)

When I met Osundare later the same day and asked him for an update on the Syndrome a decade after the publication of his essay, he did not sound any more optimistic about either the stage or the national scene:

> It is still a problem, even much more virulent now than when I wrote my article, because the more decadent the society becomes, the more pseudo-religious and hegemonic it also tends to become. I have always admired the Ibos for their republican, individualistic, independent approach to life, but in the past years we have discovered that virtually every village in Iboland now has a king! It's strange to their culture: think of *Things Fall Apart* by Achebe, where the British ask for the king and the locals don't have one. This is the decadent aspect of Yoruba culture. Why should the Ibo copy it?
>
> I think it's because of the kind of culture we are under, too. Military regimes must of necessity support patriarchy and monarchy, their hegemonic structure. They want to rule by indirect means, like the old British Indirect Rule. They are a colonial occupation force. Since you cannot talk to hundreds of thousands of people, why don't you get a representative among them, bribe him and get him to take care of the rest? After all, you use a monkey to catch other monkeys ....
>
> Of course, this has been transferred to our stage. I'm getting rather worried about what is fast becoming the Ibadan tradition of drama. But, as I said in that essay I wrote, the kabiyesi factor is very attractive because monarchy is theatre: the throne, the retinue and so on. And very Shakespearean, too. (Osundare, Ibadan, 1 August 1997)

In Chapter 7 below, the Ghanaian Mohammed ben Abdallah will frequently be associated with the Nigerian Femi Osofisan for the way in which both writers have endeavoured to overcome such shortcomings.

As for the popular theatre model outlined above, the desired increase in mass appeal was hardly attained: the failure to break the metropolitan enclosure of literary drama highlighted by Sutherland and the linguistic barriers already discussed may account for this. Nevertheless, the model does not appear to have lost its appeal among African playwrights, who are still keenly aware of the gap between their works and the people they supposedly address. The reaction of the Ghanaian Ama Ata Aidoo, for instance, seems to betray both envy and guilt when talk turns to Concert Parties: "You know, I think it is the most valid thing going. I feel almost guilty myself writing the type of thing I write, really."[132]

In Western Nigeria, the Yoruba Popular Theatre that developed from the biblical Cantatas arouses the same kind of admiration in one of the best-known literary playwrights in English, Bode Sowande, who told me:

> The Yoruba language theatre, that's where you would really find 'total theatre', even more than in the English language one. That's the aesthetic they have used over the years. Those of us in the English language theatre are just appreciating it. Total theatre is a tradition that is, was and will be, because of our cultural experience. If a play for the larger society lacks the elements of total theatre, it will be deemed inferior or inadequate, its turnout will be greatly reduced.
>
> Educated people, the middle class, are the minority here – that must be underlined. Even though we are written about in Europe and America, paradoxically we are the minority. Our audience is the minority. The majority of people watch total theatre in Yoruba. I think that this aspect of international scholarship needs to be corrected in the next millennium. I like imagining that within the first ten years of the next millennium it will be corrected. And much has been lost already, because a lot of unwritten great works have never been documented on video.
>
> They are the dramatists who have actually been able to live on their profession a hundred percent, people such as Hubert Ogunde. I mean commercially and professionally successful, accepted by the general public. The work we are doing with ODU THEMES [his company, which celebrated its Silver Jubilee in 1997] is like an approximation of this, we want to see how far we can go in society. We have our days of fasting and our days of feasting: the former are slightly more than the latter. (Sowande, Ibadan, 2 August 1997)

In his seminal book on African drama, *The Truthful Lie* (1985), Biodun Jeyifo pinpoints the dilemma touched upon by Aidoo and Sowande: the still diverging paths beaten by the two main dramatic traditions, the literary and the popular.[133] Nowadays West African popular theatres employ more and more new media such as

---

132 Maxine McGregor, "Interviews with Ama Ata Aidoo," in *African Writers Talking: A Collection of Interviews*, ed. Dennis Duerden & Cosmo Pieterse (London: Heinemann Educational, 1972): 21.

133 See Jeyifo, *Truthful Lie*, 78–79.

discs, films and TV,[134] and are still founded on unwritten plots and improvisation, a far cry from being invested with the status of 'literature.' According to Jeyifo:

> our most talented, accomplished literary dramatists do not remotely begin to approach the vast popularity of the professional theatre groups who, in the main, are not writers or producers of lasting dramatic writing.[135]

Eldred Jones has similarly declared that "Those which are popular never get published and those which are published are never popular."[136]

On the one hand, Jeyifo localizes the root of the problem in both organizational faults (ie, the absence of lasting companies[137]) and deficiencies in the contents of literary works: "The best of our literary drama" – he writes – "must be re-examined and critiqued from the perspective of a necessary convergence of the literary and the popular."[138]

At the opposite extreme of this polar opposition, popular theatre is often 'accused' of being based on stereotyped characterizations and backward morality pandering to public taste. Michael Etherton states that this theatre "is indeed very often about nothing at all."[139] With regard to the Togolese Concert, Alain Ricard concentrates on the squandering of various talents resulting from its lack of integration with literary drama: "In conclusion, the Togolese Concert Party has some marvellous comedians but it has nothing original to say, whereas several writers and playwrights have things to say but they do not know where to find their comedians."[140] The Yoruba Travelling Theatre seems to be be cultivating a popular genre that is more prone to move from improvisation to written literature, but the process is still in its conceptual stage: "a certain orientation to literacy [...] a notion of the play as a text."[141]

---

[134] See also Barber et al, *West African Popular Theatre*, 18–19.

[135] Jeyifo, *Truthful Lie*, 79.

[136] Eldred Jones, "Editorial," *African Literature Today* 8 (1976): vii.

[137] The only exception, according to him, was Rotimi's company at Ife, "our only true institution-based repertory company to date [which] reached the same scale as that encompassed by the popular Yoruba professional troupe"; Jeyifo, *Truthful Lie*, 80.

[138] Jeyifo, *Truthful Lie*, 81–82.

[139] Etherton, *Development of African Drama*, 318.

[140] "En somme le concert a des merveilleux comédiens mais n'a rien à dire d'original, alors que beaucoup d'écrivains et de dramaturges ont à dire, mais ne savent où trouver les comédiens"; Alain Ricard, *L'Invention du théâtre: Le théâtre et les comédiens en Afrique noire* (Lausanne: L'Age d'Homme, 1986): 116 (my tr.).

[141] Barber et al., *West African Popular Theatre*, 47, 48; see also Karin Barber, "Literacy, Improvisation and the Public in Yorùbá Popular Theatre," in *The Pressures of the Text: Orality, Texts*

The question closing this chapter – and tackled in the next one – is: have the younger generations of West African playwrights fared any better, in terms of their approach to the traditional and the popular dimensions of drama?

---

and the Telling of Tales, ed. Stewart Brown (Birmingham University African Studies Series 4; Birmingham: Centre of West African Studies, 1995): 23, 27.

7 Mohammed ben Abdallah's Search for an African Theatre

THIS CHAPTER FOCUSES on a Ghanaian attempt to work towards a convergence of the traditional and popular formats – the works of the playwright Mohammed ben Abdallah (b. 1944). It shows how his themes and techniques manage to maintain a difficult but creatively inspiring balance between traditional and Western elements, and attempts to place all this within the context of the contemporary state of West African theatre through comparisons with and quotations from other relevant West African authors belonging to his generation. Among these, special relevance will be granted to the much-studied and lauded Nigerian playwright Femi Osofisan (b. 1946), with his experimental techniques and socially engaged content.

The Trial of Mallam Ilya and other plays (1987)

In the brief preface to his first collection of works, *The Trial of Mallam Ilya and other plays* (1987),[1] Abdallah defines his plays as "a search for an authentic 'African Theatre'; a theatre that caters for the needs of all people, from the peasant to the University Professor." Further, he acknowledges his indebtedness to the "pioneering work" of some unspecified African playwrights. One of these inspirational sources is certainly Efua Sutherland, as he later confirms with reference to both the traditional and the popular model:

> I was thinking of some of our really serious writers like Efua Sutherland, who is very concerned with this problem, not only of authenticity but also of how to really create a 'viable' theatre, that kind of theatre that would be self-sustaining. What I keep repeating to my students of the School of Performing Arts, University of Ghana, is that I find

[1] Mohammed ben Abdallah, *The Trial of Mallam Ilya and other plays* (Accra: Woeli, 1987). Page references are in the main text.

> it unacceptable that more than 25 years after the establishment of the School, there's no linkage with the show business, between industry and theatre. It took government efforts to establish one modern professional theatre company. (Abdallah, Legon, 11 December 1993)

In another interview, with Jane Wilkinson, Abdallah seems to consider the work of Sutherland and DeGraft, too, as decisive in the birth of modern Nigerian theatre:

> [they] started the School of Music and Drama at the University of Ghana, but the interesting thing is that quite a few people came from Nigeria to study the model and then went back, and suddenly Nigeria took over. There was Wole Soyinka, J.P. Clark, Ola Rotimi, Duro Ladipo.[2]

The critic Kofi Agovi makes the Sutherland/Abdallah connection in an essay in which he defines the latter as "the carrier of the promise," the author "who seems to have dominated the Ghanaian theater since the 1980s."[3]

Abdallah, who was in the original cast of *The Marriage of Anansewa* and acted during his university years with James Gibbs's company Legon 7, began his search in a way very similar to Sutherland's, by touring Ghana with the Legon Road Theatre in the early 1970s.[4] *The Trial of Mallam Ilya and other plays* is the first complete printed outcome of Abdallah's stage productions. The first two plays in the collection, *The Alien King* and *Verdict of the Cobra*, were performed during the said tours. The long timespan between production and publication is a sign of the author's belief in the primacy of the stage over the printed word:

> My first intention was not of being published, and I refused to do that for a long time. When I write something, I consider it as a script; only when it's put on stage and people see it I possibly start thinking of its publication. (Abdallah, Legon, 11 December 1993)

The structure of each of the three plays included in the book is based on a series of alienation-effects marking a clear rejection of any notion of naturalism. The story of *The Alien King*, for instance, is enacted by some students of Sanusi's, an old *griot*: the first stage direction states: "*Sanusi's students are getting ready to rehearse a play*" (3) – the story of the Fulani king Ada. The audience witnesses how the students, thanks to Sanusi's promptings, start to perform the narrative. Salifu, a mem-

---

[2] Wilkinson, *Talking with African Writers*, 37–38.

[3] Agovi, "Towards an Authentic African Theatre," 73.

[4] See Anthony A. Aidoo & James Gibbs, "Mohammed Abdallah at Fifty," *School of Performing Arts Newsletter* (University of Ghana at Legon) 3 (July–September 1994): 20; James Gibbs, "Mohammed ben Abdallah and the Legon Road Theater," *African Arts* 5.4 (1972): 33–34.

ber of the group, acts as storyteller, and introduces the plot before the other actors / students take over with the characters' dialogue. The prelude, in verse, relates how the history of how the Fulani came to Hausaland:

> Greetings, my mothers and sisters.
> Fathers and brothers, we greet you.
> This is an old story.
> A very old story of the people of Kano.
> They tell it everyday until it has become like a book. (4)

Abdallah lays bare all the delays and decisions involved in the group's work-in-progress. When the actor impersonating the Hausa king Kumbaru sends for Sanusi, the audience realizes that the real story of the alien king and its enactment overlap:

> STORYTELLER: Wait! Wait just a moment.
> *They freeze. The Storyteller steps out of character and crosses over to Sanusi.* (11)

The action is halted so that the students can ask Sanusi to impersonate himself, and the *griot*, after some reflection, assents:

> SANUSI: All right. That is enough. Let the play continue.
> *The students are overjoyed. Salifu resumes the character of the Storyteller and crosses back to his place. King Kumbaru's chamber comes back to life.* (12)

Sanusi tells the kings Kumbaru (Hausa) and Ada (Fulani), still on brotherly terms, that he sees discord in their future. The storyteller says: "The rest is hearsay. The rest is bloodshed" (14). What has happened? At this point, the rehearsal is halted again: "*Suddenly there are sounds of distant drumming, gunshots and jubilation. The Students get out of character and run to the parapets*" (14).

A messenger says that King Ada has been captured alive, and is going to stand trial. Sanusi's words seem to put an end to the rehearsing:

> Young men and women, this is not the time to rehearse. You have heard the news. Go your ways. We will meet again here tomorrow at sunset to rehearse, by which time our story will have a true ending. (16)

From this point to the end of the play, there is no more sign of the enactment of the story: the characters carry the action forward in a very naturalistic way, without any stops or metatheatrical reflections. When reading the play, one might think that Abdallah has switched from presentation to representation, but an audience cannot help noticing that the same actors – Sanusi's students – are on stage.

The ambiguity between layers of fictional reality is maintained until the very end of the play, when it is only partially resolved by the storyteller's last intervention. "*Fade in Sanusi's roof-top. A rehearsal. The students have just come to the end of the last scene*" (54).

Verdict of the Cobra, the second play in the collection, is also founded on a storytelling structure, conducted out by a child and his grandmother, and on its estranging, denaturalizing effects. At the beginning, the child

> *sees the audience and smiles. Obviously pleased.* [...]
>
> CHILD: Look, grandmother, look! They have come! They have come to hear the dream! [...] The story of my mother, my father and my uncle. (*He picks up the miniature drum and begins to beat on it.*). (58)

The old woman speaks to the audience as well: "I know that you have not come here to listen to his story, but he does not know. Please forgive him. [...] 'The mad child' they call him" (59). She then begins her storytelling to appease him, narrating the tragic history of her two twins and of how they loved the same woman from Eweland (eastern Ghana). The plot will continue with no storytelling intrusions until its end, when the grandmother will speak to the audience again before taking her leave. Once more, therefore, the presentational frame is limited to a sort of introduction plus conclusion, without a real attempt to interact fluidly with the plot. Kofi Agovi praises the "total fusion of narrative and dramatic action" in *The Alien King* and the way in which it "achieves perfection" in *Verdict*, but he is referring to the character playing the part of the storyteller who also becomes part of the acting, not to a fusion of the two styles.[5]

In the third play in the collection, *The Trial of Mallam Ilya*, there is no proper storytelling, but alienating non-naturalistic effects continue to abound in its complex structure. When Malwal and his men seize power after their violent rebellion, they capture Mallam Ilya, accusing him of having refrained from fighting for the oppressed despite his position as a popular hero. This is why they decide to organize a trial in order to judge him:

> MALWAL: [...] Brothers, I suggest that we help Mallam Ilya to defend himself and to re-enact his famous exploits. Take your places, brothers. (85)

The rest of the play is developed through several levels of narration or acting: Ilya recounts the story of his life – thus acting as a sort of narrator – alternating with its performance by him and other characters. Sometimes the whole recollective process

---

[5] Kofi Agovi, *New Directions in the Ghanaian Theatre of the Eighties* (paper presented at a staff seminar held at the seminar room, 31 August 1989; University of Ghana at Legon, Institute of African Studies, 1989): 15.

is interrupted by Malwal and his men, whenever they do not agree with the proceedings. For example:

> MALWAL (*from his seat in the darkness of the auditorium*): Cut! Cut!! Cut!!!
> *All freeze as the court of Kumrahn fades into a tableau of silhouettes. Lights fade in on the chained Ilya and his guards on the auditorium. There is a general commotion and murmuring.* (96)

The play's complexity requires several expedients in order to ensure smooth passage from one level to another. Abdallah's stage directions attempt to organize all this, but retain the same categorizing attitude of the other two plays, as if the author wanted to make sure that the audience can distinguish among the various fictional levels: "*Whenever Ilya has to descend into the main stage action, his place in the 'tableau of silhouettes' may be taken by either a dummy or another actor*" (98). Such different levels cannot but have an estranging effect on the audience, well aware that they are just witnessing a representation. With regard to this, it is not surprising that Abdallah remembers seeing during his youth, among a dominance of British works, Luigi Pirandello's *Six Characters in Search of an Author* (1921). This experiment in metatheatre still exerts a profound influence on world drama.[6]

Storytelling and, more generally, the unmasking of naturalistic conventions is a feature Abdallah shares with other contemporary West African playwrights. The first and foremost name that comes to mind is the Nigerian Femi Osofisan, whose theatrical activities and publications are impressive both quantitatively and qualitatively. His search for new forms is unceasing, and his declared aim is to attain "new patterns of dramaturgy, derived from our African tradition."[7]

In his *Esu and the Vagabond Minstrels* (1991), for instance, the initial stage directions leave room for adaptation to the circumstances of the gathering: "*Lights come up on a festive scene. A community in obvious celebration [...] any community will do, and the appropriate vocabulary adjustments should then be made.*" The festive atmosphere is re-created with musicians and people chatting and drinking. When the leader starts his speech, a song intrudes about the latest coup d'état, "*which everybody picks up.*"[8] The community, we are told, is rehearsing a play for a competition:

---

[6] See Wilkinson, *Talking with African Writers*, 37. In 1967 the Ghanaian Company International Players staged Pirandello's *Tonight We Improvise* at the Accra Community Centre; see Lokko, "Theatre Space," 316.

[7] Muyiwa P. Awodiya, *Excursions in Drama and Literature: Interviews with Femi Osofisan* (Ibadan: Kraft, 1993): 67.

[8] Femi Osofisan, *Esu and the Vagabond Minstrels* (Ibadan: New Horn, 1991), 1.

> CHIEF: But... is it possible... I mean, can we see some bit of it before we disperse today? Just to give us a foretaste?[9]

The audience thereupon witnesses the construction of a seemingly improvised performance and its work-in-progress, akin to Abdallah's *Alien King* and *Verdict* and, going further back, Yirenkyi's *Amma Pranaa*. The stage and the play's conventions are quickly established by Ade and the Chief:

> ADE: That is, if you don't mind our doing it without costumes and the necessary props?
>
> CHIEF: Come on, what are costumes? What are props? Are they not just embellishments? It's the story we want, not so? *(Responses).*
>
> ADE: [...] Alright, alright. I think I'll ask the women present to help us. Can you please lend us your shawls? Thank you. Thank you. These people [...] When they wrap themselves, as they are doing now, they turn to stones. Yes, just like that. See?[10]

Another feature of traditional theatre that Abdallah makes lavish use of is the combination of diverse artistic forms, following the total-theatre plays written and produced by his predecessors (and mentioned in Chapter 6 above). The musical element, for instance, is employed continuously by the author, not as a mere background, but as a functional part of the story.[11]

As Kofi Agovi writes, "traditional African society recognized the importance of integrating all the senses in the communication process."[12] Abdallah strives to make the most of every facet of bodily and vocal expression. Pantomime can create a background to storytelling, as in *The Alien King*:

> STORYTELLER: The Fulani came from everywhere.
> And settled everywhere in Hausaland.
>
> *Fulani travellers enter and take their places in the acting area as they are mentioned by the Storyteller.* [...]

---

[9] Osofisan, *Esu*, 3.

[10] Osofisan, *Esu*, 3–4.

[11] Traditional archetypes aside, one cannot help likening this to the importance of music in popular theatre, already highlighted in Chapter 6. According to Kwabena N. Bamé, in Concert Parties "music and dancing also form an essential and conspicuous feature [...] contributing much of their value, meaning and attraction. Some comic play-goers attend the play principally to enjoy the ear-catching music so plentifully provided by the bands of comedians. Indeed, music is as vital a part of the play as it is of American musicals"; Bamé, *Come to Laugh: A Study of African Traditional Theatre in Ghana* (Accra: Baafour, 1981): 36.

[12] Kofi Agovi, "The Philosophy of Communication in Traditional Ghanaian Society: The Literary and Dramatic Evidence," *Research Review* (Institute of African Studies, University of Ghana at Legon) New Series 5.2 (1989): 53.

They settled everywhere and became people of Hausaland.
But one day ....
The Fulani begin to pantomime a disagreement which builds up to chaos. (5)

In the same play, the sex scene between Ada and Bagunsuwa is shown in silhouette (29–31), while in *The Trial* Kumrahn's palace walls are made up of the actors' bodies: "*they form a semi-circle around the 'Palace', forming its walls and indicating entrances and exits*" (85). At the beginning of this play, too, the whole initial scene of Malwal's revolt is to be staged in the dark. Here is the first stage direction:

Blackout in the theatre! The following action takes place in total darkness. Immediately after the blackout, a woman screams loudly and drops her water pot so that it breaks with a loud noise.

MALWAL'S VOICE: Stop that woman! Quick! (79)

Dancing is another fundamental component of this collection, as when Mairama dances for the alien king before his execution (50), or when Mallam Ilya and the traditional priest Kouyate meet again in the latter's village:

The sacred background music swells gradually and above Ilya and Kouyate. During this exchange, Ilya and Kouyate move in circles in some sort of 'Combat Dance' and the priestess dances between them and prevents them from touching. (141)

Rituals are another component of Abdallah's total art. Alongside 'narrative drama,' in fact, Nketia also considers 'ceremonial drama' as a traditional form of theatre, "dramatic expression associated with social, ritual or ceremonial occasions."[13] Abdallah often associates rituals with dancing scenes that employ little or no dialogue. In other words, there is danced and / or mimed reproduction of rites. *Verdict of the Cobra*, before the appearance of the grandmother, begins with the Ewe "Dance of the Initiation of the Virgins," described closely in a long introductory stage direction. The grandmother's twin sons are made identical by wearing masks. Having kidnapped a neophyte of the Gods, an initiate virgin of the Ewe, one of them causes the curse to be drawn upon his village, and the ritual involved is a way of restoring the link with the gods, albeit of another ethnic group. The tragic atmosphere and the end of the play envelope a society at risk of losing harmony with the metaphysical.

When they fight over the woman's love, nobody will be able to tell them apart any more, and the High Priest will decide to perform the Cobra ritual: if closed in the same hut with the twins, the sacred serpent will strike the liar. The whole scene is ritually reproduced by the Priest (holding two masks) and the woman:

[13] Nketia, *Ghana*, 29.

> *Slowly, she begins to dance as a cobra, to the tune of the xylophone and flute. First, she move only the neck, like a cobra watching an enemy. Then, as the drums join the music, her chest moves, then her belly, the waist and the hips. Slowly, she stands up, holding her hands up like two cobras. The Priest begins to dance with her. Her aim is to strike one of the masks and he avoids her strokes.[...] she strikes one of them; at the same moment, there is a loud scream from the hut.* (75)

This scene, then, integrates into his "ceremonial drama" another mode of traditional Ghanaian theatre illustrated by Nketia, "dance drama" (already mentioned in Chapter 6 with regard to Patience Addo's *Anansewa*).[14] *The Verdict*, after all, was the first production of the School of Performing Arts (University of Ghana at Legon) which incorporated the Ghana Dance Ensemble, the group that moved from traditional folk dances to dance-drama experiments in the early 1980s.[15]

Abdallah's effort to build a 'total art,' to integrate all the senses of actor and audience, does not seem to be an isolated effort in African drama. Writing about this general trend, Jeyifo notes:

> thanks also to this fusion of the textual and subtextual forms in our best plays, such dramatic modes as the representational, the presentational and the stylized modes that are usually encountered as distinct entities in Western drama are often encountered as integral elements in the best of our contemporary drama.[16]

Abdallah accordingly has full recourse to the integration of artistic forms bequeathed to him by traditional drama, popular theatre and his literary predecessors, even though some critics do not seem to be in favour of such techniques. In Ibrahim Salla's view, "These devices are mostly kept under control, although at times they seem more interesting for the spectacle they offer than for a more profound purpose."[17] The point is, where is the limit? What should be the criterion of judgement? It seems obvious that the artistic whole should never lose sight of the message, but enhance it. One could guess, for instance, that the 'Combat Dance' quoted above is supposed to bring into focus the rivalry between the two religious heads, expressed elsewhere through dialogue.

Unfortunately, other critics do not seem to appreciate the effectiveness that this many-layered theatre can acquire. Biodun Jeyifo – contradictorily, given what he says in the above quotation – employs his Marxist standpoint to criticize the Ethi-

---

[14] See Nketia, *Ghana*, 29.

[15] See Aidoo & Gibbs, "Mohammed Abdallah," 20; Agovi, "New Directions," 9.

[16] Jeyifo, *Truthful Lie*, 58.

[17] Ibrahim Salla, review of Abdallah, *The Trial of Mallam Ilya and other plays*, *Wasafiri* 9 (Winter 1988–89): 35.

opian Tsegaye Gabre–Medhin's work, on the grounds that it aspires to a Wagnerian, hence bourgeois conception of art, thereby submerging its content. He generalizes his view thus:

> This model of theatrical practice is an indulgence anywhere, but even more so in the contemporary African theatre. More pointedly, it works against the earnestness and relevance of dramatists like Gabre-Medhin, whose social vision has much to contribute to the current ideological debates in Africa.[18]

Jeyifo probably underestimates how efficaciously a total theatre can convey its message. At this point, another kind of African theatre needs to be introduced as a comparative touchstone: Theatre for Development, which organizes educational workshops for village or urban communities all over the continent and places supreme value on the successful conveyance of its messages. The efficacy of total art is demonstrated by the fact that the same techniques have been adopted by such groups in Theatre for Development as the Atelier Théâtre Burkinabé and Ngugi's Kamiirithu Theater.[19]

Another case in point is the personal experience related by Sandy Arkhurst, former leader of Efua Sutherland's Kusum Agromma and later practitioner and Professor of Theatre for Development at Ahmadu Bello University, Zaria, and the University of Ghana at Legon:

> community education must acknowledge the potency of the authentic folk forms [...] Communities at large are still strongly bound to their pristine cultural values, the influence of education, urbanization and alien religions notwithstanding. As a result, most of these folk forms hold a unique attention, bordering on reverence, for the people.

Arkhurst also cites projects where such forms were used to reinforce the message.[20]

Total theatre is far from being a recent phenomenon on West African stages, but Femi Osofisan once again provides the most suitable term of comparison for his generation. His works should be considered as highly relevant to the topic, and one of the most enjoyable is *Yungba-Yungba and the Dance Contest* (1993). This play requires an all-female cast. Aperin, interpreter of the river cult, opens the play by trying to narrate a tale, but is stopped by the women of the three leading families,

---

[18] Jeyifo, *Truthful Lie*, 96.

[19] See Joy F. Morrison, "Forum Theatre in West Africa: An Alternative Medium of Information Exchange," *Research in African Literatures* 22.3 (1991): 36; David Kerr, "Participatory Popular Theatre: The Highest Stage of Cultural Underdevelopment?," *Research in African Literatures* 22.3 (1991): 64.

[20] Sandy Arkhurst, "African Music, Dance and Drama in Community Education," unpublished paper presented at the Colloquium on African Theatre, Yaoundé (16–21 June 1997): 5, 7. Cf the use of the Concert Party format for educational campaigns by Efua Sutherland's Kusum Agromma.

who rehearse in succession their songs and dances for the oncoming contest, the Great Night of Courtship, the winner of which will marry the most eligible bachelor in the land. The atmosphere is charged with a deeply-felt rivalry which incorporates a highly proverbial language hinting at songs of abuse: "Our spindle was never cut from some inferior wood, so the ants are only wasting their time gnawing at us!"[21]

The secret cult of the Yungba–Yungba ('dream of sweetness') shifts the tension to political concerns: they want the festival to be performed according to the traditional laws, because the winner once used to become the new religious leader and was automatically elected in the legislative assembly of the land, before the priestess Iyeneri altered the rules and held the post for good. The Yungba–Yungba must overcome the eternal hatred between the families, which also constitute the main pretext used by Iyeneri to retain power. The play thus reflects on the presence of military regimes in Africa, justified by the failure of Western democracy and by ethnic divisions: "A Parable of Our Times," is the play's subtitle. In any case, the reply by the Yungba–Yungba is adamant, embodying the hope Osofisan places in the youngest generations of political activists:

> By seizing from us the right to decide for ourselves, Iyeneri, you saved us from chaos no doubt, but you have taught us nothing. You have not cured our barbarism, only postponed it. [as a worthy leader] you are the best qualified now to begin the process of returning our people to the ways of democracy.[22]

Iyeneri's plans to eliminate the Yungba–Yungba fail; in the end, the story that was stopped at the beginning can be narrated to its end: the story of Song, Drum and Dance, the three daughters of Felicity, all beautiful and very gifted weavers at the loom. But Discord, from the neighbouring stall, stirs each of them into selfishness; the house breaks down, and its unique product is lost: "Each went her separate way / With just her individual skill: / Song wandered West, Drum to the East / and Dance went up to the North."[23] The story's significance is multifaceted, hinting at various concepts: the harmony of integrated art-forms (one of the main ideas sustaining the present study), the need for democratic collaboration in achieving sociopolitical improvement, and, more specifically, the removal of the ethnic divisions that have lacerated Nigeria since its independence, with the three cardinal points symbolizing the three main ethnic groups. The fusion between form and content finds its perfect

---

[21] Femi Osofisan, *Yungba–Yungba and the Dance Contest* (Ibadan: Heinemann Educational, 1993): 5.

[22] Osofisan, *Yungba-Yungba*, 55–57.

[23] Osofisan, *Yungba-Yungba*, 117.

expression in the story, and in the play that contains it. If the winner of the contest traditionally became a political representative, it was because the foremothers

> knew the tremendous amount of training, energy and self-discipline it takes for anyone to win our championship, and they knew these were also the same qualities for responsible leadership![24]

Chris Dunton rightly states that "Osofisan stands apart from many of the other 'new wave' critics – in his insistence on foregrounding the concept of 'artistry' alongside an advocacy of clear social relevance."[25] Another implication of this story is represented by the homage Osofisan pays to Amos Tutuola through it. In Tutuola's *The Palm-Wine Drinkard*, "Drum, Song and Dance [...] were living creatures as ours" and their spell is inescapable:

> my wife, myself and spirits etc, were dancing with 'Dance' and nobody who heard or saw these three fellows would not follow them to wherever they were going. Then the whole of us were following the three fellows and dancing along with them. So we followed the three fellows and were dancing for a good five days without eating or stopping once.[26]

Osofisan, then, recontextualizes Tutuola's "three fellows" in a contemporary issue with both dramatic and political significance.[27]

Osofisan's successful fusion of theme and technique shifts attention to the value of the key themes in Abdallah's first collection, not least because both dramatists bloomed artistically in the 1970s, a decade in which "neo-colonialism also became an increasingly recognised liability in African life."[28] T*he Alien King*'s main subject – the clash of the different cultures and peoples who eventually formed Northern Nigeria – resembles *Yungba–Yungba*'s in its inter-ethnic appeal, even though it does not possess the same contemporary relevance. Here are Abdallah's remarks on how he is descended from a complex cultural mix:

> That concern, I believe, is partly a reflection of my own personality. My family has been in Kumasi since 1900, but my great-grandfather, the one who established the

24 Osofisan, *Yungba-Yungba*, 24–25.

25 Dunton, *Make Men Talk True*, 171.

26 Tutuola, *Palm-Wine Drinkard*, 38.

27 His fondness of Tutuola's work is also evident in his essay extensively quoted in Chapter 1, "Wonderland and the Orality of Prose," and in his political one-act play *The Oriki of a Grasshopper*, in *Two One-Act Plays* (also including *Altine's Wrath*) (Ibadan: New Horn, 1986): 44–45.

28 Agovi, *New Directions*, 7.

> family, had Mauritanian and Moroccan ancestors. Two of his four wives, moreover, were of Guinean origin. I myself was born with two original languages: Hausa and Twi. (Abdallah, Legon, 11 December 1993)[29]

In *The Alien King*, the Fulani king Ada rebels against the Hausa ruler Kumbaru. The latter's thirst for truth will lead him to question Ada about the reason for his deeds: "O spirit of our ancestors / Make our kings / Of men who always question!" (54) says the old griot Sanusi, paraphrasing Fanon's *Black Skin, White Masks*.[30] Ada will be executed, but out of all this a fusion between the two people is heralded:

> ADA: Take my people and make them yours. Bind them with the laws of Kano for their hearts are buried in the earth of Kano. They will always be Fulanis but they are your people. All yours. Yes? Take my hand. (*Kumbaru does so. Ada falls and dies. The distant voice of the Muezzin is heard chanting the call to prayer*). (52)

Verdict of the Cobra is centred on the same topic, this time regarding Ghanaian ethnic groups, as seen above. The peaceful cohabitation of different African peoples in the modern states has been a primary point at issue in Ghanaian arts ever since Nkrumah and his pan-Africanist vision,[31] and it has already emerged a few times in the present study in the case of some authors who display polyglot skill in various Ghanaian / African languages, such as Kojo Laing (Chapter 2 and 3) and Atukwei Okai (Chapter 4). The predominance of this approach may be linked with the low number of cases of ethnic clashes occurring in Ghana since Independence.

The same conciliatory mood is detectable in a recent unpublished Ghanaian play, Dzifa Glikpoe's *Knife in the Pocket* (1985),[32] set in a traditional environment which is a mix of different Ghanaian cultures. The play contains ritual elements together with dances, songs and drumming, and a riddling session that is open to audience involvement. At the beginning the play, the chief praises this peaceful ethnic blend, implying mixed marriage rites:[33] "we all speak and understand the three main languages our forebears who first settled here used," symbolic of the three

---

[29] Anthony A. Aidoo and James Gibbs write: "Because the house [his great-grand-father's, in Kumasi] accommodated visitors, travellers and traders from different parts of northern and southern Ghana, a variety of cultures surrounded him in his formative years" ("Mohammed Abdallah," 19).

[30] Frantz Fanon, *Black Skin, White Masks*, tr. Charles Lam Markmann (New York: Grove, 1967): 232.

[31] See Shillington, *Ghana*, 4–5.

[32] *Knife in the Pocket* was first directed by Asiedu Yirenkyi in 1985 and later performed in 1995 and 1996.

[33] In *The Trial* as well, the wedding of Ilya and Halima combines Islamic and traditional rites (128–31).

main cultures of Southern Ghana: Akan, Ga and Ewe. He continues: "Our forefathers were united. It is the only way they could have built up the treasures we are enjoying today. Let us keep the togetherness, one beam cannot build the house."[34] The plot of the play, just like that of *Verdict of the Cobra*, is structured on an illicit love-story that goes against custom. There is none of the attention that Osofisan devotes to the burning social and political issues of the day.

Fortunately, in *The Trial of Mallam Ilya* the pan-ethnic thrust of the first two plays yields to more up-to-date concerns which are "capable of addressing penetrating social and political issues,"[35] possibly because it was completed later than the first two, in 1976, when Abdallah's theatrical skills had improved. Captured by Malwal and his fellow rebels, Ilya is accused of having betrayed the responsibilities of honour, of being one of "a generation of ageless butterflies that have sucked from high places from one generation of rulers to another with amazing agility" (82). In order to defend himself, Ilya recalls his confrontation with Mwake Kumrahn, Father of the Land of Angah. The unspecified past and invented nation where the story is set cannot conceal the evident anagrams; "I have distorted events and fused characters"– says the author in his preface – "so as to arrive at what I choose to call 'true fiction' or 'faction' for short."

In this particular case, the leader in question is, of course, the still controversial figure of Nkrumah (1909–72), first president of Ghana, and of his regime. In fact, his aforesaid efforts to recover the strength and creativity of traditional culture and his mass-literacy campaigns[36] were offset by a more negative side, which emerges in Abdallah's play. Kumrahn's entries are preceded by a court crier,[37] just as Nkrumah's speeches were introduced by Boafo Akuffo, a salaried traditional poet who delivered a "well-articulated appellation performance [...] It is indeed from the lexicon of this poetic institution that Nkrumah acquired the title 'Osagyefo' ('Saviour-at-War')."[38] The same title is employed in the play for Kumrahn; his ruthless policy towards judges or artists critical of him recalls his historical counterpart's stifling domestic policy which culminated in the Preventive Detention Act.[39]

---

[34] Dzifa F. Aku Glikpoe, "Knife in the Pocket," author's typescript, 1985: 9.

[35] Appiah Sackey, review of Abdallah, *The Trial of Mallam Ilya and other plays*, *African Concord* (11 March 1988): 24.

[36] See Chapters 4 and 6 above (pp. 114, 127–29, 137–38).

[37] See pp. 91, 96, 98, 105.

[38] Yankah, "Making and Breaking," 15. See also Chapter 4.

[39] See Shillington, *Ghana*, 11–12.

The play's political theme affords useful insights into the debate over the usefulness of total theatre broached earlier in this chapter. In a long interlude (117–19), the traditional priest Kouyate is instrumental in organizing, in a village of the forest region, a satirical masquerade where Henry the Navigator, David Livingstone and Queen Victoria are associated with a cartoon of the tyrant Kumrahn. The performance reminds one of contemporary example of satirical festivals such as carnivals or the Kalakuwa festival in the village of Bomo near Zaria, Northern Nigeria, where all sorts of administrative and political personalities are role-played along the village streets and spectators can "visit them and enter into role play with them."[40] But in *The Trial* the performers are arrested by real policemen: should not this long scene, filled with music and dancing and with little dialogue, be construed as a criticism of the alleged concern for traditional culture on Nkrumah's part?

In today's Ghana, Nkrumah still arouses a lot of heated polemic,[41] and Abdallah has this acted out by the rebels' reaction when the former leader is evoked for the first time:

> *There is general commotion and murmuring as the following sentences are said by various people in the auditorium and on stage all at once.*
>
> FIRST MAN: No! No! No!! This must be stopped. We must not allow this!
>
> SECOND MAN: Can't the dead rest in peace? (96–97)

Nkrumah did not refrain from deporting leading churchmen who disagreed with his policies.[42] In the play, Mallam Ilya and the traditional priest Kouyate are likewise

---

40 Etherton, *Development of African Drama*, 30.

41 This is true outside Ghana, too, given the importance of his political figure in all of the pan-African world; after all, Ghana was the first sub-Saharan African state to achieve independence (1957) and this made Nkrumah a model for many of those involved in the anti-colonial struggle.

Among Nigerian playwrights, Bode Sowande makes him appear as a commenting spirit – together with Napoleon Bonaparte – in his *Tornadoes Full of Dreams* (1990). Femi Osofisan, in *Nkrumah Ni... Africa Ni...* (unpublished, Ghana Broadcasting Corporation video, 1994), tries to imagine what happened in Conakry, Guinea, during the six years of Nkrumah's exile, when the ousted leader often found himself discussing with Guinean president Sekou Touré and Guinea–Bissau's freedom fighter Amilcar Cabral. Their dialogue is sometimes interesting and sometimes too long – see *SPA Newletter* 2 (1994): 20–23 – but Osofisan does not renounce his usual anti-illusionist devices. In this case there is a group of masked jesters appearing on a raised platform, on the left of the audience: they leer at Nkrumah, mentioning his abuse of power. At first they seem products of Nkrumah's troubled conscience, but later they start arguing with Touré, too, and claiming the legitimacy of their presence before the audience: "You act your own parts and we act ours!"

42 See Yankah, "Making and Breaking," 19. John K. Djisenu writes that "'Mallam Ilya' rhymes with 'Mallam Tula' [...] and the seed of the idea of the play may have come from the trial

persecuted for being the mouthpieces of the oppressed, and Ilya is also falsely accused of having raped his beloved Halima, who is actually pregnant by Kumrahn.

Moreover, the oppressive workings of political power are unmasked again by a play-within-the-play, conferring on the whole work a Russian doll-like structure and intensifying its structural intricacy. When the tyrant Mwake Kumrahn and his council of sycophantic elders devise a plan to get rid of Mallam Ilya, they all role-play it in a near-farcical style, mixing acting with description:

> KUMRAHN: He must confess… publicly! You understand? [...]
>
> ABDUL KARIM: I see, Great One, it's a wonderful idea – a stroke of genius.
>
> *During the following, they all go into a mime with elaborate expansive movements and gestures.*
>
> SAMBURU: *(Pulls an imaginary scroll out of his sleeve, unrolls it, clears his throat and reads).* Mallam Muhammad Ilya, Caretaker of the Mosques, is charged with and tried for conspiracy to commit treason and treason.
>
> *(The rest gather around him, pretending to be a crowd of ordinary citizens).*
>
> SAMBURU: The verdict!
>
> ALL: Guilty!!!
>
> SAMBURU: And Ilya is sentenced to death by the highest court of the land of Angah.
>
> *(Abdul Karim elbows Samburu into the crowd and takes his place on the imaginary platform).*
>
> KARIM: But just before Mallam Muhammad Ilya is due for execution, he makes a heart-rending confession that dispels all doubts pertaining to his complicity in the abortive attempt at the elimination of the Father of Angah ....

Karim's move stage-front is a good instance of an improvised narrative where every member of the council is expected to add his own ideas to make the plot perfect. Ilya's confession, followed by Kumrahn's forgiving tears, is similarly enacted "*with great exaggeration*" (102–104).

Role-play is a device shared by several West African dramatists. Kacke Götrick finds its origin in Apidan theatre, when "a character temporarily plays the role of somebody else in order to make the latter be understood as fictional within the fiction," and she traces a connection with Soyinka's extensive use of the technique.[43]

---

following the Kulungugu bomb-throwing incident of Mallam Tula"; Djisenu, "Useful Political Lessons from Abdallah's *The Trial of Mallam Ilya*," *School of Performing Arts Newsletter* (University of Ghana at Legon) 2 (April–June 1994): 2. Kulungugu is a village in Northern Ghana: in August 1962, a small boy was killed there and Nkrumah was wounded in the back; see Shillington, *Ghana*, 12.

43 Götrick, *Apidan Theatre*, 161. For another brand of West African drama making use of this technique, see the prison play in pidgin English *Katakata for Sofahead* (London: Macmillan,

Femi Osofisan has also made the connection between traditional and modern in this regard when talking about his *Farewell to a Cannibal Rage* (1986):

> in the middle of the play everybody changes role. [my plays with large casts] are designed for multiple roles just like moonlight games when improvisation takes place. These plays are the ones which have given me more opportunity to continue in what might be called the traditional African play-making mechanics.[44]

In Osofisan's works, role-play is often a means of social satire, as the villagers re-enact as farce the policemen's bullying ignorance in *Aringindin and the Nightwatchmen* (1991);[45] or as a way to reveal a character's hidden identity, as in the play-within-the-play running throughout *The Chattering and the Song* (1976).[46] "The effect of this technique," Awodiya writes, "described as Brecht's 'alienation effect', is to avoid the possibility of emotional attachment of the audience to the actors on stage."[47] Sandra Richards elaborates on this, stressing the revolutionary, subversive element that marks Osofisan's oeuvre:

> these texts [...] focus attention on the way in which all truths are contingent stories that function to articulate an ideology in the sense in which Marxist critics Louis Althusser and Fredric Jameson define the term: a strategy of containment or essential narrative by which one knows the world. Those role-playing, storytelling and riddling foreground, on the one hand, the ways in which a hegemonic reality is constructed and presented as natural and, on the other hand, the ways in which those realities can be overturned and replaced with still other fictions. They project a dialectical perspective.[48]

1983) by the Nigerian Segun Oyekunle, where several layers of role-playing highlight the attitude imposed by economic and social constrictions; in-depth analyses of the play can be found in Etherton, *Development of African Drama*, 295–301, and in Eliane Utudjian Saint–André, "New Modes of Writing in West African Drama: Prison Plays from Sierra Leone, Ghana and Nigeria," *Commonwealth: Essays and Studies* 14.1 (Autumn 1991): 73–75. The latter traces the influence on Oyekunle of Brecht and Soyinka.

[44] Awodiya, *Excursions in Drama and Literature*, 54.

[45] Femi Osofisan, *Aringindin and the Nightwatchmen* (Ibadan: Heinemann Educational, 1991): 9–14, 62–64.

[46] Femi Osofisan, *The Chattering and the Song* (1976; Ibadan: Ibadan UP, 1977).

[47] Muyiwa P. Awodiya, "Structure and Meaning in *The Chattering and the Song*," in *Femi Osofisan: Interpretive Essays 1*, ed. Awodiya (Lagos: Centre for Black African Arts and Civilization, 1996): 120.

[48] Sandra L. Richards, *Ancient Songs Set Ablaze: The Theatre of Femi Osofisan* (Washington DC: Howard UP, 1996): 112. On the subversive potential of storytelling, see Gilbert & Tompkins, *Postcolonial Drama*, 127–28.

Abdallah, it must be said, lacks that harmonious interweaving of technical sophistication and wide political perspective shown by Osofisan, but *The Trial of Mallam Ilya* constitutes an exception in some ways. Unfortunately, the play's ending does not offer many fictional alternatives to the stagnation of African politics. Kumrahn's fall obviously leads to Ilya's rise as a hero. When accused by Malwal, he points out the impossibility of bringing about effective change: "We are all puppets. We cannot escape it, so we must live with it" (133). This vein of pessimism runs through the play: "For how long shall our people be squeezed through the fingers of one generation of leeches right into the open palms of another?" (143). Forever, the author's answer seems to be. Malwal's rebellion, in fact, will end up by using the same coercive and violent methods on innocent people as did that of his predecessors.[49] The tragic final *coup de théâtre*, where Malwal is shown to be Halima's and Kumrahn's son (and which implies that he has unwittingly killed his own mother) is followed by a fight in total darkness, just as at the beginning of the play. The cycle has come full circle in both content and form: Abdallah appears to have given up any political hope for his country.

Much more stimulating are the theatrical stratagems employed to involve the audience in Ilya's trial. When the proceedings begin, Malwal and some of his men

> *take their reserved seats in the auditorium.*
>
> MALWAL *(from his seat in the audience)*: Mallam, we are ready, be brief ....
>
> SECOND MAN (*also in the audience*): And truthful. (85)

The barrier between stage and public is broken down again when Ilya senses Halima's death and stops his narration / enactment:

> ILYA: Answer my question, young man! *(Pause. Ilya descends into the audience and stands over Malwal)* You may kill me if you wish, but until you tell me what you have done with my wife, I will not say a single word. (86)

Every time Malwal interrupts Ilya's enacted recollections, he speaks from a seat in the dark just like a director, sometimes saying "Cut!" (96, 125, 152). The audience, then, is supposed to sit next to the actors taking part in the play, and Abdallah even attempts to draw them into the trial when the Mallam is to be questioned publicly:

> *The following questions from the cast in the audience are to stimulate questions from the audience and to ensure that the pace is maintained. Ilya answers all questions. If a question is asked which he thinks will be answered in the course of the play, he simply says: 'Your question will be answered as the trial unfolds.' When a question makes him angry, he does not hide his anger. All this implies a thorough previous investi-*

---

[49] See pp. 122, 154.

> *gation into the character of Ilya by the actor playing the role. [...] The questions by the actors in the audience need not be in this order. They may be alternated with the questions from the audience. Malwal is the time keeper of the interrogation. He stops the questioning and lets the trial proceed when he thinks enough questions have been asked.* (134)

Abdallah's attempt to draw the public into the performance is to be seen as a continuation of the procedures of traditional theatres, popular Concert Parties and literary theatre inaugurated by Efua Sutherland's generation. Another potential term of comparison, in this regard, would once again be the Theatre for Development, constantly trying to involve the public in the very creation of the play by attaining the highest possible degree of "egalitarian participation from the audience, not only at the end of the play, but during the performance as well."[50]

Abdallah's efforts expose the drawbacks of that African theatre, which is 'top-down' in its attitude towards the public. The same concern is expressed by the critic Michael Etherton. According to him, the Nobel Prize winner Wole Soyinka's poetic vision is extremely powerful, but "What this vision denies the audience is their own participation in its creation. In every play performed, text published, the audience receives a completed dramatic product."[51]

Abdallah's plays look for a new conception of theatre hopefully lacking the élitist approach of much African drama. His dissatisfaction with university audiences may be seen as a sign of this: "On campus we never managed to involve the audience, I was shocked," he said to me (Abdallah, Legon, 11 December 1993). His unease could well be seen as part of a general mood of discontent, among some critics and practitioners, over the gap between contemporary theatre and its audience.

Femi Osofisan once more serves as the model for Abdallah's generation of playwrights, having always tried to involve the audience as well. If Abdallah seeks the patrons' help to unveil the personality of Mallam Ilya in all his facets, Osofisan similarly wants the principle of popular democracy affirmed in *Yungba–Yungba* to be immediately and actively applied by the people watching his production. In the play's epilogue, the dance competition finally takes place, and it includes cultural

---

[50] Kerr, "Participatory Popular Theatre," 61. See also Eugene Van Erven, "Revolution, Freedom and Theater of Liberation," *Research in African Literatures* 22.3 (1991): 21, and Penina Muhado Mlama, "Women's Participation in 'Communication for Development': The Popular Theatre Alternative in Africa," *Research in African Literatures* 22.3 (1991): 43.

[51] Michael Etherton, "African Theatre and Political Action," *Wasafiri* 6–7 (1987): 4.

quizzes and a beauty parade for the contestants. The jury panel, though, is picked from among the audience:

> *This must, needless to say, be a genuine competition, in which members of the audience should be encouraged to participate. To enhance this, actresses should be planted in the audience and give the impression of spontaneous enthusiasm which should persuade their neighbours.*
>
> *The questions asked in the first part of the competition should be about current events, or on the historical and cultural heritage of the community in which the play is being performed.*
>
> *The winner, crowned, should be led in a parade through the audience, as the play goes on and on, and becomes part of the real life, as ... the HOUSE LIGHTS come on.*[52]

Sandra Richards stresses the fluidity of roles in Osofisan's theatre, which "exists both in the sense that the narrator plays a multiplicity of characters and in the fact that all assembled are potentially performers."[53]

The search for this kind of fluid interaction – as seen in Chapter 6 – necessarily touches on matters of stage configuration, on the possibility of finding substitutes for the proscenium stage that might be more suitable for that fusion of scene and auditorium: "Rather a thousand Kodzidans than one National Theatre," Efua Sutherland might have argued.[54]

Nevertheless, Ghanaian authorities decided to pursue the opposite policy. A huge National Theatre was built in Accra in 1990, thanks to "a generous loan from the Chinese government." It was planned in China with a "distinctive Pagoda touch,"[55] and this created one of the many controversies about its construction. To add insult to injury, the site chosen in the centre of Accra was the same as that of the Drama Studio, which was consequently pulled down and rebuilt on campus, at the School of Performing Arts in Legon. In one of her collections of verses, Ama Ata Aidoo dedicates a poem to the destruction of this landmark of Ghanaian theatre:

> But the Drama Studio is gone, Robert,
> razed to the ground:
> to make way for someone's notion of
> the kind of theatre

[52] Osofisan, *Yungba-Yungba*, 122. Furthermore, Osofisan ends his famous play *Once Upon Four Robbers* in the same way; Femi Osofisan, *Once Upon Four Robbers* (Ibadan: Heinemann Educational, 1980): 96–97; in Gilbert & Tompkins, *Postcolonial Drama*, 128, this play is taken as a model for the audience's role as creator of meaning.

[53] Richards, *Ancient Songs*, 82.

[54] Gibbs, "Theatre of the Villages," 279.

[55] Ajoa Yeboah–Afari, "The Pagoda Touch," *West Africa* 3802 (1990): 2062.

> I
> should
> want.[56]

Looming over the capital, the new National Theatre has often been criticized for its detachment from the local audience, and for its desultory activities. During our interview, Abdallah complained about the unfortunate developments of the situation. He was personally caught in the polemic, having been the Chairman of the National Commission on Culture which carried out the project, and having later moved the university company Abibigromma (he had been instrumental in forming it in the early 1980s) to the new building. This created an absurd situation in which, still today, there are two Abibigrommas and two Ghana Dance Ensembles, divided between the National Theatre and the School of Performing Arts.[57] When we first met in 1993, Abdallah had just resigned, apparently torn by the contradictions of his political engagement:

> It's been a long struggle. I was playing tennis on both sides of the court. As for the rebuilding of the Drama Studio, it was a compromise I managed to reach by calling the Chinese Ambassador. It was a landmark of our theatre history, we couldn't lose it altogether. (Abdallah, Legon, 11 December 1993)

A similar event occurred earlier in Nigeria, with the construction of five multi-million-dollar theatres, of which the National Theatre in Lagos is "simply a replica of a Bulgarian model"; some committed playwrights, writes Michael Etherton, would hold that "the provision of these theatres inevitably means the exclusion of the vast mass of the population."[58]

To return to Abdallah's plays, it is noteworthy how the aforementioned scene in *The Trial* does not simply require the audience's participation, but also a different notion of actor, as the stage direction explicitly suggests. The role of Ilya necessarily approaches something similar to the Concert Party actor, required to work by deftly improvising on an unwritten plot;[59] a popular performer or comedian, in other

---

[56] Ama Ata Aidoo, *An Angry Letter in January* (Coventry: Dangaroo, 1992): 19.

[57] About this controversy, see Aidoo & Gibbs, "Mohammed Abdallah"; Kwame Nkrabeah, "Oh! Abdallah Has Resigned!," *The Independent* (Accra) (1–7 December 1993): 10; Kwesi Yankah, "Mohammed Abdallah: Is He Killing the Arts?," *Uhuru* 6 (1993): 21–25.

[58] Etherton, "Trends," 71.

[59] See Bamé, *Come to Laugh*, 27. The same could be said about the actors in Osofisan's *Yungba-Yungba*.

words, rather than a conventional actor. After all, as Peter Brook's actor Yoshi Oida said, improvisation "saves you from going mad – it makes worlds."[60]

Malwal's work from the auditorium, on the other hand, is meant to maintain an overall balance between plot and improvisation. He is akin to the director–performer of the Togolese Concert company analysed by Alain Ricard in his compelling *L'Invention du Théâtre*.[61] Therefore *The Trial* may be partly considered as the product of collective authorship, and this constitutes another similarity with Concert Parties, where "the creative energy that goes into a production is a corporate one."[62]

On the whole, then, *The Trial of Mallam Ilya* seems to elude the conception of written dramatic literature as something closed and finished, pointing to a work open to significant modifications at every performance, that freedom defined by Ricard as "freedom with regard to time."[63] The audience's role is called into play again, since their aesthetic guidance is fundamental for the 'final' printed output. The plays analysed in this chapter are probably the result of a long series of tentative corrections, as is shown by the way in which they differ substantially from the evidence of the few extracts published earlier.[64]

Notwithstanding the openness and fluidity of plays like *The Trial*, Abdallah's texts can certainly be considered as *written* dramatic literature. I analyse mainly his written works and their implications for a hypothetical performance, with a few references to videotapes of his plays and to a performance I personally witnessed. Their dynamic and manifold qualities are characteristic of works that are not limited to words, yet certainly deserving literary dignity. Their dialogue is sometimes interspersed with proverbial statements and metaphor, but on the whole they are rather straightforward, wholly different from the indirection or even obscurity of, say, some of Soyinka's plays. Jeyifo refers, among others, to *Madmen and Specialists*

---

[60] John Heilpern, *Conference of the Birds: The Story of Peter Brook in Africa* (1977; London: Methuen, 1989): 91.

[61] Ricard, *Invention du théâtre*, 100.

[62] Bamé, *Come to Laugh*, 55. See also: "The actors in concert party, like the bandsmen, seem to collaborate in an egalitarian way on the stage." In this respect, there is a marked difference from Yoruba Travelling Theatres, founded on a system of individual charismatic leaders defined "big man-ism," which "followed the lines of other social organizational patterns in Yoruba society"; Barber et al., *West African Popular Theatre*, xv, 51.

[63] "Liberté à l'égard du temps"; Ricard, *Invention du Théâtre*, 96 (my translation).

[64] See Abdallah, "The Slave," *Okyeame* 5 (1972): 41–47; James Gibbs, "Mohammed ben Abdallah and the Legon Road Theater," 33–34, and Gibbs, "But Spiritual Billionaires," *West Africa* 3865 (1991): 1680–81.

when calling for "a conscious attempt to achieve greater directness, greater clarity, greater popularity."[65]

Abdallah appears to stand between the two extremes of the literary and the popular, trying to move them closer to each other. On the one hand, he attempts to lend his plays the "greater directness" invoked by Jeyifo. On the other, he shows popular theatre a way to assume written form without stifling the open, oral dimension. Togolese Concert Parties and Yoruba Travelling Theatres, after all, are permeated by a new orientation towards literacy, by "the idea, if not the fact," of the written characteristics of their works.[66]

The Fall of Kumbi and other plays (1989)

The first play in Abdallah's second collection is *The Witch of Mopti*, his most courageous experiment in storytelling techniques. As in *The Alien King*, there is a group of storytellers, performed by the Abibigromma company. They play both the storytellers and the characters, but the latter are "*to be played interchangeably*" by the former.[67] The presentation of the story, then, is given pre-eminence over the story itself, and naturalistic action is once again discarded. Moreover, the storytellers have at their disposal on the stage seven crosses covered with costumes; each time they take on a character, they "*simply walk or dance up to the crosses and change into their costumes.*" Another estranging detail is "*the music stand with a sign that reads ABIBIGROMMA*" (3).

An opening song is followed by the Song of Welcome, during which the actors go down to shake hands with members of the audience. Abotsi then speaks directly to the people: "Good evening (*or afternoon... whatever the case may be*)" (3). The company introduces itself, trying to explain their role: players, musicians, jokers, what do they do? Their collective answer is: "We do all those things and more! (*Music grows louder and there is general dancing*)" (6). Emphasis, therefore, is

[65] Jeyifo, *Truthful Lie*, 84. The same play's reputation for being difficult is satirized in the Nigerian 'Biyi Bandele–Thomas's first novel, *The Man Who Came in from the Back of Beyond*, where it is chosen as a piece of retaliatory homework by a fifth-form literature teacher: "In school on Monday I found out that I wasn't the only one who hadn't written his essay: virtually everyone of us had not. We could not agree on what the play was all about. Some said it was about beggars, others said war. Some said it was about cannibalism, others said patricide"; Bandele–Thomas, *The Man Who Came in from the Back of Beyond* (London: Bellew, 1991): 5.

[66] Barber et al., *West African Popular Theatre*, 47.

[67] Mohammed ben Abdallah, *The Fall of Kumbi and other plays* (Accra: Woeli, 1989): 2. Further page references are in the main text.

again on a multifaceted kind of performer in accordance with the total-theatre concept dominating the West African stage, the same concept on which the School of Performing Arts of the University of Ghana at Legon (where Abdallah artistically matured) founds its education.[68] An analogous view of the actor was developed by the British director Peter Brook during his African journey in 1972, quoted at length by Abdallah in the preface to his doctoral dissertation:

> Brook's actor must be the composer, the singer, the poet, the dancer, the writer – each is a part of him, to be rediscovered, in time [...] trained to become so organically related within himself, he thinks completely with his body. He becomes one sensitive responding whole, like the cat.[69]

In *The Witch of Mopti*, after an argument about who is going to be the storyteller, they agree on everybody telling the story, and the plot can begin:

> TOGBI: A very long time ago in Mopti ....
>
> ALL: Mopti! (7)

From this point on, they take turns in speaking to the public, switching from plain narration to mimed and danced narration and to acting. All this is carried on in a quite humorous spirit:

> NII SAI: ... And don't forget the warriors of Mopti. Yes, the strong and handsome warriors who will kill even a citizen of Mopti. (*They mime a soldier bullying a citizen)* in defence of Mopti and, of course, will die for Mopti. (*A soldier is executed in public).* (8)

During the acted sections, Togbi, the main storyteller, steps in and out of the crowd of performers to continue the narration, comment on the events or attract the audience's attention: "Shh! Silence. I want absolute silence! You must listen carefully! For we have reached the crux of the matter! The eye of the storm! The knot in the heart of the story!" (79). In this case, Togbi's appeal is akin to the traditional bard's "climactic alerts," employed to communicate his "sense of moment," the importance of an incident.[70]

These storytelling techniques are also marked by a series of danced and mimed rituals with little or no words being spoken by the actors.[71] In *The Witch of Mopti*,

---

[68] One of the leading actors of SPA's Abibigromma, Atta Xornam Owusu, defined this conception of the "holistic" during a video interview with the American researcher Marion Wichmann Bailey in 1997 (personal recollection).

[69] Heilpern, *Conference of the Birds*, 62, 147.

[70] Okpewho, *Epic in Africa*, 212.

[71] See pp. 13, 17, 18–20, 25, 27–28, 30.

Abdallah's employment of storytellers certainly reaches its peak of complexity, and this can be compared to Bode Sowande's version of Amos Tutuola's novel *My Life in the Bush of Ghosts*, presented at the Africa '95 Festival, London, through a collaboration between Sowande's Odu Themes and the British Young People's Theatre. In Sowande's play Tutuola's 'Yorubanglish' is carried out by four storytellers who alternate in narrating in the first person the adventures of the protagonist: while one narrates, the other four act out what is being said, together with the rest of the cast. At the beginning the actors impersonate the narrator's audience, but as soon as the initial war starts they scatter with "a dance of rampage with vigorous drumming and full-bodied singing," and from then on they will act as characters in the protagonist's story in the forest of ghosts and / or continue to act out a listening audience. The rest of the play "for music and dance also employs other non-Yoruba cultures of Nigeria, namely Efik, Hausa and Edo,"[72] as the author's prefactory note reads, showing a pan-ethnic thrust shared with Abdallah.[73] The result, as I was personally able to verify on 14 August 1997, at the Arts Theatre (University of Ibadan),[74] is an enthralling championing of total theatre which can scarcely be conveyed on the printed page, as the author's several insertions of inverted commas indicates. When the protagonist turns into a cow, for instance, he escapes in order to avoid being sacrificed, and "*a small section of the storyteller's 'audience' on stage form and simulate a still pond, as the ritual group flees before reappearing later in search of the 'cow'.*" He realizes he is a person again when he sees himself in the water, embodied by Narrator 2 and 3 moving specularly, then he "*steps out of the 'pond', whose mimetic simulators 'flow' in movement back to the audience within the audience of the storytelling drama.*" At one point, the protagonist meets an antelope, which turns into a Superlady who will momentarily become the fifth narrator; and, leaving the land of ghosts at the end, in a sad parting that Tutuola's creative 'Yorubanglish' turns into a "bad-bye,"[75] all four narrators "mix with the party and are simultaneously bidden farewell."[76]

In *The Witch of Mopti*, Abdallah broadens the received notions of drama from a linguistic point of view as well. In the course of the play, some performers only

---

72 Bode Sowande, "My Life in the Bush of Ghosts" (author's undated typescript): 9, 3.

73 In Nigerian drama, the same thrust is evident in Wale Ogunyemi, *Langbodo* (Lagos: Thomas Nelson, 1979) and Ola Rotimi, *Hopes of the Living Dead* (Ibadan: Spectrum, 1988).

74 That version featured only two storytellers, instead of four. The performance was part of the celebrations for the Silver Jubilee of the Odu Themes.

75 For Tutuola's poetic English, see Chapter 1 (pp. 5–8).

76 Sowande, "My Life in the Bush of Ghosts," 22–23, 44.

speak Akan, and when they do so no translation is provided. Togby Onny speaks no English, and complains about its use in the play as a common language; a Ghanaian language should be employed, in his opinion. Coherently, he speaks Akan, acting as one of the storytellers and as town crier. He seems to be the most outspoken member of the group, especially when he boos the villainous witch. Furthermore, Dzifa and Adwoa's dialogue in Akan functions as a channel for popular feelings: openly discussing the king's sexual escapades, they are chased away by Onny.[77]

The linguistic variety mastered by Abdallah could be considered as a way of approaching the popular theatre's widespread use of local languages since the 1940s and the 1950s or, as Kofi Agovi writes, as an attempt to get rid of any linguistic inferiority complex.[78] Instead of opting for either English or Akan as such predecessors as Sutherland used to do, Abdallah opts for a mixture of the two. He invited me to consider this as a matter of verisimilitude:

> What turns out to be in *The Witch of Mopti* is a sort of mirror image of what is happening in Ghanaian society all the time. In some places you keep switching from one language to another. (Abdallah, Legon, 11 December 1993)

Works by other Ghanaian writers, like the poet Atukwei Okai and the novelist Kojo Laing, similarly incorporate many Ghanaian expressions, usually translated in a glossary.[79] Theatre has obviously various non-linguistic means of conveying its message, by exploiting all its potentially expressive tools, and can therefore afford to play with multilingualism unrestrictedly: "the fascination of Ghanaian and Togolese concert party plays," for instance, "comes from their incipient polyglottism."[80]

Abdallah appears to have moved a step beyond the linguistic habits of his precursors, but actually his weaving of English and Akan is reminiscent of Kobina Sekyi's *The Blinkards*, staged in 1915 – the very first Ghanaian play – almost forgotten by the mid-1930s and published only in 1974. The work, satirizing the europeanized élite of Cape Coast, was written partly in Fante, in accordance with scenic requirements and the level of education and anglicization of each individual character. Significantly, Abdallah once declared his wish to shoot a film of it.[81]

---

77 See pp. 4–5, 14, 22. These characters are not properly involved in the plot, and their commentary reminds one of Ama Ata Aidoo's similar technique in both her prose and her drama; see Chapter 1 (pp. 16–23).

78 Agovi, "Towards an Authentic African Theatre," 74–75. See also Chapter 6 above.

79 See Chapters 2, 3 and 4.

80 Barber et al., *West African Popular Theatre*, 49.

81 See Wilkinson, *Talking with African Writers*, 37.

Despite its formal and linguistic features, however, the story of *The Witch of Mopti* lacks a certain penetration and social vision. Since the king has rejected her daughter for a poor girl he loves, the witch Maimuna uses all her powers to punish the city of Mopti: assisted by the classic three witches, she makes the king impotent and afflicts his people in several ways. All her spells are nullified by the magicians summoned by the king, until she exchanges her daughter's life for the Devil's power to drive everyone mad by polluting the well water. This eventually leads to the scene being divided into four different simultaneous planes:[82] the Witches worshipping Maimuna's daughter, the anxious king who is the only sane person left, the storytellers Togbi and Onny who quietly watch, and

> *a parade of all the citizens of Mopti, lunatics of all kinds, shades, sizes and ages. [...] a cacophony of different songs, and a spectacle of fantastic and strange costumes [...] and a dance of bizarre movements, gyrations and contortions both physically and facially.* (36)

To such insane people the sane king is mad, thus cannot rule Mopti any longer, in a curious reversal of the sanity/lunacy opposition. Just when he is at a complete loss what to do

> *(Togbi and Onny step out of their corner and approach the king.)*
> KING: Oh, God! Who are you? Where do you come from? Have you come to help me? (38)

The interacting storyteller, as seen above, is a traditional feature also employed by Sutherland in *The Marriage of Anansewa*.[83] In the present case, Togbi and Onny hint at a piece of advice decisive for the whole plot:

> You see, we are not even supposed to be here. We are not part of the story. We are only storytellers from a different time and a different dimension. That well over there is the problem [...] the solution may very well lie deep inside the well. (39)

The king grasps the suggestion, drinks some water and goes mad: he has regained his 'sanity.' Togbi closes the play by commenting on the king's Pyrrhic victory: "In the struggle for Mopti .... Who was the winner .... And who the loser?" (41).

A somewhat superficial reflection on the nature of madness and power of this kind[84] may be a little disappointing, but is actually closer to the *anansesem* that Ab-

[82] In the December 1998 production that I saw (Drama Studio, School of Performing Arts, University of Ghana at Legon), such parallel enactments were also effected through a raised platform in the background, home to the witches' tricks.

[83] Sutherland, *Marriage of Anansewa*, 19–20.

dallah dramatized in his two plays for children: *Ananse and the Rain God* (1989) and *Ananse and the Golden Drum* (1994), both written in the early 1970s, probably in the wake of other writers' dramatized folktales (as seen in Chapter 6). Both plays witness the spider-trickster bringing misfortune on himself because of his greed, and employ storytelling, music and dance; in the second play, the storytelling session begins in a family whose members will perform the action. Abdallah thus shows that he also belongs among those writers interested in creating stories for children.

The lack of thematic import does not affect *The Slaves* and *The Fall of Kumbi*, contained in the same collection. These two historical tragedies, on the slave-trade and the legendary origins of the Asante kingdom, share the idea of sacrifice, of choosing a physical death instead of a spiritual one.[85] Abdallah quotes Armah's novel *Two Thousand Seasons* in his epigraph to the collection: "physical death is a necessary preparation for a profounder life, [...] life of our way, the way."[86] Despite abounding in music, dancing and, above all, rituals, however, the two plays also share a nearly total lack of presentational style, as if the author were less successful in integrating themes and techniques than in *The Trial of Mallam Ilya*.

In *The Slaves* a group of prisoners is kept in the dungeons of a coastal castle, waiting to be shipped to the Americas. The crude atmosphere of insults and dark desperation is lit by a gleam of hope when one of them devises a plan:

> No, my friends. The white man is not our man. Stop the slave trade at its source. Kill the black man who sells the slaves [...] If I can get out of here I shall be dangerous again. I have influence where I come from. (57–58)

An old Yoruba priest sets up a rite to propitiate the man's escape, but they will all be betrayed by Naa, who is pregnant by (and psychically enslaved to) the overseer. The play closes sadly amidst generally spiteful indifference with Naa's miscarriage.

The tragedy of the play derives from the characters' severance from the metaphysical: "The gods! What do the gods care what happens to us?" (50). Such a rupture, though, is shown to be caused by the black man's guilt about slavery: as Armah writes, "No one sold us but our chiefs and their hangers-on."[87]

---

[84] "Based on a traditional folk story from the Sahel," reads the programme of the December 1998 production held at the Drama Studio and directed by the author himself.

[85] Maybe this is why they were included in the same collection, even though *The Slaves* was first produced very early, in 1971.

[86] Armah, *Two Thousand Seasons*, 199.

[87] Armah, *Two Thousand Seasons*, 146. *The Slaves* thus belongs to the group of African works concerned with the devastating experience of the slave trade. The Ghanaian critic and poet Kwadjo Opoku–Agyemang has written essays and poems on the subject, and complains about the failure, on the part of most African authors, "to bring to the center of contemporary discourse the largest

The Fall of Kumbi establishes a more explicit link with Armah's novel, since it could be considered as a dramatization of the oral history narrated in its third chapter, "The Predators." The tragedy concerns the fall of the ancient empire of Ghana, and the name Kumbi refers to one of its capitals, identified by scholars with the ruins of Koumbi Saleh. In the play, Amu Diata, prince of Kumbi, elopes with Zainata, a betrothed Tuareg princess, and later attacks the Tuareg town of Audoghast. This provides Ibn Yacin's Moors with a pretext for sacking Kumbi's riches, enacted through "*a ballet depicting the attack on Kumbi by the Marabout army* [...] *characterized by pillaging and raping of women*" (85). The ancient Ghana empire was likewise overrun by the Almoravids in 1076.

As in *The Slaves*, a crudely violent tragedy is visited on a people because of their own faults (this time reminiscent of the rape of Helen in Homer's *Iliad*), as the mother of the temple virgins says: "Kumbi slapped Audoghast in the face and demanded that they should not weep! We went to shit in their courtyard and asked them to wipe our ass for us" (91). Armah's *Two Thousand Seasons* would appear to be dominated by the concept of guilt as well, about a people who have abandoned "the way."[88]

To face the danger, the High Priest of Kumbi summons the other priests. After a long ceremony of trances and praise-singing where he "*screams loudly as the spirit throws him high in the air*"(89), he tells them to lead the seven clans of Kumbi to the southern forests. As far as their Golden Stool is concerned, it "will be swallowed up into the womb of the skies" (95), and kept by God until a priest will burst the heavens open and take it back. Abdallah dramatizes what some (contentious) oral histories recount about the origins of the Asante empire: folk traditions hold that the Akans came from the eleventh-century kingdom of Ghana, and that the Golden Stool was given by the priest Anokye to the king Osei Tutu (1770–30) through thunder, to invest him with power. The Stool is believed to contain the soul of the Asante nation.[89]

---

segment and most traumatic body of events in the African experience"; Opoku–Agyemang, "A Crisis of Balance: The (Mis)Representation of Colonial History and the Slave Experience as Themes in Modern African Literature," *Asemka: A Literary Journal of the University of Cape Coast* 7 (September 1992): 66. This scholar's writings are of particular interest for his analysis of the long-term effects of the slave trade on the psyche of those who remained at home.

[88] Armah, *Two Thousand Seasons*, 37, 58.

[89] See Nina Pawlak, "Akan Folk Literature and the Beginnings of Writing in Twi," in *Literatures in African Languages: Theoretical Issues and Sample Surveys*, ed. B.W. Andrzejewski et al. (Warsaw: Wiedza Powzechna; Cambridge: Cambridge UP, 1985): 129, 145–46.

Before the destruction of Kumbi is complete, the High Priest has himself killed by the possessed Khumata, the Queen Mother's daughter, who is touched with a divine madness that allows her to utter further prophecies to her fellow captives:

> Kumbi is dead but Kumbi will rise again bearing a new name in the Rain Forest of the South. [...] This is only the beginning of a long journey for our own people. Two thousand seasons of pain and death, my sisters! (117)

The references to the Asante capital, Kumasi, and to Armah's novel are fairly obvious. In the gruesome final Initiation Dance, Khumata follows the Priest's example and commits suicide, in her case by penetrating herself with a long wooden phallus. As she says, "There is no ignorance more pathetic than the ignorance about the worth of your own soul!" (120). Such a refusal of a worthless physical survival reminds one again of Armah's third chapter, since this is a concept supporting those who decide to migrate southwards under the threat of the predators' oppression: "Absurd then for us to continue here merely for the zombi purpose of existing."[90]

The Slaves and *The Fall of Kumbi* are both collective tragedies, where no hero is singled out as the emblem of his/her people. Based on oral histories, they cannot but regard the destiny of entire collectivities. This, too, faithfully reflects the spirit pervading Armah's novel, which is narrated in the first-person plural and where fragmentation is seen as the worst danger threatening a people's integrity: "There is no beauty but in relationships."[91] The similarity with Greek theatre, too, is evident. Raymond Williams blames Western criticism for reshaping Greek tragedies by isolating single heroes and by using psychology to interpret them:

> Greek tragic action was not rooted in individuals, [but] in history, and not in human history alone. Its thrust came [...] from a man's inheritance and relationships, within a world that ultimately transcended him. What we then see is a general action specified, not an individual action generalised.[92]

The same collective outlook is detectable in Femi Osofisan's plays, which tend to point to a communal, rather than individual, heroism in search of alternative and revolutionary social configurations.

---

[90] Armah, *Two Thousand Seasons*, 39. A further characteristic shared by Abdallah and Armah's poetics is a recent interest in the culture of ancient Egypt. While the latter published his latest novel in 1995 under the title *Osiris Rising* (Popenguine, Senegal: Per Ankh), the playwright has been researching into Akhnaton (the heretical pharaoh who established monotheism) and is, he told me (Accra, 8 July 1997), planning to write a play about him called "Song of the Pharaoh."

[91] Armah, *Two Thousand Seasons*, 206.

[92] Raymond Williams, *Modern Tragedy* (1966; London: Hogarth, 1992): 87–88.

On the other hand, there is a wide gap separating Abdallah from Osofisan. As can be seen from the two historical tragedies of his second collection and also from *Verdict of the Cobra*, Abdallah holds ritual practices in deep respect, almost trying to stage them at face-value, without trying to undermine or modernize their received significance.[93] With regard to ritual, the author has declared to Jane Wilkinson:

> I can't think of a single play that I have written that doesn't have that heavy ritual aspect. Maybe because for me the ritual – the mask and the dance which are all part of the ritual anyway – provides a very important medium for the regeneration of society. I don't believe in theatre purely for entertainment.[94]

The violence in *The Fall of Kumbi* raises cries about the gods' indifference. The Queen Mother accuses them and proclaims "Then hide your face, sun! For the gods have been put to shame. The world henceforth must be ruled by men, not gods!" (113) This constitutes the root of the play's tragedy. The same attitude is displayed by Abdallah towards the received oral narratives about the power structure of the Asante kingdom, and the spiritual power of Anokye's Golden Stool.

Unlike Abdallah's, Osofisan's standpoint shatters all assumptions with regard to myth and ritual, by shedding light on the dialectical relationship between them and contemporary life. Sandra Richards writes that such a treatment differs radically from "'Zulu Sofola, Bode Sowande and Ola Rotimi who use music, dance and mask realistically as environment or as stable indices of social mores and characters."[95] Abdallah could easily be included in her list.

With regard to the present topic, Osofisan's seminal essay is undoubtedly "Ritual and Revolutionary Ethos" (1982), where he reacts to Wole Soyinka's use of myth in plays such as *Death and the King's Horseman*. In Osofisan's view, "he [Soyinka] presents the traditional Yoruba world untransmuted, [and] his art seems encompassed, his vision reactionary." In other words, what is to be refused is "the

---

[93] Another play that assigns a restorative value to ritual is certainly *Lake God* (Yaoundé: BET, 1986) by the Cameroonian Bole Butake. The historical starting point of the play is the sad and mysterious death of a whole village on Lake Nyos, which occurred on 21 August 1986; toxic volcanic gas or chemical weapons could have been the cause. Butake's work describes a community at risk of losing its traditional values. Shey Bo–Nyo, traditional priest and narrator of the play, is the last to remain faithful to his forefathers' faith. Together with the leader of the Kwifon cult, he insists that the westernized chief perform the customary sacrifice to the god of the lake. The final cataclysm is to be seen as a consequence of his refusal, of the general loss of ancestral customs. One may feel a bit disquieted by such a conservative orientation.

[94] Wilkinson, *Talking with African Writers*, 36.

[95] Richards, *Ancient Songs Set Ablaze*, 78.

art that stubbornly weaves around old mythologies, *unmediated*, [that] prolongs the unfeeble past and is anti-progress."[96]

In order to grasp fully his restructuring of myth, a detailed analysis of some of his plays is necessary. *The Chattering and the Song*, mentioned by the author himself at the end of his essay, provides a significant object of study. Its dominant mythic element is formed by Ifa, the Yoruba oracular system, and its deity Orunmila, the god of wisdom and divination consulted before taking decisions.

In the prologue, Yajin and Sontri engage in a snappy dialogue that turns out to be a poetic courtship ritual marked by the repeated formula "Iwori Otura," defined by M.P. Awodiya as "a major Ifa chant [...] Whenever the Ifa oracle prescribes love, 'Iwori Otura' signifies success in the inquirer's amorous life."[97] Yajin accordingly leaves Mokan, a good friend of Sontri's, for the love of the latter.

Part One is centred on the preparations for their wedding, where the painter Funlola teasingly recollects her friend Yajin's description of Sontri: "I am not talking now of his physical appearance. From your letter I know Sontri's the incarnation of Orunmila himself."[98] So far, no fundamental novelty is recognizable in Osofisan's approach to Yoruba myth: one deity (Orunmila) is associated with the figure of the fighter in order to reinforce it. In this case the warrior is a revolutionary one (Sontri, activist of the Farmers' Movement), rather than one or more traditional rulers. The only change would thus seem to reside in the side the author takes. The play's development, though, unveils the radical standpoint of Osofisan's dramaturgy.

In Part Two the characters enact, on Yajin's request, a short play-within-the-play written by Sontri regarding the confrontation between the famous Alafin Abiodun and Latoye. The play thus confronts itself with a written source from Yoruba history, Samuel Johnson's *The History of the Yorubas* (1921), which describes Abiodun – the man who killed the ruthless general Gaha – as "a tall and slender prince [...] a comely person, of dignified manners, and altogether fit to wear a crown [...] whose peaceful reign has passed into a proverb."[99] In Sontri's scenario, though, Abiodun's rule is exposed by Latoye, the only son of Gaha's who survived the massacre

[96] Femi Osofisan, "Ritual and Revolutionary Ethos: The Humanistic Dilemma in Contemporary Nigerian Theatre," *Okikè* 2 (September 1982): 76 (emphasis in the original). Soyinka replies to Osofisan's essay in his "Who's Afraid of Elesin Oba?," where he further explains the function he envisages for Ogun; Soyinka, *Art, Dialogue and Outrage: Essays on Literature and Culture* (Ibadan: New Horn, 1988): 118–24.

[97] Awodiya, "Structure and Meaning," 67.

[98] Osofisan, *Chattering*, 10.

[99] Rev. Samuel Johnson, *The History of the Yorubas: From the Earlier Times to the Beginning of the British Protectorate* (Lagos: C.M.S. Bookshops, 1921): 162.

thanks to Abiodun's mercy.[100] While the monarch is acted out by Sontri, the main role of the rebel Latoye is, surprisingly, given to Leje, a drunkard of no apparent moral stature. The audience is told that Latoye is popularly reputed to have been a drunkard, too.[101] In the enactment, Latoye is taken to Abiodun as a captured agitator, but the former succeeds in showing that the latter is merely another member of a long line of oppressors: "My father was a plague, and you killed him. But you, Abiodun, you are the new plague! The new spot to be scraped out! [...] Because the earth, fouled with your contagion, cries for cleansing!"[102] As Awodiya writes, "Osofisan subverts these [Johnson's] historical and mythological materials."[103]

A dialectical struggle ensues: Latoye speaks to the guards in favour of rebellion, whereas the king's motivation is based on the value of continuity: "The sea ages: / Tides do not corrode the coral: / They only add to its adornment .... / The world shall not spoil in our time!"[104] Later on, Abiodun translates his position into religious necessity: who will keep the rituals alive, he asks, who will act as a link between the human and the superhuman if the people choose freedom and revolt? Latoye's reply illuminates Osofisan's revolutionary conception of the Yoruba pantheon:

> We know how Edumare [the Yoruba supreme deity] himself arranged his heaven, on which model he moulded the earth. To each of the gods, Edumare gave power, and fragility, so that none of them shall be a tyrant over the others, and none a slave [...] all the assurance that power shall not be corrupted by abundant previlege, that neither good nor evil shall be the monopoly of a few. [...] Sango eats, Ogun eats, and so do the ebora [spirits] of the forest. But in your reign, Abiodun, the elephant eats and nothing remains for the antelope! The buffalo drinks, and there is drought in the land! Soldiers, seize him![105]

In a 1988 interview with Charles Uji, the author sets out clearly the reasons for his reworking of myth. If religion helps people deal with the environment, he says, it should change as the conditions of living vary:

> [myth] is merely history distilled, crystallised [...] just a peculiar interpretation of issues. And when you think of it, most of these interpretations, in fact, have been de-

---

100 In this case, Osofisan's source cannot have been Johnson, who never mentions Latoye but only some "surviving sons"; see Johnson, *History of the Yorubas*, 186, 194. It is curious that M.P. Awodiya should trace Latoye back to Johnson's volume; Awodiya, "Structure and Meaning," 62.

101 Osofisan, *Chattering*, 24.

102 Osofisan, *Chattering*, 39.

103 Awodiya, "Structure and Meaning," 62.

104 Osofisan, *Chattering*, 43.

105 Osofisan, *Chattering*, 45.

> cided by the ruling class, which means that they are also subject to *re-interpretations* [...] because the victims and the victors never share the same perspective.[106]

The Chattering and the Song is closed by a double *coup de théâtre*. Mokan stops the play to have Sontri and Yajin arrested as members of the seditious Farmers' Movement: the rejected lover is revenged via the secret police. Yet the revolution, as Sontri himself says, cannot be stopped: "There's nothing you can do to stop the birds from singing."[107] The epilogue – and the second surprise – further develops this statement, probably in the hope that it will not sound like an empty slogan. Once he has dropped the role of the rebel Latoye, Leje offers Funlola, whose artistic sensitivity he appreciates, a place in the Farmers' Movement: the seemingly non-descript drunkard is actually Osongongon, the Farmers' leader. Working in the background, he is hard to destroy, and not indispensable: "What is a single man in revolution?"[108] To gain her support, Leje starts the same 'Iwori Otura' ritual that occurred in the beginning between Sontri and Yajin:

> FUNLOLA: Iwori Otura: be gentle with me,
> I'm famished and weak, I'm just like a thread ....
> LEJE: A thread in a loom? The loom of the state?
> Say I am a shuttle ....
> FUNLOLA: And I the thread?
> LEJE: Iwori Otura: across the loom
> If we dance as one [...]
> We'll weave new patterns out of our world.[109]

Thus the Ifa chant, in tune with contemporary needs, has moved from its traditional amorous context to wider social preoccupations without preluding a possible romantic involvement. With Sontri and Yajin, social engagement was almost seen as menacing their bond of sentiment. There was very little harmony between Yajin's feelings and Sontri's aggressive, shouting drive towards collective struggle.[110]

---

[106] Awodiya, *Excursions in Drama and Literature*, 114 (emphasis in the original). See also Osofisan's play *No More the Wasted Breed*, a response to Soyinka's *The Strong Breed*, where the ruthless gods are rejected because of the absurd human sacrifices they requested: "Tides change for gods as they do for men"; Osofisan, *Morountodun and other plays* (Ikeja: Longman Nigeria, 1982): 110.

[107] Osofisan, *Chattering*, 47.

[108] Osofisan, *Chattering*, 53.

[109] Osofisan, *Chattering*, 55.

[110] Osofisan, *Chattering*, 4–5. Sandra Richards emphasizes Sontri's vanquishing posture towards Yajin: "Whereas at the outset the iwori otura riddling was expressed in terms of conquest,

Recourse to Ifa, rather than a tendency to rely on individual personalities endowed with its powers, is conceived by Osofisan as a collective reservoir of wisdom that could and should touch all the characters. Osofisan's idea of Ifa is a far cry from the divination priest consulted by the *kabiyesi* on the eve of a battle, and in some of his plays he has cast a negative light on such mercenary employment of the divining chain.[111] Indeed, he has always stressed the idea of Ifa as metaphor, provider of knowledge, representing no fixed truth and requiring no worship.[112]

A further development in Osofisan's remoulding of the Yoruba pantheon is evident in his *Esu and the Vagabond Minstrels*.[113] Esu, the Yoruba trickster deity oscillating between mischief and justice, was subject to thorough manipulation by Christian ideology, which identified him with absolute evil. Not surprisingly, the Reverend Samuel Johnson passively adhered to this view when writing his *History*, where he defines Esu as "Satan, the Evil One, the author of all evil."[114] Dunton writes that in 1986, notwithstanding its success, Osofisan's play provoked some controversy among conservative Christian groups on Ife campus.[115]

Actually, Esu possesses dual, ambiguous qualities. Abimbola writes that he belongs both among the *orisa* (benevolent gods) and among the *ajogun* (malevolent ones), acting as "an impartial judge who mediates between them."[116] He also mediates between men and gods, being the one who accepts sacrifices from humans on behalf of the pantheon, and is therefore worshipped as a very powerful god. In Ogunyemi's play *Eshu Elegbara* (1970), he sows discord among the gods who take part in the creation, and when expelled from their midst he becomes the divine

---

here [with Leje and Funlola] the images are of interdependence"; Richards, *Ancient Songs Set Ablaze*, 105.

[111] See his satire in *Who's Afraid of Solarin?*, a farce based on Nikolai Gogol's *The Inspector General*, where the Ifa priest Baba Fawomi performs mock rituals by chanting meaningless words, and ends up being ridiculed by the houseboy's pidgin English. Femi Osofisan, *Who's Afraid of Solarin?* (Ibadan: Scholars Press, 1978): 18, 20, 24, 53.

[112] See Awodiya, *Excursions in Drama and Literature*, 70; Osofisan, "Ritual and Revolutionary Ethos," 78.

[113] Sandra Richards aptly traces the presence of Ifa in another play by Osofisan, *Once Upon Four Robbers* (1991), especially in the character of Aafa, who performs the same function as the Old Man in *Esu*; Richards, *Ancient Songs Set Ablaze*, 125–32.

[114] Johnson, *History of the Yorubas*, 28.

[115] Dunton, *Make Men Talk True*, 85.

[116] Wande Abimbola, "Ifa: A West African Cosmological System," in *Religion in Africa*, ed. T.D. Blakely, W.E.A. van Beek & D.L. Thomson (London: James Currey; Portsmouth NH: Heinemann, 1994): 106.

intermediary. At the end of the play, Ogun aptly calls him "The versatile intimidator / Who sympathizes with / Whom he implicates."[117] Robert D. Pelton sees Esu as a catalyst of change, whose mischief disrupts the status quo and exposes its false assumptions.[118]

Femi Osofisan's view is very similar. He rejects the Christian bias, holding that Yoruba thought leaves room for nothing of the sort:

> Our traditional world-view did not have such characters who are totally one-sided, either positively or negatively; [here] you have the greatest proof that man is created in God's image. Unlike the baffling contradictions in their Christianity.

The author singles out Esu because he sees in him the turbulence necessary for improvement: "Eshu is the god of indeterminacy [...] of chance [...] if a knowledge needs to be carried forward, something must come and disturb the present stability [...] else we stagnate and die." Esu, then, represents

> constant questioning, constant challenge to authority, to orthodoxy. The restless iconoclastic spirit. But then the resolution of that comes out of the Ifa principle. The synthesis, the gathering of everything together, then, that's resolved in the Ifa principle, in the union of Eshu and Orunmila.[119]

The plot of *Esu* stages a dramatic fusion of the two religious entities. Fallen out of favour after a coup, a group of musicians used to playing for the wealthy meet an Old Man at a crossroads who claims to be Esu's priest. He gives all the minstrels the magic power to help those who come to Esu's crossroads with any kind of problem: their songs will suffice to perform the feat. The fortune of every minstrel will depend on the gratitude of the succoured person:

> Esu will multiply by two,
> Whatever you have used the power to acquire!
> But if you have gained nothing,
> If you have misused the power,
> Chosen the wrong targets, I promise
> You will be severely punished.[120]

This warning seems to hint at the Parable of the Talents in Matthew 25:29, which concerns the coming of the Day of Judgement: "For everyone who has will be given

[117] Wale Ogunyemi, *Eshu Elegbara* (Ibadan: Orisun Acting, 1970): 55.

[118] Pelton, *Trickster in West Africa*, 127–50.

[119] Awodiya, *Excursions in Drama and Literature*, 47, 81.

[120] Osofisan, *Esu*, 19.

more, and he will have in abundance. Whoever does not have, even what he has will be taken from him."

Taking the Old Man's words literally, and probably with the servants of the parable at the back of their minds, the minstrels strive to help affluent people in distress, where money or power can come in return. The only exception is Omele, who helps a poor woman to deliver her baby for a simple "thank you" and consciously takes a couple's leprosy on himself through an embrace. Just as in *The Chattering*, the play closes with unexpected turns of events. First of all, the wealthy people in need were all sent by the Old Man, who turns out to be Esu himself. In keeping with his role, the trickster god has used his mischief to expose the greedy nature of the minstrels and Omele's unadulterated compassion. But when he seems slow in judging them and prone to having some more fun at their expense, the former lepers also reveal their true identities as the gods Orunmila and Yeye Osun. The greedy are given leprosy – but the surprises do not end here.

While the divine couple are uttering the final moral, the actors reappear on stage, removing their costumes and claiming that they decided to rewrite the script because "There's no magic to the riddle of evil [...] No incantation can cure the anguish caused by the greed of politicians." But the actor playing Orunmila, too, was also just getting to the same point before being interrupted, and thus restates the author's metaphoric, conceptual notion of the Yoruba deities: "All of us, / What are we, but metaphors in a / Fading tale?" When all the actors have finally taken off their costumes, the collective song proclaims "Esu does not exist / save in your imagination!"[121]

Land of a Million Magicians (1993)

Abdallah's latest published play is set in today's Niiman, recalling Nima, a deprived urban area in Accra where he moved at the age of fourteen to live with his uncle.[122] The urban setting allows the author to depict that cultural mix typical of contemporary West African cities: the play opens with a street drowned by "*various sounds of the music and dance of the different indigenous groups that inhabit Niiman*"[123] –

---

[121] Osofisan, *Esu*, 70–72.

[122] For other descriptions of Nima's destitute landscape, see Awoonor's *This Earth, My Brother*.

[123] Mohammed ben Abdallah, *Land of a Million Magicians* (Accra: Woeli, 1993): 1. Further page references are in the main text.

Asante, Dagomba, Ga, Yoruba, Hausa. All of these cultures make their contribution to this colorful, lively and crowded play featuring music and dancing.

Among these cultural strains, Abdallah could hardly overlook the Ghanaian Concert Party, and employs the Abibiman Company guitar band as musical support – "my favourite band," says the storyteller (2).[124] The company provides a long musical introduction and some highlife interludes. When the play was first produced in Accra on 29 August 1991, "music was provided by the veteran Concert Party performer 'Lord' Bob Cole."[125] The author openly declared his love for the genre:

> It's a unique contribution to African arts that should have been nurtured and helped and studied, especially some of its parts like the acting style. Now they're slowly disappearing, but there used to be a time when they were all over the place. In *Land* I tried to see whether it is possible to salvage some of its dynamic aspects. (Abdallah, Legon, 11 December 1993)

Recently, live shows have decreased a little, but other media have taken up the Concert Party tradition. After the TV adaptations and photoplays of the 1970s and the 1980s (and later the audio cassettes), the National Theatre started a programme in September 1994 run by William Addo. In 1997 these Keysoap-sponsored shows enjoyed great success, both in their live versions on Sunday afternoons and as Friday evening TV broadcasts. Such a national revival of popular theatre goes hand in hand with the developmental issue:

> Every production has a theme, which is in line with the general theme for the year. This year, the theme is Sanitation. Last year, it was Bush Fires and Afforestation. Groups therefore craft their stories with the theme in mind.

One of the top comedians featured in the shows is Bishop Bob Okalla, who "worked with Kusum Agoromba because of Efua Sutherland of blessed memory who catered for Okalla as if she was his mother."[126]

In *Land*, Abdallah continues to employ effects of alienation, like the character/storyteller Mummuni, Niiman's water-seller, who introduces the story:

> *He notices the audience and bows to them ....*
>
> MUMMUNI: My name is Mummuni and this is Niiman, the city-within-a-city! (1)

---

[124] The Abibiman company is employed by the Ghanaian Arts Council, and has often worked with Bob Vans, a scriptwriter who composes Concert Party shows on commission, "the tentative beginning of a scripted theatre"; Barber et al, *West African Popular Theatre*, 20.

[125] James Gibbs, "Land of a Million Magicians," *School of Performing Arts Newsletter* 1 (January--March 1994): 7.

[126] Ahuma Boseo Ocansey, "The Greatest Show in Town," *Sunday Herald* (29 June 1997), Living 1: 5.

As far as estrangement is concerned, there is plenty of it in Bertolt Brecht's political works. He could be considered, alongside ancestral drama, an influential source for Abdallah. In this case there is an admitted link between the two authors, since *Land* is based on Brecht's *The Good Woman of Setzuan*. In both plays, three gods are sent to earth to find out what can be done to save our planet, and the best person they meet is a prostitute, Hasana / Shen Te. Abdallah connects them to the three main Ghanaian religions: a traditional *okomfo*,[127] an imam and a cardinal. Mummuni is the Ghanaian correspondent of Wong; they both deliver an introductory speech to the audience about the poverty of their hometowns: "I am poor, yes! But that is the fashion here. We are all poor [...] On behalf of the poor of the world I, Mummuni, welcome you" (2). Desperately trying to find a house for the gods, he even seeks the audience's help: "You there…you look like a very wise man. Please, advise me. What would you do if you were in my shoes?" (14).

Despite such poverty, a light mood of comedy prevails in the play, more markedly so than in Brecht's: "Today being Sunday, Niiman is full of music and dance. We may be poor in cash but I must say when it comes to the riches of the spirit, we are billionaires" (3). In the midst of all these bands, even the storyteller cannot resist the temptation: "Oh! God! I can't help myself .... please excuse me while I shake a bit. *(He joins the group and dances with one of the women for a few minutes and then steps out of the group.)*" (3). Later on the Concert Party band starts playing, and he *"joins the band and leads in singing that number"* (4).

The humour pervading the play is often infectious, as when Mummuni calls the cardinal "your Holiness" (9, 21) or when he leads the gods to Hasana's place while she is servicing a client:

> OKOMFO: What is that noise? Is the lady all right?
>
> MUMMUNI *(knocking harder)*: Hasana! Hasana!
>
> HASANA: Yes! .... Yes! ....
>
> CUSTOMER: Oooh! Hasana ....you are so good..oooh! aah! [...] Oh! God! .... Ooh!
>
> MUMMUNI: Hasana! Open the door ....it's me ....

---

127 In the 1991 performed version of the play, the Okomfo's lines were spoken in the vernacular, as can be noticed on the video recording. Ben Abdallah told me that the actor impersonating him belonged to the Concert Party tradition: "he doesn't speak a word of English, but he can stand on stage and entertain an audience and make them laugh! But that is not enough... someone should have the courage to create for him, otherwise he could languish there" (Abdallah, Legon, 11 December 1993). On the other hand, he strangely chose to transcribe the Okomfo's words in English in the published text, thereby passing up an opportunity to re-create the polyglot atmosphere of popular theatre as in *The Witch of Mopti*.

HASANA: O. K.! I'm coming!

CUSTOMER: Oh God! I'm coming too! She's coming! Wait .... Ooh, we're coming ....ooh. (18–19)[128]

The comic mood of the play is not a novelty for Abdallah, but unlike the folktale lightness of *The Witch of Mopti* it is coupled in this case with solid social insight. Significantly enough, this humorous turn in Abdallah's writing occurs in the same play where a Concert Party band – Ghanaian comedians' theatre *par excellence* – plays, as a further approach to the popular format. In the same manner, Osofisan's irresistibly hilarious farces,[129] which satirize the various ills of Nigerian society, are seen by Sandra Richards to follow the popular novelistic tradition of Cyprian Ekwensi and the trickster-like Baba Sala's comic performances, raising this question:

> how, in the absence of a widely supported, progressive ideology, a theatre can be both popular with a broad-based public and critical of the social order that the same public, for a variety of reasons, helps to maintain.[130]

Biodun Jeyifo, when trying to dismantle the commonplace distinction between the immediate sense of comedy and the lasting values of tragedy, emphasizes the material, everyday nature of the former, its potential "status as both a reflection and a critique of contemporary society."[131] In *Land of a Million Magicians* such a critique materializes when Hasana – like Brecht's Shen Te – has to find a way to spend the money that the gods have left her in order to improve Niiman's life.

When asked by the gods how Niiman can survive its appalling poverty, Hasana and Mummuni cannot help laughing: "It's a mystery .... it's like .... like .... everybody knows nobody's money is enough. Yet everybody survives .... it's like magic" (26). In November 1984, the author explained the origin of the title:

> there was a joke about Nigerians, how they referred to Ghanaians. In Ghana you are paid something like 20 cedis a day, and the average worker pays the equivalent of that for transportation from his house to his place of work and that doesn't take into account what he eats for breakfast, for lunch and dinner, what his wife and children eat,

---

[128] Generally speaking, Abdallah was criticized for his sexually explicit scenes; see John Djisenu, "Useful Political Lessons," 4. In his review of *The Alien King*, Ibrahim Salla notes, among other things, that one scene "is certainly over-indulgent in its detailed attention to the physical"; Salla, review of *The Trial*, 35. Personally I find this kind of critical prudery quite out of place, but generally speaking this issue certainly divides Ghanaian society.

[129] See *Who's Afraid of Solarin?*, *Midnight Hotel* (Ibadan: Evans, 1986) and *The Midnight Blackout* (Ibadan: Ibadan UP, 1994).

[130] Richards, *Ancient Songs Set Ablaze*, 45–46.

[131] Jeyifo, *Truthful Lie*, 65.

> his children's school fees, his rent and everything. But everybody still survives. So the Nigerians nickname Ghana 'the land of 12 million magicians.'[132]

It is not by chance that the play was first performed in Accra on 29 August 1991

> as part of the entertainment offered to the heads of a Non-Aligned States meeting [...] at a time when Ghana was struggling to come to terms with the Structural Adjustment Programme recommended by the International Monetary Fund.[133]

In Mummuni's initial monologue to the audience,[134] there is a satirical remark about that meeting and the construction of the new Niiman Highway:

> of course, they constructed it for themselves .... not for us .... but to accelerate their speedy passage through this.. this.. this place, to avoid the ugly sight and stench of poverty and squalor .... no .... seriously, it is very good. But why are they working so hard all over the place? It is because the gods are coming? No!!! It is because of a special gathering of third world peoples! .... And, my brothers and sisters .... if you are looking for rehabilitation and road works, don't look here! After all Niiman is not where the delegates will visit! (5)

The ironical magic concerning the play's title and Niiman's life finds a correspondence in the plot, thanks to the magic gift by the gods. On the one hand, this could be seen as a further point in common with Concert Parties, where a supernatural element can occasionally intervene.[135] On the other, the device is certainly inspired by Brecht's work, and is shared with Femi Osofisan, who employed it in *Once Upon Four Robbers* (1980) and *Esu and the Vagabond Minstrels* (1991) as part of a planned cycle of ten works called 'Magic Boon Plays'. Osofisan explains their aims in a way that could apply to Abdallah's *Land* as well:

> It is a parabolic format, because I construct most of these plays like parables, tales with moral lessons [...] some people have some crisis, they meet someone who gives them some magical power [...] In the process of using it they reveal, in fact, certain fundamental tensions about our society. They tell us very much more about the material process of our society.[136]

---

[132] Wilkinson, *Talking with African Writers*, 44. The "joke" refers to the early 1980s, the worst period in the Ghanaian economy; see Shillington, *Ghana*, 107–28.

[133] Gibbs, "Land of a Million Magicians," 7.

[134] Maybe *Land* would be even more enjoyable if Mummuni maintained his contact with the audience as Jeroboam does in Soyinka's *The Trials of Brother Jero*, in order to consolidate a non-naturalistic atmosphere.

[135] See Barber et al., *West African Popular Theatre*, 21.

[136] Awodiya, *Excursions in Drama and Literature*, 98.

Apart from the money they leave, the gods are incapable of solving people's problems. Mummuni even complains about their faults, and the cardinal's answer is surprisingly candid and helpless: "No, my son .... on the contrary, you may be right .... I do not know" (75).

Hasana is left to decide which is the best way to employ all that money. Following in Brecht's wake, the author confers the leading role on a woman. His concern for gender matters shows how he does not share the sexist attitude common in much Ghanaian popular drama.[137] Her first attempt is communal; the money is shared among everybody: "Form cooperatives! Build schools .... clinics .... Kindergartens .... chop bars .... work!" (44). The whole of Niiman is involved; even beggars, thieves and prostitutes are summoned by Hasana.

General carelessness causes the failure of Hasana's communalism or communism. She therefore resorts to disguising herself as her invented twin brother Fuseni (Brecht's Shui Ta), who tries to mend the damage by reverting to the most ruthless kind of capitalism, only to spread suffering all over the place. The popular trial eventually organized by the gods declares Fuseni guilty and Hasana good. After revealing her trick, the gods leave Niiman certain about the existence of at least one good person. Hasana is helpless, and her enthusiasm for change meets with general indifference.

Nevertheless, the one piece of advice given by the gods is significant:

> The power of authority must flow from you. As we leave you, we urge you to wake up and change the nature .... the very essence of authority. For when you have become the source of the power of authority .... only then can you hope to change the conditions in which you live! (77)

The failure of the two political structures imported from the Western blocs, then, may hint at a 'third way' based on the participatory rule typical of some traditional African societies. It also recalls the spirit of Jerry Rawlings' one-party regime, one of whose objectives was "the involvement and active participation of the people in the decision-making process" as Rawlings declared on 31 December 1981, and this "would be achieved through the setting-up of people's defence committees in the work-places and in every district and village." Abdallah's personal engagement in Rawlings' regime (1981–92) and, later, democratic government (1992–),[138] though sometimes criticized, can perhaps be construed through the gods' advice.

---

[137] See Bamé, *Come to Laugh*, 25.

[138] Shillington, *Ghana*, 82, 80. Abdallah was appointed Secretary for Culture and Tourism in 1983 and later Chairman of the National Commission on Culture. Rawlings's later switch to the guidelines of the IMF policy, though, would need further discussion.

Another laudable political choice by Abdallah concerns the publication of his plays:

> The best thing is that I could have them published in Ghana. I've always felt dubious about the philosophy of the African Writers Series by Heinemann, because it established European languages as the norm, it gave the African élite an escape from their fear to deal with the issue of language. Even now it is easier to find an African book in England or America than here. (Abdallah, Legon, 11 December 1993)

Such a move implies, on the one hand, that his books should be easier to find by Ghanaian readers (and at affordable prices); on the other, it has negatively affected Abdallah's popularity abroad: he is not even mentioned in the 1994 *Cambridge Guide to African and Caribbean Theatre.*

The 1991 performance of *Land* ended too optimistically, with Hasana and Mummuni celebrated by an enthusiastic crowd. This was not appreciated by James Gibbs in his review of the show, which complained about the lack of Brecht's "tough thinking and unsentimental stagecraft."[139] Gibbs is obviously referring to the ending of *The Good Woman of Setzuan*, where Shen Te desperately cries for help and the epilogue leaves every decision to the audience with the command: "You write the happy ending of the play."[140]

The published version of *Land* closes on a much more despondent note. Hasana turns down Mummuni's marriage proposal because of the work still to be done, but the inhabitants of Niiman refuse to take up her call for communal participation:

> *(The people have started leaving one by one.).*
>
> HASANA: Please don't leave. Don't turn your backs on me. We have work to do. [...] You can't turn your back on me .... not you, Mummuni.
>
> *(Mummuni turns away from Hasana and takes off his big fancy gown. He walks slowly towards his water containers. He picks them up and, without a glance at Hasana, he walks out.).*
>
> Mummuni! .... Mummuni! .... Magajiya, he is gone! Mummuni .... Magajiya .... my sister, they are all gone! What are we going to do? How do we change the land, Magajiya? How? How? How, Magajiya ...!
>
> FADE-OUT
>
> THE END. (80)

---

[139] Gibbs, "But Spiritual Billionaires," 1681.

[140] Bertolt Brecht, *The Good Woman of Setzuan* (1948; New York: Grove, 1966): 141.

Not surprisingly, Gibbs sounds content with the new solution: "The text is the work of a wiser, and possibly sadder, man. The published Abdallah does not present any easy solutions."[141]

Before closing, one final point needs analysing – the influence of Western drama on Abdallah and his generation of playwrights. In the preface to his doctoral dissertation, Abdallah outlines the theoretical assumptions supporting his creative output: he finds inspiration in Augusto Boal's rejection of "Aristotle's coercive system of tragedy [...] that has, for centuries, dominated dramatic theory, criticism and playwriting."[142] At the same time he recognizes that a decolonization of the African mind does not imply total rejection of Western paradigms, but should consist of indigenous ingredients plus the achievements of the 'rebels' of Western theatre. As he writes in the preface to *The Trial of Mallam Ilya and other plays*, "we must not be ashamed to take out the examples of the Western world that will help us in our bid for progress and development."

In his dissertation, Abdallah quotes at length Peter Brook's research journey through Northern and Western Africa (1972), narrated in John Heilpern's *Conference of the Birds* (1977). Brook and his troupe performed several times along their route, seeking new founts of dramatic inspiration. The results of their search often bear a resemblance to the conception of theatre developed by Sutherland, Abdallah and the other writers examined in this chapter: first of all, an "experience packed and bursting with high and low qualities, serious and comic, élitist and popular"; the double point of view on life encompassing reality and fantasy, that "for the Western audience [...] are different things. But for an African brought up in a traditional way of life, they are two aspects of the same reality"; and, finally, the emblematic conclusion of Heilpern's book:

> Brook, in search of the new, has in fact returned to theatre's oldest root and heartbeat, storytelling. His way of doing it, when all is said and done, is what the African journey was about.[143]

Apart from Brook, this chapter shows that Western models can also include authors who never investigated African traditional theatre, such as Pirandello, or

---

141 Gibbs, "Land of a Million Magicians," 9.

142 Mohammed ben Abdallah, "Kings Warriors, Slaves...! A Dramatic Trilogy" (doctoral dissertation, University of Texas at Austin, 1980): vii.

143 Heilpern, *Conference of the Birds*, 191, 71, 327.

those theatre practitioners who contributed to the development of antirealistic modes from the beginning of this century, such as Artaud, Grotowski and, above all, Bertolt Brecht. Their interest in ritual and in the techniques of Oriental theatre led them to develop aesthetics similar to African dramatic practices. Brecht is certainly the Western author who has proved most directly influential on West African theatre: see, for instance, *Opera Wonyosi* (1981), Soyinka's version of Brecht's *The Threepenny Opera* (1928), which was in turn an interpretation of *The Beggar's Opera* (1728) by John Gay. Segun Oyekunle, too, worked on another version of Brecht's opera and on a Nigerian Pidgin rendition of *The Good Woman of Setzuan.*[144]

In the light of the topics examined in this chapter, it is noteworthy to discuss the importance Brecht attributed to the unmasking of all naturalistic illusion:

> He saw the 'illusionistic' theatre as a theatre which deliberately or unconsciously keeps the social connections obscure, pursuing as it does individualistic solutions for the benefit of individuals. He developed in its place a theatre which he called 'epic theatre', in which the actors do everything in their power to prevent the audience from imagining they are playing 'fixed' or predetermined characters which they must believe are 'real.'[145]

In order to unveil the class structure and workings of capitalist societies, he devised a series of alienating effects such as role-play, storytelling, audience involvement, songs – in short, effects already encountered in the West African plays analysed in this chapter – "thereby encouraging audiences to consider alternatives to the dominant order."[146]

Aside from these formal effects, another playwright who also seems closer to Brecht's political and ideological stance is undoubtedly Femi Osofisan, as I have endeavoured to show. A further instance of Brechtian influence on his writings is represented by the farce *Midnight Hotel*, which the author himself defines as "a comic opera after Feydeau, through Brecht."[147] The songs of the play are not sung as if in a 'normal' opera, as substitutes for dialogue, but imply a disrupting of the plot thanks to the presence of a Songmaster and THE PETRONAIRA BAND, who "*must remain conspicuous throughout the play [...] be played in such a way as to*

---

[144] See Etherton, *Development of African Theatre*, 104, 295.

[145] Etherton, *Development of African Theatre*, 294.

[146] Richards, *Ancient Songs Set Ablaze*, 66.

[147] Osofisan, *Midnight Hotel*, vii.

breach the naturalistic context of the rest of the play."[148] One of the first songs is introduced thus:

> JIMOH [*to Bicycle*]: This is Lagos, man, and in Lagos sex is business. Naked women, half-naked women, women about to be naked, women who have always been naked, women who will die naked, all is money in this city. Big money! Big money! Wait! *(goes to the Songmaster).* Please Songmaster, you do have this "Song of the Lagos Woman," don't you? Thank you. Let us sing it for this idiot. *(The Songmaster gives him a large tablet, starts the orchestra, and they begin to sing. As with all songs in the play, every encouragement should be given to audience to participate, either by distributing the songs with the program, inscribing them on slides for projection on screens, etc.).*[149]

Sandra Richards precisely defines a conceptual difference between Brecht's and Osofisan's songs:

> distrustful of the appeal to emotions that was characteristic of theatre in his day, Brecht sought to focus on the political narrative of his lyrics by using melodies that his German audiences often found unpleasant and unsingable. In contrast, Osofisan reasons that if his audiences find the music appealing, they are more likely to repeat the songs and thereby integrate some of his perspectives into their own thinking.[150]

Trying to establish the pre-eminence of the traditional influence over the Brechtian (or vice versa) in Osofisan's drama is quite pointless. As Osofisan said to me, the two theatres worked on him in different ways and from different angles. With respect to this, he also establishes an interesting connection with Atukwei Okai's poetry recitals (examined in Chapter 4):

> One thing doesn't exclude the other. The importance of Brecht is that he was able to theorize many features which were already in existence here, and still exist here. We were brought up in a similar tradition that didn't leave any theories in writing, and we can use Brecht because he was the first to develop a systematic theory. Even he didn't claim he invented it, he got them from the theatre of the Far East. But he made it a self-conscious thing. The same happened to Atukwei Okai in Ghana: he became more conscious of his performance theory in Russia, where he took part in public readings. (Osofisan, Ibadan, 2 August 1997)

Therefore, keeping in mind both of these influential sources, Osofisan's plays espouse a total conception of drama which comprises diverse instruments of expression. This, in turn, encapsulates the fluidity among literary genres proposed

---

148 Osofisan, *Midnight Hotel*, ix.

149 Osofisan, *Midnight Hotel*, 4.

150 Richards, *Ancient Songs Set Ablaze*, 68.

in this study. In her book on Òsofisan's drama, Sandra Richards envisages this principle as reflected in Yoruba epistemology, where "experience is dynamic, characterized by discrete, contradictory force fields that may nonetheless achieve equilibrium and are best understood holistically."[151]

<>

[151] Richards, *Ancient Songs Set Ablaze*, 154.

Conclusion: Holistic Perspectives

And so are we the vulgarians
craving the message and the morality.
(Chinua Achebe)

As I HOPE TO HAVE SHOWN, in anglophone West African literature prose, poetry and theatre display their protean qualities to the full. They constantly gesture towards each another, spinning connecting threads and thereby forming a web which covers the terrain of anglophone West African literature – there is nothing better than this image (evoking the metamorphic Ananse) to capture the phenomenon under scrutiny.

The novel and the short story have been moving towards the musical intimations of poetical soundscapes: abandoning the reassuring firmness of realistic narratives for the pleasure of more unstable grounds. They have shattered the linearity of a form of art which reflects a similarly non-linear reality. All of the authors discussed in Chapters 1–3 have their own peculiar traditional sources of inspiration, including the precursors of such a course: the Yoruba language for Tutuola, the bardic utterance for Armah, the techniques of orality for Aidoo, the Ewe dirge for Awoonor.

Starting from those models, the novelists of the 1980s inaugurated the mode of magical realism in West Africa. In this study, an effort has been made to define and categorize this manifold mode in its various manifestations. It would be excessively simplistic, however, to group Cheney–Coker, Okri and Laing under the same general label. Their writing is affected in different ways not only by their West African predecessors, but also by illustrious Latin American magical-realist novelists. Cheney–Coker's Latin American bent, for instance, is a far cry from Okri's hallucinatory style and from Laing's linguistic experimentalism. Okri and Laing have also tried to push the boundaries of their prose some steps further into utopian worlds, other dimensions and future ages. They have challenged received notions about what African novels should be like, expectations that less than two decades ago seemed unshakeable. In 1983, Charles E. Nnolim complained rather bluntly about the lack of daring in Nigerian prose, arguing that the country's novelists had not experimented with "the novel of ideas, the epistolary novel, science fiction, the utopian novel, the stream of consciousness novel, the futuristic novel. [...] What kind of society would Nigeria have in the year 2080?"[1] Even though his curiosity has not been satisfied to the letter, the bleak scenario he depicted has certainly undergone some changes.

So immersed in poetry are the authors analysed in Chapters 1–3 that the movement to Chapters 4–5 must have seemed to most readers rather hard to perceive, at least in terms of the style of the works. "It is not rhyming or versing that maketh a poet [...] But it is that feigning notable images," wrote Sir Philip Sidney[2] – but that was an age that did not know the novel as we know it. The primary criterion guiding Chapters 4–5, therefore, is the delivering act, both in the performance potentiality inherent in the discussed poems and in the actual stage events which have taken place in Ghana, introduced first by Okai, then taken up by Anyidoho, Acquah and others. Live Ghanaian poetry started in the 1970s, reached its apex in the 1980s and seems to have waned in the 1990s. It offers no fixed data as an object of study and certainly needs constant monitoring. contemporary Ghanaian poetry in English thus proves to be closer to a conception of process, performance, happening, rather than to the art-object as a finished work.

Its stage dimension represents a projection towards the genre of anglophone drama which, in turn, projects itself towards other, non-literary kinds of theatre while drawing inspiration from them at the same time. The unwritten status of traditional theatre, popular plays and theatre for development constitutes a deep reservoir to be tapped by contemporary authors and practitioners. This is where total theatre, total art, the holistic perspective proper, finds its home. Such a wide range of references is traceable in both the authors examined and the origin of this very volume: writers like Efua Sutherland, turned in their search for new forms during the enthusiasm of the Independence years, to traditional and popular paradigms, just as the writing of this volume found an inspiring parallel drive in Karin Barber's studies of traditional genres and popular forms of art.[3] During the following decades, Abdallah and Osofisan politicized their precursors' formal research.

---

[1] Charles Nnolim, "Nigerian Tradition in the Novel," 36–37.

[2] Sir Philip Sidney, *An Apology for Poetry*, ed. Geoffrey Shepherd (1580; Nelson's Medieval & Renaissance Library; London: Thomas Nelson, 1965): 103.

[3] See Introduction.

This general phenomenon of generic porosity, though, interacts with and is sustained by other elements which contribute to widening the scope of this book further. First of all, many of the writers taken into consideration have shown a lively interest in writing for children and producing critical literature alongside their creative output, as if guided by a strong will to maintain their educational role on various levels. Okai's nonsensical verses for children, Aidoo's folktales, Sutherland and Abdallah's Ananse plays for the young, to mention only a few, testify to how these writers have adapted the usual thrust of their art to didactic purposes. Their activity is to be considered part of a wider social concern for the reformation of their society. This book has attempted to keep this concern firmly in view, unlike certain sections of contemporary literary criticism. The epigraph to this chapter is to be construed in this light. Secondly, some playwrights have staged theatrical renditions of well-known West African novels – Sowande with Tutuola's *My Life in the Bush of Ghosts* and Abdallah re-creating Armah's *Two Thousand Seasons* in his *The Fall of Kumbi* – thereby showing that generic porosity in West Africa is not necessarily unidirectional towards total theatre, and kindling the hope that drama might help the novel to overcome its limited popularity among West African audiences.

As specified in the Introduction, the writers and their works examined here are inextricably linked with their national and historical context, and so they are not likely to be approached through vague theories of hybridity: national projects and questions of national identities have not been marginalized.[4] The ubiquitous presence of the controversial figure of Kwame Nkrumah testifies to this. He surfaces in almost every chapter of this book, with special reference to the effects of his policies: on the one hand, his recovery of traditional arts; on the other, his despotic, neocolonial domestic policy (as this impinged on Armah and Abdallah).[5] Another significant instance is the engagement of Osofisan's *The Chattering and the Song* with one of the figureheads of Yoruba written history, Samuel Johnson.[6]

In any case, looking back at this research I realize how its most surprising outcome is undoubtedly its geographical connections with other literatures, reaching out well beyond the horizon of the West African coastline, all the way to diverse

[4] See Slemon & Tiffin, *After Europe*, vi.

[5] See Chapter 1 and 7. In one play dated 1983 but performed in 1976–77, *The Trial of Kwame Nkrumah* by Kwaku Mensa-Bonsu, the Osagyefo is tried in the After-World by the Supreme God himself. This work, which includes a storyteller, seems to draw inspiration from Anyidoho's poem "In the High Court of Cosmic Justice" (see Chapter 4, pp. 149–50) and from Ali Mazrui's novel *The Trial of Christopher Okigbo*, but it lacks their debating subtleties and ends up sounding too eulogistic.

[6] See Chapter 7 (p. 252).

literary *aburokyire.*[7] One cannot but wonder at the number of world literary currents that have nourished the growth of anglophone West African genres. In some cases, elements of African culture which had developed on the American continent after the Middle Passage have returned to their original soil to play an inspirational role. Barber, Collins and Ricard define this phenomenon as a 'transatlantic feedback cycle,' when delving into the origins of West African popular theatre and into its rapport with the American vaudeville artists who toured West Africa in the 1920s; the same label could be attached to Latin American magical realists (and their relationship to African culture) and used as a model for the novelists discussed in Chapter 2 and, to a lesser extent, to the works of Langston Hughes in relation to some of the poets examined in Chapters 4–5.

In some cases, however, other literary connections have no African source whatsoever. Despite being imbued with their traditional cultures and national histories, some novelists make free use of the most diverse literary models: Awoonor quotes (among others) Dante to convey his pessimistic outlook on independent Ghana; Okri's utopian island reminds one of Calvino's fantasy; one of his novels is interspersed with both overt and covert references to the most diverse sources, such as Blake, Fanon, Herodotus, Novalis and Ovid;[8] Laing does not hesitate to borrow an image from Melville's *Bartleby* in order to make his point about the contemporary state of Western culture; Okai acknowledges the importance of Russian performance poetry on his rediscovery of traditional modes of oral delivery; Osofisan does the same with regard to Brecht's epic theatre (which in turn has Eastern origins); finally, Abdallah rewrites one of Brecht's works in a Ghanaian context and pays homage to Pirandello and the experiments of Peter Brook.

Such foreign connections all appear to have a catalytic function, speeding up a process of rediscovery of traditional lore and its adjustment to contemporary needs, especially in the case of Latin American magical realism, Russian performance

---

[7] In Twi, '*aburokyire*' means 'beyond the horizon': ie 'overseas' (usually Europe, Britain and North America); see Florence Abena Dolphyne, *A Comprehensive Course in Twi (Asante)* (Accra: Ghana Universities P, 1996): 15.

[8] Okri, *Infinite Riches*, 313, 185, 140, 186 respectively. Okri also playfully subverts Conrad and Huxley: "Heart of the World" is employed as a definition for the African continent, whereas "Brave New Darkness" concerns the exploitative activities of neocolonialism; Okri, *Infinite Riches*, 235–38. See also the following encounter experienced by Azaro, resonant with Tutuolan and Achebian echoes: "I came to the forest of shadows. I met a man who was hallucinating about his favourite palm-wine. Still searching for a dead tapster. Further on I encountered the stuttering spirit of a grim man. His machete was still bloody with the murder of an outcast": Okri, *Infinite Riches*, 308.

poetry and Brechtian theatre. An observation by Osofisan is worth quoting again here: "We were brought up in a similar tradition that didn't leave any theories in writing, and we can use Brecht because he was the first to develop a systematic theory" (Osofisan, Ibadan, 2 August 1997). Similarly, when asked about the influence of European surrealism on Caribbean literature, Aimé Césaire said: "Surrealism offered me what I was confusedly looking for. I welcomed it gladly because I found in it an adaptation, rather than a revelation."[9]

This wide net of non-African literary connections was unintended (at least to such an extent) by the original project that led to the writing of this book. It is a feature that has slowly revealed itself in progress, in keeping with the performative orientation of Chapters 4–7. In a way, to use Homi Bhabha's definition, these works, too, "contest the meaningfulness of culture as being embodied in idealized models of representation."[10] In other words, something akin to Bhabha's notorious categories of 'third space,' 'interstitial space,' of culture as a never-ending negotiation certainly surfaces in this book, but in its own peculiar way – a way that departs from the model of postcolonial 'high theory' in crucial respects.

Why, for instance, should contemporary negotiations be necessarily located in the cosmopolitan cities of the West? Why privilege the "hybrid cosmopolitanism of contemporary metropolitan life"[11] or, in Edward Said's terms, those subjects who have embarked on 'the voyage in'? Why give pre-eminence to writers who have overtly answered back to colonial and neocolonial texts?[12] This work has, I trust, demonstrated how the same negotiations can be effected in cultures and literatures with strong national leanings, collective visions and, to use a term that must sound shocking to many postcolonial critics, with firm *roots*.

At the bottom of it all, the real problem is that such literatures and such writers need researching; they require careful and detailed analysis both in their written testimonies and in the contextual field of their creativity. This is what I understand to be, as far as the critic's role is concerned, the practice desired by Homi Bhabha: "To shift the definition of the cultural process from the point of expression to articulation [...] articulation rather than authentication."[13] The latter critic is here taken to

---

[9] "El surrealismo me ha proporcionado lo que yo buscaba, confusamente. Lo he recebido con alegría porqué he encontrado en él más una conformación que una revelación"; René Depestre, "Entrevista con Aimé Césaire," *Casa de Las Américas* 9.49 (July–August 1968): 138 (my tr.).

[10] Homi Bhabha, "The Manifesto" and "Reinventing Britain: A Forum," *Wasafiri* 29 (Spring 1999): 39.

[11] Bhabha, "Manifesto," 38.

[12] My observations are not meant to include the work of Gayatri Spivak.

[13] Bhabha, "Manifesto," 39.

task for not putting into practice this process of articulation, for remaining contradictorily frozen at the level of his carefully woven concepts, for not delving enough in the various 'postcolonial' actualizations of his theory, be they hybrid and cosmopolitan or still residing in some God-forsaken former colony that high theorists do not seem to be very interested in. An instance of this is Bhabha's essay "Postcolonial Criticism," which was published "in almost identical form, under three different titles, in a period of eighteen months between 1992 and 1994."[14] I am referring here to the version included in the volume *Redrawing the Boundaries*, a book intended as a collection of essays examining the various areas of Anglo-American literary criticism with a special focus on recent significant developments in each one.[15] In most essays, contributors prove to be genuinely helpful in tracing the several currents and undertows criss-crossing their realms of specialization. Bhabha could have done the same with reference to postcolonial theory and criticism, possibly outlining the workings of postcolonial perspectives in other fields such as Renaissance and Victorian literature. Instead, he resorted to a disappointing enunciation of theories following *his own* paradigms – that is, which conformed to his principle of refusing fixed polarities and stable identities. The thinkers he quotes are mostly templates of Western theory such as Arendt, Bakhtin, Barthes, Derrida, Eagleton, Lacan, Jameson, Said, Spivak, with the exception of the Afro-Caribbean critics C.L.R. James and Frantz Fanon. For the vast mass of literature coming from the various areas of the former empires, for the numberless primary and secondary sources that such areas engender, there seems to be no space in Bhabha's vision. Unfortunately, this attitude runs the risk of creating new marginalized subjects, new outsiders.

---

[14] Moore–Gilbert, *Postcolonial Theory*, 186.

[15] Stephen Greenblatt & Giles Gunn, *Redrawing the Boundaries: The Transformation of English and American Literary Studies* (New York: Modern Language Association of America, 1992): 3.

Bibliography

Primary Sources

Abdallah, Mohammed ben. *Ananse and the Golden Drum* (Accra: Woeli, 1994).

——. *Ananse and the Rain God* (Accra: Woeli, 1989).

——. *The Fall of Kumbi and other plays* (Accra: Woeli, 1989).

——. "Kings Warriors, Slaves...! A Dramatic Trilogy" (doctoral dissertation, University of Texas at Austin, 1980).

——. *Land of a Million Magicians* (Accra: Woeli, 1993).

——. "The Slave," *Okyeame* 5 (November 1972): 41–47.

——. *The Trial of Mallam Ilya and other plays* (Accra: Woeli, 1987).

Acquah, Kobena Eyi. *The Man Who Died* (Accra: Asempa, 1984).

——. *Music for a Dream Dance* (Accra: Asempa, 1989).

——. *No Time for a Masterpiece* (Accra: Woeli, 1995).

Addo, Patience Henaku. *Company Pot*, in *Nine African Plays for Radio*, ed. Gwyneth Henderson & Cosmo Pieterse (London: Heinemann, 1973): 163–85.

——. "Nyankonkra" and "Nea Ohwehwe Annya," *Okyeame* 4.1 (1968): 16–19.

Agbadja, Adolph. "Down Below the Volta River," in *Voices of Ghana: Literary Contributions to the Ghana Broadcasting System, 1955–57*, quoted in Kofi Agovi, "A Dual Sensibility: The Short Story in Ghana, 1944–1980," in *Literature and Black Aesthetics*, ed. Ernest N. Emenyonu (Calabar Studies in African Literature 5; Ibadan: Heinemann, 1990): 257–58.

Agovi, Kofi. *A Wind from the North and other stories* (Tema: Ghana Publishing Corporation, 1989).

Aidoo, Ama Ata. *An Angry Letter in January* (Coventry: Dangaroo, 1992).

——. *Anowa* (1970; Harlow, Essex: Longman, 1980).

——. *Changes* (1991; Accra: Sub-Saharan, 1994).

——. *The Dilemma of a Ghost* (1965; Harlow, Essex: Longman, 1980).

——. *The Eagle and the Chicken and other stories* (Accra: Afram, 1989).

——. *The Girl Who Can and other stories* (Accra: Sub-Saharan, 1997).

——. *Our Sister Killjoy or Reflections from a Black-Eyed Squint* (Harlow, Essex: Longman, 1977).

——. *No Sweetness Here* (1970; Harlow, Essex: Longman, 1970).

Al-Hassan, Selma. "Tanofia," in Various Authors, *The Cowrie Girl and Other Stories* (Tema: Ghana Publishing Corporation, 1971): 8–11.

Angelou, Maya. *All God's Children Need Travelling Shoes* (1986; London: Virago, 1991).

Anyidoho, Kofi. *AncestralLogic and CaribbeanBlues* (Trenton NJ: Africa World Press, 1993).

——. *Earthchild with Brain Surgery* (Accra: Woeli, 1985).

——. *A Harvest of Our Dreams with Elegy for the Revolution* (1984; London: Heinemann & Accra: Woeli, 1985).

Appiah, Peggy. *The Children of Ananse* (London: Evans, 1968).

——. *Gift of the Mmoatia* (1972; Accra: Quick Service Books, 1996).

Armah, Ayi Kwei. *The Beautyful Ones Are Not Yet Born* (Oxford, Heinemann, 1968).

——. *Fragments* (1969; London: Heinemann, 1974).

——. *The Healers* (1978; Oxford: Heinemann, 1979).

——. *Osiris Rising* (Popenguine, Senegal: Per Ankh, 1995).

——. *Two Thousand Seasons* (1973; Oxford: Heinemann, 1979).

Asare, Yaw. "Ananse in the Land of Idiots." Undated typescript.

——. "The Secret of the Ancient Well." Undated typescript.

Awoonor, Kofi Nyidevu. *Comes the Voyager at Last: A Tale of Return to Africa* (Trenton NJ: Africa World Press, 1992).

——. *Night of My Blood* (Garden City NY: Doubleday, 1971).

——. "Lament," in *Short African Plays*, ed. Cosmo Pieterse (London: Heinemann. 1972): §§–§§.

——. *This Earth, My Brother* (London: Heinemann, 1971).

——. *Until the Morning After: Collected poems 1963–1985* (Accra: Woeli, 1987).

Bandele-Thomas, 'Biyi. *The Man Who Came in from the Back of Beyond* (London: Bellew, 1991).

Bell, Madison Smartt. *All Souls' Rising* (New York: Pantheon, 1995).

Brecht, Bertolt. *The Good Woman of Setzuan* (1948; New York: Grove, 1966).

Busia, Abena Pokua Adompim. *Testimonies of Exile* (Accra: Woeli, 1990).

Butake, Bole. *Lake God* (Yaoundé: BET, 1986).

Calvino, Italo. *Invisible Cities*, tr. William Weaver (San Diego CA: Harcourt, Brace, 1972).

Carpentier, Alejo. *The Kingdom of This World*, tr. Harriet de Onís (1949; London: André Deutsch, 1990).

Casely Hayford, Joseph Ephraim. *Ethiopia Unbound: Studies in Race Emancipation* (1911; London: Frank Cass, 1969).

Cheney–Coker, Syl. *The Last Harmattan of Alusine Dunbar* (Oxford: Heinemann, 1990).

Clark, John Pepper. *Ozidi* (London: Oxford UP, 1966).

Cobby, Anne Elizabeth, ed. *Aucassin et Nicolette* with *The Pilgrimage of Charlemagne*, tr. & intro. Glyn S. Burgess (Garland Library of Medieval Literature, A47; New York: Garland, 1988).

De Graft, Joe. "Ananse and the Gum Man." Undated typescript, Library of the Institute of African Studies, University of Ghana at Legon.

Dei-Anang, Michael. *Okomfo Anokye's Golden Stool* (Accra: Waterville, 1963).

Ebisike, Eze. *Money Marriages: Mammon Marriages (Stop Mammon Marriages)* (Lagos: Beteze, 1992).

Eliot, Thomas Stearns. "The Love Song of J. Alfred Prufrock" (1917), in Eliot, *Collected Poems 1909–1962* (London: Faber & Faber, 1963): 11–15.

Ellison, Ralph. *Invisible Man* (New York: Random House, 1947).

García Márquez, Gabriel. *Of Love and Other Demons*, tr. Edith Grossman (1994; Harmondsworth: Penguin, 1994).

——. *One Hundred Years of Solitude*, tr. Gregory Rabassa (1967; Harmondsworth: Penguin, 1972).

Glikpoe, Dzifa F. Aku. "Knife in the Pocket." Author's typescript, 1985.

Iyayi, Festus. *Violence* (London: Longman, 1979).

Kayper–Mensah, Albert W. *Sankofa: Adinkra Poems* (Tema: Ghana Publishing Corporation, 1976).

Kyei, Kojo Gyinaye. *The Lone Voice* (Accra: Ghana Universities P, 1969).

——, with Hannah Schreckenbach. *No Time to Die* (privately printed, 1975).

Laing, Kojo. "Festival" and Grasscutters in the West," *West Africa* (19 March 1984): 617.

——. *Godhorse* (Oxford: Heinemann, 1989).

——. "If You Dare to Swim," *West Africa* (22 June 1981): 1422.

——. "Jaw," *Lines Review* (Edinburgh) 24 (1968), repr. in *Scottish Poetry* 4, ed. George Bruce, Maurice Lindsay & Edwin Morgan (Edinburgh: Edinburgh UP, 1969): 59–67.

——. *Major Gentl and the Achimota Wars* (London: Heinemann, 1992).

——. "Resurrection," *Okyeame* 5 (November 1972): 23–40.

——. *Search Sweet Country* (London: Heinemann, 1986).

——. "Vacancy for the Post of Jesus Christ," in *The Heinemann Book of Contemporary African Short Stories*, ed. Chinua Achebe & C.L. Innes (Oxford: Heinemann, 1992): 185–96.

——. *Woman of the Aeroplanes* (London: Pan / Picador, 1989).

Leigh, Mike. *Naked and other screenplays* (London: Faber & Faber, 1995).

Mazrui, Ali. *The Trial of Christopher Okigbo* (London: Heinemann, 1971).

Melville, Herman. "Bartleby, the Scrivener" (1856), in *The Portable Melville* (New York: Viking, 1952).

Mensa–Bonsu, Kwaku. *The Trial of Kwame Nkrumah: A Play Dedicated to a Soul at Rest* (Accra: Black Mask, 1983).

Milton, John. *Paradise Lost* (1667; London: Longman, 1971).

Nazareth, Peter, ed. *African Writing Today*, special issue of *Pacific Quarterly Moana* 6.3–4 (July–October 1981).

Nketia, Kwabena H. "A Poem in Praise of Osei Tutu: from Traditional Apaee," *Okyeame* 2.1 (1964): 21.

Ogunyemi, Wale. *Eshu Elegbara* (Ibadan: Orisun Acting, 1970).

——. *Ijaye War (in the nineteenth century): A Historical Drama* (Ibadan: Orisun Acting, 1970).

——. *Kiriji: An Historic Drama on Ekiti Parapo War in the Nineteenth Century* (Lagos: African Universities P, 1976).

——. *Langbodo* (Lagos: Thomas Nelson, 1979).

Okai, Atukwei. "All the Suicides in Heaven." Undated typescript.

——. "And Now to End the World News: Agegeyan Gethsemane." Typescript, 1980.

——. *The Anthill in the Sea (Verses and Chants for Children)* (Tema: Ghana Publishing Corporation, 1988).

——. "The Calabash Elegy for Lady Victoria Opoku–Ware." Typescript.

——. "Fanfare for Oduduwa," in *African Writing Today*, ed. P. Nazareth, 37–44.

——. *Flowerfall* (London: Writers Forum, 1969).

——. "Freedom Symphony," *Atlantic Monthly* (May 1969): 60; repr. in *African Voices*, ed. Howard Sergeant (London: Evans, 1973): 21; *West Africa* (19 January 1987): 115.
——. "Fugue for Waterfrogs," *Okyeame* 4.2 (1969): 27–34.
——. "In the Stool Room of the Soul: A Concerto for Black Satellites," *Weekly Spectator* (1 May 1993): 5.
——. *Lorgorligi Logarithms and other poems* (Tema: Ghana Publishing Corporation, 1974).
——. "Mandela the Spear," *West Africa* (26 March–1 April 1990): 495.
——. [as "John Okai"]. *The Oath of the Fontomfrom and other poems* (New York: Simon & Schuster, 1971).
——. "A Pharaonic Fandango for Ataa Odartey Lamptey," unspecified newspaper (15 June, 1996): 18.
——. "The Rosetta Stone in the Meantime of Eternity," *Ghana Association of Writers Commemorative Brochure* (23 November 1991): 42–45.
——. "Sakumo Concerto," *Callaloo* 3.1–3 (February–October 1980): 139–55.
——. "To the Chlorophyll of Hope: An Elegy for Ayikaikai (Mrs. Regina Ayikaikai Annan)." Undated typescript.
——. "Watu Wazuri," *West Africa* (15 December 1986): 2612.
Okigbo, Christopher. *Labyrinths* (London: Heinemann, 1965).
Okri, Ben. *An African Elegy* (London: Jonathan Cape, 1992).
——. *Astonishing the Gods* (London: Phoenix House, 1995).
——. *The Famished Road* (London: Jonathan Cape, 1991).
——. *Incidents at the Shrine* (1986; London: Flamingo, 1987).
——. *Infinite Riches* (London: Phoenix House, 1998).
——. *Songs of Enchantment* (London: Jonathan Cape, 1993).
——. *Stars of the New Curfew* (1988; Harmondsworth: Penguin, 1989).
Omotoso, Kole. *The Combat* (London: Heinemann, 1972).
——. *Memories of Our Recent Boom* (Harlow, Essex: Longman, 1982).
Opoku–Agyemang, Kwadjo. *Cape Coast Castle* (Accra: Afram, 1996).
Osei–Boahene, Kwabena. *The Day of the Dancing Gods* (Accra: Woeli, 1995).
Osofisan, Femi. *Aringindin and the Nightwatchmen* (Ibadan: Heinemann, 1991).
——. *The Chattering and the Song* (1976; Ibadan: Ibadan UP, 1977).
——. *Esu and the Vagabond Minstrels* (Ibadan: New Horn, 1991).
——. *Farewell to a Cannibal Rage* (Ibadan: Evans, 1986).
——. *Kolera Kolej* (Ibadan: New Horn, 1975).
——. *The Midnight Blackout* (Ibadan: Ibadan UP, 1994).
——. *Midnight Hotel* (Ibadan: Evans, 1986).
——. *Morountodun and other plays* (including *No More the Wasted Breed* and *Red Is the Freedom Road*) (Ikeja: Longman Nigeria, 1982).
——. *Once Upon Four Robbers* (Ibadan: Heinemann, 1980).
——. *Two One-Act Plays* (including *The Oriki of a Grasshopper* and *Altine's Wrath*) (Ibadan: New Horn, 1986).
——. *Who's Afraid of Solarin?* (Ibadan: Scholars, 1978).
——. *Yungba–Yungba and the Dance Contest* (Ibadan: Heinemann, 1993).
Osundare, Niyi. *Songs of the Marketplace* (Ibadan: New Horn, 1983).

Owusu, Martin. *The Story Ananse Told* (London: Heinemann, 1971).
——. *The Sudden Return and other plays* (London: Heinemann, 1973).
Oyekunle, Segun. *Katakata for Sofahead* (London: Macmillan, 1983).
Rotimi, Ola. *The Gods Are Not to Blame* (London: Oxford UP, 1971).
——. *Hopes of the Living Dead* (Ibadan: Spectrum, 1988).
——. *Ovonramwen Nogbaisi* (Benin City: Ethiope & Oxford: Oxford UP, 1974).
Salkey, Andrew. *Anancy's Score* (London: Bogle–L'Ouverture, 1973).
Sekyi, Kobina. *The Blinkards* (London: Heinemann, 1974).
Sowande, Bode. "My Life in the Bush of Ghosts." Author's undated typescript.
——. *Tornadoes Full of Dreams* (Ikeja & Lagos: Malthouse, 1990).
Soyinka, Wole. *Aké: The Years of Childhood* (Ibadan: Spectrum, 1981).
——. *A Dance of the Forests* (1963), in *Collected Plays 1* (Oxford: Oxford UP, 1973): 1–77.
——. *From Zia, with Love* (Ibadan: Fountain, 1992).
——. *Kongi's Harvest* (London: Oxford UP, 1967).
——. *The Trials of Brother Jero* (1964), in *The Jero Plays* (Ibadan: Spectrum, 1973): 6–44.
Sutherland, Efua Theodora. *Foriwa* (Accra: State Publishing, 1967).
——. *The Marriage of Anansewa* (Harlow, Essex: Longman, 1975).
——. "New Life at Kyerefaso" (1960), in *Unwinding Threads: Writing by Women in Africa*, ed. Charlotte H. Bruner (London: Heinemann, 1994): 17–23.
——. *Vulture! Vulture!* [and *Tahinta*]: *Two Rhythm Plays* (Accra: Ghana Publishing House, 1968).
Tutuola, Amos. *My Life in the Bush of Ghosts* (London: Faber & Faber, 1954).
——. *The Palm-Wine Drinkard* (1952; London: Faber & Faber, 1961).
Wells, Herbert George. *The Invisible Man* (1897; New York: Dover, 1992).
Wosornu, Ladé. *Eté: A Woman of Africa & other poems* (Accra: Woeli, 1995).
Yeats, William Butler. *Collected Poems* (London: Macmillan, 1978).
Yirenkyi, Asiedu. "Dasebre." Unpublished typescript, 1975.
——. *Kivuli and other plays* (London: Heinemann, 1980).

Secondary Sources

Abimbola, Wande. "Ifa: A West African Cosmological System," in *Religion in Africa*, ed. T.D. Blakely, W.E.A. van Beek & D.L. Thomson (London: James Currey & Portsmouth NH: Heinemann, 1994): 101–16.
Abodunrin, 'Femi. "Black Literature and Literary Theory," *Wasafiri* 14 (Autumn 1991): 7–11.
Achebe, Chinua, ed. *Beyond Hunger in Africa: Conventional Wisdom and a Vision of Africa in 2057* (London: James Currey; Nairobi& Portsmouth NH: Heinemann, 1990).
——. *Morning Yet on Creation Day* (London: Heinemann, 1975).
Acquah, Kobena Eyi. "'Na My Mouth Be Gun?'," *West Africa* (12 May 1986): 23–25.
Acquaye, Saka. "Folk Opera in Ghana and Nigeria," paper delivered at the Symposium on African and Afro-American Music (1–6 March 1972), Institute of African Studies, University of Ghana.
——. "The Problems of Language in the Development of the African Theatre," *Okyeame* 4.2 (1969): 70–76.

Adedeji, Joel A. "The Alarinjo Theatre: The Study of a Yoruba Theatrical Art from Its Earliest Beginnings to the Present Times" (doctoral dissertation, University of Ibadan, 1969).

Adelugba, Dapo. "Kíriji: the Concept of Theatre as Exploration," *African Notes* (Institute of African Studies, University of Ibadan) 7.1 (1971): 107–16.

——. *Towards a Theory and Criticism of Theatre Arts* (Discourse 3; lecture delivered in the Postgraduate School Forum for Interdisciplinary Discourse, University of Ibadan, 25 July 1991; University of Ibadan, 1991).

Adil, Alev. "More Narnian than Olympian," *Times Literary Supplement* 4797(10 March 1995): 23.

Adjei, Mawuli. "Tradition and Continuity in Contemporary African Poetry in English: The Case of Kofi Awoonor and Anlo–Ewe Oral Tradition" (M.Phil. thesis, Department of English, University of Ghana at Legon, 1994).

Afolayan, A. "Language and Sources of Amos Tutuola," in *Critical Perspectives on Amos Tutuola*, ed. Bernth Lindfors, 148–62.

Agovi, Kofi. "A Dual Sensibility: The Short Story in Ghana, 1944–1980," in *Literature and Black Aesthetics*, ed. Emenyonu, 247–71.

——. *New Directions in the Ghanaian Theatre of the Eighties* (paper presented at a staff seminar held at the seminar room, 31 August 1989; University of Ghana at Legon, Institute of African Studies, 1989).

——. "The Origin of Literary Theatre in Colonial Ghana, 1920–1957," *Research Review* (Institute of African Studies, University of Ghana at Legon) 6.1 (1990): 1–23.

——. "The Philosophy of Communication in Traditional Ghanaian Society: The Literary and Dramatic Evidence," *Research Review* (Institute of African Studies, University of Ghana at Legon) New Series 5.2 (1989): 52–59.

——. "The Poet's Politics in African Society," *Legon Journal of Humanities* 4 (1988): 1–17.

——. "The Political Relevance of Ghanaian Highlife Songs since 1957," *Research in African Literatures*, 20.2 (Summer 1989): 194–201.

——. "Preliminary Observations on the Modern Short Story and the African Folktale Tradition," *Research Review* (Institute of African Studies, University of Ghana at Legon) 9.1 (1973): 123–29.

——. "Towards an Authentic African Theatre," *Ufahamu* 19.2–3 (Spring–Fall 1991): 67–79.

——. "Traditional Storytelling and the Modern Short Story" in *Out of the Writers' Workshop* (Accra: Arts Council of Ghana, 1974): 11–25.

Agyemang–Duah, Ivor. *Some African Voices of Our Time* (Accra: Anansesem, 1995).

Ahmad, Aijaz. *In Theory: Classes, Nations, Literatures* (London: Verso, 1992).

Aidoo, Anthony A., & James Gibbs. "Mohammed Abdallah at Fifty," *School of Performing Arts Newsletter* (University of Ghana at Legon) 3 (July–September 1994): 19–22.

Alexis, Jacques–Stephen. "Du réalisme merveilleux des Haïtiens," *Présence Africaine* 9–10 (juin–novembre 1956): 245–71.

Amoako, A.A. "Kojo Laing's *Search Sweet Country*," *Journal of the University of Science and Technology* (Kumasi, Ghana) 8.2 (October 1988): 91–94.

——. "*Search Sweet Country*: B. Kojo Laing," *Legon Journal of the Humanities* (University of Ghana) 4 (1988): 102–106.

Amuta, Chidi. "Ayi Kwei Armah and the Mythopoesis of Mental Decolonization," *Ufahamu*.3 (Spring 1981): 44–56.

——. *The Theory of African Literature: Implications for Practical Criticism* (London: Zed, 1989).

Anderson Imbert, Enrique. "'Magical Realism' in Spanish-American Fiction," *International Fiction Review* 2.1 (January 1975): 1–8.

Andrzejewski, B.W. *Literatures in African Languages: Theoretical Issues and Sample Surveys* (Warsaw: Wiedza Powzechna & Cambridge: Cambridge UP. 1985).

Angmor, Charles. *Contemporary Literature in Ghana 1911–1978: A Critical Evaluation* (Accra: Woeli, 1996).

Anyidoho, Kofi. "Atukwei Okai and His Poetic Territory," in *New West African Literature*, ed. Kolawole Ogungbesan (London: Heinemann, 1979): 45–59.

——. "Ayi Kwei Armah and Our Journey of the Mind," in *Literature and National Consciousness*, ed. Emenyonu, 108–120.

——. The Complex Simplicity of Children's Literature: A Reading of *Ghana Motion* and *The Brassman's Secret*," *Legon Journal of the Humanities* 6 (1992): 51–63.

——. "Divine Drummer: Drum Poetics in Brathwaite and Okai," in *Black Culture and Black Consciousness in Literature*, ed. Emenyonu, 197–210.

——. "Historical Realism and the Visionary Ideal: Ayi Kwei Armah's *Two Thousand Seasons*," *Ufahamu* 11.2 (Fall 1981): 108–130.

——. "The 6th Ibadan Annual African Literature Conference: The Oral Performance in Africa," *Research in African Literatures* 13.2 (Summer 1982): 225–26.

——. "Kofi Awoonor," in Lindfors & Sander, *Dictionary of Literary Biography* 117, 77–92.

——. "Mythmaker and Mythbreaker: The Oral Poet as Earwitness," in Julien et al., ed. *African Literature in its Social and Political Dimensions*, 4–14.

——. "National Identity and the Language of Metaphor," in Anyidoho & Gibbs, ed. *FonTom-From*, 1–22.

——. "Oral Poetics and Traditions of Verbal Art in Africa" (doctoral dissertation, University of Texas at Austin, 1983).

——. *The Pan African Ideal in Literatures of the Black World* (Accra: Ghana Universities P, 1989).

——. "Poetry as Dramatic Performance: The Ghana Experience," *Research in African Literatures* 22.2 (Summer 1991): 41–55.

——, & James Gibbs, ed. *FonTomFrom: Contemporary Ghanaian Literature, Theatre and Film* (*Matatu* 21–22; Amsterdam & Atlanta GA: Rodopi, 2000).

Appiah, Kwame Anthony. *In My Father's House* (London: Methuen, 1992).

Apronti, Jawa. "Ghanaian Poetry in the 1970s," in *New West African Literature*, ed. Kolawole Ogungbesan (London: Heinemann, 1979): 31–44.

——. "John Atukwei Okai: the Growth of a Poet," *Universitas* 2.1 (October 1972): 117–29.

Arkhurst, Sandy. "African Music, Dance and Drama in Community Education," unpublished paper presented at the Colloquium on African Theatre, Yaoundé, 16–21 June 1997.

Armah, Ayi Kwei. "Battle for the Mind of Africa," *South* (August 1987): 62.

——. "The Caliban Complex: 2," *West Africa* (25 March 1985): 570–71.

——. "The Definitive *Chaka*," *Transition* 50 (October 1975): 10–13.

——. "Masks and Marx," *Présence Africaine* 131 (1984): 35–65.

Assimeng, Max. *Social Structure of Ghana* (Tema: Ghana Publishing Corporation, 1981).

Ashon, Enimil. "Atukwei Drops a Seed into Young Fertile Minds," *Weekly Spectator* (23 March 1989): 7.

Awodiya, Muyiwa P. *Excursions in Drama and Literature: Interviews with Femi Osofisan* (Ibadan: Kraft, 1993).

——. "Structure and Meaning in *The Chattering and the Song*," in *Femi Osofisan: Interpretive Essays 1*, ed. Awodiya (Lagos: Centre for Black African Arts and Civilization, 1996): 54–68.

Awoonor, Kofi. *The Breast of the Earth: A Survey of the History, Culture and Literature of Africa South of the Sahara* (Garden City NY: Doubleday / Anchor, 1975).

——. "The Poem, the Poet, the Human Condition," *Asemka: A Bilingual Literary Journal of the University of Cape Coast* 5 (September 1979): 1–23.

Azodo, Ada Uzoamaka, & Gay Alden Wilentz, ed. *Emerging Perspectives on Ama Ata Aidoo* (Trenton NJ: Africa World Press, 1999).

Bakhtin, Mikhail. *L'Œuvre de François Rabelais et la culture populaire au Moyen Age et sous le Renaissance* (Paris: Gallimard, 1965).

Balzer, Cam. "M.me —dolph and the Question of (Postcolonial) Art," *Commonwealth: Essays and Studies* 18.2 (Spring 1996): 13–20.

Bamé, Kwabena N. *Come to Laugh: A Study of African Traditional Theatre in Ghana* (Accra: Baafour, 1981).

——. *The Concert Party in a Birth Control Campaign Programme: A 1975 Report Project* (a paper prepared for the 4th International Conference on Popular Music Studies at Accra Arts Centre on 12th–19th August, 1987; Institute of African Studies, University of Ghana at Legon, 1988).

Banham, Martin et al., ed. *The Cambridge Guide to African and Caribbean Theatre* (Cambridge: Cambridge UP, 1994).

Barber, Karin. "Literacy, Improvisation and the Public in Yorùbá Popular Theatre," in Brown, ed. *The Pressures of the Text*, 6–27.

——. "Multiple Discourses in Yoruba Oral Literature," *Bulletin of the John Rylands University Library of Manchester* 73.3 (Autumn 1991): 11–24.

——. "Popular Arts in Africa," *African Studies Review* 30.3 (September 1987): 1–78.

Barber, Karin; Collins, John; Ricard, Alain. *West African Popular Theatre* (Bloomington & Indianapolis: Indiana UP& Oxford: James Currey, 1997).

Bardolph, Jacqueline. "Azaro, Saleeem and Askar: Brothers in Allegory," *Commonwealth: Essays and Studies* 15.1 (1992): 45–51.

Bender, John. "Eighteenth Century Studies," in Greenblatt & Gunn, ed. *Redrawing the Boundaries*, 79–99.

Benjamin, Walter. "The Storyteller: Reflections on the Works of Nikolai Leskov," in *Illuminations*, ed. Hannah Arendt, tr. Harry Zohn (1955; London, Collins / Fontana, 1992): 83–107.

Bertinetti, Paolo. "Reality and Magic in Syl Cheney–Coker's *The Last Harmattan of Alusine Dunbar*," in Linguanti et al., ed. *Coterminous Worlds*, 197–207.

Bhabha, Homi. *The Location of Culture* (London: Routledge, 1994).

——. "The Manifesto" and "Reinventing Britain: A Forum," *Wasafiri* 29 (Spring 1999): 38–43.

——. *Nation and Narration* (London: Routledge, 1990).

——. "Postcolonial Criticism," in Greenblatt & Gunn, ed. *Redrawing the Boundaries*, 437–65.

Birmingham, David. *Kwame Nkrumah* (London: Cardinal, 1990).

Bjornson, Richard. "Theory and Moral Commitment in the Study of African Literature," in Gugler et al., ed. *Literary Theory and African Literature*, 31–41.

Bleich, David. *Utopia: The Psychology of a Cultural Fantasy* (Studies in Speculative Fiction 5; Ann Arbor MI: UMI Research, 1970).

Bowler, Berjouhi Barsamian. *The Word as Image* (London: Studio Vista, 1983).

Brathwaite, Edward Kamau. *History of the Voice: The Development of Nation Language in Anglophone Caribbean Poetry* (London & Port of Spain: New Beacon, 1984).

Breitinger, Eckhard, ed. *Theatre and Performance in Africa: Intercultural Perspectives* (Bayreuth African Studies 31; Bayreuth: Bayreuth University, 1994).

Brown, Stewart. "Daring the Beast: Contemporary Nigerian Poetry," in Gurnah, ed. *Essays on African Writing 2*, 58–72.

——. "Dreams, Godhorses and Vultures," *Planet: The Welsh Internationalist* (June–July 1990): 97.

——. "Writing in Light: Orality-through-typography, Kamau Brathwaite's Sycorax Video Style," in Brown, ed. *The Pressures of the Text*, 125–36.

——, ed. *The Pressures of the Text: Orality, Texts and the Telling of Tales* (Birmingham University African Studies Series 4; Birmingham: Centre of West African Studies, 1995).

Buckley, David. "Full Diddly Delirium," *Observer* (16 March 1995): 19.

Carter, Angela. "Gaudy Metaphysics," *Sunday Times* (31 March 1991): 8.

Cezair–Thompson, Margaret. "Beyond the Postcolonial Novel: Ben Okri's *The Famished Road* and its Abiku Traveller," *Journal of Commonwealth Literature* 31.2 (1996): 33–57.

Chanady, Amaryll Beatrice. *Magical Realism and the Fantastic: Resolved Versus Unresolved Antinomy* (New York & London: Garland, 1985).

——. "The Origins and Development of Magic Realism in Latin American Fiction," in *Magic Realism and Literature: Essays and Stories*, ed. Peter Hinchcliff & Ed Jewinski (Proceedings of the Conference on Magic Realist Writing in Canada; Waterloo: University of Waterloo / Wilfrid Laurier University, May 1985): 49–60.

Chauduri, Amit. "Immoral, Invisible, God Only Wise," *Spectator* (1 April 1995): 33.

Chinweizu, Onwuchewka Jemie & Ihechukwu Madubuike. *Toward the Decolonization of African Literature*, 1: *African Fiction and Poetry and Their Critics* (Enugu: Fourth Dimension, 1980).

Collins, John. *Highlife Time* (Accra: Anansesem, 1994).

Cooper, Brenda. *Magical Realism in West African Fiction: Seeing with a Third Eye* (London & New York: Routledge, 1998).

——. "Syl Cheney–Coker: *The Last Harmattan of Alusine Dunbar*, and an Interview," *African Literature Association Bulletin* 20.3 (Summer 1994): 3–17.

Cumale, Kwame, & Batilloy Warritay. "Theatre for the People," *West Africa* (16 December 1985): 2641–42.

Dabydeen, David. "Freedom's Slave," *Observer* (8 August 1999): 23.

Danow, David K. *The Spirit of Carnival: Magical Realism and the Grotesque* (Lexington: UP of Kentucky, 1995).

Deandrea, Pietro. "Between Page and Stage: Reflections on Contemporary Ghanaian Poetry through Conversations with Atukwei Okai, Efua Sutherland, Kojo Gyinaye Kyei, Kofi Agovi, Kofi Anyidoho, Kobena Eyi Acquah and Kojo Laing," in *Cross-Cultural Voices: Investigations into the Post-Colonial*, ed. Claudio Gorlier & Isabella Maria Zoppi (Rome: Bulzoni, 1997): 19–58.

——. "From a Different Dimension: Mohammed ben Abdallah's Search for an African Theatre," *Quaderni del Centro Piemontese di Studi Africani* 3 (1998): 91–124.

——. "Gorges to Be Gored, Wisdom to Be Wielded: Figures from Yoruba Myth and History in Some Anglophone Yoruba Writers," in *Yoruba/English: Strategies of Mediation*, ed. Stewart Brown (Birmingham: Centre of West African Studies, University of Birmingham, forthcoming).

——. " 'History Never Walks Here, It Runs in Any Direction': Carnival and Magic in the Novels of Kojo Laing and Mia Couto," in Linguanti et al., ed. *Coterminous Worlds*, 209–225.

——. "An Interview with Ben Okri," *Africa America Asia Australia* 16 (1994): 55–82.

——. "Man Meaning to Man: A Close Encounter with Niyi Osundare's Poetry," in *Emerging Perspectives on Niyi Osundare*, ed. Abdul–Rasheed Na'Allah (Lawrenceville NJ: Africa World Press, forthcoming).

——. " 'New Worlds, New Wholes': Kojo Laing's Narrative Quest for a Social Renewal," *African Literature Today* 20 (1996): 158–78.

——. "The Scented Unknown: Beyond the Fourth Dimension in Three African Novels," in *Routes of the Roots: Geography and Literature in the English-Speaking Countries*, ed. Isabella Maria Zoppi (Rome: Bulzoni, 1999): 595–615.

Dei–Anang, K.K. "Discipline in the Making of Poetry," *Universitas* 2.1 (October 1972): 102–116.

Dekutsey, Atsu. "Poetry as Theatre," *West Africa* (24 March 1986): 618–19.

Depestre, René. "Entrevista con Aimé Césaire," *Casa de las Américas* 9.49 (July–August 1968): 137–42.

Djisenu, John K. "Performing Spaces and Institutional Organisation in Ghana," *Journal of Performing Arts* (School of Performing Arts, University of Ghana at Legon) 2.1 (1996): 22–27.

——. "Useful Political Lessons from Abdallah's *The Trial of Mallam Ilya*," *School of Performing Arts Newsletter* (University of Ghana at Legon) 2 (April–June 1994): 2–4.

Dogbe, Esi. review of Awonoor, *Comes the Voyager at Last*, *Uhuru* 5 (1994): 56–57.

Dolphyne, Florence Abena. *A Comprehensive Course in Twi (Asante)* (Accra: Ghana Universities P, 1996).

Dorkenoo, Kodzo Tom. "Ayi Kwei Armah, Winner of Ghana's Highest and First Literary Prize," *Growth: Literary Magazine for Young Writers* (Accra: Arts Council of Ghana / Young Africans Writers' Club) 3 (September 1973): 68–71.

Duerden, Dennis. *African Art and Literature: The Invisible Present* (1975; London: Heinemann, 1977).

Dunton, Chris. "Far-Flung Vision," *West Africa*.3783 (26 February–4 March 1990): 317.

——. *Make Men Talk True: Nigerian Drama in English since 1970* (London: Hans Zell, 1992).

——. "Wale Ogunyemi," in Lindfors & Sander, *Dictionary of Literary Biography* 157, 251–61.

Elder, Arlene. "Ama Ata Aidoo: The Development of a Woman's Voice," in Azodo & Wilentz, ed. *Emerging Perspectives on Ama Ata Aidoo*, 157–69.

Emenyonu, Ernest N., ed. *Black Culture and Black Consciousness in Literature* (Calabar Studies in African Literature 2; Ibadan: Heinemann, 1987).

——, ed. *Literature and Black Aesthetics* (Calabar Studies in African Literature 5; Ibadan: Heinemann, 1990).

——, ed. *Literature and National Consciousness* (Calabar Studies in African Literature 4; Ibadan: Heinemann, 1989).

Essien, Arit Essien. "Symbiotic Unity in Oral Performance," in Emenyonu, ed. *Literature and National Consciousness*, 89–96.

Etherton, Michael. "African Theatre and Political Action," *Wasafiri* 6–7 (1987): 3–6.

——. *The Development of African Drama* (Hutchinson University Library for Africa; London: Hutchinson, 1982).

——. "Trends in African Theatre," *African Literature Today* 10 (1979): 57–85.

Ezenwa Ohaeto. *Contemporary Nigerian Poetry and the Poetics of Orality* (Bayreuth African Studies Series 45; Bayreuth: Eckhard Breitinger, 1998).

Fanon, Frantz. *Black Skin, White Masks*, tr. Charles Lam Markmann (1952; New York: Grove, 1967).

——. *Les damnés de la terre* (Paris: Maspero, 1961).

——. *The Wretched of the Earth*, preface by Jean–Paul Sartre, tr. Constance Farrington (tr. 1965; Penguin Twentieth-Century Classics; Harmondsworth: Penguin, 1990).

Faris, Wendy B. "Scheherazade's Children: Magical Realism and Postmodern Fiction," in Zamora & Faris, ed. *Magical Realism*, 163–90.

Finley, Jeanne, with Cynde Gregory. "Okai Mixes Africanisms with Street Lingo in Skidmore Reading," *Kite* (14 February 1979): 4.

Fraser, Robert. "Kojo Laing: Profile and Extract," *Wasafiri* 3 (Autumn 1985): 9–11.

——. *The Novels of Ayi Kwei Armah: A Study in Polemical Fiction* (London: Heinemann, 1980).

——. review of Ato Quayson's *Strategic Transformations in Nigerian Writing* and Ben Okri's *Infinite Riches*, *Wasafiri* 29 (Spring 1999): 86–87.

——. *West African Poetry: A Critical History* (Cambridge: Cambridge UP, 1986).

Garuba, Harry. "Ben Okri," in Lindfors & Sander, *Dictionary of Literary Biography* 157, 277–85.

——. "Ben Okri's Animist Realism and the Famished Genre," *Guardian* (Lagos) (13 March 1993): 23.

Gates, Henry Louis, Jr. "Between the Living and the Unborn," *New York Times* (6 August 1992): 20.

Gawuga, Emmanuel. "Remembering the Dismembered Continent.. Ayi Kwei Armah," *Pan African Capital of the World: Newsletter of the W.E.B. Du Bois Memorial Centre for Pan African Culture* 1.1 (January–March 1997): 1, 11.

Gbadamosi, Gabriel. Review of Okri, *The Famished Road*, *Wasafiri* 14 (Autumn 1991): 35.

Genette, Gérard. *Palimpsestes: La Littérature au second degré* (Paris: Seuil, 1982).

Gibbs, James. "But Spiritual Billionaires," *West Africa* 3865 (1991): 1680–81.

——. "Land of a Million Magicians," *School of Performing Arts Newsletter* 1 (January–March 1994): 7–9.

——. "Mohammed ben Abdallah and the Legon Road Theater," *African Arts* 5.4 (1972): 33–34.

——. "Theatre of the Villages," *West Africa* (19–25 February 1996): 278–79.

Gilbert, Helen, & Joanne Tompkins. *Postcolonial Drama: Theory, Practice, Politics* (London & New York: Routledge, 1996).

Glover, Ablade. "Contemporary Art in Ghana," *Sunday Herald* (6–12 July 1997), Living: 2.

Gorlier, Claudio. "The Haunted House of National Literature: Individual Malaise and Communal Plight in the Making of a Literary Discourse in A.K. Armah's Novels and G. Okara's *The Voice*," in Emenyonu, ed. *Literature and National Consciousness*, 14–25.

Götrick, Kacke. *Apidan Theatre and Modern Drama* (Stockholm: Almqvist & Wiksell, 1984).

Grant, Linda. "Long Walk of Men and Angels," *The Independent* (31 March 1991): 31.

Greenblatt, Stephen, & Giles Gunn. *Redrawing the Boundaries: The Transformation of English and American Literary Studies* (New York: Modern Language Association of America, 1992).

Gugler, Joseph, Hans–Jürgen Lüsebrink & Jürgen Martini, ed. *Literary Theory and African Literature* (Beiträge zur Afrikaforschung 3; Münster & Hamburg: LIT, 1994).

Gurnah, Abdulrazak. "The Accidental Tourist," *Sunday Times* (12 March 1995): 21

——, ed. *Essays on African Writing 2: Contemporary Literature* (Oxford: Heinemann, 1995).

Gyekye, Kwame. *An Essay on African Philosophical Thought: The Akan Conceptual Scheme* (Cambridge: Cambridge UP, 1987).

Hadjor, Kofi Buenor. *Nkrumah and Ghana: The Dilemma of Postcolonial Power* (London & New York: Kegan Paul International, 1988).

Hagan, W.B. "Profile: Saka Acquaye Blends the Arts in Ghana," *Africa Report* (January 1971): 34–35.

Hagher, Iyoruese O. "The Kwagh Hir: An Analysis of a Contemporary Indigenous Puppet Theatre and Its Social and Cultural Significance in Tivland in the 1960s and 1970s" (doctoral dissertation, Ahmadu Bello University, Zaria, 1981).

Hawley, John C. "Ben Okri's Spirit-Child: *Abiku* Migration and Postmodernity," *Research in African Literatures* 26.1 (1995): 30–39.

Haynes, John. "Surreal Connections," *West Africa* 3768 (5–12 November 1989): 1853.

Heilpern, John. *Conference of the Birds: The Story of Peter Brook in Africa* (1977; London: Methuen, 1989).

Hill–Lubin, Milfred A. "The Storyteller and the Audience in the Works of Ama Ata Aidoo," *Neohelicon* 16.2 (1985): 222–45.

Hume, Kathryn. *Fantasy and Mimesis: Responses to Reality in Western Literature* (New York: Methuen, 1984).

Idowu, E. Bolaji. *African Traditional Religion: A Definition* (1973; Lagos: Fountain, 1991).

Igwe, Dimgba. "Armah: The Reluctant Novelist," *African Concord* (7 May 1987): 17–19.

Innes, C.L. "Conspicuous Consumption: Corruption and the Body Politic in the Writing of Ayi Kwei Armah and Ama Ata Aidoo," in Gurnah, ed. *Essays on African Writing 2*, 1–18.

Jackson, Rosemary. *Fantasy: The Literature of Subversion* (London: Methuen, 1981).

James, C.L.R. *Nkrumah and the Ghana Revolution* (London: Allison & Busby, 1977).

Jameson, Fredric. "On Magic Realism in Film," *Critical Inquiry* 12 (1986): 301–25.

Jemie, Onwuchewka. "Hughes's Black Esthetic," in *Critical Essays on Langston Hughes* (Boston MA: G.K. Hall, 1986): 95–120.

Jerimah, Ahmed. "The Guerrilla Theatre as a Tool for National Re-Awakening: A Study of the Soyinka Experiments," in Emenyonu, ed. *Literature and National Consciousness*, 181–204.

Jeyifo, Biodun. "Literary Theory and Theories of Decolonization," in Gugler et al., ed. *Literary Theory and African Literature*, 17–30.

——. *The Truthful Lie: Essays in a Sociology of African Drama* (London & Port of Spain: New Beacon, 1985).

Johnson, Rev. Samuel. *The History of the Yorubas: From the Earlier Times to the Beginning of the British Protectorate* (Lagos: C.M.S. Bookshops, 1921).

Jones, Eldred. "Editorial," *African Literature Today* 8 (1976): vii–viii.

Jowitt, David. "Structure and Meaning in Ben Okri's Magic Fiction," *Guardian* (Lagos) (9 October 1993): 20.

Julien, Eileen. *African Novels and the Question of Orality* (Bloomington: Indiana UP, 1992).

——, M. Mortimer & C. Schade, ed. *African Literature in its Social and Political Dimensions* (Annual Selected Papers of the ALA; Washington DC: African Literature Association / Three Continents, 1986).

Kerr, David. "Participatory Popular Theatre: The Highest Stage of Cultural Underdevelopment?," *Research in African Literatures* 22.3 (1991): 55–75.

King Reidt, Kelly. Review of Awonoor, *Comes the Voyager at Last*, *Wasafiri* 20 (Autumn 1994): 78–79.

Konrad, Zinta. *Ewe Comic Heroes: Trickster Tales in Togo* (New York & London: Garland, 1994).

Korang, Kwaku Larbi. "Ama Ata Aidoo's Voyage Out: Mapping the Coordinates of Modernity and African Selfhood in *Our Sister Killjoy*," *Kunapipi* 14.3 (1992): 50–61.

Kropp–Dakubu, Mary Esther. "Kojo Laing," in Lindfors & Sander, *Dictionary of Literary Biography* 157, 140–49.

——. "Kojo Laing's Poetry and the Struggle for God," in Anyidoho & Gibbs, ed. *FonTomFrom*, 235–41.

——. *Language and Community: The View from Accra* (Accra: Ghana Universities P, 1996).

——. "The Language of Being in the Poetry of B. Kojo Laing," *Legon Journal of the Humanities* 5 (1991): 79–62.

——. "*Search Sweet Country* and the Language of Authentic Being," *Research in African Literatures* 24.1 (Spring 1993): 19–35.

——. "The Significance of Language, or Why Spider Must Be Punished in Ga Tales," in *Sprache, Symbole und Symbolverwendungen in Ethnologie, Kulturanthropologie, Religion und Recht: Festschrift für Rüdiger Schott zum 65. Geburtstag*, ed. Werner Krawietz, Leopold Pospisil & Sabine Steinbrich (Berlin: Duncker & Humbolt, 1993): 489–507.

——. "The Trope of the Nation in Kojo Laing's Poetry," in Kropp–Dakubu, ed. *English in Ghana*, 275–85.

——, ed. *English in Ghana* (Accra: Black Masks / Ghana English Studies Association, 1997).

Kubayanda, J. Bekunuru. "Dream, Betrayal and Revolution: Independent Ghana in the Poetry of Kofi Anyidoho," *Legon Journal of Humanities* 3 (1987): 62–78.

——. "Polyrhythmics and African Print Poetics: Guillén, Césaire and Atukwei Okai," in *Interdisciplinary Dimensions of African Literature*, ed. Kofi Anyidoho et al. (Washington DC: Three Continents, 1985): 155–69.

Kyerewaa–Gyapon, Amma. "Drama and Theatre in Post-Independent Ghana," BA thesis, Institute of African Studies, University of Ghana, undated.

Lasagna, Laura. "The Logos of the African Trickster," *Africa America Asia Australia* 16 (1994): 29–40.

La Rose, John. "About *New Beacon Review*: A Statement," *New Beacon Review* 1 (July 1985): 2.

Lim, Michael. "Written Communication: Ghana and the Fiction of Kojo Laing," *New Literatures Review: Factions and Fictions* 28–29 (Winter 1994 – Summer 1995): 46–54.

Lindfors, Bernth. "Amos Tutuola: Debts and Assets," in Lindfors, ed. *Critical Perspectives on Amos Tutuola*, 224–55.

——. "Armah's Histories," *African Literature Today* 11 (1980): 85–96.

——. *Comparative Approaches to African Literatures* (Cross / Cultures 14; Amsterdam & Atlanta GA: Rodopi, 1994).

——, ed. *Critical Perspectives on Amos Tutuola* (London: Heinemann, 1980).

Lindfors, Bernth, & Reinhard Sander, ed. *Dictionary of Literary Biography*, 117: *Twentieth Century Caribbean and Black African Writers, First Series* (Detroit MI: Bruccoli Clark Layman / Gale, 1991).

——. *Dictionary of Literary Biography*, 125: *Twentieth Century Caribbean and Black African Writers, Second Series* (Detroit MI: Bruccoli Clark Layman / Gale, 1993).

——. *Dictionary of Literary Biography*, 157: *Twentieth Century Caribbean and Black African Writers, Third Series* (Detroit MI: Bruccoli Clark Layman / Gale, 1996).

Linguanti, Elsa, Francesco Casotti & Carmen Concilio, ed. *Coterminous Worlds: Magical Realism and Contemporary Post-Colonial Literature in English* (Cross / Cultures 39; Amsterdam & Atlanta GA: Rodopi, 1999).

Lodge, David. "Magic Realism," in Lodge, *The Art of Fiction* (Harmondsworth: Penguin, 1992): 113–16.

Lokko, Sophia D. "Theatre Space: A Historical Overview of the Theatre Movement in Ghana," *Modern Drama* 23 (1980): 309–319.

Maduakor, Obi. "Novel (West Africa): Magical Realism," in *Encyclopedia of Postcolonial Literatures in English*, ed. Eugene Benson and L.W. Conolly (London & New York: Routledge, 1994): 1162–63.

Maduka, Chidi T. "African Religious Beliefs in Literary Imagination: *Ogbanje* and *Abiku* in Chinua Achebe, J.P. Clark and Wole Soyinka," *Journal of Commonwealth Literature* 23.1 (1987): 17–30.

Maja–Pearce, Adewale. "Interview with Kojo Laing," *Wasafiri* 6–7 (Spring–Autumn 1987): 27–29.

——. *A Mask Dancing: Nigerian Novelists of the Eighties* (London: Hans Zell, 1992).

——. Review of Laing, *Woman of the Aeroplanes*, *Wasafiri* 10 (Summer 1989): 23.

Marcus, Mordecai. "Melville's Bartleby as a Psychological Double," in *Bartleby the Inscrutable*, ed. M.T. Inge (Hamden CT: Archon, 1979): 114–26.

Mbiti, John S. *African Religions and Philosophy* (London: Heinemann, 1969).

McCaffery, Larry, ed. *Storming the Reality Studio: A Casebook of Cyberpunk and Postmodern Science Fiction* (Durham NC: Duke UP, 1991).

McCaskie, Tom C. "Armah's *The Healers* and Asante History," in *Images of Africa* (Stirling: University of Stirling / Centre of Commonwealth Studies, 1990): 42–60.

——. "Asantesem: Reflections on Discourse and Text in Africa," in *Discourse and Its Disguises: The Interpretation of African Oral Texts*, ed. Karin Barber & P.F. de Moraes Farias (Birmingham University African Studies Series 1; Centre of West African Studies, University of Birmingham, 1989): 70–86.

——. "Komfo Anokye of Asante: Meaning, History and Philosophy in an African Society," *Journal of African History* 27 (1986): 315–39.

McGregor, Maxine. "Interview with Ama Ata Aidoo," in *African Writers Talking: A Collection of Interviews*, ed. Dennis Duerden & Cosmo Pieterse (London: Heinemann, 1972): 19–27.

Mensah, A.N. "Kofi Anyidoho," in Lindfors & Sander, *Dictionary of Literary Biography* 157, 3–16.

Menton, Seymour. "Jorge Luis Borges, Magic Realist," *Hispanic Review* 50 (1982): 411–26.

Mimicks, David. "Derek Walcott and Alejo Carpentier: Nature, History and the Caribbean Writer," in Zamora & Faris, ed. *Magical Realism*, 371–404.

Mlama, Penina Muhando. "Women's Participation in 'Communication for Development': The Popular Theatre Alternative in Africa," *Research in African Literatures* 22.3 (1991): 41–53.

Mobolade, Timothy. "The Concept of Abiku," *African Arts* 7.1 (Autumn 1973): 62–64.

Moore, Gerald. "Amos Tutuola: A Nigerian Visionary," in Lindfors, ed. *Critical Perspectives on Amos Tutuola*, 34–42.

——. *Twelve African Writers* (Hutchinson University Library for Africa; London: Hutchinson, 1980).

Moore–Gilbert, Bart. *Postcolonial Theory: Contexts, Practices and Politics* (London: Verso, 1997).

Morrison, Joy F. "Forum Theatre in West Africa: An Alternative Medium of Information Exchange," *Research in African Literatures* 22.3 (1991): 29–40.

Mukherjee, Arun P. "Whose Postcolonialism and Whose Postmodernism?," *World Literature Written in English* 30.2 (1990): 1–9.

Muir, Kate. "An Author in Search of Humility," *The Times* (25 October 1991): 15.

Nazareth, Peter. "Time in the Third World: A Fictional Exploration," in *Awakened Conscience: Studies in Commonwealth Literature*, ed. C.D. Narasimhaiah (New Delhi: Sterling, 1978): 195–205.

Newell, Stephanie. "Anatomy of Masculine Power: Three Perspectives on Marriage and Gender in Nigerian Non-Fiction," in Newell, ed. *Writing African Women*, 170–90.

——. "From the Brink of Oblivion: The Anxious Masculinism of Nigerian Market Literatures," *Research in African Literatures* 27.3 (Fall 1996): 50–67.

——, ed. *Writing African Women: Gender, Popular Culture and Literature in West Africa* (London: Zed, 1997).

Nketia, J.H. Kwabena. "Akan Poetry," in *Introduction to African Literature: An Anthology of Critical Writing from 'Black Orpheus'*, ed. Ulli Beier (London: Longmans, 1967): 23–33.

——. *Ghana: Music, Dance and Drama; A Review of the Performing Arts of Ghana* (Tema: Ghana Publishing Corporation, 1965).

Nkrabeah, Kwame. "Oh! Abdallah Has Resigned!," *The Independent* (Accra; 1–7 December 1993): 10.

Nnolim, Charles E. "The Nigerian Tradition in the Novel," *The Commonwealth Novel in English* 2.2 (1983): 22–39.

Novicki, Margaret A. "Interview with Mohammed ben Abdallah, Secretary of Education and Culture, Ghana," *Africa Report* 32.4 (July–August 1987): 14–22.

Nwanko, Chimalun. "The Feminist Impulse and Social Realism in Ama Ata Aidoo's *No Sweetness Here* and *Our Sister Killjoy*," in *Ngambika: Studies of Women in African Literatures*, ed. Ann Adams Graves & Carol Boyce Davies (Trenton NJ: Africa World Press, 1986): 149–61.

——. Review of *The Last Harmattan of Alusine Dunbar*. *African Studies Review* 35.1 (1992): 134–35.

Nwoga, Donatus. "Modern African Poetry: The Domestication of a Tradition," *African Literature Today* 10 (1979): 32–56.

Nzewi, Meki. "Music, Dance, Drama and the Stage in Nigeria," in *Drama and Theatre in Nigeria: A Critical Source Book*, ed. Y. Ogunbiyi (Lagos: Nigeria Magazine, 1981): 433–56.

Obiechina, E.N. "Amos Tutuola and the Oral Tradition," in Lindfors, ed. *Critical Perspectives on Amos Tutuola*, 84–105.

Ocansey, Ahuma Boseo. "The Greatest Show in Town," *Sunday Herald* (29 June 1997), Living 1: 4–7.

Ofeimun, Odia. "Surrealistic Power-Play," *West Africa* 3918 (19–25 October 1992): 1794.

Ofori Akyea, E. "The Atwia–Ekumfi Kodzidan: An Experimental African Theatre," *Okyeame* 4.1 (1968): 82–84.

Ofosu–Appiah, L.H. *Joseph Ephraim Casely Hayford: The Man of Vision and Faith* (J.B. Danquah Memorial Lectures, Series 8; Accra: Academy of Arts and Sciences, 1975).

Ogede, Ode S. "Armah as a Literary Critic," *Savanna* 10.1 (June 1989): 84–92.

——. "The Rhetoric of Revolution in Armah's *The Healers*: Form as Experience," *African Studies Review* 36.1 (April 1993): 43–58.

Ogunsanwo, Olatubosun. "Intertextuality and Postcolonial Literature in Ben Okri's *The Famished Road*," *Research in African Literatures* 26.1 (1995): 40–52.

Ogunyemi, Chikwenye Okonjo. "Efua Theodora Sutherland," in Lindfors & Sander, *Dictionary of Literary Biography* 117, 284–89.

Okai, Atukwei. "Vision, Image and Symbol in Ghanaian Literature," in *African Writing Today: A Special Issue of Pacific Moana Quarterly*, ed. Peter Nazareth, 6.3–4 (July–October1981): 51–61.

Okpewho, Isidore. *African Oral Literature: Backgrounds, Character and Continuity* (Bloomington & Indianapolis, Indiana UP, 1992).

——. "African Poetry: The Modern Writer and the Oral Tradition," *African Literature Today* 16 (1988): 3–25.

——. *The Epic in Africa: Towards a Poetic of the Oral Performance* (New York: Columbia UP, 1975).

——. "Myth and Modern Fiction: Armah's *Two Thousand Seasons*," *African Literature Today* 13 (1983): 1–23.

Okri, Ben. "A Poet in Search of Arcadia," *European* 346 (26 December 1996), Magazine: 16–19.

——. *A Way of Being Free* (London: Phoenix House, 1997).

Olayemi, Val. "The Supernatural in the Yoruba Folktale," in *Yoruba Oral Tradition: Poetry, Music, Dance and Drama*, ed. Wande Abimbola (Ife African Languages and Literatures Series 1; Department of African Languages and Literatures, University of Ife, 1975): 953–71.

Oliva, Renato. "Re-Dreaming the World: Ben Okri's Shamanic Realism," in Linguanti et al., ed. *Coterminous Worlds*, 171–96.

Omotoso, Kole. *The Form of the African Novel* (Akure & Ibadan: Fagbamigbe, 1979).

Opara, Chioma. "Narrative Techniques and the Politics of Gender: Ama Ata Aidoo's *Our Sister Killjoy* and *No Sweetness Here*," in Newell, ed. *Writing African Women*, 137–46.

Opoku, Kofi Asare. *West African Traditional Religion* (Accra: FEP, 1978).

Opoku–Agyemang, Kwadjo. "A Crisis of Balance: The (Mis)Representation of Colonial History and the Slave Experience as Themes in Modern African Literature," *Asemka: A Literary Journal of the University of Cape Coast* 7 (September 1992): 63–77.

——. "The Logic of Escape in the Akan Trickster Tale," *Asemka: A Literary Journal of the University of Cape Coast* 8 (1995): 101–12.

Opoku–Agyemang, Naana Jane. " 'A Girl Marries a Monkey': The Folktale as an Expression of Value and Change in Society," *Asemka: A Literary Journal of the University of Cape Coast* 7 (September 1992): 5–12.

——. "Lest We Forget: A Critical Survey of Ghanaian Women's Literature," *Asemka: A Literary Journal of the University of Cape Coast* 8 (1996): 61–84.

——. "Narrative Turns in Ama Ata Aidoo's *No Sweetness Here*," in Azodo & Wilentz, ed. *Emerging Perspectives on Ama Ata Aidoo*, 127–44.

O'Shaughnessy, Kathy. "A Real Nowhere Man," *Sunday Independent* (23 April 1995): 12.

Osofisan, Femi. "Ritual and Revolutionary Ethos: The Humanistic Dilemma in Contemporary Nigerian Theatre," *Okikè* 2 (September 1982): 72–81.

——. "Warriors of a Failed Utopia? West African Writers since the '70s," *Leeds African Studies Bulletin* 61 (1996): 11–36.

——. "Wonderland and the Orality of Prose: A Comparative Study of Rabelais, Joyce and Tutuola," in *The Genre of Prose Fiction: Two Complementary Views* (Ife Monographs on Literature and Criticism, 4th series, 3, 1986): 2–60.

Osundare, Niyi. *African Literature and the Crisis of Poststructuralist Theorising* (Ibadan: Options Book and Information Services, 1993).

——. "Theatre of the Beaded Curtain: Nigerian Drama and the Kabiyesi Syndrome," *Okikè* 27–28 (March 1988): 99–113.

Otu, John. "Beyond Okri's Surrealism: A Gestalt Perspective," *Guardian* (Lagos) (10 April 1993): 19.

Owusu, Kofi. "Canons under Siege: Blackness, Femaleness and Ama Ata Aidoo's *Our Sister Killjoy*," *Callaloo* 13.2 (Spring 1990): 351–63.

Owusu, Martin. *Drama of the Gods: A Study of Seven African Plays* (Roxbury MA: Omenana, 1983).

Pawlak, Nina. "Akan Folk Literature and the Beginnings of Writing in Twi," in Andrzejewski et al., ed. *Literatures in African Languages*, 128–56.

Pelton, Robert D. *The Trickster in West Africa: A Study of Mythic Irony and Sacred Delight* (Berkeley: U of California P, 1980).

Pollard, Phyllis. "Meditations on Time and Exile," *CRNLE Reviews Journal* 2 (1994): 126–29.

Portelli, Alessandro. *Il testo e la voce* (Rome: Manifestolibri, 1992).

Porter, Ed. "Invisible Men Lost in a Fog," *Evening Standard* (6 March 1995): 15.

Priebe, Richard K. "Kofi Awoonor's *This Earth, My Brother* as an African Dirge," *Ghanaian Literatures* (Contributions in Afro-American and African Studies 120; Westport CT: Greenwood, 1988).

——. *Myth, Realism and the West African Writer* (Trenton NJ: Africa World Press, 1988).

Profumo, David. "From Sublime Dreaminess to Radical Chic," *Daily Telegraph* (11 March 1995): 27.

Quayson, Ato. "Esoteric Webwork as Nervous System: Reading the Fantastic in Ben Okri's Writing," in Gurnah, ed. *Essays on African Writing 2*, 144–58.

——. "Orality – (Theory) – Textuality: Tutuola, Okri, and the Relationship of Literary Practice to Oral Tradition," in Brown, ed. *The Pressures of the Text*, 96–117.

——. *Strategic Transformations in Nigerian Writing: Orality and History in the Work of Rev. Samuel Johnson, Amos Tutuola, Wole Soyinka and Ben Okri* (Oxford: James Currey & Bloomington & Indianapolis: Indiana UP, 1997).

——. "Tradition(s) And the Individual Talent: The Development of a Nigerian Literary Tradition with Special Reference to the Works of Rev. Samuel Johnson, Amos Tutuola, Wole Soyinka and Ben Okri" (doctoral dissertation, Pembroke College, University of Cambridge, September 1994).

Radin, Paul. *The Trickster: A Study in American Indian Mythology* (London: Routledge & Kegan Paul, 1956).

Rattray, R.S. *Ashanti* (New York: Negro UP, 1923).

Ricard, Alain. *L'Invention du théâtre: Le théâtre et les comédiens en Afrique noire* (Lausanne: L'Age d'Homme, 1986).

Richards, Sandra L. *Ancient Songs Set Ablaze: The Theatre of Femi Osofisan* (Washington DC: Howard UP, 1996).

Robson, David. "Keep Off the Spirits," *Sunday Telegraph* (19 March 1995): 25.

Sackey, Appiah. Review of Abdallah, *The Trial of Mallam Ilya and other plays*, *African Concord* (11 March 1988): 24.

Sackey, Edward. "Oral Tradition and the African Novel," *Modern Fiction Studies* 37.3 (Autumn 1991): 389–407.

Said, Edward. "Yeats and Decolonization," in *Nationalism, Colonialism, and Literature*, ed. Terry Eagleton, Fredric Jameson & Edward W. Said (Minneapolis: U of Minnesota P, 1990): 65–95.

Salla, Ibrahim. Review of Abdallah, *The Trial of Mallam Ilya and other plays*, *Wasafiri* 9 (Winter 1988–89): 35–36.

Schipper, Mineke. *Beyond the Boundaries* (Chicago: Ivan R. Dee, 1989).

——. *Theatre and Society in Africa* (Johannesburg: Ravan, 1982).

Sekyi–Baidoo, J.Y. "A Study of Kobena Eyi Acquah's Use of Antecedents to *Music for a Dream Dance*," in Kropp–Dakubu, ed. *English in Ghana*, 248–62.

Sekyi–Otu, Ato. "'Toward Anoa... Not Back to Anoa': The Grammar of Revolutionary Homecoming in *Two Thousand Seasons*," *Research in African Literatures* 18.2 (Summer 1987): 192–214.

Sey, Kofi A. *Ghanaian English* (London: Macmillan, 1973).

Shillington, Kevin. *Ghana and the Rawlings Factor* (London: Macmillan, 1992).

Sidney, Sir Philip. *An Apology for Poetry*, ed. Geoffrey Shepherd (1580; Nelson's Medieval & Renaissance Library; London: Thomas Nelson, 1965).

Slemon, Stephen. "Magic Realism As Postcolonial Discourse," *Canadian Literature* 16 (Spring 1988): 9–24.

Slemon, Stephen, & Helen Tiffin, ed. *After Europe: Critical Theory and Postcolonial Writing* (Mundelstrup & Sydney: Dangaroo, 1989).

Smith, Arthur E.E. "Dreams from the Mind," *West Africa* 3842 (22–28 April 1991): 632.

Soyinka, Wole. *Art, Dialogue and Outrage: Essays on Literature and Culture* (Ibadan: New Horn, 1988).

——. *Myth, Literature and the African World* (Cambridge: Cambridge UP, 1976).

Spitzer, Leo. *The Creoles of Sierra Leone* (Madison: U of Wisconsin P, 1974), quoted in Cooper, "Syl Cheney–Coker: *The Last Harmattan of Alusine Dunbar*."

Sutherland, Efua Theodora. *The Original Bob: The Story of Bob Johnson, Ghana's Ace Comedian* (Accra: Anowuo Educational, 1970).

——. "Venture into Theatre," *Okyeame* 1 (1961): 47–48.

Sutherland–Addy, Esi. "Narrative Technique and the Role of Commentators in Ama Ata Aidoo's Works," *Research Review* (Institute of African Studies, University of Ghana at Legon) New Series 5.2 (1989): 60–70.

Taiwo, Oladele. *Female Novelists of Modern Africa* (London: Macmillan, 1984).

Tekpetey, Kwawisi. "The Trickster in Akan–Asante Oral Literature," *Asemka: A Bilingual Literary Journal of the University of Cape Coast* 5 (September 1979): 78–82.

Therson–Cofie, Larweh. "Life Is War in Achimota City," *People's Daily Graphic* 9 (September 1993): 7.

Utudjian Saint–André, Eliane. "New Modes of Writing in West African Drama: Prison Plays from Sierra Leone, Ghana and Nigeria," *Commonwealth: Essays and Studies* 14.1 (Autumn 1991): 70–77.

Uwatt, Efiok B. "Towards a New Form of African Theatre: Theatre-in-the-Round Performance in Ola Rotimi's Drama," in Emenyonu, ed. *Literature and Black Aesthetics*, 177–93.

Van Erven, Eugene. "Revolution, Freedom and Theater of Liberation," *Research in African Literatures* 22.3 (1991): 11–27.

Vincent, Theo. *Seventeen Black and African Writers on Literature and Life* (Lagos: Centre for Black African Arts and Civilization / Cross Continent, 1980).

Waters, Harold H. Review of *Major Gentl and the Achimota Wars*, *World Literature Today* (Spring 1993): 427.

Watt, Ian. *The Rise of the Novel: Studies in Defoe, Richardson and Fielding* (1957; Harmondsworth: Penguin, 1963).

Weisgerber, Jean. "Le réalisme magique: La locution et le concept," *Rivista di Letterature Moderne e Comparate* ns 35 (January–March 1982): 27–53.

Wilentz, Gay. "Writing for the Children: Orature, Tradition and Community in Efua Sutherland's *Foriwa*," *Research in African Literatures* 19.2 (Summer 1988): 182–96.

Wilkinson, Jane. Interview with Ben Okri, *Guardian* (24 October 1991): 19.

——. "Kofi Anyidoho: An Ewe Poet between Tradition and Change," *Africa* (Rome: Bulzoni) 43 (December 1988): 543–72.

——. *Talking with African Writers* (London: James Currey; Portsmouth NH: Heinemann, 1990).

Williams, Raymond. *The Country and the City* (1973; London: Hogarth, 1993).

——. *Modern Tragedy* (1966; London: Hogarth, 1992).

Wilson, Rawdon. "The Metamorphoses of Fictional Space: Magical Realism," in Zamora & Faris, ed. *Magical Realism*, 209–33.

Wright, Derek. *Ayi Kwei Armah's Africa: The Sources of His Fiction* (New Perspectives on African Literature 1; London: Hans Zell, 1989).

——. "Comes the Novelist at Last: Some Long-Awaited Works of African Fiction," *CRNLE Reviews Journal* 2 (1994): 167–74.

——. "Returning Voyagers: The Ghanaian Novel in the Nineties," *Journal of Modern African Studies* 34.1 (1996): 179–92.

——. "Whither Nigerian Fiction? Into the Nineties," *Journal of Modern African Studies* 33.2 (1995): 315–32.

Yankah, Kwesi. "Creativity and Traditional Rhetoric: Nkrumah's Personal Poet and His Son," in Emenyonu, ed. *Literature and National Consciousness*, 78–88.

——. "The Making and Breaking of Kwame Nkrumah: The Role of Oral Poetry," in Eileen Julien et al., ed. *African Literature in Its Social and Political Dimensions*, 15–21.

——. "Mohammed Abdallah: Is He Killing the Arts?," *Uhuru*.6 (1993): 21–25.

Yankson, Kofi. "*This Earth, My Brother*: A Study in Despair," *University of Cape Coast English Department Workpapers: Critical Essays and Reviews* 4 (July 1972): 67–71.

Yeboah–Afari, Ajoa. "The Pagoda Touch," *West Africa* 3802 (1990): 2062–64.

Zabus, Chantal. *The African Palimpsest: Indigenization of Language in the West African Europhone Novel* (Cross / Cultures 4; Amsterdam & Atlanta GA:, Rodopi, 1991).

Zamora, Lois Parkinson, & Wendy B. Faris, ed. *Magical Realism: Theory, History, Community* (Durham NC: Duke UP, 1995).

Interviews

(My interviews with Ben Okri were integrally published in issue 16 of *Africa America Asia Australia*; listed above under Secondary Sources: page numbers refer to this journal.)

Abdallah, Mohammed Ben: South Legon, Accra, 11 December 1993 & Drama Studio, University of Ghana at Legon, 8 July 1997.

Acquah, Kobena Eyi: PAWA House, Accra, 13 December 1993 & Du Bois Centre, Accra, 13 August 1997.

Addo, Patience Henaku: Ansaa Villa, Madina New Road, Accra, 18 August 1997.

Agovi, Kofi Ermeleh: Little Legon, Accra, 18 December 1993.

Aidoo, Ama Ata: East Legon, Accra, 10 June 1997 & 3 July1997.

Anyidoho, Kofi: Department of English, 19 November 1993 & School of Performing Arts, 30 May 1997, University of Ghana at Legon.

Arkhurst, Sandy: School of Performing Arts, University of Ghana at Legon, 8 May 1997.

Kyei, Kojo Gyinaye: Osu, Accra, 17 December 1993.

Laing, Kojo: St. Anthony Primary School, South Odorkor, Accra, 15 December 1993.

Ogunyemi, Wale: Institute of African Studies, University of Ibadan, 1 August 1997.

Okai, Atukwei: PAWA House, Accra, 22 November 1993 & Institute of African Studies, University of Ghana at Legon, 19 August 1997.

Okri, Ben: Notting Hill Gate, London, 17 December 1990 & Rome, 15 October 1992.

Osofisan, Femi: University of Ibadan campus, 2 August 1997.

Osundare, Niyi: Department of English, University of Ibadan, 1 August 1997.

Sowande, Bode: Odu Themes headquarters, Agbowo, Ibadan, 2 August 1997.

Sutherland, Efua Theodora: Accra, 17 December 1993.

Yirenkyi, Asiedu: School of Performing Arts, University of Ghana at Legon, 23 November 1993.

Videotapes

Video Archive of the W.E.B. Du Bois Memorial Centre for Pan-African Culture, Accra

DuBois Night at the Drama Studio, Accra, 28 August 1986, code G7.

Birth and Rebirth: The Living Echoes in Poetry Dramatisation, 27 January 1988, Du Bois Centre, code G14.

5th DuBois-Padmore-Nkrumah Pan-African Lecture, by Ayi Kwei Armah, 18 & 20 August 1996, Du Bois Centre, code G15.

Maya Angelou in Performance with the Ghana Dance Ensemble, produced by Ghana Broadcasting Corporation for the African Heritage Series, Ghana National Theatre, Accra, date unspecified, code G25.

Children of the Land, by Kofi Anyidoho, University of Ghana Primary School, Legon, 11 July 1987, code K8.

Nkrumah Ni... Africa Ni, written and directed by Femi Osofisan, produced by Kofi Anyidoho, performed by the National Theatre ABIBIGROMMA for Ghana Broadcasting Corporation TV, code O5.

K.E. Acquah's private collection

Music for a Dream Dance, 29 July 1988, Du Bois Centre, Accra.

M. Abdallah's private collection

The Fall of Kumbi, 23 April 1993, National Theatre, Accra.

Land of a Million Magicians; a National Commission on Culture production, produced by Kofi Boateng.